# Caribbean Heritage

Brimstone Hill, St Kitts: the citadel viewed from below the archways of the infantry officers' quarters with the canteen and gift shop centre left. Photo by Kathleen Orchard, May 2004.

# Caribbean
## Heritage

Edited by

## Basil A. Reid

**University of the West Indies Press**

Jamaica • Barbados • Trinidad and Tobago

The Reed Foundation, Inc.

University of the West Indies Press
7A Gibraltar Hall Road Mona
Kingston 7 Jamaica
www.uwipress.com

The Reed Foundation, Inc.
500 Fifth Avenue, Suite 2222
New York, NY 10110-2202
www.thereedfoundation.org

A catalogue record of this book is available from the
National Library of Jamaica.

ISBN: 978-976-640-264-8

*Cover illustration*: *Port Antonio*, by J.B. Kidd, circa 1830.
Courtesy of the National Library of Jamaica.

Cover and book design by Robert Harris
Set in Plantin Light 10/14.5 x 24
Printed in the United States of America

# Contents

# Acknowledgements

I WISH TO THANK ALL OF THE AUTHORS for their seminal contributions. It was a pleasure working with such fine scholars, whose rich expertise in their respective fields was critical to the overall quality of the volume. I am also grateful to Kevin Farmer, Alexandra Sajo, Maria Peter-Joseph, Shinelle Martin, Onika Mandela, Lystra Baksh-Moti, Daren Dhoray, Christopher Thomas, Kerry Bullock and Cecil Hodge for assisting with various aspects of the project such as the printing, collating and formatting of chapters and the converting of maps and figures. I wish to thank both Olivier Cole and his wife, Karen Sanderson-Cole, for twice delivering two hard copies of the manuscript to the University of the West Indies Press during their travels from Trinidad and Tobago to Jamaica. Thanks to Margaret Rouse-Jones for assisting with the editing of the Notes on Contributors. Jo-Anne Ferreira provided constructive comments on the table of contents; her input is gratefully acknowledged. I am grateful to Zara Ali, my research assistant, for proofreading the manuscript.

Rabia Ramlogan (Alma Jordan Library, University of the West Indies, St Augustine) and David Uzzell (professor of Environmental Psychology at the University of Surrey, Guildford, United Kingdom) both provided me access to a number of articles and Internet links relating to my research. Their generosity is well appreciated. Johann Bennett of the Marketing and Communications Office, University of the West Indies, St Augustine, should be thanked for graciously providing photographs of the Alma Jordan Library for chapter 10 in this volume. Thanks to the University of the West Indies, St Augustine, Research and Publication Committee, for partially funding this volume. I am especially grateful to the Reed Foundation, Inc., for their generous financial support, without which this publication would not have been possible.

I am thankful to my beloved wife, Joan, and our son, Gavin, for their encouragement as I edited this volume. Finally, I gratefully acknowledge the sterling efforts of Linda Speth and her staff at the University of the West Indies Press for supporting this project from beginning to end.

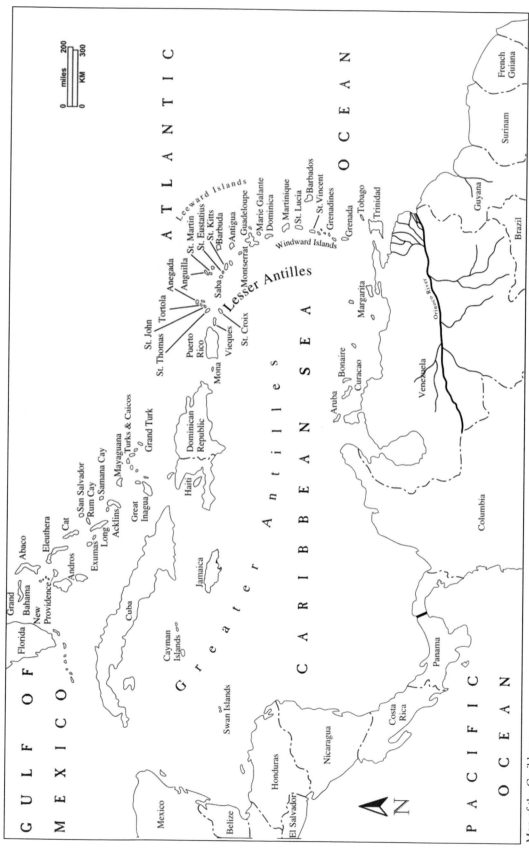

Map of the Caribbean.

# Caribbean Heritage

## An Introduction

PATRICK BRYAN AND BASIL A. REID

## Introduction

This volume provides an important entrée into the current thinking and rethinking on Caribbean heritage. Included are several topics that represent the rich plurality of the Caribbean experience, such as symbolism, popular culture, literature, linguistics, pedagogy, philanthropy, natural history, land tenure, townscapes, archaeology and museology. Although some chapters specifically relate to Jamaica, St Lucia, Barbados, St Kitts, Dominica and the Cayman Islands, with a significant number trained on the wider Caribbean, most of the volume's contributions focus on Trinidad and Tobago.

## Defining Heritage

Heritage is commonly defined as a legacy, birthright or property that descends to an heir (Langenscheidt Merriam-Webster Dictionary 1994; Oxford English Dictionary 2009). It is also defined as that which comes from circumstances of birth; an inherited lot or portion; the condition or state transmitted from ancestors (OED 2009). Issues of birthright and property are clearly reflected in Griffith-Charles and Lallo's interesting chapter on "family" land in St Lucia.

However, the foregoing definitions are never wholly satisfactory at reflecting both the substance and meaning of a complex subject such as the concept of heritage. Twenty years ago, Davidson and McConville (1991, 4) posited that "the users of this newly popular word [heritage] were often more confident of its acceptability than its precise meaning". In his discussion of the Japanese concept of heritage in its global politico-cultural context, Pettman (2001, 2) correctly asserts that *heritage* is never neutral, since in this regard at any rate, "'reality' does not exist in itself, we create it". As such, "each society and each age has different versions of what 'reality' might be", versions that serve contemporary purposes, some of which might be at odds with each other (so that in practice *heritage* can convey several different meanings at once), and some of which will always prevail over others (so that in practice *heritage* means that some people get their own way while others do not) (Pettman 2001, 2). Pettman further argues that the heritage that does get chosen is invariably that of the dominant group. Others get disinherited in the process. Heritage as a globalist concept is not only a construct, therefore, but a highly political construct, involving what is aptly called the "contemporary use of the past" (ibid.). Laurajane Smith is of the view that nothing is inherently "heritage": "there is rather a hegemonic discourse about heritage, which acts to constitute the way we think, talk and write about heritage" (cited in Anico and Peralta 2009, 16).

The process of identifying, recognizing and managing heritage is always political, partial and contested. This is especially the case for the anglophone Caribbean, whose history and ethnic composition have been the result of conquest, immigration, dominance, resistance and creolization (Agorsah 1994; Delle, Hauser and Armstrong 2011; Bryan 2000; Higman 2010).

## Nationalism and Heritage

The people of the British Caribbean committed themselves hesitantly to Caribbean nationhood during the years of the federation between 1958 and 1961. In spite of some institutional representation in West Indies cricket and the University College of the West Indies, territories of the federation broke away to establish nation-states. That political decision, hurried along by the referendum in Jamaica in 1961, ensured that after the 1960s Caribbean heritage became not so much a concern with the "collective social memory" (Hall 2008) of the Caribbean as a dedication to heritage within each Caribbean state.

For some nationalists, the search for a Caribbean heritage meant drawing a line between the European and the non-European heritage (with a preference for the latter). But rejection was not easy, because the existence of a European heritage in Georgian architecture, in forts and fortifications that speak to the military history of the Caribbean (once described by Dominican historian Juan Bosch as the "Imperial Frontier"), and in shipwrecks and other vestiges of the colonial period was a tangible reminder that the colonial period had created a significant institutional, linguistic and constitutional framework within which the contemporary national heritage (however defined) was born and developed.

Caribbean peoples have their origins in all continents and sometimes view their heritage of conflicting and still evolving cultures under the broad rubric of "creolization", which offered the option of harmony rather than the conflict inherent in ethnic nationalism. The new Caribbean nation-states faced the challenge of creating a national identity: having established themselves as nation-states, the question of *whose* heritage within the nation-state became important. However, defining heritage apart from the strictly European heritage was not sufficient to determine the heritage of the new states in the face of profound race, class and cultural contradictions within Caribbean societies. In Jamaica the nationalist model derived from the European nation-state and the Westminster constitutional model; the cultural driving force behind it was a creole nationalism which emphasized the blending of races and cultures in Jamaica. But, as Anthony Bogues (2002, 363–67) notes, creole nationalism in Jamaica ran parallel to black nationalism, which before independence in 1962 had projected itself through Marcus Garvey's Universal Negro Improvement Association and African Communities League and in the millenarian Rastafarian movement. The latter's religious base, its Afrocentricity in art, sculpture and music and its rejection of Jamaica ("Babylon") in favour of repatriation to Africa contradicted creole nationalism in many ways and demonstrated the tensions between creole nationalism and black nationalism, and to some extent, black internationalism.

## Ethnicity and Heritage

In answering the question "Whose heritage?" it was assumed that *heritage* would place less emphasis on the European colonial background. In this sense, heritage corresponded to the "new regime of truth" anxiously being sought after political independence. To some extent, cultural autonomy replaced economic independence as a national priority. Within Caribbean territories where one particular ethnic group constitutes the overwhelming majority, the assumption was that the national heritage would be a conscious recording and approval of the culture of that majority. Thus, for territories such as Jamaica there has been significant emphasis on the African background – once treated as secondary to European culture – of Jamaican cultural identity. The African-Caribbean Institute of Jamaica and the Memory Bank gave institutional representation to that particular focus. But within the structure of the Caribbean nation-state, ethnicity also emerged as a strongly divisive, rather than integrative, force in cultural nationalism. Yet ethnic diversity, for all its divisiveness, has served to enrich rather than impoverish Caribbean heritage.

In Trinidad and Guyana, African and Indian ethnicities vie for dominance, or at least for equality in symbolic recognition. This issue is echoed in Bridget Brereton's chapter, where Indian ethnicity in Trinidad successfully challenges the Christian symbolism of the Trinidadian state. (Ethnicity has also proved a difficult issue in North American heritage with respect to Native American and African-American heritage.) Insofar as identification of heritage is related to the invention of tradition – defined by the Jamaican Norman Manley as an "act of intelligence" – there are subjective judgements as to what constitutes a nation's heritage. To some extent heritage is a "political idea" (Jameson 2008, 36).

The Caribbean heritage is not only mixed – given the participation of different ethnic groups in the creation of that heritage – it also poses a challenge to identification of historical and cultural continuity in a complex ethnic framework in which the majority of people came from different continents. They had to adapt to a completely new economic and social system dominated by the export-oriented plantation, with all the agonies associated with the intense abuse of labour. In a real sense, the search for a Caribbean heritage is in part a challenge to the plantation complex, which has morphed but has not disappeared.

Not only is the study of Caribbean heritage partly rooted in nationalism and ethnicity, it has also been influenced by concerns that were initially specific to the industrialized countries. There, urbanization and industrialization threatened a never-ending struggle between development (modernization) and conservation (preserving the past); the developer, measuring the gap between a rural and an industrial landscape, saw the former as a sign of backwardness and the latter as proof of progress. On the other hand, some preservationists with essentially politically conservative views considered industrialization as disturbance of an idyllic rural past. To some extent, these concepts of heritage management and conservation, derived from a different geographical space, have been successfully transferred to the Caribbean. Although it is true that the Caribbean has gone through a less rigorous industrialization process, it confronts a future in which heritage preservation must cope with unregulated urbanization.

## Museums and Heritage

The Caribbean has imitated metropolitan conduct by establishing museums, national trusts, libraries and institutions designed to promote a national culture or, initially, to project "local colour". Metropolitan heritage preservation has been stimulated by urbanization and industrialization which threaten the landscape (both the cultural landscape and the environment), even at the risk, for example, of projecting the British country mansion as the soul of British heritage. The Caribbean has no such illusions. The history of the rural Caribbean was a mixture of blood, sugar and rum, supervised from the great house which overlooked precarious wattle-and-daub slave cottages.

At the centre of cultural policy in some territories is the establishment of museums, whose development has been uneven across the region. Museum development is associated with public education and seeks to represent all layers of society. Kevin Farmer and Alessandra Cummins's co-authored essay (chapter 25) frankly sees museum development as an aspect of identity and nation-building. But it is also spoken about in light of another matter of urgency: the growth of the Caribbean tourist industry. Ideally, museums present the heritage of a nation to the public. For the more materialistic, museums make no sense unless they add positively to the national accounts. On the one hand, heritage tourism can be seen as a form of "collaboration between conservationists and commercial promotion" (Jameson 2008, 59); on the other hand, the tourist industry can pose a challenge to maintenance of authentic heritage (Thompson 1997; Lowenthal 1993, 275–76). Allison Dolland and Clement Sankat's chapter on industrial heritage features a motley collection of forts, ruins and sites throughout the region that have much potential for heritage tourism.

## The Natural Environment and Heritage

Another aspect of heritage is related to the environment and sustainable development. From the environmental point of view, heritage is no longer a matter of national sentiment. The environmental issue is a global one and has attracted the attention of essays in this book on the Caribbean Sea (chapter 14) and the flora and fauna of Trinidad (chapter 15), for example. Environmentalists, by quietly reminding us of the destruction of tropical rainforests, the pollution of oceans, rivers and underground water supplies, the melting of the Arctic and Antarctic ice, emphasize the reality that heritage – in its environmental aspects – is related to sustainable development and the survival of planet Earth. In this sense, heritage for some is protection of the environment and represents good stewardship of Earth's resources. For others, ecotourism is a major justification for protecting the environment in the first place. But the Caribbean environment is becoming polluted: coral reefs are being destroyed; agricultural land is being washed into the sea.

One area of heritage that has received much attention recently is medicine and medicinal plants and the diversity of flora and fauna in the Caribbean. The contribution by Gregor Barclay (chapter 16) notes that there are more than three hundred different plant species with "reputed" medicinal properties in Trinidad alone. This area of heritage has received abundant attention in Jamaica, in the works of Arvilla Payne-Jackson and Mervyn Alleyne (2004) and Henry Lowe (2001) on Jamaican folk medicine and ethno-medicine. Writing on the history of food in the Caribbean has been growing in volume and sophistication (Higman 2004), and Laura Roberts-Nkrumah (chapter 17) has added to our knowledge of food plants, starting from pre-Columbian times.

## The Built Environment and Heritage

Heritage comes with other challenges, some of them legal. Archaeological sites have been looted; there has been illegal international trade in artefacts which can be reduced only by thorough national inventories of artefacts. According to the study by Andrea Richards (chapter 23), it would appear that the Caribbean is not fully prepared for those challenges, despite the efforts of the United Nations Educational, Scientific and Cultural Organization (UNESCO) to generate an interest in world heritage. The notion of world heritage – the idea that some aspects of heritage belong to mankind as a whole and not only to a particular nation – collapses amidst vandalistic tendencies that thrive on the greedy quest for quick profits from the red bricks of "old" buildings. On the other hand, although the Caribbean is not faced with the issue of "Elginism", the regulations of the splendid British Museum are of interest to a region from which artefacts were taken during the colonial period: "On the other hand, the British Museum is not allowed under its statute to dispose of parts of its collection, and in any case, so it argues, it is a world museum which happens to be in Britain, not the British *sensu* 'National British' Museum, holding material from the world for the world at a convenient place on the global tourist routes" (Boniface and Fowler 1993, 135).

## Intangible Heritage

Partly because Caribbean resources are limited, the preservation and conservation of heritage poses challenges to hard-pressed ministers of finance faced with competing demands. It is fortunate, however, that in areas such as music, gifted Caribbean musicians with entrepreneurial abilities have seized the initiative, and have thereby crowned with glory governments with limited resources that applaud from the sidelines. Calypso, mento and reggae, artists such as the Trinidadian Sparrow, the Jamaicans Bob Marley and Peter Tosh and the steel bands of Trinidad have dazzled the international world of music.

Archaeological work has increased in the Caribbean over the past forty years, but perhaps it is not the highly visible structural remains of the colonial period that dominate Caribbean heritage but its so-called intangible heritage. Claudius Fergus's chapter on Anansi and Ian Robertson and Beverley-Anne Carter's chapter on proverbs cut to the heart of popular discourse in the Caribbean and bring into sharp perspective the cultural continuities that exist between Africa and its Caribbean diaspora. Both Gerard Rogers's and Lorraine Nero's chapters on libraries (chapters 10 and 11) underscore the extent to which indigenous repositories continue to be effective purveyors of information.

This book focuses on the anglophone Caribbean, and its themes range from ecology and folklore to shipwrecks, museums and architecture. These themes are to be expected in a volume on heritage. However, the inclusion of essays on philanthropy (chapters 12 and 13) will encourage a more rigorous discussion of what constitutes heritage, particularly the distinction between "heritage as ideals and heritage as things" (Schofield 2008, 17). By including essays on both intangible heritage and philanthropy, this volume underscores both the creativity and self-reflexiveness of social actors in Caribbean heritage. This approach also undercuts the prevailing modernist view that the concept of heritage is exclusively about "the past as a place, as a 'thing' with other things in it" (Pettman 2001, 1), as part of an "objectifying, reifying, parks-and-museums-making process" (Pettman 2001, 6). In her discussion of Trinidad's ethnicity (chapter 2), Béatrice Boufoy-Bastick calls for a more postmodernist Caribbean heritage, one that challenges "the modernist view of cultural heritage as 'the unchanging meaning of representational objects'" while embracing multiple perspectives and multivocality (see Knapp 1996).

## Conclusion

Given its multidisciplinary approach, *Caribbean Heritage* should appeal to a wide range of scholars. The book will be of particular interest to folklorists, environmentalists, heritage professionals, linguists, librarians, cultural studies experts, historians, archaeologists, museologists and students involved in heritage studies in the region. Readers also stand to benefit from the several images and tables included in this volume.

# References

Agorsah, Kofi E., ed. 1994. *Maroon Heritage: Archaeological, Ethnographic and Historical Perspectives*. Kingston: Canoe Press.

Anico, Marta, and Elsa Peralta, eds. 2009. *Heritage and Identity: Engagement and Demission in the Contemporary World (Museum Meanings)*. London: Routledge.

Bogues, Anthony. 2002. "Nationalism and Jamaican Political Thought". In *Jamaica in Slavery and Freedom: History, Heritage and Culture*, edited by Kathleen Monteith and Glen Richards, 363–87. Kingston: University of the West Indies Press.

Boniface, Priscilla, and Peter Fowler. 1993. *Heritage Tourism in the Global Village*. London: Routledge.

Bryan, Patrick E. 2000. *The Jamaican People, 1880–1902: Race, Class and Social Control*. Kingston: University of the West Indies Press.

Davison, Graeme. 2008. "Heritage: From Patrimony to Pastiche". In *The Heritage Reader*, edited by Graeme Fairclough et al., 31–41. London: Routledge.

Davidson, Graeme, and Chris McConville, eds. 1991. *Heritage Handbook*. New South Wales, Australia: Allen and Unwin.

Delle, James A., Mark W. Hauser and Douglas V. Armstrong, eds. 2011. *Out of Many, One People: The Historical Archaeology of Colonial Jamaica*. Tuscaloosa: University of Alabama Press.

Hall, Stuart. 2008. "Whose Heritage? Un-settling 'The Heritage', Re-imagining the Post-Nation". In *The Heritage Reader*, edited by Graham Fairclough et al., 219–28. London: Routledge.

Higman, B.W. 2004. *Jamaican Food: History, Biology, Culture*. Kingston: University of the West Indies Press.

———. 2010. *A Concise History of the Caribbean*. Cambridge: Cambridge University Press.

Jameson, John, Jr. 2008. "Cultural Heritage Management in the United States". In *The Heritage Reader*, edited by Graeme Fairclough et al., 42–61. London: Routledge.

Knapp, A.B. 1996. "Archaeology Without Gravity: Postmodernism and the Past". *Journal of Archaeological Method and Theory* 3: 127–58.

*Langenscheidt Merriam-Webster English Dictionary*. 1994. Springfield, MA: Merriam-Webster; New York: Langenscheidt.

Lowe, Henry. 2001. *Jamaica's Ethnomedicine: Its Potential in the Healthcare System*. Kingston: Pelican.

Lowenthal, David. 1993. *The Past Is a Foreign Country*. Cambridge: Cambridge University Press.

*Oxford English Dictionary OED Online*. 2009. Oxford: Oxford University Press. http://oed.com (accessed 13 January 2010).

Payne-Jackson, Arvilla, and Mervyn Alleyne. 2004. *Jamaican Folk Medicine: A Source of Healing*. Kingston: University of the West Indies Press.

Pettman, Ralph. March 2001. *The Japanese Concept of Heritage in Its Global Politico-cultural Context*. http://www.victoria.ac.nz/slc/asi/publications/14-japanese-concept-of-heritage.pdf (accessed 6 February 2011).

Schofield, John. 2008. "Heritage Management: Theory and Practice". In *The Heritage Reader*, edited by Graham Fairclough et al., 15–30. London: Routledge.

Smith, Laurajane. 2006. *Uses of Heritage*. London: Routledge.

Thompson, Alvin. 1997. *The Haunting Past: Politics, Economics and Race in Caribbean Life*. Kingston: Ian Randle.

**Part 1.**

INTANGIBLE HERITAGE

# 1.

# Anansi

## An African Legacy Bridging Time, Spaces and Spirits

CLAUDIUS FERGUS

------------------------------------------------------------

*The expression "nansi story" to describe an incredibly fantastic and unrealistic tale is deeply embedded in Creole lexicons across the Caribbean; yet, outside Jamaica, its provenance in Anansi, the Ashanti spider god, is almost unknown or forgotten. The retention of Anansi in the African diaspora from earliest transatlantic forced migrations and enslavement to the present day is one of the amazing stories of African cultural resilience. Regardless of the subsidiary characters in Anansi stories among Caribbean folklorists and storytellers, the didactics remain intact: wit triumphs over brawn, the downtrodden over the mighty, justice over injustice. This chapter connects Anansi in his African homeland with the African diaspora in the colonial slavery era and the post-slavery circum-Caribbean.*

## Introduction

Any meaningful investigation into the cultural history of the African diaspora must follow the contours of the cultural landscape of Africa. However, scholars in various disciplines are challenged by well-established Eurocentric assertions and usurpations of Africa's cultural legacy in the Atlantic diaspora. Notwithstanding, one of the earliest cultural products to be branded with an indisputable African stamp is the folklore of Anansi. Anansi folklore embodies the divine and the profane in a single character, an ideal intellectual construct that engages the ontology of Africanness through time and space (Bascomb 1992, 3–4; Jekyll 1907, ix–xvi, 5). Anansi stories mythologize creation, the origins of various types of misfortunes, death, diseases and natural phenomena. Equally significantly, these stories mythologize humanity's awesome potentialities and frailties and the morality and depravities of civil society (Jarmon 2003, 35–53). The skilfully crafted seminal tales explaining how all animal stories became known as "Anansi stories" has become a signature expression for fantasia and incredulity in the lexicon of languages throughout the anglophone Caribbean. Orthographic variations of *Anansi* in the diaspora include Anansy, Anancy, Annancy, Nansy, Nansi and Xanci – all derivatives of *ananse*, the Twi-Akan word for spider (Werner 1907). Africans from this linguistic region were known collectively to European slave traders and colonists as Koromantis, Kromantins or Coromantees.

## Anansi in Africa

The Twi-Akan region was dominated by the great Ashanti (Asante) empire and Fante kingdoms, where our folk hero is known as Kwaku Ananse, Kweku Ananse, Ananse Kokroko or simply Ananse the spider god. Ananse is also known in the folklore of other culture groups from Togo to Hausaland (northern Nigeria), a legacy of migrations from the Ashanti-Fante region (Gayibor 1997, 33–34). Other spider stories that survived the Middle Passage could easily have become Anansi stories – part of the repertoire of Anansi – as suggested by the wide distribution of Anansi folktales in the Caribbean and Central and South America. As a personal name, Anansi is equivalent to "First Spider", the Adam of the spider race. As a deity or semi-deity (the spider god, son of the high god Nyame), Anansi is the father of the human race and a trickster. In a word, Anansi folklore is the Ashanti's *Animal Farm*, with a liberal touch (Orwell 1993). In Anansi's world, Lion, Tiger, Alligator and other predators and poisoners are reflections of the economic and political elites and oppressors in human society. Rabbit, Tortoise and other traditional prey are the peasants and common folk (Terrell et al. 2004).

Anansi is not the only trickster hero, nor the only spider trickster, in Africa, but he is certainly the most famous mythical trickster hero of sub-Saharan Africa, from Sierra Leone to the Democratic Republic of the Congo (Knappert 1971, 169–74). Other leading animal tricksters in Africa include the rabbit and the tortoise, most popular among the Yoruba, the Igbo and culture groups in Central Africa; the monkey, among the Fon of Togo; and the rat, in the Democratic Republic of the Congo (Knappert, 169–74; Ogunmefe 1984, 65–87; Peek and Yankah 2004, 4). Just as Akan emigration facilitated the migration of Anansi to Hausaland, Togo and other states of West Africa, wherever Akans were concentrated in the Caribbean or played a leading cultural role, their trickster heroes also assumed some degree of hegemony. Thus, while Anansi achieved legendary folk-hero status in Jamaica, Brer Rabbit is best known to the African diaspora in St Lucia and Tortoise (or Turtle) in

Cuba (Brailsford 2003, iv; Lee 1979, 4; Bueno 2003, 63–67; Cabrera 2008, 45–47). Storytellers in both Africa and the diaspora brought rival tricksters and formidable animals such as Lion and Elephant into the stories (Anansi versus Rabbit; Anansi versus Tortoise, etc.). This juxtaposition underscores the primacy of Anansi as a master trickster (David 1985, 19). The pitting of these major tricksters from different culture areas against one another also raises questions of ethnic accommodation and rivalry between migrant Africans and their autochthonous hosts, as well as among African diaspora communities during and after the slavery era.

Storytelling in Africa, as elsewhere, combines instructional objectives with social entertainment; as stated by Peek and Yankah, "Anansi personifies possibilities" while "his preposterous adventures are the stuff of humour with a didactic edge". Folktales introduce listeners (and readers) to a variety of cultural practices, standards of behaviour and beliefs; they inculcate in the very young "the power of rhetorics [sic] and repertoire". As Brathwaite succinctly states of enslaved diasporan Africans in the Caribbean, "the word was held to contain a secret power". Likewise, Anansi stories "sharpen the intellect and power of memory" of adult listeners and participants (Peek and Yankah, 4; Ogungini and Na'Allah 2005, 76; Brathwaite 1971, 237). To Africans in particular, Anansi was a vehicle of socialization into call-and-response behaviours, which manifest in diverse African cultural spaces and group activities, including religion, politics and music.

Although Alice Werner, in her introduction to Walter Jekyll's seminal collection of folktales, pronounced, "His [Anansi's] moral character is consistently bad all through", there is strong evidence for a split personality. As the quintessential trickster, he is the epitome of wit and cunning, manifesting the most negative and abhorrent qualities of human nature: he is lazy, adulterous, selfish and greedy to the extreme. Stories feature Anansi cheating his own family of their food and plotting to sell his wife to the fruit demon. Such extreme "character flaws" compel reflection in storytelling audiences or readers of folk literature. In order to protect children against "Anansi morality", storytellers in Jamaica end their tales with "Jack Mandora, me no choose none" – Mandora is heaven's gatekeeper, to whom the tellers disavow condoning Anansi's amorality (Jekyll 1907, xv–xvi; Barker and Sinclair 1972, 69–72; Bennett 2005; Beckwith 1969, 16, 31).

Notwithstanding his boastful self-proclamation as "the cleverest of the animals", Anansi sometimes makes errors of judgement, though he often redeems himself by sheer inventiveness (Ogungini and Na'Allah, 80–81; Barker and Sinclair; Salkey 1980, 79–80; Halsworth 1972, 71–75). Thus the abiding attractiveness of Anansi to storytellers and listeners is his identification as an underdog with a determination to survive and thrive against the greatest odds, transforming defeatist expectations into monumental victories. In such instances, the listening audience invariably identifies with Anansi as hero. Listeners' loyalty to Anansi is assured by pitting him against the largest, most ferocious and most cunning forest animals, the most notable antagonists from land, water and air, such as Lion, Tiger, Leopard, Snake, Crocodile, Elephant, Fox and Gnat. Storytellers also manipulate loyalty in order to emphasize moral values. At such times Anansi's opponents are other trickster animals of lesser stature, such as Rabbit, Tortoise and Rat, among other common prey of the great hunters and foragers. The audience switches their identification to the beleaguered antagonists or victims of Anansi's greed and trickery. Rex Nettleford assures us that, notwithstanding Anansi's flaws, "in the end he is always the audience's hero. He has to be!" (Nettleford 1966, xiv).

Anansi embodies intangible continuities with African cosmology going back to antiquity. This aspect is attested to in Anansi's ability to transform into human or semi-human form or into other creatures, while still retaining the virtues of the traditional trickster. Evidence abounds that Saharan rock art dating as far back as the fifth millennium BCE portrayed human figures with totemic animal heads. This mythological genetic fusion is even more prominent and emphatic in ancient Egypt's anthropomorphic cosmology. The goddess Hathor manifested as a cow; Horus, the son of Re, manifested as a falcon or a human with a falcon's head; Thoth, the god of wisdom, was always portrayed with the head of an ibis; the goddess Isis was commonly portrayed with outstretched wings. It was also customary to portray animals with human heads – a sculptural art form generically termed sphinxes. During the Iron Age in sub-Saharan Africa, blacksmiths were vested with supernatural powers to transform into animals. Diasporan folklore of the *lagahoo* and *soucouyant*, creatures of the night, engaged this transformative power of humans (Ottley 1979, 19–21).

## The Diasporan Anansi

Oral tradition was the principal medium for transmission and preservation of many African cultural practices among the African diasporas. The literary tradition of African Muslims who survived the Middle Passage did not find an accommodating environment in European plantation colonies. On the other hand, to survive chattelization, Africans successfully incorporated "traditional" African song patterns independently and as accompaniment to African dance rhythms. Songs, with their repertoire of dances, were regularly featured on weekends and feast days and during wakes. The spoken word was also the medium for transmission of religious, medical and esoteric knowledge. Against the concerted dehumanization strategies of plantation enslavement, African folklore was the most effective medium for preserving and transmitting Africa's oral literature and moral/ethical values. In short, the spoken word *was* power, and recognized as such by enslaved and enslavers alike.

To West Indians the expression *nansi story* usually means "nonsense story", one which carries "little or no truth"; alternatively it is "any folk tale, a lie" (Abrahams 1982, 389; Warner-Lewis 1991, 168). Notwithstanding, Jamaican folk memory of Anansi is not that of the "negative tricksters"; to them the "real Anansis" are "creatures, who are thinkers and planners" (Marshall 2007, 50). Thus the Maroon expression "doing an Anansi" conveys the meaning of "victory or advantage by outsmarting another" (Zips 1999, 165). Although *nansi story* is embedded in the lexicons of the Caribbean, speakers are not always aware of its provenance in Akan/Ashanti folklore.

The Akan/Koromanti presence in Jamaica predated English colonization. The Jamaica Maroons, who defeated the English and had their freedom and sovereignty recognized by treaty, were largely Akan. Many of the names of leaders such as Kojo/Cudjoe, Kofi/Cuffee and Tacky; lesser mortals such as Cubba, Memba and Fibba; and townships such as Accompong and Cudjoe's Town (now Trelawny Town) attest to this fact. The strength of Akan/Koromanti influence elsewhere is similarly attested to in the leadership of major revolts and maroon communities in Demerara and Suriname. Although creolized by the plantocracy into the quintessential negative stereotype, the name Quashie (Akan for "born on Sunday") is also significant of the Koromanti presence.

The infamous diarist, planter and overseer Thomas Thistlewood, of Jamaica, left us the name Vine (possibly from the Igbo Ifine) as one of the great practitioners of Anansi storytelling during the slavery era. Indeed, Vine was an oral specialist in the true tradition of the West African griot, though more particularly engaged in "communicative cultural and symbolic recounting of stories of Anansi" and other folklore (Asante 2007, 125; Zips 1999, 165; Hale 1998). An object of attraction to many white plantation males, Vine told her "Nancy stories" in the evenings at Thistlewood's house, sometimes sharing the stage with Abba, another female (Akan) storyteller. Thistlewood confirmed that the stories were always "entertaining" and "very cleverly" composed and delivered (Hall 1999, 159–60).

The trickster as hero was destined to become psychological therapy as well as revolutionary ideology in the culture of resistance of enslaved peoples in European colonies. In Carriacou, Anansi is venerated in the Big Drum rites. Songs such as "Anancy" and "Anancy-O, Sari Baba" recall the Akan spirit of resistance in Carriacou from at least the seventeenth century (David 1985, 19; Hill 1999; Lomax 1999). In Jamaica Anansi quickly became the quintessential Maroon, a master planner and organizer of camouflage and ambush.

As told by a Maroon descendant, Mr Bernard of the Windward Maroons, "Anansi started to talk his story . . . Through we Maroon" (Marshall 2007, 53); on the plantation of the enslaved he remained a free spirit, a missionary of freedom, cementing the community through the voices of storytellers. Many historians attest to the wit and cunning of enslaved Africans in contradiction to the Quashie/Sambo stereotype of the lazy, servile moron. It is also well-known that the enslaved exploited this stereotypical characterization while using their wit to procure advantages proscribed by plantation authorities.

The Maroons of Jamaica were a major conduit for the transmission, survival and status of Anansi as a virtual national hero. They also testify to Anansi stories' possessing "latent possibilities that frightened the colonists" (James 1963, 18). Based on field work among the Jamaican Maroons, anthropologist Emily Marshall agrees: "The stories of Anansi's skill inspired Maroon survival tactics" (2007, 53). Indeed, during the Maroons' eighty years of warfare with the British (c. 1660–1739), Anansi's wit and cunning provided ideological fodder for guerrilla warfare, particularly the secrets of camouflage and ambush – basics of guerrilla warfare introduced to the Caribbean by African survivors of the Middle Passage (Marshall 2007, 53; Thompson 2006, 148). In the popular imagination of Maroons and their descendants, Anansi was the primary inspiration for military intelligence and martial science. As with many African deities, Anansi transcends sexual definitions. Thus the Maroon queen Nanny was reincarnated as Anansi in the legends of her exploits against the colonial forces sent to destroy her and her people (Marshall 2007, 53).

Enslaved Africans gathered round their campfires at night to tell stories. C.L.R. James agrees that this was the main cultural space for storytelling and thus for building community among enslaved Africans in Saint-Domingue/Haiti. This sense of community is also evident in the account by Captain Smith of the Jamaican township of modern-day Moore Town, founded by Maroons in the eighteenth century, where moonlight was a substitute for the campfire of slavery. Smith testified that during moonlit nights his grandmother and grandfather "would take you up in an Anansi story. You would have children coming from other homes to listen, and that would last for late night" (Marshall 2007, 52).

Two layers of preservation and transmission of folklore existed: (1) within the socializing spaces of children and (2) in adult culture spaces, especially during wakes. At bedtime the mother of well-known Jamaican Anansi story-teller Louise Bennett would read Anansi stories, all of which had their repertoire of songs (Bennett 1966, ix). Stella Bouville, a long-time resident of three different cultural milieus in Trinidad, recalls in a 2008 interview in Mayaro that her parents' house in central Trinidad was a meeting place for storytelling; invariably the favourite genre was Anansi, told in the classic dramatic style

(Opekwho 1992, 43–46). Bouville recalls, "The older ones tell us stories but we too tell our stories to them." Children were also allowed to share the company of elders at village wakes, where stories were told to appease the spirits of the dead as much as to entertain the living (Herskovits and Herskovits 1934, 4; Elder 1970, 8). However, she affirms that adults also had exclusive spaces where Anansi stories were told. In Guyana the inclusion of African Creole oral tradition added a touch of spice to Amerindian trickster storytelling. Edna La Fleur, of Kwakani, in Guyana's hinterland, affirms that her grandmother was the principal storyteller at family gatherings (interview with author, 2008); although mostly Amerindian stories were told, the repertoire also included Anansi. On the contrary, Scholastique Thomas of St Lucia recollects that as a child she was not privileged to listen to storytelling: "These people did not even want you to come round them." This generational exclusivity may not have been the general rule, however. Sandra Evans, of St Augustine, Trinidad and Tobago, recalls that an uncle from the south of St Lucia would tell of spending his childhood in the company of elders during storytelling (interview with author, 2008).

Age stratification of storytelling audiences in African diaspora communities is indicative of major changes in the upbringing of children in the last quarter of the twentieth century, prior to which children were generally not allowed to participate in the leisure activities of elders. During the slavery era, the prime cultural space created by enslaved Africans was the campfire, which was enriched by funerary wakes. The post-slavery diaspora transformed the wake-house into the primary cultural space for *esprit de corps* among village folk. The dedication of space and time to honour the dead as central to the community of the living goes far back into African antiquity. That this cultural feature transcended time and space in Africa is attested to by several scholars. Herskovits (1941, 63) assures us that the cultural orientation of modern West Africa maintained the eschatological focus of ancient Egypt: "the funeral is the true climax of life, and no belief drives deeper into the traditions of West African thought". Oral evidence abounds that wakes played a critical role in the preservation and vitalization of African folktales in the post-slavery era. The testimony of Herskovits and Herskovits (1934, 4) on Saramakan practice supports this cultural experience: "While the body lies in the open house of the dead, relatives and the village elders are in attendance on the spirit night and day. It is they who all night tell stories about the trickster, spider Anansi, to amuse the spirit, and they who play traditional games."

Bouville (interview, 2008) testifies to a remarkably similar cultural phenomenon. She recalls that, during her childhood, the corpse was kept in the house of mourning until the hour of the funeral. The main features of the first wake, held on the night before the funeral, were storytelling, songs and the playing of traditional indoor games. The bereaved were completely freed of the emotional and financial burdens commonly associated with funerals and wakes – the community "took charge of everything". More storytelling and games featured in the commemorations called "nine nights" and "forty days". She laments, "All this now disappear; it is only your food visitors coming for, and to gamble." In speaking of the "New World" African diaspora in general, J.D. Elder (1970) confirms this funerary experience as a victory of African "psychic sciences" over colonial Christianity: "After near to 500 years of theological confrontation from pulpit, crusade and camp-meeting, the Negroes still regard it as their duty to 'feed the spirits' in return for their guardianship, guidance and protection." Anansi folklore was a libation reconcilable to all faiths in the diaspora.

The ontology of the crossroads also facilitated the retention of Anansi and other trickster stories. According to Jarmon (2003, xiii), the crossroads, like the wishbone, is a "site of power", but also a point of "indeterminacy". In this sense one may locate Anansi, Brer Rabbit and other trickster heroes as links between the esotericism of obeah practitioners and other plantation-based anti-slavery resistance specialists on the one hand and the military culture of Maroon guerrillas on the other. For example, having won the copyright to the folktales of the Ashanti, Anansi "taught Awo, a human, the knowledge of medicine", which undoubtedly was a forte in obeah practices. This assertion is supported by Warner-Lewis (1991, 134); she compares the high-pitched prophesying of "diviners and herbalists in Yorubaland" with "the vocal quality ascribed to Anansi the spider in Jamaica oral narratives". Like Anansi, obeah specialists were feared for their intellect and special gift for accomplishing the impossible. The compelling place of obeah in Jamaican creole ontology led to its becoming the first subject of Jamaican literature (Pradel 2002, 262).

African folklore attracted its fair share of hostility from cultural assassins during the slavery era. According to Mary Turner (1998, 65), one of the primary challenges of Christian missionaries to Jamaica was "to replace Anansi, the supreme ginal, with Christian the Pilgrim, who fought his way through life". Yet in contradiction of the spirit of contemporary Western Christianity, the missionaries condemned running away, and all other forms of resistance to enslavement, as sin (Nisbett 1970, 95). David Braidsford (2003, iv) has affirmed the continuing war against Anansi by Christian churches. He asserts that one of the reasons Anansi is "no longer at the centre of Jamaican culture" is because Christian authorities considered Anansi pagan. Notwithstanding, urbanization, the digital revolution and new expressions of popular culture have proven a greater threat to survival of the oral tradition as a whole. Television has largely replaced the yard and the campfire as a cultural space of communal entertainment (Joseph 1979, 1). As mentioned earlier, older folk also lament that modern wakes have lost their communal impulse and degenerated into an avenue for free meals and unlicensed gambling.

Although Anansi grew out of and thrived in preliterate oral cultures, the emergence of literacy among the emancipated, however sanitized of African content, did not bring about the death of African folklore, or even lessen the taste for it. A major reason for this is that folklore is best digested in the dialect in which it was originally constructed and transmitted. So long as a sense of community existed among rural folk – sustained by cooperation in wakes, sou-sou, lend-hand/gayap and other forms of communalism – Anansi tales and other folklore were assured continuity and currency. Scholars recognize that oral literature "also provides students a frame of reference to bring to the literature and the cultures they will later encounter" (Greene 1996, 33–34; Young et al. 2004).

The practice of call and response in storytelling is integral to audience/spectator participation within African communities. In diasporan storytelling it testifies to the syncretism of ethnicities and languages in the making of a pan-African creole Caribbean. One of the most recognized expressions associated with storytelling in the eastern Caribbean is the teller's final call, "Crick!" and the audience's response, "Crack!" Often the Trinidadian storyteller would end with "Crick-crack!" and the audience would respond, "Monkey break his back!" (la Fortune 1980, 63). In St Lucia, kwéyòl (patois) storytellers end with the call, "I di kwik!" while the audience responds, "Kwak!" (Thomas 2008; Samantha Mitchell, personal communication, 2008). To diasporan storytellers and even anthropologists, *crick-crack*, and its kwéyòl variant, is not translatable. On the contrary, a clue to its etymology comes from Saramaka storytellers of Suriname. The Saramaka have preserved the teller's call "Kri-kra!" to begin their stories and summon the audience to attention. This expression is unmodified Akan, and still used in Ghana today by storytellers. *Kra* has the sense of "send the message" (Agnes Akwele Olemoh, interview with author, Tema, Ghana, 2008); therefore the audience's response, "Will it go?" makes perfect sense (Herskovits and Herskovits 1934, 104). *Crick-crack* and *kwik-kwak* are clearly derived from Akan, though with changed positions in the story.

Another Saramakan storyteller's opening call, "Er-tin-tin", is used mainly in stories told to children; the young audience responds, "Tin-tin-tin." These are very common Fante expressions and can still be heard from storytellers in Ghana (Herskovits and Herskovits 1934, 103; Olemoh, interview). The phrase "tin-tin-tin" is also a common chorus line in *zouk*, a popular genre of songs in the French Antilles. In St Lucia the opening phrase "Tim Tim!" is so well-established that the expression "Tim-Tim stories" is used instead of

"Anansi stories" (Lee 1979, 4). Less popular storytelling calls and responses recorded by Herskovits and Herskovits (1934, 103) among the Saramaka are "Hireti!" and "Daieti!". "Hireti" comes from the Yoruba word *ireti*, meaning "to anticipate", while "daieti" derives from the Yoruba word *areti*, meaning "we remember" (Olemoh, interview). This call-and-response behaviour in Anansi stories was successfully transferred to other aspects of diasporan life, including missionary Christianity, which Africans modified to produce unique forms of Christian worship for the Caribbean region and the wider world. African-influenced call and response has also influenced the music genres of the Americas, as well as politics and other areas of popular culture.

One of the first compilations of African diaspora folktales was included in the seminal volume by Walter Jekyll (2007). Other compilers were active during the interwar period in the Caribbean as well as in Africa (Beckwith 1924; Ogunmefe 1929). J.O. Cutteridge, first as deputy director and later as director of education in Trinidad and Tobago, made an invaluable contribution to creole culture by breaking the hegemony of European content in school texts, incorporating into his *West Indian Reader* series folktales of the African diaspora. For a whole generation these readers were the prescribed texts for all levels in primary schools in British West Indian colonies. Together with other pioneers of folk literature, Cutteridge was responsible for accelerating the transformation of Anansi, Brer Rabbit and other African stories from oral tales to written literature.

## Beyond Folklore

On a lone stele in Cape Coast Castle is a painted image of Anansi standing watch over one of the main points of embarkation of Africans during the European slave trade. Among other prominent Ghanaian buildings featuring Anansi designs are the Cape Coast Hotel and the mausoleum of W.E.B. Du Bois in Accra. Spider designs are also common in Caribbean architecture, although the extent to which they are directly influenced by Anansi folklore is uncertain. However, many scholars agree "that a certain level of Anancy represents the character of the Caribbean people" (Prahlad 2006, 28). This assertion leaves scope for debate on the extent to which Anansi shaped or reflects this character. Yet the combination of storytelling, enslavement, colonialism and neo-colonialism surely had an impact on oral art forms and the "love of eloquence" in general (Rohlehr 1990, 66). The Caribbean persona may be expressed in a variety of art forms, but arguably the most pervasive is the calypso. Writing in 1962, V.S. Naipaul (1962, 70) asserted, "It is only in the calypso that the Trinidadian touches reality"; this judgement could now be aptly extended to the wider anglophone Caribbean. Calypsonians – combinations of folk-poet, singer and performer – consciously glorify "anansy-ism"; they also proudly represent themselves – and are seen as such by the public – as the voice of the voiceless, the champion of political, economic and social underdogs. Calypsos proliferate, for example, about cricket heroes who engineer victory for their territorial or regional teams against the might of imperial England and the formidable Australians.

The word power of enslaved Africans, preserved through Anansi stories, flourished in both nineteenth-century folk poetry and educated oratory and writings. Conscious of this legacy, rapso artist Brother Resistance (in *When De Riddum Explode*, 2001) affirms in his composition "Nzobu": "Rhythm is the voice of rebellion / The power of the word . . ." In another composition, "Aluta Continua", he is the griot, master of the word, but also a Maroon for whom the struggle for freedom is a vocation: "I refuse to write words / That will negotiate / Instead of advocate / For freedom from oppression / I will not write poetry / For peaceful coexistence with the oppressors."

Several scholars and storytellers affirm that Anansi "was one of the trickiest guys around"; he was also "as lazy as could be" (Hagerty and Perham 2006, 91). Greed and selfishness are other character flaws explored earlier in this essay. Whereas the Jamaican storyteller repudiates Anansi's amorality, the calypso tradition glorifies these negative traits – invariably in humorous compositions. The Mighty Sparrow may be considered at the top of this class that praises the gifted liar; one of his most memorable compositions is "Lying Excuses" (1987). Similar classics were sung by the Mighty Zandolie ("Too Much Man Family", 1967) and Lord Nelson ("King Liar", 1977). Anansi's cunning is celebrated in calypsos acclaiming the "smartman", or conman, with the Barbadian (Bajan) often being held above the Trinidadian as the quintessential conman. Examples of these songs include "Smart Bajan" by Mighty Sparrow (2000) and "Take Yuh Meat Out Meh Rice" by Lord Kitchener (1967); "Pyramid Scam" by Mighty Sparrow (2000), a calypso documentary of a nation-wide financial swindle during the 1990s.

Anansi's greed finds expression in several calypsos, an example of which is King Fighter's composition on being the uninvited guest at an Indian wedding. In his analysis of the song, Rohlehr (1990, 25) asserts, "he knowingly assumes the role of trickster in order to penetrate into the secret or private lifestyle of the Other", a risky business, fraught with danger. Rohlehr then makes a more direct allusion to Anansi: "His behaviour follows the shape of archetypal myth. Anansi is depicted as a gate-crasher, disguiser and trickster. He is also frequently threatened with violence." Thus it owes more to the self-discovery of character of the people than to the popularity of the trickster hero that the expression "nansi story" has assumed epistemological status in the lexicon of Caribbean Creole.

# References

Abrahams, Roger D. 1982. "Storytelling Events: Wake Amusements and the Structure of Nonsense on St. Vincent". *Journal of American Folklore* 95, no. 378: 389–414. http://www.questia.com/PM.qst?a=o&d=95178256 (accessed 20 January 2010).

Asante, Molefi Kete. 2007. *The History of Africa: The Quest for Eternal Harmony.* New York: Routledge.

Barker, W.H., and Cecilia Sinclair. 1972. *West African Folk-Tales.* Northbrook, IL: Metro Books.

Bascomb, William. 1992. *African Folktales in the New World.* Bloomington: Indiana University Press.

Bennett, Louise. 1966. "Me and Annancy". Introduction to *Jamaican Song and Story: Annancy Stories, Digging Sings, Ring Tunes, and Dancing Tunes,* edited by Walter Jekyll. New York: Dover.

———. 1973. *Anancy Stories and Dialect Verse,* new series. Kingston: Pioneer Press.

———. 1980. "Anancy and Common Sense". In *Caribbean Folk Tales and Legends,* edited by Andrew Salkey. London: Bogle-L'Ouverture.

———. 2005. *Anancy and Miss Lou.* Kingston: Sangster's Book Stores.

Brailsford, David. 2003. *Confessions of Anansi.* Kingston: LMH.

Brathwaite, Edward. 1971. *The Development of Creole Society in Jamaica, 1770–1820.* Oxford: Clarendon Press.

Bueno, Salvador. 2003. *Cuban Legends.* Translated by Siegfried Kaden. Jamaica: Ian Randle.

Cabrera, Lydia. 2008. *Afro-Cuban Short Stories.* Translated by Marieta A. Gutiérrez. New York: Edwin Mellen.

David, Christine. 1985. *Folklore of Carriacou.* Barbados: Coles Printery.

Elder, Jacob Delworth. 1970. "The New World Negroes' Search for Identity". Public lecture, Barbados.

Gayibor, N.L. 1997. *Histoire des Togolais de 1884 à 1960.* Vol. 1, *Des origines à 1884.* Lomé, Togo: Presses de l'Université de Lomé.

Greene, Ellin. 1996. *Storytelling: Art and Technique.* New Providence, NJ: R.R. Bowker.

Hagerty, Timothy, and Mary Gomez Parham. 2006. *If de Pin Neva Bend: Folktales and Legends of Belize.* Benque Viejo del Carmen, Belize: Cubola.

Hale, Thomas A. 1998. *Griots and Griottes: Masters of Word and Music.* Bloomington: Indiana University Press.

Hall, Douglas. 1999. *In Miserable Slavery: Thomas Thistlewood in Jamaica, 1750–1786.* Kingston: University of the West Indies Press.

Hallworth, Grace. 1977. *Listen to This Story: Tales from the West Indies.* London: Cox and Wyman.

Herskovits, Melville J. 1941. *The Myth of the Negro Past.* Boston: Beacon Press.

Herskovits, Melville J., and Frances Shapiro Herskovits. 1934. *Rebel Destiny: Among the Bush Negroes of Dutch Guiana.* New York: McGraw-Hill.

Hill, Donald R. 1998. "West African and Haitian Influences on the Ritual and Popular Music of Carriacou, Trinidad and Cuba". *Black Music Research Journal* 18, nos. 1–2: 183–201. http://www.questia.com/PM.qst?a=o&d=5001415051 (accessed 2 July 2010).

James, C.L.R. 1963. *The Black Jacobins: Toussaint L'Ouverture and the French Revolution*. New York: Random House.

Jarmon, Laura C. 2003. *Wishbone: Reference and Interpretations in Black Folk Narrative*. Knoxville: University of Tennessee Press.

Jekyll, Walter, ed. 1907. *Jamaican Song and Story: Annancy Stories, Digging Sings, Ring Tunes, and Dancing Tunes*. London: David Nutt.

Knappert, Jan. 1971. *Myths and Legends of the Congo*. Nairobi: Heinemann Educational.

La Fortune, Knolly. 1980. "Bre'r Tacooma in Trouble". In *Caribbean Folk Tales and Legends*, edited by Andrew Salkey, 59–63. London: Bogle-L'Ouverture.

Lee, Jacintha A. 1979. *Give Me Some Sense*. N.p.

Marshall, Emily Zobel. 2007. "Tracking Anansi". *Caribbean Beat* 88 (November–December).

Naipaul, V.S. 1962. *The Middle Passage*. London: Andre Deutsch.

Nettleford, Rex. 1966. "Jamaican Song and Story and the Theater". Introduction to *Jamaican Song and Story: Annancy Stories, Digging Sings, Ring Tunes, and Dancing Tunes*, edited by Walter Jekyll. New York: Dover.

Nisbett, Richard. [1789] 1970. *The Capacity of Negroes for Religious and Moral Improvement Considered: with Cursory Hints, to Proprietors and Governments, for the Immediate Amelioration of the Condition of Slaves in the Sugar Colonies: to which are subjoined Short and Practical Discourses to Negroes, on the Plain and Obvious Principles of Religion and Morality*. Reprint, New York: Negro University Press.

Ogungini, Bayo, and Abdul-Rasheed Na'Allah. 2005. *Introduction to African Oral Literature and Performance*. Trenton, NJ: Africa World Press.

Ogunmefe, M.I. [1929] 1984. *Yoruba Legends*. London: Sheldon Press.

Okpewho, Isidore. 1992. *African Oral Literature: Backgrounds, Character, and Continuity*. Bloomington: Indiana University Press.

Ottley, C.R. 1979. *Folk Beliefs, Folk Customs, and Folk Characters Found in Trinidad and Tobago*. Diego Martin, Trinidad: Crusoe.

Orwell, George. [1945] 1993. *Animal Farm*. London: David Campbell.

Peek, Philip M., and Kwesi Yankah, eds. 2004. *African Folklore: An Encyclopedia*. New York: Routledge.

Pradel, Lucie. 2002. "African Sacredness and Caribbean Cultural Forms". In *Questioning Creole: Creolisation Discourses in Caribbean Culture*, edited by Verene A. Shepherd and Glen L. Richards, 257–64. Kingston: Ian Randle.

Prahlad, Anand. 2006. *The Greenwood Encyclopedia of African American Folklore*. Westport, CT: Greenwood Press.

Rohlehr, Gordon. 1990. *Calypso and Society in Pre-independence Trinidad*. Port of Spain, Trinidad: G. Rohlehr.

Thompson, Alvin. 2006. *Flight to Freedom: African Runaways and Maroons in the Americas*. Kingston: University of the West Indies Press.

Turner, Mary. 1998. *Slaves and Missionaries: The Disintegration of Jamaican Society, 1783–1834*. Kingston: University of the West Indies Press.

Warner-Lewis, Maureen. 1991. *Guinea's Other Suns: The African Dynamic in Trinidad Culture*. Dover, MA: Majority Press.

Werner, Alice. 1907. Introduction to *Jamaican Song and Story: Annancy Stories, Digging Sings, Ring Tunes, and Dancing Tunes*, edited by Walter Jekyll. London: David Nutt.

Young, Terrel A., et al. 2004. "Folk Literature: Preserving the Storytellers' Magic". *Reading Teacher* 57: 782. http://www.questia.com/PM.qst?a=o&d=5005902743 (accessed 20 January 2010).

Zips, Werner. 1999. *Black Rebels: African-Caribbean Freedom Fighters in Jamaica*. Translated by Shelley L. Frisch. Kingston: Ian Randle.

# 2.

# Measuring the Postmodern Dynamics of Trinidadian Cultural Heritage

BÉATRICE BOUFOY-BASTICK

*This chapter explores changing representations of cultural heritage in Trinidad. It challenges the modernist view of cultural heritage as the unchanging meaning of representational objects, as epitomized by the museum exhibit. Whilst from a postmodernist perspective it recognizes the modernist view of cultural heritage as an official construction, it questions the authority of that construction, the purposes of official interpretations of selected objects and why those objects, rather than others, have been selected. From the perspective of radical constructivism, it questions the agenda of institutions in defining the cultural heritage of Trinidadians. The chapter operationalizes this postmodernist view using the cultural index, a measurement method of Culturometrics. Culturometrics views an individual's cultural heritage as a continued personal re-construction of trans-generational ethnic identity components. In multicultural societies such as Trinidad this is achieved via a sociocultural bricolage. Culturometrics views the cultural heritage of a group as a socially negotiated aggregation of individuals' cultural heritages. These re-constructions and negotiations then produce a dynamic cultural heritage that exhibits both developmental and historical change. This chapter demonstrates the dynamics of cultural heritage in Trinidad using ethnic comparisons of trans-generational cultural identity components of 348 Trinidadians. As presented in this chapter, the significance of the modernist culturometric perspective is that it stresses the changing meanings of cultural heritage and formalizes its dynamic historically revisionist nature.*

## Introduction

This chapter presents changing representations of cultural heritage in Trinidad and supports a postmodernist definition of cultural heritage. It argues against the traditional view of cultural heritage as an unchanging meaning of representational objects and presents cultural heritage as a dynamic social process enhancing cultural and civic identity. This chapter then focuses on one aspect of that process. It defines cultural heritage as the trans-generational components of cultural identity and focuses on individuals' constructions of their cultural heritage. This radical-constructivist postulate was tested in the culturometric study reported in this chapter. It shows changes in the ideological conceptualization of cultural heritage: from a positivist modernist view to a postmodernist social-constructivist perspective and ultimately to the radical-constructivist definition proposed here. This chapter reports both empirical qualitative evidence that tests the radical-constructivist definition of cultural heritage and the quantitative empirical evidence that verifies its social-constructivist perspective.

## Reconceptualizing Cultural Heritage: A Diachronic Perspective

Reviewing the literature on cultural heritage highlights manifest changes in ideological thinking. It shows that cultural heritage evolved from a traditional modernist construct into the current postmodernist construct. The literature review presented here illustrates the original positivist modernist definition of cultural heritage in terms of institutionally selected and authorized artefacts. It then illustrates that this top-down hegemonic characterization is contested and renegotiated by groups within a social-constructivist perspective. Finally, it shows cultural heritage being assembled from the bottom up from individuals' constructed trans-generational identity components (Abu-Khafaj 2010; von Glaserfeld 1998).

### Expounding a Politically Guided Hegemonic Definition of Cultural Heritage

Cultural heritage is traditionally epitomized by the museum exhibit: a rare, valued, protected and presumably cherished artefact representing valued characteristics of a cultural group. The object, its choice and the laws, rules, policies and circumstances enforcing its protection give authority to the valuing of the cultural characteristics it represents. This traditional meaning of cultural heritage both affirms the positive value of those who identify with the cultural group and further empowers the authority that defines it through their allegiance. This positive empowerment loop encourages the accretion of more objects into what we refer to here as a monolith of cultural heritage, spreading protection to those objects and benefiting those people and institutions that control access to the cultural heritage. These monoliths typically comprise objects such as those that define cultural heritage in UNESCO's 2005 and 2008 *Operational Guidelines for the Implementation of the World Heritage Convention*:

> Article 1
> For the purposes of this Convention, the following shall be considered as "cultural heritage":
>> monuments: architectural works, works of monumental sculpture and painting, elements or structures of an archaeological nature, inscriptions, cave dwellings
>> . . .
>> groups of buildings: groups of separate or connected buildings which, because of their architecture, their homogeneity or their place in the landscape, are of outstanding universal value from the point of view of history, art or science;
>> . . . (WHC 2005, 13, para. 45; WHC 2008, 13, para. 45)

This monolithic, modernist conception of cultural heritage is evidenced in numerous works titled "*The* Cultural Heritage of . . ." which seek to narrowly define a single official cultural heritage specified as authoritatively selected and preferred objects to which individuals should socially or historically relate. Illustrative examples are *The Cultural Heritage of India* by Haridas Bhattacharyya, *The Cultural Heritage of Pakistan* by S.M. Ikram and P. Spear, *The Cultural Heritage of Africa* by Pascal James Imperato, *The Cultural Heritage of Malaya* by N.J. Ryan, *The Cultural Heritage of the Himalayas* by Kishori Lal Vaidya, *The Cultural Heritage of Malaysia* by Yahaya Ismail and so forth.

## Proposing a Social-Constructivist Definition of Cultural Heritage

Subsequent cultural heritage definitions are best appreciated through a contested authoritative inclusion of the "objects" they comprise. These definitions question and contest the political motivations for including some of these so-called defining objects, creating cracks in the cultural heritage monoliths (Smith 2004; Thomson 1978) and suggesting wider social constructions (Dann and Seaton 2002; Graham 1996; Kreamer 2006; Hou 2004; Olwig 2005; Sculthorpe 2005; Worden 1996). For example, a UNESCO glossary of traditional knowledge gives a more recent definition of cultural heritage:

> Having at one time referred exclusively to the monumental remains of cultures, heritage as a concept has gradually come to include new categories such as the

intangible, ethnographic or industrial heritage. A noteworthy effort was subsequently made to extend the conceptualization and description of the intangible heritage. This is due to the fact that closer attention is now being paid to humankind, the dramatic arts, languages and traditional music, as well as to the informational, spiritual and philosophical systems upon which creations are based. (UNESCO 2003)

Article 2 of UNESCO's 2003 *Convention for the Safeguarding of the Intangible Cultural Heritage* includes these social intangible "objects" as part of its definition of cultural heritage.

> For the purposes of this Convention,
> 1. The "intangible cultural heritage" means the practices, representations, expressions, knowledge, skills – as well as the instruments, objects, artefacts and cultural spaces associated therewith – that communities, groups and, in some cases, individuals recognize as part of their cultural heritage. This intangible cultural heritage, transmitted from generation to generation, *is constantly recreated by communities and groups* [my emphasis] in response to their environment.
> 2. The "intangible cultural heritage", as defined in paragraph 1 above, is manifested inter alia in the following domains:
>    (a)  oral traditions and expressions, including language as a vehicle of the intangible cultural heritage;
>    (b)  performing arts;
>    (c)  social practices, rituals and festive events;
>    (d)  knowledge and practices concerning nature and the universe;
>    (e)  traditional craftsmanship. (UNESCO 2003, 2)

Further, Tongyun Yin (2006, 2) instructively identifies two social subcategories of intangible cultural heritage, the second of which refers to the personal lived culture of individuals:

> I prefer to divide the Intangible Cultural Heritage into two groups: one is the Intangible Cultural Heritage that used to live and be practiced within original natural and social contexts. . . . The other one is the Intangible Cultural Heritage that is still living and being practiced within its natural and social contexts. This type of Intangible Cultural Heritage is viewed as both traditional and contemporary in the sense that the traditional culture and folklore form a living culture that is still a vibrant and self-identified part of cultural communities' lives.

However, cultural heritage has been much more narrowly defined for specific social purposes. "The idea of cultural heritage means not only separate objects or places, but also their place – the environment related to the history of the civilization. A cultural monument cannot be separated from its history – a witness of which it is and where it is located" (Dambis 2001, 218); this bears on the rival Greek and British claims to the Elgin Marbles as cultural heritage (Merryman 2000, 165). One of the narrowest definitions of cultural heritage is constructed by the US Code, title 18, section 668, Theft of major artwork: "'object of cultural heritage' means an object that is: (a) over 100 years old and worth in excess of $5,000; or (b) worth at least $100,000" (Chaffinch 2002, 96–97).

With these various social extensions, cultural heritage may be considered as a postmodern social construction that varies markedly between societies and their subgroups. Cultural heritage as a postmodern construct is supported by Uffe Juul Jensen, who writes: "Yet the analogy between cultural heritage and heritage in the primary sense of inheritance has its limitations. Heritage is not always something already present in a culture. It is, on the contrary, selected, negotiated, and perhaps even *constructed by the heirs*" (2000, 38; my emphasis). Besides showing that cultural heritage is a contested social construction in terms of what objects it authoritatively comprises, the UNESCO convention quoted above also emphasizes the role of cultural heritage in "identity construction". This role of cultural heritage in the construction of identity is central to the culturometric derivation of the definition of cultural heritage that is propounded in this chapter: "This intangible cultural heritage, transmitted from generation to generation, is constantly recreated by communities and groups in response to their environment, their interaction with nature and their history, and *provides them with a sense of identity*" (UNESCO 2003, 2; my emphasis).

## Contesting a Hegemonic Cultural Heritage from a Radical-Constructivist Standpoint

The above supports a socially constructed cultural heritage, albeit as a meta-narrative used for social cohesion and civic identity, one that serves hegemonic political purposes. However, nowadays, particularly in multicultural and ethnically diverse societies such as Trinidad and Tobago, the authority and the intentions of official constructions of cultural heritage are being questioned, and one group's genetic ancestry or ethnic history is no longer considered the sole influence on cultural heritage construction. Individuals construct their cultural heritages to express the trans-generational components of their identities. Objects such as heirlooms, old family photographs, stories, or an ancestor's birth certificate can help an individual to construct that part of his or her identity that represents his or her personal cultural heritage. As Susan Pearce writes in "The Making of Cultural Heritage", "cultural heritage is cognitively constructed, as an external expression of identity, operating in a range of ways and levels. It is a social fact" (2000, 59).

A noteworthy example is the current digital archiving of personal cultural heritages which allows personal objects of identity to be recorded and arrogated as a record of valued subgroup cultural heritage and identity, while enabling the organizations that produce these memorabilia to implicitly claim democratic authority in defining cultural heritages. This process implicitly gives the archiving institution democratic authority to define cultural heritage, because the individuals whose cultural heritage is being defined participated in the institution's definition of their cultural heritage. While they agreed to contribute their personal memorabilia as a representation of their cultural heritage, the archiving institution retains the prerogative of accepting or rejecting contributions in forming its own definition of cultural heritage. This seemingly overt "democratic" authorization contrasts with the traditional covert "autocratic" definition of cultural heritage: a definition based on an institution's non-participatory choice of public objects to define a group's cultural heritage.

The Great Rivers Cultural Heritage Network Project is an example of such a participatory definition of cultural heritage (Minnesota Historical Society 2007). Museum collection management software such as PastPerfect enables the public to contribute heirlooms for digitizing into virtual artefact databases. Wikis such as Placeography (2010) allow the public to incorporate their user-created content into theme-based cultural heritage databases. The public can also contribute trans-generational family stories and oral histories to theme-based cultural heritage databases, for example, stories that have been passed down through generations about the Great Depression (Minnesota Historical Society, 2009). The available software promotes the positive empowerment loop described above, by allowing "branding" of the cultural heritage by participating institutions – such as with the use of a "skin" or logo, by identifying an institution and promoting its authority through individuals' accepting its definition of their group's cultural history, and by the branding institution's validating for individual contributors the value of their personal trans-generational "identity".

In concluding, the literature attests to a cultural heritage *bricolage* whereby individuals select trans-generational objects from across diverse sociocultural influences to forge self-defined cultural identities. The aggregation of these identities in turn allows for a consensually negotiated group cultural heritage evincing the individual's group membership. It is important to note that group membership is then socially and culturally defined rather than determined by an ethnic genetic ancestry. For example, a "white Rasta" will be categorized as more Rastafarian in Manchester, England, than in Manchester, Jamaica. A mixed Afro-Indo-Trinidadian will be categorized as more "Afro" in an Indo-Trinidadian community than in an Afro-Trinidadian community. Hence this assertion supports the use of a culturometric classification, rather than ethnic genetic ancestry, for defining cultural identity constructs such as Afro-Trinidadianness, Indo-Trinidadianness and the trans-generational cultural identity components of cultural heritage. These classifications of Trinidadian cultural identity can be compared to Caribbean creole markers of national identity in both Jamaica and Guyana (Boufoy-Bastick 2009a) and culturometric classifications of cultural identity within Jamaican society (Boufoy-Bastick 2010a), as well as Indo-Fijian and indigenous Fijian cultural identity in Fijian society (Boufoy-Bastick 2010b, 2010c).

## Methodological Overview of the Research: Contrasting Afro-Trinidadian and Indo-Trinidadian Constructions of Cultural Heritage

A brief overview of this research is now provided to explain how Afro-Trinidadian and Indo-Trinidadian constructions of cultural heritage were investigated. The research used a representative household survey of Trinidadian respondents (N = 348) to conduct a culturometric analysis comparing ethnic constructions of the different components of Trinidadian cultural heritage, selecting for interview respondents who exhibited very different identity components. These interviews were subsequently transcribed, and the content analysis of the transcripts sought to demonstrate how Afro-Trinidadians and Indo-Trinidadians differentially construct the components of their Trinidadian cultural heritage. Classification of respondents into Afro-Trinidadian or Indo-Trinidadian was based upon cultural affiliation rather than genetic/ethnic endowment, using Boufoy-Bastick's culturometric methodology (2003, 2007). An overview of the quantitative and qualitative methodologies is now presented.

## Quantitative methodology

### Sample

The data was collected in 348 Trinidadian households in November 2007. The households formed a random sample stratified by population density and ethnicity from ten major Trinidadian constituencies across the island. The interviews were conducted by thirty-three trained interviewers who read the questions, instructions and explanations to respondents. The mean interview duration was thirty-four minutes. The sample comprised 152 males and 196 females, with an average age of forty-six, of whom 56 per cent (195) were heads of households. Respondents were asked to rate the importance of different components of their cultural heritage and report the following educational, economic and societal demographic information: their highest educational level, the income of the highest wage-earner in the household, property value, and their major cultural/ethnic identity and allegiances. The culturometric analysis identified respondents by cultural affiliation as either Afro-Trinidadian or Indo-Trinidadian and compared Trinidadian cultural heritage components for the respondent groups. Based on these demographic sections of Trinidadian society, respondents were selected for interview to elicit different constructions of their Trinidadian cultural heritage components.

## Using a Culturally Sensitive Culturometric Classification of Ethnicity

Trinidadians recognize two main ethnic groups: Afro-Trinidadians and Indo-Trinidadians (Brereton 2002, 2–3). Trinidadians have come to label themselves based on their self-perception of visual genetic endowments from African and Indian ancestral groups as either Afro-Trinidadian, Indo-Trinidadian or mixed (England 2008). For example, the 2002 Central Statistical Office population figures for Trinidad and Tobago indicate that 40 per cent of the 1.3 million population were considered to be of Indian descent, 37.5 per cent of African descent and 20 per cent of "mixed race" (Trinidad and Tobago 2003). Ethnic categorization based on socially relative self-labelling of stereotypical genetic endowment is inaccurate, and an immutable, socially divisive method of classification which is theoretically less relevant to cultural heritage behaviour options than ethnicity based on cultural allegiances. Hence this study employed a more culturally sensitive culturometric classification of ethnicity using cultural index (CI) regulators.

Technical details for using CI regulators have already been explained by Boufoy-Bastick (2001, 2009b, 2010d). The following is designed to show in sufficient detail for critical understanding and replication how this culturometric technique was applied to this study.

Respondents were asked to use their cultural values consistently in answering the following questions:

J2. How Indo-Trinidadian do you feel (0 to 10)?
J3. How Afro-Trinidadian do you feel (0 to 10)?
J6. How Indo-Trinidadian is George Maxwell Richards (0 to 10)?
J7. How Afro-Trinidadian is George Maxwell Richards (0 to 10)?
J10. How Indo-Trinidadian is calypso (0 to 10)?
J11. How Afro-Trinidadian is calypso (0 to 10)?

George Maxwell Richards, then president of Trinidad and Tobago, and calypso were chosen as benchmarking public objects (Boufoy-Bastick 2010c, 524). To avoid subsequent divisions by zero, all responses were rescaled by adding one. Each respondent's Afro-Trinidadian cultural index (ACI1) and Indo-Trinidadian cultural index (ICI1) were calculated using Indo-Trinidadian CI as $ICI1 = (mean\ j6) \times j2/j6$, and Afro-Trinidadian CI as $ACI1 = (mean\ j7) \times j3/j7$ (Boufoy-Bastick 2002, 2003, 2007). The culturometric value-added proportion (VAP), an alternative to value consistency, was used to calculate the absolute respondent error for how consistently respondents used their Afro-Trinidadian cultural values (AfrValE) and their Indo-Trinidadian values (IndValE) using $(AfrValE) = abs(AfrVal–AfrValT)/AfrValT$ and $(IndValE) = abs(IndVal–IndValT)/IndValT$, where $AfrVal = j7/j11$ and $AfrValT = (mean\ j7)/(mean\ j11)$, and $IndVal = j6/j10$ and $IndValT = (mean\ j6)/(mean\ j10)$.

Reliable respondents – those with less than 80 per cent inconsistency in applying their Afro-Trinidadian cultural values – were classified as Afro-Trinidadians if they were above the median of ACI1 and below the median of ICI1. Similarly reliable respondents with less than 80 per cent inconsistency in applying their Indo-Trinidadian cultural values were classified as Indo-Trinidadians if they were above the median of ICI1 and below the median of ACI1. All other reliable respondents with $j2 > 1$ or $j3 > 1$ were classified as mixed and, because of limitations of space, were not used for this report.

## Cultural Heritage Components

Five components of cultural heritage in Trinidad were identified. The dependent variables were self-ratings of the importance of these five components of cultural heritage given in answer to the following four questions:

With reference to your cultural heritage (legacy of values/artefacts/traditions):

h1. How important to you is your cultural heritage (0 to 10)?
h2. How important to you is your Trinidadian cultural heritage (0 to 10)?

All Trinidadians have a mixed cultural heritage

h3. How important to you is your Indo-Trinidadian cultural heritage (0 to 10)?
h4. How important to you is your Afro-Trinidadian cultural heritage (0 to 10)?
h5. How important to you is your American-Trinidadian cultural heritage (0 to 10)?

Importance was chosen as an intuitively rateable indicator of cultural heritage (CH) difference. Although respondents who rate their CH of equal importance might have different cultural heritages, it can be argued that different ratings of importance do not necessarily imply differences in CH, as cultural heritage could be the same set of authorized objects for each respondent and each respondent could give varying importance to this same set. However, importance is part of an individual's construction of his or her CH, and so qualitatively alters it. To test the social-constructivist perception of CH, $t$ tests were used to assess possible differences in how the two ethnic groups constructed the five components of their cultural heritage. To test the radical-constructivist perception of CH, respondents who gave different ratings of importance to their cultural heritage were interviewed to verify that their individual cultural heritages were differently constructed in terms of the objects included and the authorization of those objects.

## Quantitative Results

The quantitative results attest to a social-constructivist perception of cultural heritage. Table 2.1 shows significant differences between the mean importance ascribed to each of the five CH components by the two ethnic groups. These ethnic differences are displayed in figure 2.1.

**Table 2.1** Significant Differences between Two Ethnic Groups in the Construction of Their Cultural Heritage (CH)

| Independent Variables | Ethnicity: CI regulated | N | Mean | Diff | t-value | Sig |
|---|---|---|---|---|---|---|
| h1 How important to you is your cultural heritage? | 1 Afro-Trinidadian | 37 | 6.919 | | | |
| | 2 Indo-Trinidadian | 38 | 7.763 | 0.844 | -2.344 | *0.022 |
| h2 How important to you is your Trinidadian cultural heritage? | 1 Afro-Trinidadian | 39 | 7.077 | | | |
| | 2 Indo-Trinidadian | 44 | 7.750 | 0.673 | -2.227 | *0.029 |
| h3 How important to you is your Indo-Trinidadian cultural heritage? | 1 Afro-Trinidadian | 57 | 4.789 | | | |
| | 2 Indo-Trinidadian | 40 | 7.150 | 2.361 | -6.413 | **0.000 |
| h4 How important to you is your Afro-Trinidadian cultural heritage? | 1 Afro-Trinidadian | 50 | 6.260 | | | |
| | 2 Indo-Trinidadian | 59 | 4.746 | 1.514 | 4.143 | **0.000 |
| h5 How important to you is your American-Trinidadian cultural heritage? | 1 Afro-Trinidadian | 42 | 3.833 | | | |
| | 2 Indo-Trinidadian | 54 | 3.519 | 0.315 | 0.808 | 0.421 |

* Difference is significant at the 0.05 level (2-tailed)
** Difference is significant at the 0.01 level (2-tailed)

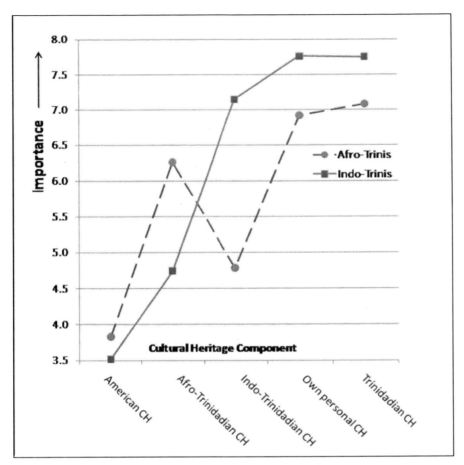

**Figure 2.1** Differences between two ethnic groups in the construction of their cultural heritage (CH)

There were differences between how the two ethnic groups constructed their CH. All differences were statistically significant except for how the two groups constructed their American-Trinidadian CH. American-Trinidadian CH was more important to Afro-Trinidadians, but this difference (0.315) did not reach statistical significance. Indo-Trinidadians awarded significantly higher importance to their own personal CH and to their national Trinidadian CH than did the Afro-Trinidadians, with differences of 0.844 and 0.673 respectively. As would be expected, each group valued its own ethnic CH significantly more than it was valued by the other group. The bigger difference was in how the two groups valued their Indo-Trinidadian CH as opposed to their Afro-Trinidadian CH (2.361 versus 1.514 respectively).

## Qualitative Methodology

In order to demonstrate the radical-constructivist nature of cultural heritage, a list was made of Afro-Trinidadian and Indo-Trinidadian respondents representing the high and low groups for each independent variable. The qualitative interviews comprised six questions such as the following:

Q1  What do you mean by your cultural heritage?

Q2  What do you mean by your Indo-Trinidadian cultural heritage? In what ways are your parents' Indo-Trinidadian cultural heritage different from your own? (What do they value that you don't and why?)

Q3  What do you mean by your Afro-Trinidadian cultural heritage? In what ways are your parents' Afro-Trinidadian cultural heritage different from your own? (What do they value that you don't and why?)

This questionnaire was administered to the listed respondents and their answers were compared in order to demonstrate how individuals construct different CHs. This was done by (1) transcribing each interview, (2) selecting key sections and developing keyword (KW) codes to identify the objects and authorities that respondents used to construct their CHs, (3) tabulating these objects and authorities by respondent category, and (4) contrasting these tabulations with evidence from different personal CH constructions.

## Qualitative Results

The following is an example of responses to Q2. These responses are from a young female low-income Indo-Trinidadian.

Q2  What do you mean by your Indian cultural heritage?

Answer: For me, more a race. Indian when we have Hindu festivals like Diwali. If they have prayer I go; it's my only link with my Hindu cultural heritage. They are my Hindu religious – Hindu rites. Right now, Diwali not very important; when my mother was alive – she died ten years ago. So now we kind of lost that link and don't carry on with the fasting. But the celebration carried on. . . . Prayer sessions, it is more like a bonding experience with my cousins but now, not very important for the Hindu cultural heritage. . . . For Indo-Christians, because difference is education. Education creates a hierarchy. Like people in Caroni, lots of them don't have much education. It's the only difference, but although I am spiritual, there's some duality between the two sides. What is good, I did not have to choose: I am always completely welcome in both.

I have no idea how to describe myself. Being part of both worlds. I am East Indian descent because of race. More and more young are open-minded and westernized.

To objectively clarify constructed responses for comparisons, transcripts were coded for *objects* and *authorities,* as in the following coding of the above example:

KW: ancestry; CH Indo; festivals; religion; rituals

*For me, more a race. Indian when we have Hindu festivals like Diwali. If they have prayer I go; my only my link with my Indian heritage is Hindu. They are my Hindu religious – Hindu rites.*

KW: ancestry; CH Indo; festivals; religion; rituals; parents; rating low; cultural loss

*Right now, Diwali not very important; when my mother was alive – she died ten years ago. So now we kind of lost that link and don't carry on with the fasting. But the celebration carried on.*

KW: CH Indo; rating low; rituals; religions; cultural evolution

*Prayer sessions, it is more like a bonding experience with my cousins but now, not very important for the Hindu CH.*

NB: religious meaning lost but used as a family tie.

Table 2.2 shows an example of the keyword listings developed for coding.

**Table 2.2** Partial List of Keywords Developed for Coding

| | | | | |
|---|---|---|---|---|
| Africa | carnival | Civic identity | dance definition | modernist |
| Afro TT | Catholic | Colonial | demographics | Multicultural |
| Afro to Afro | CH | corruption | dressing | Multiethnic |
| Afro to Indo | CH Afro | Creole | drumming | music |
| age | CH alien | Cultural blending | economics | Muslim |
| ancestry | CH Indo | Cultural evolution | education | oral traditions |
| Baptist | CH tangible | Cultural identity | Language | parents |
| Caribbean | CH TT | Cultural loss | male | postmodern |

Summaries, similar to the following summary from the above example, were then used to identify and extract objects and authorities for tabulation, as shown below.

*CH Indo*
- most important: race; Hindu festivals (e.g., Diwali); Hindu prayers and rites
- kept use of Indian Bojphuri terms (she refers as Indian creole) in the home which are not known by Africans (e.g., nani, nana; dabla used for making rotis, belna for rolling pin)

- education and family values (parents spend time with children)
- saving and working hard

*cultural loss:* fasting before Diwali

*loss of meaning:* prayers not for religion but for family bonding

The following two tabulations of constructed responses from two different Afro-Trinidadian male educated respondents illustrate different personal constructions of the same components of cultural heritage.

**Afro-Trinidadian Male Respondent 1** (see table 2.3)

Interview conducted 8 May 2008, 3:45–5:00 p.m.

African male (high Afro-Trinidadian cultural identity)

DOB: 22/03/1956 (52 years old); married with four children

Education: master's degree

Salary: TT$18,000 monthly

Religion: born-again Christian; prayed for 12 hours last week

Genetic ethnic mix: 0 Indo, 10 Afro, 0 other

Sociocultural mix: 10 TT, 0 Indo, 5 Afro, 0 American, 0 British

Feels: – TT, – Indo, – Afro, – American

CH importance: 10, 10 TT, 7 Indo-TT, 9 Afro-TT, 1 American-TT

**Table 2.3** CH Personal Construction of Afro-TT Male Respondent 1

| | |
|---|---|
| CH Afro | Music, calypso, steelpan, drums, mouth organ, tambour bamboo; food; Spiritual Baptist religion; limbo; best village tradition; stories of African slaves, stories of resistance of slaves |
| CH Indo | Music, chutney, tassa drums; food; rituals (marriage), religion; clothes |
| CH Afro tangible valued | Food |
| CH Indo tangible valued | Food |
| CH Afro intangible not valued | Religious values, e.g. Shango, Yoruba (elements of worship) |
| CH Indo intangible not valued | Religious, e.g. Hinduism (elements of worship) |
| TCH intangible valued | National anthem, calypso, steelband, chutney |

*Comments:* The national anthem and the saying/singing of the words are very important to him (100%). Sees it as the element that everyone in the country has in common.

He was born in a time of transition.

**Afro-Trinidadian Male Respondent 2** (see table 2.4)

Interview conducted 4 May 2008, 9:50–10:30 a.m.

African male

DOB: 21/04/1970 (38 years old); single

Education: bachelor of science

Salary: TT$7,000 weekly

Religion: Methodist; prayed 1 hour last week

Genetic ethnic mix: 0 Indo, 9 Afro, 1 Spanish

Sociocultural mix: 10 TT, 1 Indo, 8 Afro, – American

Feels: 10 TT, 0 Indo, 10 Afro, 0 American

CH importance: 10, 10 TT, 8 Indo-TT, 8 Afro-TT, 1 American-TT

**Table 2.4** CH Personal Construction of Afro-TT Male Respondent 2

| | |
|---|---|
| CH Afro | Religious beliefs, values, practices, behaviour |
| CH Indo | Religious beliefs, values, practices |
| CH Afro tangible valued | |
| CH Indo tangible valued | |
| CH Afro tangible not valued | Food |
| CH Indo tangible not valued | Food |
| TCH intangible valued | Music, socializing |

*Comments:* Religion and religious beliefs play an important role in his notion of CH.

Their qualitative responses illustrate how two Afro-Trinidadian males construct different self-defined representations of cultural heritage. However, although both placed a high importance on their cultural heritages, they gave different emphases, authorities and interpretations to the objects they comprised. The overall qualitative results of the study showed that individuals construct their cultural heritages with their own tangible and intangible objects. The qualitative results also showed that cultural heritages as constructed by individuals differ in terms of the authority they accept for including cultural objects. It was interesting to note that, other than Carnival, few Trinidadian respondents reported traditional museum-type objects or government-designated objects – such as the national bird, the national flower, ecological sites and so on – as representations of their CH. In contrast, respondents gave examples of ecological utilization and explained that Trinidadians, like other diasporic peoples, expect to "use up" their environment and move on. Respondents' authorities for their CH objects were mainly their community and parents.

## Conclusions: Social-Constructivist and Radical-Constructivist Perspectives of Cultural Heritage

The literature abounds with qualitative position papers, expert opinion and academic reflection on cultural heritage. This literature is presented here to support the original postmodernist interpretation of cultural heritage presented in this chapter. In particular, the research reported in this chapter proposed a dynamic social-constructivist definition of cultural heritage that is negotiated from radical-constructivist cultural heritages of individuals. This definition of cultural heritage and subsequent measures of cultural heritage were derived from the culturometric perspective of cultural identity. The culturometric approach used here allowed for additional quantitative insights, which is not usual in the research literature on the meaning of cultural heritage. The proposed postmodern dynamics and culturometric definition of cultural heritage, being the trans-generational components of cultural identity, were tested and evidenced by the empirical qualitative and quantitative results for five fundamental components of Trinidadian cultural heritage.

This study showed that each main Trinidadian ethnic group held a different social construction of both Afro-Trinidadian and Indo-Trinidadian cultural heritages. In particular, the qualitative and quantitative results authenticated the radical definition of cultural heritage by demonstrating that individuals construct the same components of their personal cultural heritages using differently authorized objects. Likewise, the quantitative results tested and endorsed the social-constructivist nature of cultural heritage by indicating significant differences in how Afro-Trinidadians and Indo-Trinidadians constructed the same components of their group cultural heritages. Both the empirical qualitative and quantitative results of this study have expressly validated the new postmodern definitions of cultural heritage and formalized the dynamic nature of cultural heritage expounded in this chapter.

# References

Abu-Khafaj, S. 2010. "Meaning-Making and Cultural Heritage: The Local Community, the Context and the Archaeological Sites in Khreibt al-Suq". *International Journal of Heritage Studies* 16, no. 1: 123–39.

Bhattacharyya, H., ed. 1953. *The Cultural Heritage of India*. Calcutta: Ramakrishna Mission Institute of Culture.

Boufoy-Bastick, B. 2000. "The Cultural Index as a Predictor of Culturally-Determined Behaviours in Multicultural Societies". Educational Resource Information Center, ED450063; SO032590. http://www.eric.ed.gov.

———. 2001. "Introduction to Culturometrics: Measuring the Cultural Identity of Teachers and Children". Educational Resource Information Center, ED460044; SO033462. http://www.eric.ed.gov.

———. 2002. "Measuring Cultural Identity in Culturally-Diverse Societies". *World Cultures* 13, no. 1: 39–47.

———. 2003. *Academic Attainments and Cultural Values*. Munich: Lincom Europa.

———. 2004. "Promoting Pan-Caribbean Cultural Identity in the Multilingual Caribbean". *Caribbean Educational Research Journal* 1: 66–82.

———. 2007. "Culturometrics: Quantitative Methodology for Measuring Qualitative Judgements". *International Journal of the Humanities* 5, no. 10: 1–10.

———. 2009a. "Creoles as Linguistic Markers of National Identity: Examples from Jamaica and Guyana". In *The African-Caribbean Worldview and the Making of Caribbean Society*, edited by H. Levy, 203–10. Kingston: University of the West Indies Press.

———. 2009b. "A Culturometric Analysis of Fear of Crime in Trinidad". *Caribbean Journal of Criminology and Public Safety* 14: 1–48.

———. 2010a. "A Culturometric Exploration of Intrusions of Globalization on Transnational Identities: The Jamaican Example". *Journal of Identity and Migration Studies* 4, no. 1: 91–109.

———. 2010b. *Language Education and Policy in Fiji: A Culturometric Investigation of Ethnic Values*. Vol. 1, *Discovering the Cultures of Fiji*. Saarbrücken, Germany: Lambert Academic.

———. 2010c. *Language Education and Policy in Fiji: A Culturometric Investigation of Ethnic Values*. Vol. 2, *How Culture Determines Language Attainment*. Saarbrücken, Germany: Lambert Academic.

———. 2010d. "A Culturometric Exploration of the Changing Language Identities of French and Spanish Undergraduate Students in Trinidad". In *Proceedings of the 2nd Paris International Conference on Education, Economy and Society*, vol. 2, edited by G. Tchibozo, 78–92. Strasbourg: Analytrics.

Brereton, B. 2002. *Race Relations in Colonial Trinidad, 1870–1900*. Cambridge: Cambridge University Press.

Brothman, B. 2001. "The Past That Archives Keep: Memory, History, and the Preservation of Archival Records". *Archivaria* 51: 48–80.

Bruce, D., and O. Creighton. 2006. "Contested Identities: The Dissonant Heritage of European Town Walls and Walled Towns". *International Journal of Heritage Studies* 12, no. 3: 234–54.

Chaffinch, L. 2002. "The Federal Bureau of Investigation's Art Theft Program". In *The Strategic Stewardship of Cultural Resources: To Preserve and Protect*, edited by A.T. Merrill, 95–100. Philadelphia: Haworth Press.

Civallero, E. 2007. "When Memory Turns into Ashes . . . Memoricide during the XX Century". *Information for Social Change* 25: 7–22.

Crownshaw, R. 1999. "Cultural Heritage and Ethnic Identity: Belsen in the Museum". In *Developments in British Media*, edited by J. Tokes and A. Reading, 295–303. London: Macmillan.

Dambis, J. 2001. "Latvia". In *Policy and Law in Heritage Conservation*, edited by R. Pickard, 207–26. London: Spon Press.

Dann, G.M.S., and A.V. Seaton, eds. 2002. *Slavery, Contested Heritage, and Thanatourism*. New York: Haworth Press.

de Condappa, P. 2006. "Cultural Genocide in Bosnia-Herzegovina: Destroying Heritage, Destroying Identity". Genocide Studies seminars, Genocide Studies Program, Yale University. http://www.yale.edu/gsp/past/spring2006.html.

England, S. 2008. "Reading the Dougla Body: Mixed Race, Post-race, and Other Narratives of What It Means to Be Mixed in Trinidad". *Latin American and Caribbean Ethnic Studies* 3, no. 1: 1–31.

Graham, B. 1996. "The Contested Interpretation of Heritage Landscapes in Northern Ireland". *International Journal of Heritage Studies* 2, no. 1: 10–22.

Hou, J. 2004. "Preserving for Multiple Publics: Contesting Views of Urban Conservation in Seattle's International District". Open Journal Systems 1, no. 1 (October 20). http://www.ct.ceci-br.org/novo/revista/viewarticle.php?id=8.

Ikram, S.M., and P. Spear, eds. 1955. *The Cultural Heritage of Pakistan*. London: Oxford University Press.

Jensen, U.J. 2000. "Cultural Heritage, Liberal Education and Human Flourishing". In *Values and Heritage Conservation: Research Report*, edited by E. Avrami, R. Mason and M. de la Torre, 38–43. Los Angeles: Getty Conservation Institute.

Kreamer, C.M. 2006. "Shared Heritage, Contested Terrain: Cultural Negotiation and Ghana's Cape Coast Castle Museum Exhibition". In *Museum Frictions: Public Cultures/Global Transformations*, edited by Ivan Karp and Corinne Kratz, 435–68. Durham, NC: Duke University Press.

Lorkovic, T. 1993. "Destruction of Libraries in Croatia and Bosnia-Herzegovina". *International Leads* 7, no. 2: 1–2.

———. 1995. "Wounded Libraries in Croatia". Book review. *Libraries and Culture* 30: 205–6.

Merryman, J.H. 2000. *Thinking about the Elgin Marbles: Critical Essays on Cultural Property, Art and Law*. The Hague: Kluwer Law International.

Minnesota Historical Society. 2007. Collections. http://www.mnhs.org/collections/projects/.

———. 2009. "Minnesota's Greatest Generation: The Depression, the War, the Boom". *Experiencing Their Past, Learning for Our Present*. CCH Veterans' Gallery. http://cchsvetsgallery.blogspot.com/2009/05/minnesotas-greatest-generation.html.

Olwig, K.R. 2005. "The Nature of Cultural Heritage and the Culture of Natural Heritage: Northern Perspectives on a Contested Patrimony". *International Journal of Heritage Studies* 11, no. 1: 3–7.

Osborne, B.S. 1996. "Figuring Space, Marking Time: Contested Identities in Canada". *International Journal of Heritage Studies* 2, no. 1: 23–40.

Pearce, S.M. 2000. "The Making of Cultural Heritage". In *Values and Heritage Conservation: Research Report*, edited by E. Avrami, R. Mason and M. de la Torre, 59–64. Los Angeles: Getty Conservation Institute.

Rogister, Y., and C. Ruelle. 2001. *The City of Tomorrow and Cultural Heritage*. Theme 4.2.3: *Foster Integration of Cultural Heritage in the Urban Setting*. Sustainable Development of Urban Historical Areas Through an Active Integration Within Towns (SUIT). Luxembourg: European Communities.

Roussin, L. 2003. "Cultural Heritage and Identity". *Cardozo Journal of International and Comparative Law* 11: 707–10.

Sculthorpe, G. 2005. "Recognising Difference: Contested Issues in Native Title and Cultural Heritage". *Anthropological Forum* 15, no. 2: 171–93.

Shozimov, P. 2004. "Tajikistan: Cultural Heritage and the Identity Issue, Central Asia and the Caucasus". *Journal of Social and Political Studies*. http://www.ca-c.org/journal/2004-06-eng/18.shoprimen.shtml.

Smith, L. 2004. *Archeological Theory and the Politics of Cultural Heritage*. Abingdon: Routledge.

Thomson, B. 1978. "Lot's Wife and the Venus of Milo: Conflicting Attitudes to the Cultural Heritage in Modern Russia". *Minnesota Review* 11: 137.

Trinidad and Tobago. 2003. *Population and Vital Statistics: Pocket Digest*. Republic of Trinidad and Tobago, Central Statistical Office.

UNESCO. 2003. *Convention for the Safeguarding of the Intangible Cultural Heritage*. Paris: UNESCO.

———. 2005. *Operational Guidelines for the Implementation of the World Heritage Convention*. Paris: UNESCO World Heritage Centre.

———. 2008. *Operational Guidelines for the Implementation of the World Heritage Convention*. Paris: UNESCO World Heritage Centre.

von Glaserfeld, E. 1998. "Why Constructivism Must Be Radical". In *Constructivism and Education*, edited by M. Larochelle, N. Bednaz and J. Garrison, 23–28. Cambridge: Cambridge University Press.

Worden, N. 1996. "Contested Heritage at the Cape Town Waterfront". *International Journal of Heritage Studies* 2, no. 1: 59–75.

Yin, T. 2006. "Museums and the Safeguarding of Intangible Cultural Heritage". *Ethics Arts* 6: 1–4.

# 3.

# Our Cross to Bear

## The Trinity Cross, Heritage and Identity in Trinidad and Tobago

BRIDGET BRERETON

*This chapter looks at the formation of attitudes towards heritage and national identity in Trinidad and Tobago, through a study of the controversy about the nation's highest award (up to 2008), the Trinity Cross. Established in 1969, its name recalls the Holy Trinity, for which Columbus named the larger island in the nation, and the medal was cruciform. It was challenged by Hindu and Islamic spokesmen, and by others, as inappropriate for a secular democracy with a large non-Christian population, and in 2006 the High Court ruled that it could be regarded as constituting indirect discrimination against non-Christian citizens. A committee chaired by the author was appointed to review all the issues and make recommendations. There was considerable public debate between 2006 and 2008, conducted in the newspapers and also through written submissions to the committee in response to newspaper advertisements. These materials form the basis of this study, which considers the ways in which ideas about heritage and nationalism are embedded in symbols such as national awards, and what these ideas reveal about contested narratives of the nation's past.*

## Introduction

Historians and social scientists agree that nationalisms and national identities are constructed at specific historical conjunctures, and that the creation of narratives about the past – the "invention" of a heritage – is nearly always an important part of this process. To recall the past is to place it in the service of the conceptions and needs of the present. Postcolonial states in particular

*46*

have undergone a process of national self-creation, of identity formation, involving a recasting of history to produce a usable past. The concept of nations as imagined communities is especially applicable to states, like Trinidad and Tobago, which were "colonially created" – places with virtually no pre-colonial past on which to draw for images and traditions from ancient inhabitants of the national space. In such countries there can be no depicting the nation as a primordial community; it must be defined from scratch, as it were. Moreover, the process of identity formation is complicated when the modern population is ethnically diverse, with nearly all descended from groups brought into the national space in colonial times. Such is the case of Trinidad and Tobago, which consists of two islands with very different historical trajectories that were joined by imperial fiat at the end of the nineteenth century, and which has two "majority" ethnic communities (persons of African and South Asian, or "Indian", descent) as well as several smaller ethnicities and many of mixed origins (Brereton 2007, 169–96).

Competing historical narratives of the nation are important in the process of identity formation, and ideas about the national "heritage" are embedded in these contestations. They are reflected not only in written accounts of the nation's past, whether academic or not, but also in public debates about national symbols and observances. Symbols such as national awards are seen as embodying the country's heritage, and debates about them may reveal attitudes to the past, and contestations about the present and future, among different ethnic, religious and class fractions of the population. They often illuminate a society's ideas about its intangible heritage: its traditions, its iconic cultural forms, its mores, through which a nation develops its sense of identity and its interpretation of the past.

## The Trinity Cross

This chapter examines public debates in Trinidad and Tobago in 2006–8 over the nation's highest award, the Trinity Cross. In 1969, seven years after national independence, a system of national honours was established by letters patent to the Constitution. The "order" to which all awardees would belong was the Order of the Trinity, and the highest award was the Trinity Cross. It should be noted that the larger island, Trinidad, was named by Columbus, when he sighted it in 1498, after the Holy Trinity, and three low hills along the southern coast, the first part of the island he saw, are called the Trinity Hills. The medal for the Trinity Cross was designed as a cruciform shape.

The person responsible for the name and design of the Trinity Cross in 1969 has made it clear that she did not intend to produce a specifically Christian medal, and that "religion or Christianity never entered [her] mind"

(McDowell Benjamin 2006). However, doubts about the suitability of the Trinity Cross and the Order of the Trinity for a multi-religious nation with a large population of Hindus and Muslims (nearly all Indo-Trinidadians) were expressed at the outset. These doubts were somewhat muted at first. In 1977 a prominent Muslim public figure, Wahid Ali, overcame his initial reluctance to accept the award only when he was assured by the prime minister, Eric Williams, that the whole issue would be reviewed very soon. Williams, in fact, did nothing. In 1995 a Hindu religious leader, Pundit Krishna Maharaj, refused to accept the Trinity Cross, and this (unlike Ali's reservations) became public knowledge. A committee chaired by the Chief Justice in 1997 considered the issue and made a majority recommendation to change the name of the highest award to the Order of Trinidad and Tobago. In 1997 the party in power was based mainly on Indo-Trinidadian support and was led by a Hindu prime minister, Basdeo Panday, who decided, perhaps understandably, not to implement that recommendation.

Eventually the organization representing orthodox Hindus, the Sanatan Dharma Maha Sabha (SDMS), and a smaller Islamic body brought an action challenging the constitutionality of the Trinity Cross. In a landmark judgement delivered in May 2006 (Jamadar 2006), a judge of the Trinidad and Tobago High Court ruled that in his view, "the creation and continued existence of the Trinity Cross, given the historical, religious and sociological context of Trinidad and Tobago, combined with the experiences, as well as the religious beliefs of Hindus and Muslims, amount to indirect adverse effects discrimination against Hindus and Muslims". Since, however, the Trinity Cross was entrenched in the Constitution, the judge ruled that he could not order the government to replace it with an award which would be non-discriminatory.

Soon after the ruling, the prime minister, Patrick Manning (an Afro-Trinidadian Christian), made a statement in Parliament: his government accepted that it was morally obliged to "comply with this ruling and remove this anomaly from our national life. We shall do it". He grounded this determination in the explicit statement "Trinidad and Tobago is a secular democracy" (Manning 2006). To this end he announced the creation of a committee to review all aspects of the nation's highest award, and any other national symbols and observances which might be considered discriminatory.[1]

## Debates

With respect to the first remit, the committee recommended that the Trinity Cross be replaced by the Order of the Republic of Trinidad and Tobago, that its design should be circular in shape and feature various secular symbols of the nation (figure 3.1), and that the Order of the Trinity should be replaced by the Distinguished Society of Trinidad and Tobago (Committee 2006; Committee 2007). It was not until June 2008, however, that it was announced that amendments to the letters patent would be made to allow for the recommended changes in the name and design of the highest award and of the Order of the Trinity. The first awards of the Order of the Republic of Trinidad and Tobago were made on 31 August 2008 (Loubon 2008). The rest of this chapter examines the public debate on the Trinity Cross which took place in 2006–8, in the nation's newspapers and via written submissions to the committee, which were solicited from the public late in 2006. This voluminous material will be sampled to indicate the arguments and issues articulated and to analyse what they reflect about concepts of history, heritage and nationalism.[2]

**Figure 3.1** Order of the Republic of Trinidad and Tobago

Those who wished to retain the Trinity Cross – probably the majority of the population, according to a poll by a University of the West Indies centre in July 2006 – tended to make two arguments diametrically opposed to each other but, ironically, leading to the same conclusion. First, the cross is not exclusively a Christian symbol but is universal and pre-Christian, and the concept of a trinity also exists in Hinduism, so there was no discrimination against non-Christians. Second, both the cross and the Trinity are Christian symbols and concepts and should be retained because they reflect the nation's history and heritage, and the majority of the population is at present Christian, encompassing many denominations.

Representative of the first line of argument was a letter by Karen Bart-Alexander:

> It is more than a deep intuitive feeling that there is a special reason why the cross is the symbol of this nation's highest award and it has nothing to do with Christianity. It has to do with the fact that the cross is a world symbol as ancient as creation itself . . . found in every world culture. Hindus who call for a removal of the cross as the nation's highest award either do not understand Hinduism or they are so consumed by their desire to "de-Christianise" Trinidad and Tobago that they are willing to blind themselves to their own beliefs. (Bart-Alexander 2006)

The second argument – that the Trinity Cross reflects the history and heritage of the nation, though only one part of it (a point I will return to) – is well made by Gilbert Joseph: "The Trinity Cross was named after this island [Trinidad] whose rediscovery and our consequent existence here are due to the afore-mentioned Columbus and the Christian Spaniard crew he brought with him." Consequently, the symbol "has echoes of Christianity but the true voice of our collective history attached to it" and should be retained (Joseph 2006).

D.J. Ganteaume insisted that to remove the Trinity Cross was to "deny our history": "Our country has at its foundation the pioneering drive of the Catholic powers of Renaissance Europe and do what you will, that is the unalterable truth . . . All the Trinity Cross does . . . is to honour and acknowledge that historical past". No court or committee, he felt, had the right "to strip me of my heritage". "Are we of the Christian community", he asked, "not to be able to celebrate and commemorate those historical antecedents of the country's history that (particularly but not exclusively) pertain to us? To deny any aspect of our history in any way, shape or form is like denying our parents" (Ganteaume 2006).

It is clear from the letters quoted above that the argument that the Trinity Cross properly reflected the history of the nation (or at least of Trinidad) easily slid into the assertion that to abolish it would be an attack on Christianity. Ganteaume described the removal of the Trinity Cross as "a kind of cultural annihilation being focussed on members of the Christian faith" (Ganteaume 2006). Some Christian clergy articulated the same general point. An Anglican canon described the move to change the award as a sin, an attack on "the nation's constitutionality of the highest order, which is sacred and holy" (Homer 2006). A Pentecostal pastor thought that a radical "anti-God/anti-Christian group" was behind "the removal of not only the TC, but also anything Christian from our land, as they aggressively seek to undermine all our cherished values" (Cuffie 2006b). Lay Christians followed the same line. Joseph, in the letter already quoted, called the removal of the Trinity Cross "clearly an anti-Christian move . . . but another form of Christian persecution" (Joseph 2006).

Many of the individuals who wished to retain the Trinity Cross argued for two equal highest awards: the Cross, for all Christians, and a new "secular" medal which could be chosen by future awardees. The head of the local Catholic church, the largest Christian denomination, made this recommendation (Gilbert 2006). Pentecostal pastor Winston Cuffie, who rarely agrees with the Catholics on anything, argued for the Trinity Cross for Christians and a "neutral" award for all others (Cuffie 2006a). Perhaps more surprisingly, ASJA, the largest Muslim body, and Imran Hosein, a well-known local Muslim, took the same position. Hosein called for "parallel awards of equal status for Muslims and Hindus while retaining the Trinity Cross for all others" (Hosein 2006).

Many other voices, however, as well as (eventually) the national government, agreed with the recommendation of the committee: removal of the Trinity Cross, to be replaced by a single award whose name and design were secular. Some argued that the Trinity Cross reflected the supremacy of Christianity under the colonial and immediate postcolonial regimes, a situation no longer acceptable nearly fifty years after national independence and in a modern secular democracy. In other words, it did indeed reflect the nation's history and heritage, but in a way that could no longer be reconciled with current values and aspirations for the country. One citizen (who made sure to state he was a Catholic, probably because he had an "Indian" surname) took on the Anglican canon quoted above who thought abolishing the Trinity Cross would be sinful: "A sin? Changing the nation's history? . . . There is a large difference, sir, between history and progress. History is history, nothing we do can change that. What we can change is our confinement to history, particularly when it allows real or perceived dominance of one group in society over another" (Bhaggan 2006).

Other writers made the same kind of point about the nation's history. "To claim that the Christian foundations of T and T demand the retention of the TC", wrote one, "is to argue that slavery and indentureship should never have been abolished because of reverence for their Christian origin . . . And to claim sanctification from historical establishment is to worship the errant past instead of God" (Rahman 2006). Anand Ramlogan, the lead attorney who argued the suit before the High Court, put it this way: "The Trinity Cross was perceived as a manifestation or symptom of what was, in substance if not in form, a Christian state that tolerated non-Christians" (Ramlogan 2006). This legacy of colonialism was perpetuated, in his view, by the long years of rule by the People's National Movement after independence: the party was led by and based its support on mainly Christian African-Trinidadians. So the impulse to challenge the constitutionality of the award "had to do with the sense of belonging and being able to identify with the newly adopted motherland far away from India" (virtually all Hindus and most Muslims in Trinidad and Tobago are descended from Indian immigrants).

Some of those who wanted to keep the Trinity Cross because it reflected the national heritage had argued that if it was to go, then logically so must the name of the larger island, since *Trinidad* means the Trinity, a Christian concept. A prominent attorney, also a newspaper columnist, took this on:

> Trinidad is a name coined over 500 years ago. In those intervening hundreds of years any original linking of the name to the concept of the Holy Trinity would have become merely a historical fact, at a time when no ancestor of any of the current inhabitants of this island lived here. They came long, long afterwards. In a way it would be presumptuous of any of us today to seek to quarrel with the name given in 1498 (albeit in Spanish). In contrast, the Trinity Cross is an appellation chosen at a time when we were actually in the process of forming the independent nation we are today, a nation of many creeds, races and religions. We

should have had the foresight and sensitivity then to designate our highest award by a less exclusionary and more "all-inclusive" name. We did not. It is not too late to correct that faux pas. (Seetahal 2006)

It is interesting that no one argued publicly for renaming the nation-state, despite the historical fact that the larger island was indeed named after the Christian Trinity, or for the adoption of its putative Amerindian (Arawak) name, Kairi (often spelled Iere). Folk tradition has it that this word means "land of the hummingbird", but recent scholarship is clear that it should be translated as "the island" (Boomert 2010, 29–42). Of course, such a renaming would have created enormous practical difficulties, and one significant, if not insuperable, political obstacle: Kairi was the name given to Trinidad, and the nation is a two-island state. (*Tobago* probably derives from a Carib word meaning either a cigar-like roll of tobacco leaf or a pipe used to smoke it, perhaps because of the island's elongated shape [Winer 2009, 445, 481, 903]).

Most commentators who agreed that the Trinity Cross should be replaced by a single "neutral" award grounded their opinion in a defence of secularism in a multi-ethnic and multi-religious democracy, which consciously broke with its colonial legacy of Christian supremacy. It was a necessary step towards "a society in which every creed and race can one day genuinely find an equal place", wrote Reginald Dumas, echoing a line in the national anthem, "and in which much more energy is exerted on nation-building than on fevered exaltation of one's racial, ethnic, religious or political affiliations, beliefs and prejudices" (Dumas 2006a). Why, Patrick Watson asked, should "the symbol of one group alone be engraved on the country's highest award? In a society like ours, we *must* choose something that is neutral from a religious point of view, something that may reflect the secular and the multicultural" (Watson 2006). And a letter writer who self-identified as a Christian declared that the highest award was "a secular honour granted in recognition of secular achievement or service to the nation. Neither the symbol nor the award is proprietary to Christianity . . . As a Christian I affirm that the Trinity Cross is discriminatory to citizens of other faiths and should be removed as a national award" (Bosland 2006). These and many other commentators rejected the idea of two parallel highest awards as divisive and objectionable. Dumas considered that, if implemented, it would inevitably "further divide an already fragmented society" (Dumas 2006a). Watson regarded it as absurd: "such an action would give pride of place to our religious convictions which is unbecoming of a secular society" (Watson 2006). One of the nation's top dailies, in an editorial headed "Only One Top National Award", rejected "two or three and, before we know it, as many such awards as there are races and creeds in this country". The paper believed that "national awards are unifying symbols in a country precisely because they are one and the same for everybody, which is why they are particularly meaningful in multi-ethnic societies which need as many cohering instruments as they can get" (*Trinidad Express* 2006).

One aspect of the Trinity Cross related to the nation's heritage which had nothing to do with religion, and which few people noted, was the extent to which, if at all, it symbolically comprehended the smaller island, Tobago. After all, as so many noted, "Trinity" was the name given to the larger island and has no resonance or connection with Tobago. Reginald Dumas, a high-profile public figure from Tobago, wrote: "I continue to be amazed by the argument of those who insist that the name of this country is 'Trinidad', which was bestowed on it by Columbus, and that 'Trinity', the English translation of the word, is consequently sacrosanct. The name of the country is 'Trinidad and Tobago' " (Dumas 2006b). Ganteaume, whose letter defending the Trinity Cross was quoted earlier, was one of those subsuming Tobago under the name Trinidad: "The country is named for The Trinity!" he wrote. "Are we to change the name of the country also? . . . What about the Trinity Hills, are they to be renamed also?" (Ganteaume 2006). Dumas's point was reiterated by Watson, who observed: "if there is a problem with the word 'Trinity' in Trinity Cross, it is that it means, quite literally, Trinidad Cross: only one of the islands making up a two-island Republic is represented in the highest award of that Republic. At best it should be the Trinidad and Tobago Cross – if we are willing to bear the Cross" (Watson 2006). The nation's oldest newspaper recognized that "Trinity is capable of alienating the affections of citizens . . . simply belonging to Tobago, where identification with the Trinity Hills may not come naturally" (*Trinidad Guardian* 2006). If the nation's heritage was to genuinely embrace Tobago – the very different island annexed to Trinidad by Britain at the end of the nineteenth century, purely for imperial administrative and financial convenience – then an award named after the Trinity – Trinidad – could never be appropriate.

In the many submissions to the committee and newspaper articles and letters on the Trinity Cross, two other issues relating to heritage and national identity may perhaps be singled out. Both had to do with the proposed design for the new Order of the Republic. This featured an Amerindian feathered headdress as the crest, in order to acknowledge the first inhabitants of the two islands. Stephen Kangal argued that while Amerindians were being recognized by the headdress and Africans by the representation of a steelpan (a point I will take up shortly), no "visible homage" was being paid to the "cultural emblems" of Indo-Trinidadians. The design, Kangal claimed, "deliberately excludes from its mosaic the representation of any clear and precise motif depicting any aspect of the outstanding cultural and other contributions made by the Indian community". How, he asked, could "an Amerindian feathered headdress take precedence over an Indian symbol such as the turban or 'pagree' or the tassa?" For that matter, what of the Chinese community? Did it not make an "exemplary" contribution to the nation "that may surpass that of the Amerindians"? "Is the distinctive tribute paid to the Amerindians in the depiction of the headdress", Kangal went on, "an emotional response and/or a compensating factor to mitigate for past historical neglect by the ethno-nationalist movement [i.e., the People's National Movement]?" (Kangal 2006). But most of those who felt the point was worthy of comment believed that explicit recognition of the aboriginal inhabitants was fitting.

The second element in the design of the new award to provoke some debate was the steelpan theme. The circular configuration of the pan informs the overall shape of the medal, with its twelve notes and a pair of "pan sticks" just below the crest. In the letter already quoted, Kangal argued robustly that the pan is "an Afro–T and T symbol", not a "neutral" or national one, because it is "an African-invented artefact". To use the steelpan as the dominant motif was to see the nation "through the eyes of an Afro-Trinbagonian" by elevating an "outstanding cultural creation of the African community in T and T, even if an increasing amount of non-Africans play the pan with distinction". The tassa drum should have "equal billing" in the design, Kangal argued (2006). This provoked several responses, which essentially argued that the pan was by then an authentic national symbol, even if it had originally been developed by African-Trinidadians. "Why can't the national instrument be representative of Syrians, Chinese, Indians, Africans, and those nationals that have just been fused in the callaloo melee?" asked one letter writer, reflecting the popular view; "the pan isn't an African symbol, it's Trinbagonian!" ("Phantom Scribbler" 2006). Ironically, Kangal's position on the steelpan motif – grounded in a sense of grievance about the Indo-Trinidadian profile and representation in the national discourse – was not supported by the most prominent defender of Hindu Trinidad, Satnarayan Maharaj. The long-serving secretary-general of the SDMS, the body representing orthodox Hindus in Trinidad and Tobago and the lead plaintiff in the suit challenging the Trinity Cross, gave his explicit blessing to the steelpan motif for the new award, proposing that "the steelpan should form the base/background of the emblem" (Maharaj 2006). Kangal, it seems, was being more Catholic than the pope.

## Conclusion

This brief study of the public debate on the Trinity Cross in Trinidad and Tobago in 2006–8 (and which is still continuing) reveals that discussions about national symbols such as awards, anthems, flags and so on speak to important issues related to history, heritage and identity formation. Many of these issues focus on religion and its place in a secular democracy, which the then prime minister of Trinidad and Tobago, Patrick Manning, declared his country to be in his statement on the Trinity Cross in June 2006. However, it should be noted that the preamble to the national constitution begins: "Whereas the people of Trinidad and Tobago have affirmed that the nation of Trinidad and Tobago is founded upon a principle that acknowledges the supremacy of God . . .". The nation has a historical legacy of Christian supremacy, reflected in overt discrimination against non-Christian faiths and practitioners throughout the colonial era, and persisting even after independence in 1962. This is reflected, for instance, in the nation's public holidays, with several representing the Christian calendar and only two from Hinduism and Islam, as well as in the Trinity Cross itself. Except for a few years (1995–2001), the party in power since independence has always been led by Christian citizens. At the beginning of the twenty-first century, how far should national symbols reflect that historical legacy? The "discovery" by Columbus, in the service of their Catholic Majesties, the naming of the larger island after the Holy Trinity, the role of Catholic Spanish conquistadors and priests and equally Catholic French settlers in creating the society – how far (if at all) should this heritage continue to be represented in national symbols and observances?

The debate clearly resonates with the overall issue of managing religious diversity. However, it also has regional implications, as Tobago, the smaller island, was hardly represented in the name and design of the Trinity Cross. And the discussion of the steelpan and headdress motifs reflects ethnic contestations in the modern state. As previously indicated, the recommendation of the committee was implemented in August 2008, when the first three awards of the Order of the Republic were made (in August 2009 one was made posthumously, to a young sportswoman tragically killed in an accident). Essentially, the often intense public debate of the years up to 2008 had ended; most seemed to accept the change, either because they saw it as the correct decision or simply in resignation to a *fait accompli*, boredom or indifference. In sharp contrast, there was considerable public discussion in 2009 about the methods and criteria for selection of the national awardees and the apparent politicization of that process.[3] But the decision in favour of a "neutral", secular, inclusive name and design to replace the Trinity Cross was final. Bland and boring, probably (as several critics have said), and lacking in glamour, but sometimes bland is best after all.

## Notes

1. The author was appointed chair of this committee.
2. This chapter will not consider the public debate on other national symbols and observances (including public holidays), the subject of part 2 of the committee's report (29 December 2006), which has apparently not yet been formally considered by the national government.
3. There was considerable newspaper discussion on this issue in September 2009, including editorials in the *Express* and the *Guardian*, as well as many articles and letters to the editor.

## References

Bart-Alexander, K. 2006. Letter to *Trinidad Express*, 7 June.

Bhaggan, A. 2006. Letter to *Trinidad Express*, 7 June.

Boomert, A. 2010. "Kairi, Trinidad: The One True Island". *Archaeology and Anthropology* 16, no. 2: 29–42.

Bosland, D. 2006. Letter to *Trinidad Express*, 25 July.

Brereton, B. 2007. "Contesting the Past: Narratives of Trinidad and Tobago History". *New West Indian Guide* 81, nos. 3 and 4: 169–96.

Committee to Review All Aspects of the Nation's Highest Award [Committee]. 2006. *Report*, part 1, 15 July.

———. 2007. Letter from committee chair to prime minister, 8 June.

Cuffie, W. 2006a. "Great Wisdom from Archbishop Gilbert". *Trinidad Express*, 25 July.

———. 2006b. "Trinity Cross Remains Firmly Intact". *Trinidad Express*, 1 September.

Dumas, R. 2006a. "Ministry, Mandir and Masjid". *Trinidad Express*, 8 June.

———. 2006b. Letter to acting chair of the committee, 14 June.

Ganteaume, D. 2006. Letter to committee chair, December.

Gilbert, E.J. (Archbishop). 2006. Statement on the Trinity Cross, 18 July.

Homer, L. 2006. "To Rename Award a 'Sin' ". *Trinidad Express*, 6 June.

Hosein, I. 2006. "A Muslim Response to the 'Trinity Cross' Problem". *Trinidad Guardian*, 21 July.

Jamadar, Peter (Justice). 2006. Ruling on Trinity Cross suit, 26 May. HCA No. Cv.S.2065/2004: 80.

Joseph, G. 2006. Letter to *Trinidad Guardian*, 9 June.

Kangal, S. 2006. Letter to committee secretary, 14 December.

Loubon, M. 2008. "Prof Lauds Order of Republic of T and T". *Trinidad Guardian*, 3 September.

Maharaj, Satnarayan. 2006. Secretary-general of SDMS to Cabinet Secretariat, 6 July.

Manning, P. 2006. "Statement to the House of Representatives by the Prime Minister". 2 June.

McDowell Benjamin, W. 2006. Letter to *Trinidad Express*, 9 June.

"Phantom Scribbler". 2006. Letter to *Trinidad Express*, 12 December.

Rahman, M.F. 2006. Letter to *Trinidad Express*, 8 June.

Seetahal, D. 2006. "A Rose by Any Other Name". *Trinidad Guardian*, 4 June.

*Trinidad Express*. 2006. Editorial, 21 July.

*Trinidad Guardian*. 2006. Editorial, 4 June.

Watson, P. 2006. Letter to *Trinidad Express*, 1 August.

Winer, L. 2009. *Dictionary of the English/Creole of Trinidad and Tobago*. Montreal: McGill-Queen's University Press.

# 4.

# Population Dynamics and Temporal Impact on Popular Culture

## The Case of Trinidad Carnival

GODFREY ST BERNARD

*Tangible and intangible elements of culture are manifestations of temporal changes that impact sub-populations with different consequences dependent upon one's age. The evolution of such cultural artefacts is a function of population dynamics which transcend age and also hinge upon other social and demographic attributes, such as sex composition, educational characteristics, religious affiliation, ethnic distributions and nativity. Using data emanating from five population censuses from 1960 to 2000 inclusively, changing population dynamics are examined in accordance with documented changes in critical non-material elements of Trinidad Carnival. Population projections are also used to generate plausible prospective scenarios that may characterize such non-material elements of Trinidad Carnival during the second and third decades of the twenty-first century. Altogether, this chapter embraces C. Wright Mills's notion of a sociological imagination based on reliable manifestations of population dynamics in the past, which, by virtue of their observed implications across time, permit the use of critical sensibilities to project insights into future outcomes based on prospective population dynamics. This chapter serves to reinforce the critical nexus between population dynamics and the evolution of cultural manifestations. Moreover, it strives to avert surprises among cultural activists and allied personnel, alerting them so that they can embrace more proactive positions towards the preservation of aspects of non-material culture in Trinidad Carnival. However, cohort experiences and exposure shape the reality of such cultural manifestations, a fact that all generations have to live with, given that change is the most constant feature across time.*

## Historical Forces and the Primacy of Population Dynamics

Trinidad Carnival is a major cultural phenomenon that evolved over the course of the nineteenth and twentieth centuries in the twin-island Republic of Trinidad and Tobago. Historical antecedents characteristic of Catholicism, pre-emancipation plantation society and the experience of freedom have largely been attributed as important factors in the formation of early Carnival expressions in Trinidad (Van Koningsbruggen 1997). As a medium of cultural expression, early Carnival celebrations were shaped by these cultural vestiges and, in particular, the peoples that occupied Trinidad during the mid to late nineteenth century. In those days Trinidad was home to a French Creole community of planters, freed slaves of African origin and an emergent group of East Indian, Chinese and Portuguese indentured labourers.

Demographics such as population size and other attributes of its composition, including sex ratios, age distribution, ethnic identities, religious affiliation and socio-economic status, operate independently and jointly to influence the evolution of cultural expression in all spheres of life. In the context of Trinidad and Tobago, the primacy of such factors in the evolution of a "Trini" way of life should be evident, yet it appears to go unnoticed. This chapter treats with Trinidad Carnival as a cultural phenomenon that has evolved and continues to evolve in response to temporal changes in such demographics.

As a cultural phenomenon, the construct would not have been labelled "Trinidad Carnival" had it not been for participation of the peoples of Trinidad and Tobago and the persistence of a format with inherent elements that define the essence of the construct, despite obvious changes across time in the configuration of the format and the significance of its elements. With reference to the participation of the peoples of Trinidad and Tobago, it should be understood that some sub-populations participate while others do not participate in the Carnival phenomenon. Among those who do participate, in any given period there are obvious variations in the intensity and nature of the participation of different sub-populations, and across different time periods for all sub-populations in general.

## A Review of Past Studies

Trinidad Carnival conjures up a range of interesting images that may vary across individuals, though Mason vividly captures the essence of this awesome national phenomenon. In his words,

> Trinidad carnival is one of the most photographed festivals in the world, yet not even glorious Technicolor can convey the orgy of excitement, the smells, the heat,

the confusion, the heart pounding noise, the sexual energy, the pepper sauce wit, the aching limbs and the sense of mental release. No photograph can reveal just how much this festival is woven into the fabric of one of the most vibrant, obstinate and engaging nations in the world. Many countries have a carnival, but carnival is Trinidad – and Trinidad is carnival. (Mason 1998, 7)

Grant (2004) presents Carnival as an infection: "carnivalitis" spreading across the globe largely because of individuals' exposure to it. In addressing the contemporary format of Trinidad Carnival – "Trinival", as he calls it – Grant (2008) recognizes the impact of East Indian involvement in the national festival. Other scholars such as Mason (1998) and Sankaralli (1998) have also alluded to outcomes associated with the growing East Indian presence in Trinidad Carnival.

Scholars associated with a range of academic disciplines have sought to construct reality and contribute to further understanding of Trinidad Carnival, using a host of qualitative insights. This is evident in the work of Stuempfle (1995), in the case of the steel band movement, and Cowley (1996), in the case of the development of Carnival music. Moreover, a considerable amount of Carnival research has focused on the historical antecedents of the festival (Crowley 1956; Hill 1984, 1997; Anthony 1989; Liverpool 1998, 2001; Riggio 1998). Some writers and scholars have sought to capture temporal changes in the context of different facets of Carnival. An historico-cultural approach is evident in the works of Henry (2008), who provides an account of his interpretation of the people's masquerade in transition. In a similar vein, Lovelace (1998) accounts for the decline of what he labels as the "emancipation-jouvay" that was concomitant with the loss of pan, signalling a transition from a jouvay catering primarily to the working-class African masses. Slater (1984) has also traced the decline of the steel band in Carnival from a historico-cultural perspective.

With respect to steel band, calypso and the masquerade (also known as the Carnival trinity), some scholars have provided ethno-historical interpretations to trace the evolution of the different media. This is evident in the works of Blake (1995) and Bellour et al. (2002) in the context of the emergence of a drum culture, and Rohlehr (1984, 1990) and Guilbault (2007) in the context of Carnival music genres. With respect to the masquerade, scholarly accounts of temporal changes have been documented in the work of Hill (1984, 1997) and Henry (2008). Most of these works have provided comprehensive historical accounts of Trinidad Carnival. However, they have not ventured to comment overwhelmingly on its state in the early years of the new millennium or, in particular, about prognoses for its future.

# Branding Trinidad Carnival

## Trinidad Carnival as a Unique Cultural Phenomenon

Notwithstanding its evolution across time, this cultural phenomenon has persisted and has its own customized format on an annual basis. "Trinidad Carnival" has become a brand name that connotes a real phenomenon that is structurally different from Carnival in Rio, Mardi Gras in New Orleans or other carnival experiences with historico-cultural roots. To this extent, "Trinidad-style" carnivals have emerged in a number of countries in the anglophone Caribbean and in major metropolitan cities such as New York, Miami, Washington, DC, and Baltimore in the United States, Toronto and Montreal in Canada and London, England. As has been the case in Rio de Janeiro and New Orleans, Trinidad Carnival is not simply a tourism product that generates revenue for stakeholders; it is also predicated upon symbolic historical and cultural antecedents that have persisted inter-generationally.

## Essence and Tradition

Trinidad Carnival is a pre-Lenten festival of song, music, dance, masquerade and commerce. The season usually gains momentum in January every year and culminates in two days of revelry on Carnival Monday and Carnival Tuesday, the two days preceding Ash Wednesday, which falls in either February or March. The season lasts between one and two months and is usually punctuated by attendance at Carnival fetes,[1] visits to calypso tents, the hosting of a range of competitions, visits to pan yards, and the culmination in total abandon and revelry during a nationwide street party on Carnival Monday and Carnival Tuesday.

Public participation is variable, ranging from absolutely no participation for religious and other reasons to consummate participation, with some individuals earning their livelihood from activities associated with Carnival. Among persons who choose to participate, their participation varies according to their preference for various combinations of Carnival events and the nature of their participation, whether as patrons, spectators, performers, masqueraders, workers or possibly some combination of participatory roles. In each case, participation may vary in intensity. In Trinidad and Tobago, Carnival is a hybrid industry that feeds on satellite industries such as hospitality, transport and communications, distribution and so on. From a sociological standpoint, Carnival is a major social institution with its own social order, norms, values and systemic relations.

## The Research Problem: Rationale and Scope

This chapter argues that temporal changes in the format of Trinidad Carnival and its inherent elements are inevitable, and that it is useless to resist them. At the same time, it recognizes that retentions associated with the sentiments and actions of different generations of participants are worthy and deserve a place in Carnival, despite inevitable changes in its format. With regard to the former, this chapter highlights temporal changes in demographic attributes and how they have likely been associated with qualitative changes in the format of Carnival and its elements between the 1960s and the 2000s. It also relies on projections of population dynamics and discusses their implications for the evolution of Trinidad Carnival, especially during the second and third decades of the new millennium.

## Population Dynamics: Retrospective and Prospective

### Retrospective View

Table 4.1 shows population sizes as well as age and sex compositions of the population of Trinidad and Tobago in 1960, 1970, 1980, 1990 and 2000. According to the available census data, in 1960 the population of Trinidad and Tobago comprised 827,957 persons; in 2000 the population was 1,262,366, signalling growth in general population across the period. Between 1960 and 2000 there is evidence of increases in the size of populations of persons 15 to 44 years old, 45 to 64 years old and 65 years or older, with the respective numbers of persons 45 to 64 years old and 65 years or older being more than twice the corresponding numbers observed in 1960. Such a pattern is indicative of the onset of population ageing in Trinidad and Tobago.

According to table 4.2, persons of African and East Indian origins have consistently accounted for about 80 per cent of the national population. Throughout the 1960s and 1970s, census data reveal that there were more persons of African origin than persons of East Indian origin. However, during the 1980s and throughout the 1990s, the evidence suggests that persons of East Indian origin constituted the majority. The sizes of these two population groups grew consistently throughout the 1960s to 1990s, as is also true for the population of mixed origin. During the same period there were consistent declines in the collective size of other sub-populations, whose origins were principally Chinese, "White", Syrian, Lebanese, Portuguese and Amerindian.

Despite observed increases since the 1960s, table 4.3 indicates declines in the size of the population identifying with Hinduism from the 1990s onward, the populations identifying with Roman Catholicism and Presbyterianism

**Table 4.1** Key Population Variables, Trinidad and Tobago, Selected Census Years

| Population Variables | 1960 | 1970 | 1980 | 1990 | 2000 |
|---|---|---|---|---|---|
| **Population Characteristics** | | | | | |
| Total population size | 827,957 | 931,071 | 1,079,791 | 1,213,733 | 1,262,366 |
| Population less than 15 years | 351,051 | 391,713 | 369,711 | 406,155 | 319,937 |
| Population 15–44 years | 336,731 | 376,580 | 513,027 | 571,629 | 632,199 |
| Population 45–64 years | 106,484 | 121,438 | 136,877 | 160,208 | 220,862 |
| Population 65 years or older | 33,691 | 41,340 | 60,176 | 75,741 | 89,368 |
| **Age Composition – Percentage** | | | | | |
| Less than 15 years | 42 | 42 | 34 | 34 | 26 |
| 15–44 years | 41 | 41 | 47 | 47 | 50 |
| 45–64 years | 13 | 13 | 13 | 13 | 17 |
| 65 years or older | 4 | 4 | 6 | 6 | 7 |
| **Sex Ratios (males per 100 females)** | | | | | |
| Less than 15 years | 101 | 101 | 102 | 102 | 102 |
| 15–44 years | 97 | 95 | 101 | 101 | 102 |
| 45–64 years | 107 | 104 | 100 | 97 | 102 |
| 65 years or older | 74 | 77 | 81 | 86 | 86 |

*Source:* Population and Housing Census Reports, 1960, 1970, 1980, 1990 and 2000.

**Table 4.2** Ethnic Origin, Population of Trinidad and Tobago, Selected Census Years

| Ethnic Origin | 1960 | 1970 | 1980 | 1990 | 2000 |
|---|---|---|---|---|---|
| **Ethnic Origin – Number** | 827,957 | 931,071 | 1,055,763 | 1,125,128 | 1,114,772 |
| African origin | 358,591 | 398,765 | 430,864 | 445,444 | 418,268 |
| East Indian origin | 301, 948 | 373,538 | 429,187 | 453,069 | 446,273 |
| Mixed | 134,750 | 131,904 | 172,285 | 207,558 | 228,089 |
| Other | 32,668 | 26,864 | 19,372 | 14,226 | 13,655 |
| Ethnic origin not stated | – | – | 4,055 | 4,831 | 8,487 |
| **Ethnic Origin – Per Cent** | | | | | |
| African origin | 43 | 43 | 41 | 40 | 38 |
| East Indian origin | 37 | 40 | 41 | 40 | 40 |
| Mixed | 16 | 14 | 16 | 18 | 20 |
| Other | 4 | 3 | 2 | 1 | 1 |
| Ethnic origin not stated | – | – | – | 1 | 1 |

*Source:* Population and Housing Census Reports, 1960, 1070, 1980, 1990 and 2000.

**Table 4.3** Religious Affiliation, Population of Trinidad and Tobago, Selected Census Years

| Religious Affiliation | 1960 | 1970 | 1980 | 1990 | 2000 |
|---|---|---|---|---|---|
| **All Religious Affiliations – Number** | 827,957 | 931,071 | 1,055,763 | 1,125,128 | 1,114,772 |
| Roman Catholic | 299,627 | 331,733 | 347,740 | 330,655 | 289,711 |
| Anglican | 175,044 | 168,521 | 155,155 | 122,787 | 86,792 |
| Methodist | 18,220 | 15,507 | 15,118 | 13,448 | 10,396 |
| Presbyterian | 32,413 | 39,363 | 40,275 | 38,740 | 36,710 |
| Seventh-Day Adventist | 12,631 | 16,673 | 26,268 | 41,631 | 44,147 |
| Jehovah's Witness | – | – | 8,021 | 14,713 | 17,948 |
| Pentecostal | – | – | 36,451 | 84,066 | 79,327 |
| Baptist | – | – | 25,333 | 33,689 | 79,899 |
| Hindu | 190,424 | 230,097 | 262,917 | 267,040 | 250,760 |
| Muslim | 49,736 | 58,252 | 63,333 | 65,732 | 64,648 |
| Other religion | – | – | 54,039 | 88,203 | 119,124 |
| No religious affiliation | – | – | 10,392 | 13,691 | 21,598 |
| Religion not stated | – | – | 10,721 | 10,721 | 15,170 |
| **All Religious Affiliations – Per Cent** | | | | | |
| Roman Catholic | 36 | 36 | 33 | 30 | 26 |
| Anglican | 21 | 18 | 15 | 11 | 8 |
| Methodist | 2 | 2 | 1 | 1 | 1 |
| Presbyterian | 4 | 4 | 4 | 3 | 3 |
| Seventh-Day Adventist | 2 | 2 | 3 | 4 | 4 |
| Jehovah's Witness | – | – | 1 | 1 | 2 |
| Pentecostal | – | – | 3 | 8 | 7 |
| Baptist | – | – | 2 | 3 | 7 |
| Hindu | 23 | 25 | 25 | 24 | 22 |
| Muslim | 6 | 6 | 6 | 6 | 6 |
| Other religion | – | – | 5 | 8 | 11 |
| No religious affiliation | – | – | 1 | 1 | 2 |
| Religion not stated | – | – | 1 | 1 | 1 |

*Source:* Population and Housing Census Reports, 1960, 1970, 1980, 1990 and 2000.

from the 1980s onward, and for Anglicans and Methodists from the 1970s onward. During the 1980s and 1990s there were also increases in the number of persons declaring no religious affiliation. However, despite the falling away that has been characteristic of Roman Catholicism and Hinduism, these two belief systems have persisted as the principal religious denominations claimed by the national population.

## Prospective View

Population sizes have been projected for Trinidad and Tobago across five-year intervals between 2000 and 2025 (see table 4.4). The number of persons 65 years or older is projected to increase on a continuous basis across the projection period. The rate of growth is likely to be slower in the case of 45- to 64-year-olds, among whom the numbers are likely to change very little between 2015 and 2025. In contrast, the number of children under 15 years old is projected to decline on a continuous basis across the projection period. Outcomes consistent with each of these projection assumptions highlighted also show that the number of persons 15 to 44 years old will likely have peaked around 2005; between 2005 and 2010 their numbers will probably stabilize before continuously declining thereafter up to 2025.

**Table 4.4** Projected Population Characteristics, Trinidad and Tobago, Selected Census Years

| Assumptions | 8 June 2000 | 8 June 2001 | 8 June 2005 | 8 June 2010 | 8 June 2015 | 8 June 2020 | 8 June 2025 |
|---|---|---|---|---|---|---|---|
| High | 1,262,366 | 1,267,866 | 1,285,718 | 1,312,259 | 1,347,174 | 1,379,331 | 1,398,947 |
| Constant | 1,262,366 | 1,264,613 | 1,266,147 | 1,260,585 | 1,247,294 | 1,219,573 | 1,174,665 |
| Low | 1,262,366 | 1,264,613 | 1,266,707 | 1,258,745 | 1,237,531 | 1,198,894 | 1,143,457 |
| Medium | 1,262,366 | 1,264,610 | 1,268,439 | 1,268,642 | 1,265,430 | 1,252,654 | 1,228,675 |
| Medium-High | 1,262,366 | 1,267,866 | 1,284,652 | 1,300,288 | 1,310,888 | 1,309,589 | 1,294,347 |
| Medium-Medium | 1,262,366 | 1,267,866 | 1,284,303 | 1,298,648 | 1,306,920 | 1,302,196 | 1,282,384 |
| Medium-Low | 1,262,366 | 1,264,613 | 1,266,468 | 1,259,377 | 1,243,051 | 1,211,067 | 1,161,638 |

*Source:* Central Statistical Office, Trinidad and Tobago

Whether as masqueraders, spectators or workers, the vast majority of persons pursuing such activities are likely to be drawn from the 15- to 64-year-old population. In general, the projections suggest that between 2010 and 2025 the number of persons 15 to 64 years old is likely to be at least 800,000 and at most 943,000. These numbers are substantially larger than the corresponding numbers for 1960 (443,215 persons), 1980 (649,904) and 1990 (731,837). Moreover, the forces of globalization and trans-nationalism have spawned Trinidad-style carnivals in North America, Europe and the Caribbean sub-region (Scher 1997); these are likely to continue contributing to large numbers of visitors and returning residents participating in Trinidad Carnival on an annual basis during the first twenty-five years of the new millennium. This popularity is being intensified by individual and collective expressions that deem Trinidad Carnival a phenomenon to behold. The city of Port of Spain has become the primary stage of Trinidad-style carnival celebrations, to the extent of a virtual pilgrimage during the first quarter of every calendar year that is likely to continue. Additionally, several websites exist where one can find the scheduled dates for Trinidad Carnival even beyond the 2020s.

## Population Dynamics and Prospects for Trinidad Carnival

### The Spatial Context

Since the 1990s and especially since the 2000s, Port of Spain has been stifled and choked, largely by four factors: (1) phenomenal increases in population size, primarily among persons 15 to 64 years old, (2) an overwhelming influx of visitors, precipitated by technological advancement associated with the World Wide Web and other elements of the telecommunications revolution since the late 1980s, (3) the primacy assigned to Port of Spain as the principal showpiece of Trinidad Carnival, and (4) the inability of regulatory agencies such as the National Carnival Commission to adequately manage the dispersion of crowds during Carnival celebrations, especially on Carnival Monday and Carnival Tuesday.

Prospects for changes in population size indicate that there are likely to be no major differences in the impact of population size in a spatial context, as decreases in the size of the 15- to 44-year-old population during the first three decades of the 2000s are projected to be virtually offset by increases in the size of the population of 45- to 64-year-olds. Assuming that there is an intensification of overseas visitors to Trinidad Carnival during the first three decades of the new millennium, and assuming that persons 15 to 64 years old are the major participants in Carnival activity, revellers' mobility will continue to be stifled on Carnival Tuesdays in particular, unless the relevant authorities embark upon appropriate strategies geared towards decongestion in Port of Spain. With respect to the street parades that traverse Port of Spain on Carnival Monday and Carnival Tuesday, some degree of spontaneity within a quasi-regulated environment is evident in Trinidad Carnival. Perhaps the time has come for more complete regulatory standards to be embraced to achieve some modicum of decongestion.

As Port of Spain maintains and enhances its status as the hub of Trinidad Carnival, local authorities in other urban domains, including San Fernando, are likely to pursue strategies to bolster Carnival celebrations in their locales in order to attract crowds and expand the revenue base for their respective communities. Such ventures may target specific niche groups predicated on age and ethnicity. This can be accomplished by either highlighting some of the more traditional elements of Trinidad Carnival or offering variant experiences that are less likely to be experienced in Port of Spain. The latter ought to be considered, as the Carnival phenomenon has tended to become more static and homogeneous in Port of Spain, especially since the 1990s. Thus spatial constraints could be overcome by the emergence of parallel Carnival celebrations in different locales, an outcome that could introduce divisions along ethnic, class and age lines. The prominence of chutney music and East Indian artists and the concentration of East Indians in central and parts of south Trinidad have already been deemed instrumental in the evolution of Carnival celebrations in central Trinidad, particularly on Carnival Mondays and Tuesdays.

## The Evolution of Music Genres and Delivery Media

In the 1960s, Carnival events were driven primarily by traditional music genres, principally calypso, which was delivered vocally and through the medium of the steel drum. Throughout the forty-year period between 1960 and the close of the twentieth century, the phenomenon of the calypso tent thrived in Trinidad and Tobago, having its roots in earlier periods. During the 1960s and the 1970s, street parades were predominantly driven by a wide-ranging repertoire delivered by numerous steel bands that accompanied the revellers, mainly in Port of Spain and San Fernando. Invariably, calypso renditions from famous exponents of the art form, in particular the Mighty Sparrow and Lord Kitchener, ruled supreme on the streets. During the same period, numerous satellite Carnival events, such as the seasonal dances better known as fetes and customized competitions, were also driven by the calypso genre. In the context of Carnival music genres, calypso music was the format that remained relatively homogeneous during the 1960s and 1970s, despite greater hetero-geneity that had become evident by the mid-1970s.

A major phenomenon characterizing the demographic landscape of Trinidad and Tobago since the 1970s has been noteworthy increases in the size of the population aged 15 to 44 years and, to a somewhat lesser extent, the size of the population aged 45 to 64 years. This has largely been a function of the assumption of adulthood among members of the post–Second World War baby boom, and is manifested by increasingly large population sizes that are likely to be sustained well beyond the first decade of the new millennium. Since the 1970s these dynamics have emerged in tandem with the different genres of Carnival music that have been emerging in the region. Carnival music genres became more variable, with the evolution of soca as a parallel medium driving Carnival events, a phenomenon that gained momentum throughout the rest of the twentieth century. Thus it is quite likely that phe-nomenal increases in population sizes spawned a critical mass which in turn facilitated the spread of ideas leading to a wider array of Carnival music gen-res. To this end, idiosyncratic cultural influences and island-specific "vibes" have further influenced the evolution of Carnival music genres, resulting in such derivatives as "chutney soca", "ragga soca" and "groovy soca", among others. As early as the 1970s this process would have been propelled by the fuller participation and contributions of artists from the wider Caribbean region, for example, Arrow from Montserrat, Swallow and Short Shirt from Antigua and Barbuda, Gabby from Barbados and Becket from St Vincent and the Grenadines.

The post–Second World War baby boomers emerged as popular artists during the 1980s and into the early 1990s. Trinidad-based artists such as Blue Boy/Super Blue, David Rudder, Carl and Carol Jacobs, Crazy, Colin Lucas and Chris "Tambu" Herbert were among those who assumed stardom during this period. They experimented with calypso and soca melodies, the latter being brought to the fore by earlier artists of the 1970s, in particular, Ras Shorty I and Maestro. Super Blue, in particular, was primarily responsible for introducing the "power soca" medium to Carnival music genres. Power soca was embraced by younger artists throughout the 1990s and persisted through the early years of the new millennium. The style constitutes a critical cohort influence among not only younger artists but also younger revellers; both groups came of age in the 1990s and are invariably the offspring of the post–Second World War baby boomers.

By the 1990s the children of the baby boomers had swelled the ranks of persons 15 to 44 years old. Their lifetime cohort experiences, including expo-sure to a dynamic Jamaican popular culture, the impact of globalization on Caribbean popular culture and their exposure to power soca, had a profound influence on the production of Carnival music genres. These experiences persisted throughout the 1990s and gained momentum in the 2000s. In the 1990s and 2000s, artists from Trinidad and Tobago, in particular, Machel Montano, Shurwayne Winchester, Bunji Garlin and Destra Garcia, assumed stardom. A similar fate was characteristic of artists from Barbados, in particular, Rupee and Alyson Hinds. Observed declines in the annual number of births since the 1980s has been reflected in observed decreases in the projected size of the population aged 15 to 44 years. The power soca phenomenon has persisted for more than twenty years. Despite recent thrusts towards groovy soca, a style propelled primarily by Shurwayne Winchester, Rupee and, to a somewhat lesser extent, Machel Montano, power soca has constituted a major cohort influence on the lives of children of post–Second World War baby boomers. This trend may persist even beyond 2010, among younger children as they assume teenaged status.

Socio-demographic trends and projected outcomes are consistent with the persistence of power soca and groovy soca during the second and third decades of the 2000s. Persons 15 to 44 years, and a substantial proportion of those aged 45 to 64 years, will comprise relatively larger proportions of persons who would have come of age having had exposure to such genres. Moreover, decreases in the annual number of births since the 1980s are consistent with observed decreases since 1990 in the size of the population under 15 years old, such decreases being projected to persist during the third decade of the 2000s. Even if global, regional and cultural influences foster the emergence of novel music genres among such younger cohorts as they enter the ranks of the 15- to 44-year-olds in the second and third decades of the 2000s, power soca, groovy soca and other derivatives based on fusion are likely to persist across the same period. This outcome could be realized especially because of the prominence and fanfare that characterized competitions for such positions as Power Soca Monarch and Groovy Soca Monarch in the early years of the 2000s. Moreover, the primacy placed upon power soca as the genre of choice for Road March renditions reinforces the likelihood of its persistence during the second and third decades of the new millennium, when cohorts nurtured on power soca and groovy soca come of age and join the 15- to 64-year-olds.

Since the 1990s, and intensifying in the early 2000s, the primacy of power soca has had a negative impact on the fate of the steel band and of calypso tents in the landscape of Trinidad Carnival. In addition to the Panorama competition, which has been responsible for the decline of the steel band in street parades and other major Carnival events, the evolution of melodic elements associated with emergent music genres has posed challenges to arrangers and pan players, further limiting the repertoire that can be presented in public arenas. To this end, younger generations, including large proportions of those aged 15 to 44 years, have never been exposed to cohort influences featuring the primacy of the steel band in street parades and other Carnival events. As a result, throughout the 1990s and 2000s there were observed declines in the presence of steel bands in street parades; in cases where steel bands were present, they attracted more mature revellers, who would have had fuller exposure to steel bands as a major phenomenon in Trinidad Carnival dating back to before the 1980s.

In the 1990s and 2000s, the manoeuvrability of steel bands in street parades depended upon motorized rather than human power. This was due principally to substantial declines in participation and demographic ageing among the revellers who continue to be drawn and mesmerized by the sound of the steel band in the street parades of Carnival Monday and Tuesday. In the 2000s, revellers in steel bands have been principally persons in their forties, fifties and sixties. As such, they would have experienced the sound of steel bands in the street parades during their youth, an experience that undoubtedly contributed to their primary socialization as participants in Carnival. Thus, projected increases in the size of the population 45 to 64 years old during the second and third decades of the 2000s seem consistent with the persistence of steel bands in street parades and, in particular, the ageing of such revellers. Compared to the 1960s, 1970s and 1980s, steel bands in more recent times are rarely contracted to perform at major Carnival events such as fetes. During the second and third decades of the 2000s, this is likely to intensify because of the ageing of persons who were 45 to 64 years old in the first decade of the 2000s.

Compared to the 1980s and the 1990s, the phenomenon of the calypso tent has been struggling for survival during the 2000s, primarily for the same reasons attributed to the decline of the primacy of the steel band. There has been noteworthy attrition among traditional exponents of calypso, principally from mortality, ill health or retirement. At the same time there are competing influences, including a range of alternative music genres – in particular, power soca – that appear more attractive and rewarding to "new-age" artists. Rather than perform in calypso tents, younger artists have been attracted by the potential rewards associated with novel music genres and their more positive impact on individual socio-economic well-being, shaped principally by earnings from local and international performances and by the fame associated with winning the Road March and such coveted titles as Power Soca Monarch and Groovy Soca Monarch. With the passage of time, in the early 2000s patrons of calypso tents became primarily persons aged 45 to 64 years, notwithstanding some attendance by younger persons. With the ageing of persons 45 to 64 years old and the intensification of competition with regard to

attracting new talent, the decline of the primacy of the calypso tent as a phenomenon associated with Trinidad Carnival is imminent, unless creative
entrepreneurial instincts offer a viable alternative catering to new-age artists
and their emergent profiles.

## Carnival Parade: Presentation and Spirit

Between 1960 and 2000, Trinidad Carnival became much more commercial-
ized, despite efforts in various quarters to retain the deeply rooted cultural
foci that have traditionally been central to the festivities. In this regard, several
commentators would argue that a noteworthy casualty reflecting a departure
from cultural roots has been the display of modern costumes on Carnival
Tuesdays. In the 1960s, 1970s and early 1980s, such commentators would
argue that the display of costumes richly reflected the remarkable themes portrayed by band leaders and their masqueraders on Carnival Mondays and
Tuesdays and was indicative of the creative artistic skills of the leaders and
their assistants, who had toiled long and hard and took great pride in present-
ing their portrayals to the world.

In the late 1980s, however, the band Savage introduced the "swimwear
phenomenon" to the display of costumes. Oftentimes public sentiment has
been that this transition quelled creativity and cultural expression, resulting
in content that has been deemed stagnant despite efforts to sustain annual
themes in Trinidad Carnival. This paradigm shift was evident throughout the
1990s, with the reign of bands such as Poison, Barbarossa, Legends and
Young Harts. It persisted into the first decade of the 2000s and is likely to
continue despite years of resistance, mainly evident in the presentations of
band leaders such as Peter Minshall and Brian MacFarlane and Associates.
Having gained momentum during the 1990s, this paradigm shift may have
precipitated the inevitable retirement of ageing band leaders who presented
bands for older masqueraders.

Since the 2000s, modern bands such as Tribe and Island People, among
others, have embraced the "all-inclusive" concept that provides all the masqueraders' needs under one roof. In principle the all-inclusive concept means
that patrons, having become members of a band, can enjoy an unlimited supply of alcoholic and non-alcoholic beverages, breakfast, lunch and an assortment of snacks. Additionally, provisions are made to reinforce security for
band members, while features such as mobile restrooms and first-aid services
complete the package. These modern bands have embraced a corporate culture that reinforces optimal service delivery and strives for the maxim "value
for money". Ultimately the experience is costly, and indicative of a transition
that has classist tendencies.

During the first decade of the 2000s, older adult masqueraders, particularly those in their forties, fifties and sixties or even older, were observed revelling in overwhelming numbers in steel bands, which they consider to be their principal medium for participating in the street parades on Carnival Mondays and Tuesdays. This segment of masqueraders has been successful in encouraging and fostering the retention of the steel band in street parades in Trinidad Carnival. On Carnival Mondays and Tuesdays they continue to patronize the traditional costumes that characterize the presentations of some of the more popular and older steel bands, and by so doing have fostered such retentions. In essence, the retention of the steel band in street parades reinforces the notion of the Carnival experience as a classless phenomenon: virtually anyone is able to participate, given that costs are minimal and established at a level to facilitate maximal participation. In contrast, the all-inclusive concept reflects classist tendencies, facilitating participation among the haves and alienating the have-nots. The persistence of traditional formats such as the steel bands is concomitant with spectators and vendors having a greater stake as participants when compared to emergent formats such as the all-inclusive concept.

The all-inclusive concept is indicative of an "ultramodern" conception of the Carnival parade that is often characteristic of portrayals in which the "swimwear phenomenon" prevails and represents the further feminization of the masquerade. With the prospective ageing of the young adult crowd that embraced this ultramodern concept during the first decade of the 2000s, its survival becomes a more likely outcome in the second and third decades of the 2000s. Alternatively, evolutionary processes may spawn novel "new wave" formats that challenge thrusts towards retention. These outcomes, along with the ageing of persons who were in their forties, fifties or older during the first decade of the 2000s, could hasten the demise of the steel band as a viable medium in Carnival parades during the second and third decades of the 2000s.

While several traditional elements of Trinidad Carnival have not been salvaged and are not likely to be regained, this chapter signals a warning that the role of the steel band in the parade of bands could be lost if the relevant interest groups ignore demographic and other social trends. In the absence of the steel band, classist tendencies become a real possibility. They have already been evident in other dimensions of the Carnival experience, whether in the context of the decline of the calypso tent, the emergence of the all-inclusive concept during major Carnival events, or the cost of entertainment, the latter being a function of global forces. Moreover, as attempts to cater to overseas visitors intensify, the costs of the Carnival product will increase, thereby making it more prohibitive for the average "man in the street". This will reinforce classist notions of Carnival which have been known to facilitate more broad-based participation and, as such, engendered notions of a society that can boast of an experience for which class need not preclude participation.

## Conclusion

Sociologically, Trinidad Carnival has been a mega-social institution in its own right. There seems to be a common understanding of roles and expectations which are manifested differentially across time and space. Competition has persisted as a critical feature of the Carnival landscape in the past, and with the passage of time it continues to prevail as a prominent feature. Notwithstanding the disorder that is often associated with Trinidad Carnival, not to mention the potential for such disorder, there have always been thrusts towards the establishment of order. Such thrusts are justified in the quest to brand Trinidad Carnival as safe and worthy of being embraced internationally. Such depictions portray Trinidad Carnival as a deeply rooted cultural phenomenon that must be preserved inter-generationally to avert threats to its hegemony as a world-class event.

The population of Trinidad and Tobago will peak during the first three decades of the new millennium. Such knowledge permits one to make inferences about public participation in Trinidad Carnival during the 2010s and 2020s. Specifically, it is expected to be equivalent to or eclipse that which was characteristic of the 2000s. Emergent population dynamics are likely to pose challenges that have implications for the spatial context of Carnival activities, the evolution of music genres and delivery media, and the presentation and spirit of the Carnival parade. Drawing on population projections and other critical sensibilities, this chapter has provided prospective scenarios for likely outcomes.

The ministry responsible for science, technology and tertiary education, in collaboration with key government agencies charged with responsibility for culture and tourism, should provide greater support for academic departments that focus on Carnival studies, whether in the context of the University of the West Indies, the University of Trinidad and Tobago or both. This would enhance opportunities to capture critical elements of institutional memory that persist, despite some loss due to the passing of earlier Carnival performers. To this end, degree programmes should be strengthened in the area of Carnival studies. These should be supported by systematic scholarly research reflecting every dimension of the social institution that Trinidad Carnival has been, has become, and is likely to become. Such research could be complemented by an annual conference, which should be an international event showcasing Trinidad and Tobago as the international flag-bearer of "Trini-style" carnivals.

In closing, this chapter is based on the premise that change is the most constant process in life, and the evolution of Trinidad Carnival as a process is no different. It recognizes Trinbagonian pride regarding the status of Carnival as a world-class event, and a desire to retain that status. Such a desire is extremely critical, given the proliferation of Trini-style carnivals globally. These strong nationalistic tendencies ought to be sustained among local stakeholders in order to reinforce the image of Trinidad and Tobago as the mother of all destinations that showcase Trini-style carnival. Visitors and locals alike could witness traditional elements that would surely provide a means of distinguishing Carnival in Trinidad and Tobago from Trini-style carnivals in other countries. Processes should also be established to ensure that institutions in Trinidad and Tobago continue to shape the future of Trinidad Carnival.

This chapter is deemed to be critical in using demographics to examine the retention of traditional artefacts in Trinidad Carnival. At the same time, it recognizes that change is inevitable and that the evolution and content of phenomena such as Trinidad Carnival are functions of technological advancement and period and cohort experiences. Such experiences will evolve in a global village that comprises foreigners yet to visit Trinidad, foreign visitors, residents domiciled in Trinidad and Tobago, and natives living overseas.

## Note

1. Parties that attract large crowds of patrons who dance to the various types of Carnival music and derive substantial enjoyment from mingling with friends. These events are usually scheduled anytime during the day, though mostly late at night and in the dawn hours of the morning.

## References

Anthony, Michael. 1989. *Parade of the Carnivals of Trinidad, 1839–1989*. Port of Spain: Circle Press.

Bellour, Helene, Jeffrey Chock, Kim Johnson and Milla Riggio. 2002. *Renegades: The History of the Renegades Steel Orchestra of Trinidad and Tobago*. London: Macmillan Caribbean.

Blake, Felix I.R. 1995. The *Trinidad and Tobago Steel Pan: History and Evolution*. Port of Spain: Circle Press.

Cowley, John. 1996. *Carnival, Canboulay and Calypso Traditions in the Making*. Cambridge: Cambridge University Press.

Crowley, Daniel J. 1956. "The Traditional Masques of Carnival". *Caribbean Quarterly* 4, nos. 3 and 4: 192–223.

———. 1984. "Carnival as an Instrument of Education". *Carnival Seminar Papers* with *Recommendations: The Social and Economic Impact of Carnival*, 219–25. St Augustine: University of the West Indies.

Grant, Trevor. 2004. *Carnivalitis: The Conflicting Discourse of Carnival*. Jamaica, NY: Yacos.

———. 2008. *Trinival: Carnival of the Gods*. Jamaica, NY: Yacos.

Guilbault, Jocelyne. 2007. *Governing Sound: The Cultural Politics of Trinidad's Carnival Musics*. Chicago: University of Chicago Press.

Henry, Jeff. 2008. *Under the Mas: Resistance and Rebellion in the Trinidad Masquerade*. San Juan: Lexicon Trinidad.

Hill, Errol. 1984. "The History of Carnival". *Carnival Seminar Papers with Recommendations: The Social and Economic Impact of Carnival*, 6–39. St Augustine: University of the West Indies.

———. 1997. *The Trinidad Carnival: Mandate for a National Theatre*. London: New Beacon Books.

Liverpool, Hollis. 1998. "Origins of Rituals and Customs in the Trinidad Carnival: African or European". *Drama Review* 42, no. 3: 24–37.

———. 2001. *Rituals of Power and Rebellion: The Carnival Tradition in Trinidad and Tobago, 1763–1962*. Chicago: Frontline Distribution International.

Lovelace, Earl. 1998. "The Emancipation-Jouvay Tradition and the Almost Loss of Pan". *Drama Review* 42, no. 3: 54–60.

Mason, Peter. 1998. *Bacchanal! The Carnival Culture in Trinidad*. Kingston: Ian Randle.

Riggio, Milla. 1998. "Resistance and Identity: Carnival in Trinidad and Tobago". *Drama Review* 42, no. 3: 7–23.

Rohlehr, Gordon. 1984. "An Introduction to the History of the Calypso". In *Carnival Seminar Papers with Recommendations: The Social and Economic Impact of Carnival*, 40–120. St Augustine: University of the West Indies.

———. 1990. *Calypso and Society in Pre-independence Trinidad*. San Juan: Lexicon Trinidad.

Sankeralli, Burton. 1998. "Indian Presence in Carnival". *Drama Review* 42, no. 3: 203–12.

Scher, Philip. 2003. *Carnival and the Formation of a Caribbean Transnation*. Gainesville: University Press of Florida.

Slater, Leslie. 1984. "The Music of Carnival: Some Thoughts on the Decline of the Steel Band". *Carnival Seminar Papers with Recommendations: The Social and Economic Impact of Carnival*, 121–29. St Augustine: University of the West Indies.

Stuempfle, Stephen. 1995. *The Steelband Movement: The Forging of a National Art in Trinidad and Tobago*. Philadelphia: University of Pennsylvania Press.

Van Koningsbruggen, Peter. 1997. *Trinidad Carnival: A Quest for National Identity*. London: Macmillan Education.

# 5.

# Hispanic Heritage in Trinidad

SYLVIA MOODIE-KUBLALSINGH

*Trinidad, a Spanish colony from 1498 to 1797, is located just 11 kilometres off the northeast coast of Venezuela. So it is not strange to find some evidence of Hispanic culture there. The author traces the Hispanic presence and highlights the toponyms, family names and language, focusing on parang music and Hispanic prayers, two aspects of Trinidad's Hispanic heritage practised by local rural Hispanics up to the 1970s. The music has survived but Hispanic prayers have largely disappeared. This is one example of the loss of Hispanic features in Trinidad culture and is linked to the decline or obsolescence of the local variety of Spanish. The folk knowledge available in the past too has been disappearing with the demise of the older generation. The survival of parang, with its songs in Spanish, is exceptional. It is recommended that this tradition be exploited in the teaching of the language at all levels of the education system.*

## Introduction

Trinidad's Hispanic heritage is present in the toponyms, family names, language, song, music and beliefs of its people. This heritage can be traced to the pre-British period, when Trinidad was a Spanish colony, but most of it is due to the contribution of Venezuelan peons who arrived during the nineteenth century, when the island was already British. Parang music and song constitute a prominent aspect of that heritage. This is a dynamic art form, a bridge between the rural past of its Hispanic origins and modern, multicultural, urbanized Trinidad. The total Hispanic heritage is a reminder that the Spanish language is not foreign to Trinidad and that it should serve as a base and reference point to reinforce language teaching.

## The Pre-British Period

The name *Trinidad* – Trinidad del Dorado, or Trinidad de Guayana, then Trinidad de Barlovento – has survived in its original Spanish form. On the other hand, the name of the first town established by the Spaniards in 1592, San José de Oruña, was translated into English: the town is now known as St Joseph. Many of the early Spanish toponyms were retained in their original form, partially translated or influenced by French pronunciation (Laurence 1975), for example, San Fernando, Montserrat, Entrada Point, Point Fortin, Los Bajos, Rio Claro, Punta Blanca, San Francique, Blanquizales (changed to the French Blanchisseuse). Some remarkable retentions in the original Spanish include the northwestern sea passages known as the Bocas: Boca Grande, Boca de Navios, Boca sin Entrada, Boca de Huevos and Boca de Monos, as well as Frontón de Salina, on the north-western coast between Saline and Balandra (Trinidad and Tobago 1986). The Royal Road of today (in San Fernando, Maracas and Caura) was the Camino Real of the Spanish era. Amerindian and Spanish forms are combined in Cerro del Aripo and El Tucuche, the names of the two highest mountains of the island, as well as in Gran Curucaye (towards the north of San Juan), Vega de Oropuche in the south and others. Mamural, Morichal, Bejucal, Carapal and Cocal are examples of a blend of Amerindian and the Spanish suffix *–al*; all refer to places where there is an abundance of particular vines and trees.

From 1498 to 1784 Trinidad, the Spanish colony, remained a deserted island in terms of its exploitation and colonization (Brereton 1981). However, its proximity to the mainland and the coveted El Dorado made it an important strategic possession, so continuous attempts were made to conquer and subjugate the indigenous people and introduce Spanish settlers (Morales Padrón 1957, 1960). In 1570, for example, Juan Trejo Ponce de Leon was commanded by King Philip II not to abandon his obligation of populating Trinidad until further orders. However, nine months later, unable to maintain new settlers on the island, he did abandon his task. During the next two hundred years Trinidad continued to have few white settlers. In 1784, at the apogee of Spanish language and culture in Trinidad, the total Hispanic population consisted of only 335 Spanish Creoles, 765 "mixed" Spaniards, 260 "Spanish slaves" and 1,495 Amerindians (Brereton 1981, 15). This is the population through which the Hispanic heritage of Trinidad would be channelled into the future. From all accounts, contact with the indigenous population was realized mainly through the *encomiendas* and missions which were the foundation of some of our present communities, villages and towns. The Hispanicized Amerindians referred to were most likely descendants of those who had been in contact with the colonizers either in the early *encomiendas* or the missions. In addition, we note a small number of Africans present on the Spanish colony.

The Spaniards introduced their religious and secular institutions at an early stage despite the paucity of population and resources. It is recorded that in 1644 Don Manuel Farfan de los Godos founded a significant religious confraternity, the Hermandad del Santísimo Sacramento, in St Joseph; the name Farfan is one of the oldest Spanish and European surnames in Trinidad (Borde 1876). Yet in 1684 the governor complained that for twelve years there had been an absence of priests and catechists for the Indians. Eventually Spanish Capuchin missionaries, who had undertaken the work of evangelization in the region, arrived in 1687 from Aragon and Catalonia and established missions in the north, centre and south of the island: at Tacarigua, Caura, Arauca, Sabana Grande, Montserrat and Sabaneta (Anguiano 1928). However, by 1708 the missions had been abolished. We do not know what might have been achieved in twenty-one years to have had an impact on the beliefs, religion and culture, music and traditions of the local Indian people. Brereton (1981, 5) states: "At the end of the seventeenth century the great majority [of Indians] were still living in the forest and in independent settlements, unconverted and beyond the reach of the Spaniards." Even though initially several thousands had been ostensibly Christianized, many resented this change and control and were unwilling to accede to acculturation, as evidenced in a 1699 rebellion that ended in murder and suicide (Anguiano 1918). The site of the bloodbath was San Francisco de los Arenales; according to legend some of the Amerindians hurled themselves into the sea at the place called Rampanalgas (Rompenalgas) on the northeast coast.

In 1712 only a fraction of the total Indian population was controlled by the Spaniards in four *encomiendas*: San Agustin de Arauca, San Pablo de Tacarigua, San Juan de Aricagua and Caura, all located in the north of the island. Having been exposed to some degree of indoctrination and acculturation, these Indians may have been able to impart the Spanish language and transfer aspects of Hispanic culture to younger generations. However, the Amerindian population of Trinidad steadily diminished. We may still discover remnants of colonial Spanish culture among their descendants, most of whom are now of mixed blood and are identified as Arima Caribs (Verteuil 1884). Traditionally they spoke Spanish, professed the Catholic faith and were aligned with the Venezuelan peons who arrived later in the nineteenth century (Brereton 1981, 21).

Later, in 1783, when the cedula of population came into effect, there was a dramatic change in the demographics of the colony and the nature of its society. Hispanics, whether European, Amerindian or among the few Africans who were acquired late in the history of the Spanish colony, were very much outnumbered by French-speaking newcomers of European and African origin. After 1783 Spanish language and culture were also threatened. Upon the arrival of the French, the "old Spanish Creoles of St. Joseph, impoverished and isolated, lost all influence over the affairs of their native island" (Brereton 1981, 20). This loss was further compounded by the surrender of the island to the British in 1797 (Pérez Aparicio 1965).

St Joseph – San José de Oruña – is by vocation the old Spanish capital. Notwithstanding its fall from its former favoured position, the town has always boasted of its Spanish past and the townsfolk have been proud to claim their bond with its Hispanic heritage. However, there are no artefacts to link the town with its early Spanish history. None of the original buildings of the colonial Spanish era remain; none were constructed to endure the passage of time. The present church is presumably in the same spot where the first one stood, opposite the square, and its cemetery contains some tombstones with Spanish texts, a symbol of the old capital's Hispanic heritage.

Port of Spain, which became the capital in 1757 precisely because of the dilapidated condition of St Joseph, contains a building on Sackville Street known as the Cabildo, or Town Hall. Ironically, it was erected during the early British colonial period but it serves as a reminder of an era when the few streets existing in Puerto de España bore Spanish names: Calle del Infante, Calle Príncipe, Calle de San José, Calle de Santa Ana, Calle Herrera, Calle de San Carlos, Calle de Chacón, Calle de San Luis, Calle de Santa Rosa and Calle de Princesa de Asturias (Mavrogordato 1977). (The streets are still there, with English names. The old Spanish names, as part of the island's Hispanic heritage, should really be highlighted.) However, Puerto de España, or Puerto de los Hispanioles, became Port d'Espagne, a French *ville*, then Port of Spain, an English town. In the memory of the population it was no longer Spanish. The original Spanish name of one of its neighbourhoods, La Ventilla – referring to an inn on the outskirts of the capital – was converted to the French Laventille (Pérez Aparicio 1965, 126).

## Spanish in the British Period

Trinidad became a British colony in 1803. By then the lingua franca was already French Creole or patois; French continued to increase in prestige while Spanish lost importance both numerically and socially. English became the official language in 1823 but Spanish institutions and laws were retained until between 1832 and 1840. The Spanish system of government and names of bureaucrats were retained until the middle of the century: Ilustre Cabildo, Junta Municipal, Alcalde Ordinario, Regidores, Sindico, Junta Superior de

Hacienda, escribano, depositor general, auditor and so on. English had been introduced in 1814 as the language of the tribunals, the law indicating that one needed to be fluent in English in order to fill high positions or to be elected to serve as a councillor. As the nineteenth century progressed, Spanish became increasingly marginalized. Could it survive as the language of the ordinary Hispanic folk?

The 1869 Keenan report on education revealed that Spanish was still the language of a large number in the Hispanic population (Gordon 1962). In the College of the Immaculate Conception, popularly called "the French School" because of its strong French element, a little less than 30 per cent of the pupils were from Spanish-speaking families. However, like German, it was an optional subject in the curriculum, while English and French were obligatory. It is likely that many of those Spanish speakers were descendants of the old Spanish Creoles (the Basanta, Centeno, Farfan, Hospedales, Llanos and Sorzano families), while others were probably the children of Venezuelan families that had arrived during the Independence and Federal Wars being waged on the mainland. On the other hand, some of the old Trinidadian Hispanics were surely simple folk who resided in both urban and rural areas, not members of the elite class.

## Hispanic Immigrants from the Mainland

Louis de Verteuil (1884, 288) reported a predominance of Spanish speakers of mixed race in the ward of Montserrat. He also noted that in the Northern Range the inhabitants of the Caura Valley were mostly of Spanish descent and Spanish was universally spoken. These are precisely the areas where missions and *encomiendas* were established in the seventeenth century.

From the early to mid-nineteenth century onwards, during the period of political upheaval in South America, agricultural labourers, peasants, businessmen and professionals arrived on the island. They increased the extant Hispanic population, the large numbers that de Verteuil mentioned probably being due to newcomers who gravitated to Spanish-speaking communities. After the official end of the Spanish colony in 1797, the Venezuelans assumed the responsibility, so to speak, of ensuring that Trinidad did not lose its Hispanic flavour altogether. This role was undertaken primarily by the rural folk familiarly called *cocoa panyols*, who lived and worked in the valleys and foothills of the cacao-producing areas of the island. Language, customs, occupation and even place of residence distinguished them from the rest of the society. They often looked different too, as they were mostly of mixed race: Amerindian, African and European (Spanish). They were referred to politely as Spanish and sometimes derogatorily as *cocoa panyols*. Among them was a strong group consciousness and pride in their folk knowledge: language, music, song, prayers and beliefs.

By 1967 to 1987 so-called Spanish villages and areas were already very mixed, with a diminishing core of Spanish speakers. These communities included Lopinot, Santa Cruz, Maracas, Blanchisseuse, Arima, Valencia and Las Cuevas in the north, places to which former residents of Caura had migrated in 1945 to make way for the construction of a dam (Lewis 1982). Further south, Spanish speakers resided in Erin and Cedros, Moruga, Siparia and Rio Claro and in the central Montserrat hills: in Tamana and Tabaquite, Tortuga and Gran Couva. Their family names also contributed to the island's Hispanic heritage, among them Acevero, Boneo, Castillo, Díaz, Espinosa, Guerra, Guerrero, Herrera, Lezama, Lopez (López), Luces, Marcano, Martínez, Pacheco, Peña, Pérez, Ramos, Reyes, Rodríguez, Ruiz, Salinas, Vialva (Villalba) and Villarroel. They probably also contributed "Spanish" toponyms such as El Rincón, Cambural, Brasso (Brazo) Seco, Brasso Venado, Tumbazón, La Verónica, Cabecero, La Pastora and Rancho Quemado, most of which were secluded hamlets in the Northern Range. Their presence on the island may have helped to reinforce some of the toponyms in the high woods of the interior: the *quebradas* (valleys) and *rios* (rivers) such as Rio Grande, Rio Seco and Rio Negro (note the retention of *rio* in the names). Their Spanish enriched the local vernacular with words such as these:

| Local Vernacular | Spanish Source |
| --- | --- |
| *ayo* | *adiós* |
| *lanyap* | *la ñapa* |
| *mamaguy* | *mamar el gallo* |
| *marcha palantay* | *marcha para adelante* |
| *payol, pañol* or *panyol* | *español* |
| *parang* | *parranda* |
| *pastelle* | *pastel* |
| *picong* | *picón* |
| *piong* | *peon* |
| *pokapok* | *poco a poco* |

*Source:* Allsopp 1996

*Marcha palantay* – to go ahead or move on – is now obsolete (Winer and Aguilar 1991), but the other words are still in current use.

## Language and Culture

The variety of Spanish spoken in Trinidad during the Spanish colonial period would hardly have differed from the language of the region as a whole. It would have been similar to the speech of the nineteenth-century immigrants from the mainland. In addition, there is no evidence of a Spanish-based pidgin, *bozal* or creole language in Trinidad. No local expressions used by the Trinidad Spanish Creoles or the Hispanicized Indians and their offspring in the pre-British era have been recorded. However, there is verification that the Spanish spoken by rural folk born in Trinidad in the late nineteenth and early twentieth centuries was "normal". This was the opinion of Pedro Henriquez Ureña, a renowned Hispanist from the Dominican Republic, who visited the island in 1922 and 1931. Although the local language has been influenced by French and English vocabulary (Thompson 1956), similar influence on its syntax has been negligible (Moodie 1982). The local variety is now virtually obsolete, since fluent speakers have died.

Through the *cocoa panyols* the songs, poetry and music that were perhaps introduced into Trinidad directly from Spain were revived and retained (Moodie-Kublalsingh 1994). Undoubtedly their folklore enriched local culture, and Spanish is the preferred language of local Hispanic song and the music known as parang (Allard 2000). The musical instruments are also played on the mainland: the *cuatro,* a small guitar-like instrument, and maracas (also called *shac-shac*) which, with the voice, form the core of parang. Other instruments include guitar, mandolin, violin and box bass. Some Venezuelan Spanish culture-bound words in current use in Trinidad vernacular include *aguinaldo, castellan, estribillo, ensaladilla, galerón, joropo, manzanare, sabana blanca, serenal* and *warap* (from *guarapo*), all of which refer to different types of songs. Velorio de Cruz gave rise to Cross Wake, a folk religious ritual formerly held in the month of May. *Arep* (from *arepa*), *pastelle* (from *pastel*) and *sancoch* (from *sancocho*) are popular foods of Venezuelan origin. Others less known today are *gofio, papelon, mazamorra* and *tasajo* (Thomas [1869] 1969).

Parang, an expression of Trinidad's *mestizo* culture, is the most significant aspect of the island's Hispanic heritage and is now an essential part of annual Christmas celebrations in the country. It is a performance involving family, friends and community. It transcends ethnicity, crosses racial boundaries and is universally appreciated and acknowledged by a broad spectrum of classes and age groups. It was not originally confined to the Christmas season. In fact, in Venezuela *parranda* is still a spontaneous folk celebration with typical instruments and traditional songs which people enjoy at any time of the year and for any reason. In Trinidad, as it continues to evolve and is renewed to suit modern musical styles, there have been conscious attempts to blend the traditional parang with other local and Latin American rhythms. Parang is attaining its own character, distinct from that of the Spanish Venezuelan music from which it originated. In parang we find the promise of an indigenous musical tradition that is emblematic of a fusion of the cultures and interests of a single Trinidad nation (Allard 2000).

Conversely, younger generations have lost the repertoire of prayers known to their forefathers. They are hardly aware of words such as *owezon* (from the French *oraison* and Spanish *oración*, prayer) and *santiwai* (Spanish *santiguar*, to bless), which pertain to the world of prayers and healing in which the panyol played a dominant role. *Oraciones* were cherished by the "Spanish" folk as powerful spiritual tools, veiled in secrecy and revealed to the privileged few. The rural folk in particular appealed to panyols to heal children stricken with epileptic fits (or *malkadi*, in the vernacular) and other ailments that were difficult to treat. Most of the prayers were in verse and took the form of the *romance* or ballad (Moodie 1986; Moodie-Kublalsingh 1994).

These prayers and parang songs connect Trinidad to Spain via Venezuela, but variations can be found in all Spanish-speaking countries (Moodie-Kublalsingh 1994). The range of Spanish folklore available in the past – stories, proverbs, riddles, diversions and masquerades – has been disappearing with the demise of the older generation; in addition, the names and use of medicinal plants are also being lost. In that context, the survival and flourishing of parang is truly exceptional. The following are two traditional verses of parang still sung in Trinidad, and a fragment of a prayer that is hardly remembered.

**Parang Verse 1**
*Al subir los altos montes*
*A ver si la divisaba*
*Solamente vide el humo*
*Del vapor que la llevaba*

**Parang Verse 2**
*El Ángel Gabriel*
*Le anunció a María*
*En su vientre santo*
*Un Niño nacía*

**Oración (fragment)**
*Quien esta oración rezare*
*Todos los viernes del año*
*Sacará un alma de pena*
*Y la suya de pecado*

## Conclusion

Every year participants in the national parang competitions are required to compose new songs in Spanish. This is a very demanding task, since most of the composers lack the level of competence necessary to create new songs comparable to the traditional ones. This requirement has forced practitioners to pay greater attention to the language as they become more sensitized to the rules governing versification and pronunciation. Young people are also becoming involved in parang as more and more primary and secondary school students participate in the annual schools competitions. This is positive for the development of the genre. However, a link is not always being made between the Spanish in the curriculum and the Spanish of the parang. The language of the traditional parang *is* Spanish; as the most significant part of Trinidad's Hispanic heritage, it should play a prominent role in the Spanish-language classroom.

## References

Allard, F.C. 2000. "The Evolution of Parang (Music and Text) in Trinidad, 1900–1997". Master's thesis, University of the West Indies, St Augustine.

Allsopp, R. 1996. *Dictionary of Caribbean English Usage*. London: Oxford University Press.

Anguiano, M. 1918. "Misiones de la isla de la Trinidad en las actas y muerte de los siervos de Dios Fr. Félix, Raimundo Figuerola y Marcos de Vich", Relación 8. In *Relaciones de las misiones de los padres capuchinos de Fr. Froylan de Rionegro*. Sevilla.

———. 1928. "Misión apostólica en la isla de Trinidad de Barlovento" (Madrid, 1702). In *Relaciones de los padres capuchinos de Venezuela*. Madrid.

Borde, P.G.L. 1876, 1883. *L'histoire de l'île de la Trinidad sous le gouvernement espagnol*. 2 vols. Paris: Maisonneuve.

Brereton, B. 1979. *Race Relations in Colonial Trinidad, 1870–1900*. Cambridge: Cambridge University Press.

———. 1981. *A History of Modern Trinidad, 1783–1962*. London: Heinemann.

Gordon, S.C. 1962. "The Keenan Report, 1869: Part 1, The Elementary School System in Trinidad". *Caribbean Quarterly* 8: 3–16.

Laurence, K. 1970. "Spanish in Trinidad: The Survival of a Minority Language in a Multilingual Society". Doctoral thesis, University of London.

———. 1975. "Continuity and Change in Trinidadian Toponyms". *Nieuwe West-Indische Gids* 50: 139–42.

Lewis, K. 1982. "The History of the Caura Dam Project: Its Impact upon a Village Community". Paper, University of the West Indies, St Augustine.

Mavrogordato, O. 1977. *Voices in the Street*. Port of Spain: Inprint Caribbean.

Moodie, S. 1973. "The Spanish Language as Spoken in Trinidad". *Caribbean Studies* 13, no. 1: 88–98.

———. 1982. "Trinidad Spanish Pronouns: A Case of Language Death". In *Readings in Spanish English Contrastive Linguistics*, edited by R. Nash and D. Belavel, vol. 3, 206–28. San German, Puerto Rico: Inter American University Press.

———. 1983. "Survival of Hispanic Religious Songs in Trinidad Folklore". *Caribbean Quarterly* 29: 1–31.

Moodie-Kublalsingh, S. 1994. *The Cocoa Panyols of Trinidad: An Oral Record*. London: British Academic Press.

Morales Padrón, F. 1957. "Descubrimiento y papel de Trinidad en la penetración continental". In *Anuario de estudios americanos*, vol. 14. Sevilla.

———. 1960. "Trinidad en el siglo XVII". In *Anuario de estudios americanos*, vol. 17. Sevilla.

Pérez Aparicio, J. 1965. "Pérdida de la isla de Trinidad". In *Anuario de estudios americanos*, vol. 22. Sevilla.

Thomas, J.J. 1869. *The Theory and Practice of Creole Grammar*. Port of Spain. Reprint, 1969. London: New Beacon Books.

Thompson, R.W. 1956. "Préstamos lingüísticos en tres idiomas trinitarios". *Estudios americanos* 61: 249–54.

———. 1959. "Pre-British Place Names in Trinidad". *De West-Indische Gids* 39. Reprint.

Trinidad and Tobago. 1986. Map of Trinidad. Ministry of Agriculture, Lands and Food Production, Lands and Survey Division.

Verteuil, L. de. 1884. *Trinidad, Its Geography, Natural Resources, Administration, Present Condition and Prospects*. London: Cassell.

Winer, L., and E.L. Aguilar. 1991. "Spanish Influence on the Lexicon of Trinidadian English Creole". *New West Indian Guide* 65, nos. 3 and 4: 153–91.

# 6.

# The Politics of Perspective

## Counter-Discourse and Popular Romance within the Caribbean

KAREN SANDERSON COLE

*The importance of reinventing history and counteracting dominant ideologies is an important aspect of reclaiming identity. Ideology concerns the assumptions, beliefs and rules which govern the way in which reality is interpreted by a society. Through the propagation of ideology, the disadvantage of certain groups by sex, colour or economic standing can seem commonplace and acceptable. Within the field of literature, counteracting debilitating stereotypes of black personhood has been foregrounded largely in the work of male writers. Only recently, particularly in the Caribbean, black women writers have been acknowledged as significant contributors to this struggle. Popular romance within the Caribbean also symbolizes "patterns of power" that exist between postcolonial societies and their former "owners", and these tensions are evident in the way generic traditions are transposed in a non-European setting. The development of the Caribbean-centred romance charts an increasing politicization of the genre in a growing sensitivity to the needs of the nation, which, this chapter argues, finds fullest expression in the historical/popular romance* Ti Marie, *by Valerie Belgrave. This work is of pioneering significance in this area in its attempt to combine popular romance and historical romance frameworks to indicate a changed perspective reflecting a Caribbean consciousness.*

## Introduction: Ideology

Ideology concerns the assumptions, beliefs and rules which govern the way in which reality is interpreted by a society. It is commonly believed that the powerful groups in a society construct its ideological beliefs. And it is through the propagation of ideology that the disadvantage of certain groups, whether by sex, colour or economic standing, can be made to seem commonplace and acceptable. According to Zinn et al. (1997, 441), "ideology manipulates cultural symbols and images . . . with the goal of influencing public opinions". Stereotypes are a significant aspect of ideology because they often embody a society's view of what it either lauds or disparages. Within the context of a novel, these stereotypes become evident through the ideological perspective from which the activities of the text are narrated and in the ways in which certain people, ethnic groups or cultural practices are portrayed. Within the romance in particular, a set of assertions or assumptions, implicated or presupposed, comprises stereotypes of romance characters.

Examining the structure of a Caribbean historical romance such as Valerie Belgrave's *Ti Marie* (1988) involves an analysis of the underlying departures in the romance structure as having ideological implications. Popular romance has its own, specially crafted role in society. It provides an index of what in the West has come to be defined as appropriate roles for men and women. Ideology, as articulated by Sara Mills (1995, 149), is something to be affirmed, negotiated or resisted, and while popular culture is not traditionally held to be worthy of the attention of literary critics – and romance of the kind showcased in Mills and Boon books or the works of Barbara Cartland even less so – advocates of popular fiction point not to the merit of its literary output but to its significance as a repository of underlying assumptions about the ideological beliefs that a society holds (Nachbar and Lause 1992, 33). *Romance* in this chapter is defined in its popular, or "low", sense as the chronicle of a heterosexual relationship based on an attraction – primarily physical – that culminates (or promises to) in marriage.

This chapter also attempts to bring attention to another dimension of romance, that is, the power relationships that exist in the wider society which the romance symbolizes (Christian-Smith 1998) – in a colonial environment, particularly between whites and blacks. The characteristic mode of portraying the colonies and its inhabitants primarily by means of the stereotypical represents important ideologies which can be countered through perspectival shifts in discourse. Examination of the relationship between stereotypes and ideology is important because discourse and power undergird each other in an imperial context. Zinn et al. (1997, 441) argue:

> Dominant ideas are often imposed on subordinate groups to control them. Sometimes, subordinate groups of people internalize these dominant ideas, essentially accepting the definition of the dominant group that they are, indeed, naturally inferior. However, the existence of social movements, such as the civil rights movement . . . and anti-colonial movements demonstrate that subjugated people have the ability to resist dominant ideologies, at times even forging their own, oppositional system of beliefs and values.

With regard to the study of romance fiction within the Caribbean, Edmond-son (1999, 4) makes two points that are particularly relevant here. One is that, since "[t]he Caribbean itself has historically functioned as the matrix of European eroticized romantic fantasies, it seems fitting that a critique of the clichés of Caribbean discourse should focus on the particular genre as well".

Her second point is that Caribbean peoples need to ask: "How do the old romanticized images of the region, initially constructed in the imperial European or American imagination, reinvent themselves in discourse that apparently come from the newly independent, decolonized Caribbean subjects themselves?" (Edmondson 1999, 6).

Therefore, popular romance that has a counter-discursive focus shares with other forms of counter-discursive material a concern with redefining official versions of history, re-inscribing women's role in history and society, and renegotiating male–female relationships within a colonial setting. In her rewrite of the relationship between a white man and a coloured woman in eighteenth-century Trinidad, in *Ti Marie* Belgrave is countering a heritage dominated by a prevailing ideology of the superiority of all whites and the inferiority of all blacks. *Black* here is used in two senses: as an identity based on African heritage and as a term used for "Asians, Caribbean and Latin American peoples" who are politically known as "people of colour". The deliberateness of this attempt to indigenize the genre of popular romance is an important indicator of the development of a national/Caribbean ideological perspectival shift in popular culture. An evaluation of Belgrave's attempt must, however, first be seen against the backdrop of colonial society within which the novel is set, to establish the significant ideologies which are countered.

## Popular Romance and Ideology in the Nineteenth-Century English-Speaking Caribbean

Lalla (1996) observes that the travel journal and the romance were both popular forms of writing that disseminated European views about the colonies. Indeed, the author of *Marly* (1828), in a somewhat defensive manner, asserts in his preface that he chose the novel form for his story because he "imitates the principal writers of the present day, who perhaps not unwisely imagine that to awaken the interest and engage the attention of the mass of readers, there is nothing so effectual as the machinery of a novel".

Despite the intention of the author of *Marly* to use a novel to reach a "mass of readers", the high level of illiteracy within colonial society meant that the dominant ideology about the inadequacies of the black majority was not for the most part transmitted through written material. But, like popular education, popular romance would be important as "an instrument of social control

– a means by which the established classes could tame the multitudes, repress social barbarism, and preserve their own superior status" (Green 1976, 327). In *Hamel* (1827, 31–32), Roland the missionary tells Hamel the witch doctor: "You can never be happy, at least for some years, without white men, who shall teach your children to read, to write, to pray to the only true God; the knowledge of the only means of salvation". The body of colonial romances is therefore not large, but it remains a valuable resource for evaluating the ideology of the society at the time. Context of production becomes an integral aspect of interpretation. Fowler (1986, 81), for example, argues that "[n]arrative discourse is created out of the interaction of the culture's conventions, the author's expressive deployment of these conventions as they are coded in language, and the reader's activity in releasing meaning from the text".

Popular romance valorizes the characteristics and ideals of the society it portrays. It is this feature that made it a valuable ally in the discourse of empire building, especially after emancipation. Among colonized people who comprised the Empire by the late eighteenth century, Pratt (1992, 100) argues, a significant proportion were of "mixed blood": "From the viewpoint of European hegemony, romantic love was as good a device as any for 'embracing' such groups into the political and social imaginary – as subalterns". This embracing of the inferior or the subaltern was particularly evident in the "trans-racial stories" that flourished. Pratt observes that John Stedman's *Narrative of a Five Years' Expedition Against the Revolted Negroes of Surinam* (1796) was one of the most famous love stories of this genre in the early Caribbean. In Europe "its love plot was played and replayed as drama, poetry, story and novel" (Pratt 1992, 91). The tradition established was one in which the relationship of the interracial couple challenged the status quo yet was resolved with each party returning to the fold of his or her racial group. The male protagonist would be white while the female protagonist would be "mulatta or mestizo", depending on the race of the subjugated group (Pratt 1992, 100). The female's physical features would be distinctly European; bell hooks (1998, 119) writes that "[a]s sexist/racist sexual mythology would have it, she is the embodiment of the best of the black female savage tempered by those elements of whiteness that soften this image, giving it an aura of virtue and innocence".

Belgrave's novel, therefore, is not unique in its presentation of an interracial relationship. Green (1976, 20) acknowledges that "informal liaisons between white men and coloured women were commonplace, not only for single adult males but also for resident married proprietors and their adolescent sons". What is unusual given the historical context is its culmination in marriage. According to Green (1976, 20), "Marriage between whites and non-whites continued to be considered anathema by Europeans, and the courageous few who undertook such unions courted instant social ostracism." What is interesting in *Ti Marie* are the ways in which the traditional characteristics of the trans-racial romance are presented but counteracted, signalling a crucial perspectival shift.

## Stereotypes and Ideology in the Caribbean-Centred Romance

The characterization and structure of the early Caribbean romance embody the concerns of a society in crisis. Clatterbaugh (1996, 295) argues that the system of slavery dehumanized the black majority by "deny[ing] that the members of that group possess the complete range of human abilities, needs, and wants that are valued at that time as important to being a human being". Stereotypes provided a mechanism for managing the potential threat that freedom for the slaves posed to the social structure. According to Walder (1998, 129), stereotypes reflect a system of "patriarchy resisting the autonomy of those it has long tried to marginalize".

*Hamel* (1827), *Marly* (1828), *The Maroon* (1860), *Adolphus* (1853) and *The Slave Son* (1854) are some of the earliest romances written by Europeans with a working knowledge of the West Indies – Jamaica and Trinidad in particular. The pervasiveness of the ideology that promoted the superiority of the European is evident in the fact that romances written by local whites or Creoles do not differ from those by foreign-born whites in terms of their assessments of the black or coloured characters. Fully black women appear in traditional roles as servants, house slaves or market vendors. Coloured women are usually painted as superstitious and sexually passionate.

Much of the force of the stereotype in literature lies in the fact that it is couched in the form of a generic statement which is a "generalized proposition claiming universal truth and usually cast in a syntax reminiscent of proverbs or scientific laws" (Fowler 1986, 132). Within the colonial setting, these generic statements, as Spencer-Strachan (1992, 42–43) observes, serve to highlight "[one, t]he gulf between the culture of the colonialist and the colonized; two, the exploitation of these differences for the benefit of the colonist; three, the use of these supposed differences as standards of absolute facts".

One stereotype was that blacks were lazy. "They are an indolent race – the general body of slaves have not reached that stage in society, where luxury, interest or ambition, stimulate men to exertions for the purpose of accumulating wealth or gaining celebrity" (*Marly*, 92). Another was that their physical appearance was an indicator of lack of intelligence. At a slave auction, "[t]he Mandingos, Foulahs, and Mozambiques [are] known by their more regular features. . . . The effeminate race of Loango . . . The stupid-looking Eboes,

Quaquas, and Mokos . . . while the Koromantyns . . . looked on in dogged silence" (*Slave Son* 1854, 29). Another stereotype, of significance to the analysis of *Ti Marie* below, was the belief that for Trinidad blacks life was easy: "Of all the colonies ever visited by the Abolitionists there is none where the slave was found so happy in his condition as in that most fertile and beautiful of the Antilles, the fair island of Trinidad" (*Slave Son* 1854, 5).

Conversely, it was believed that miscegenation would lead to an improvement in the physical appearance of the population of the Caribbean, and thus their intelligence. According to the author of *Marly*,

> The Maroons and the long-creolized Negroes, have greatly improved, both in features, in size and in strength from the African race; and in the course of years they will become the Georgians of the negro race. The thick lips, and the broad nose, are giving place to what Europeans consider beauty; and probably, after two or three generations have elapsed, they will have a resemblance to their masters in every respect, except the colour. (1828, 87)

There were stereotypes associated with the coloured population as well. One was that those of "mixed blood" were obsessed by love. According to one character in *Hamel* (1827, 193), "These Mulattos and Mestees think of nothing else from the hour on which they are weaned from their mothers' breast until time has wasted away every trace of their beauty; and then they console themselves with the recollection of all the transports they have enjoyed."

The uncertain ground occupied by coloureds in the romance is a reflection of their position in colonial society, which is echoed in the stylized portrayals of the romance. Green (1976, 11) concludes that "[t]he coloured population occupied an insecure middle ground between the dominant whites and servile blacks, scorned socially by the former and despised by the latter". It is interesting to observe that this viewpoint has undergone a certain amount of perspectival shift today. In fact, Edmondson (1999) argues that the coloured woman is now the obvious choice in a regional beauty competition. At first glance Belgrave's choice of a coloured heroine would appear to be an appeasement of current taste, but her selection has to be read against the criteria of the trans-racial romance. It is the way in which these expectations are countered, therefore, that is of central interest.

Counter-discourse involves transformation of an identity imposed through a Western inheritance. As Boyce-Davies (1994, 12) asserts, "Caribbean culture needs to be seen not only as oppositional or resistance but as transformational if we are to recoup any identities beyond the ones imposed." The issue of representation also takes place within popular culture. The importance of reinventing history is an important aspect of reclaiming identity.

Campbell (1986, xi) writes: "Despite the charges of sentimentality and escapism leveled at romance, it is potentially a radical literary mode, for it dares to posit a world of infinite possibility, a world in which cultural heroes and heroines come to grips with those negative forces, or villains, that interfere with the attainment of an ideal world. Romance can be used, in short, to reinvent reality." Belgrave's historical romance shows how this quest for voice resounds within a Caribbean context.

## A Non-European World View: The Significance of Parody

Valerie Belgrave's *Ti Marie* (1988) exploits many aspects of the trans-racial romance in its portrayal of Trinidad as a lush pastoral paradise, the European-style beauty of its main protagonists and the accuracy of its historical detail. It also incorporates concern for some of the dilemmas faced by the contemporary romance-novel writer of the Caribbean in indigenizing a heroine. Belgrave, who is also a batik artist, has admitted that she wrote the novel in an attempt to do away with the simplistic side of the typical romance, identified as "[t]he world of obvious villains and heroes, backward petty racism, love stories that turn on silly misunderstandings, mysteries that draw on and on into melodrama, or even in total submergence of the reader in the period" (Belgrave 1995).

Significantly, therefore, the novel attempts to return to the plantation, a symbol of slavery and degradation, and propose a new ending – one respectful of the innate humanity of the principal characters. It attempts to accomplish this through the stylized conventions of the popular romance form, based on the belief that the best way to mitigate its damaging effects is by transforming the conventions that sustain it. LaFollette argues that "[w]e cannot escape the power of the culture by separating ourselves from it . . . since the culture perpetuates itself by shaping desires, values, and attitudes, removing ourselves from the culture after these have been formed will not free us from their sway . . . The best way to eradicate racism and sexism is to transform the dominant culture that formed and sustains them" (1996, 123). Belgrave herself has argued that "[o]ne has to empathize with the people's values even as one seeks to re-orient them . . . one of the things I was trying to do was to prompt my readers to visualize their real world and their natural allegiances in terms of their fictitious world without condemning anybody but the real villains" (Belgrave 1996).

The storyline is fairly simple. Set in eighteenth-century Trinidad, *Ti Marie*, which is divided into four books, develops a romance between a young coloured girl and an English nobleman. In the context of the times, the differences of race and class are significant. The couple, however, manages to surmount these barriers and eventually settle in England, on the nobleman's estate. Belgrave's desire is to ameliorate rather than dispense with the popular romance form. The intention is to parody. Kiremidjian (1996, 18) states that "a parody is indeed not a work of art, since it does not imitate an action in nature: it imitates another work of art". A parody comprises two dimensions. The first aspect is where the parodist imitates as closely as necessary the style, diction and vocabulary of the original work. The second aspect is where the parodist inserts other subject matter into the original form, creating a disjunction between form and content.

Kiremidjian (1996, 1) highlights the general disregard for work that is parodic, which is often seen as a "trivial" exercise: "purely literary in a sterile sort of way, and entirely dependent for its own significance on the model whose significance the parody would mock. . . . Parody has then been largely seen as an aberration, an illegitimacy, or heresy." This view is consistent with a very limited interpretation of the significance of this strategy. Kiremidjian makes the point that parody differs from travesty in that the latter makes fun of the original by using the original content in another style or form, which creates humour. It also differs from caricature in that the latter relies for effect on the exaggeration of certain features of the original. But parody can also be used to create irony: "Thus parody can act as irony has, namely as a means of counterpoising elements to create a significant context without the sentimentality of appeal or commitment to meanings which are invalid or alien to the context" (Kiremidjian 1996, 53).

The tension between form and content in *Ti Marie* is evident in the play between its parodic nature and the genre of the romance. Bhatia (1993, 21) observes that genre provides the comfort of a certain amount of predictability in a recognized established form, content and audience. He points to two possibilities: one is that of "non-discriminative strategies", which replicate the conventional expectations of the genre, and the other is "discriminative strategies", which vary the nature of the genre by introducing new or additional content into the communicative purpose of the text. It is through using these discriminative strategies that Belgrave introduces perspectival shift within the text. This process of reinventing reality must of necessity interact with accepted notions of history.

## The Importance of Critical History

Price (1999, 9) identifies three features that are characteristic of the critical historical approach that Belgrave employs in popular romance: "a lack of emphasis on major historical figures; a central focus on a mediocre main character; and most important of all, a depiction of the class struggle". Liberation is also received "[f]rom characterizations that appear in dominant forms of historical representation. Critical history gives a free voice to those who want to make themselves anew and plot for themselves their own destiny" (Price 1999, 33).

Historical detail is used to provide the context that brings to Trinidad the cosmopolitan population about whom Belgrave writes: "Some of the immigrants were white families, but by far the greater number consisted of free blacks and mulattos . . . with all these immigrants came thousands of African slaves" (Belgrave 1988, 11). Historical personages are woven into the lives of the inhabitants of the plantation of Santa Clara. Don Chacon, a frequent visitor, is described as "a linguist and a liberal" who promotes adoption of an "equitable land distribution policy" which benefits settlers to the island. Canning, one of the architects of the abolition movement in Britain, meets Barry, the male protagonist, and they discuss legislation.

Much emphasis is also placed on establishing the island of Trinidad as a place where a more humane form of slavery was practised. This argument may have some credibility. Brodber (1982, 46–47) comments on the absence in nineteenth-century Trinidad newspapers of racially biased employment advertisements for women, as well as the presence of a large number of educated and leisured women, both white and, possibly, coloured. This would seem to imply that attitudes towards people of colour were an extension of a more liberal attitude prior to the abolition of slavery. At the same time, the brutality of slavery is not minimized in the text. Instead, the eighteenth-century world is presented as one of conflict – Spain against Britain, blacks against whites, free versus bonded. There is a determined attempt to establish a sense of history as a living, breathing entity that permeates the lives of all the characters.

## Parody and the Role of the Narrator

In popular romance, the narrator often accords primacy to the female protagonist's point of view. In this novel, however, the narrator's function is to balance the different points of view that are represented in the cosmopolitan society. The narrator assumes a position of authorial omniscience operating outside the time frame of the novel, with knowledge of past, present and future events. The central progressive conscience belongs to the main protagonists, who are willing to embrace the humanity of each other in spite of their differences in race and social station.

The novel employs a series of perspectival shifts which emphasize an essentially non-European world view. It is explicitly critical of European control. Slave societies are accordingly described as "horrendously oppressive" and "decidedly bigoted". Spain, a colonial power, is alternatively described as "lazy", taking "weary notice" and trying to "rouse herself from years of lethargy and incompetence". There is a juxtaposition of the native perspective on historical events against that of the imperial: "While the children of Africa . . . were writhing under the boot of the most brutal form of slavery ever known to mankind, and some were already struggling under fierce tropical skies to free themselves from that unholy bondage, certain young aristocrats in Britain untouched by those eventualities . . . were wallowing in the excesses initiated by the Prince of Wales" (Belgrave 1988, 29).

Within the generic constraints of the novel there is a constant play between the reality of social conditions and the fantasy of the romance, but in the function of the narrator, problems with the parodic structure of the text become evident. Inadvertently perhaps, there is an ideological distance between coloured people such as Eléna and the mass of Africans, and also between individual Africans such as Antoine (leader of a doomed revolt) and Fist (Barry's servant), based on their degree of socialization to white norms. Antoine's presentation is the more stereotypically negative and Fist's the more positive. In the limited scope appointed to Africans, who still make up a large proportion of Caribbean peoples, the novel falls short of using narratorial omniscience to truly capture the complexity of the points of view inherent in this context.

In the major scene in which blacks feature – the kidnapping of Eléna during the slave rebellion – they are characterized from a viewpoint that does not seem consistent with the equality of all men under the sun, a major theme of the novel. The narrator assumes the position of detached observer. Antoine and his "devotees" are seen at the end of one of their religious ceremonies. Antoine, the leader of the group, speaks in a language that is full of images of "curses", "beasts", "murder", "devils" and "hate". There is none of the "distorted but vibrant, rhythmic, musical, sensuous and expressive" language (Belgrave 1988, 44) which Barry earlier in the text applies to blacks. The difference between the voice of Antoine and that of the narrator is clearly evident in the Creole of Antoine and the standard English of the narrator.

Even though Eléna refers to herself as black in the course of the novel, it is apparent in the rescue scene that she is not part of Antoine's blackness. Yei, who rescues her daughter, argues with Antoine that "she has helped *your people* all her life" (Belgrave 1988, 269; my emphasis). The narrator describes the group's discussion of whether or not they should let her go as a "babble" of confusion. The "battle" is over when Yei reminds them that her daughter is one of twin girls. The African superstition that twins are bad luck becomes the "master stroke" that convinces them to let her go. The exchange between Yei and Antoine is reminiscent of the traditional characterization of those between masterful explorer and superstitious natives, who can be made to follow instructions through manipulation of their beliefs.

## Parody and Characterization: Eléna's Mixed Race and Implications for Presenting a Caribbean Reality

The parodic structure is employed in the text through substitution or shifts of the qualities of characterization usually seen in the genre. Both Eléna and Barry to a certain extent exist outside the norm. A look at the romance genre reveals a prescription for femininity based on a standard of race, size, height and age. Masculinity is grounded in the same categories but includes economic wealth and power. These criteria, according to Illouz (1997), define a "romantic competence" that effectively precludes all non-white groups. The importance of race cannot be denied in a slave society. By the nineteenth century, medical and scientific discourse had cemented racial mixing in the popular imagination as abhorrent. Tizard and Phoenix observe: "To maintain the superiority of the white race it was important to keep it 'pure'. Hence the opposition to, and often outrage at, the idea of marriage between white people and those of other races. It was feared that their offspring would not only dilute 'white blood', but that they would disgrace the family by inheriting and transmitting the bad qualities of the inferior race, including their stigmatized appearance" (1993, 2).

Therefore, to present a coloured woman as heroine involves changing the terms of reference in which she is seen. In the trans-racial romance, coloured female protagonists approximate European ideals. In *Adolphus* (1853, 4), Antonia is described as the colour of a "light Italian *brunette* which commands admiration throughout the world; her hair of a glossy black floated gracefully in a profusion of curls around her spotless and well formed neck, and contrasted most beautifully with her high and well organized forehead".

In *Ti Marie*, the criteria for beautiful heroines is met not so much by creating new phrases as by causing old ones to shift reference. The unfamiliar darkness is downplayed against the more customary perfection of her physical features:

> The very olive brown of her flawless skin gave her a special radiance which was rivaled only by the luster in her large round eyes whose pupils were as black and as bottomless as the night. The nose, which she had obviously inherited from that unknown white father, was straight and turned up lightly at the tip. But it was her lips that stole Barry's heart. Her full lips tilted up at the corners and could not help but smile. . . . He thought nothing of her race, her colour or her nationality. His only thought, as he finally rode away was . . . "Velvet . . . her skin is like velvet!" (Belgrave 1988, 46–47)

There is an obvious interest in the text in emphasizing a Caribbean reality grounded in the culture of the people, who include Europeans and Amerindians as well as Africans. This points to one of the central dilemmas of the novel: how to balance between the danger of re-inscribing prevailing stereotypes and at the same time to work within the acknowledged structure of a genre – especially knowing that within a slave society, colour had important social implications. A liberal, wealthy white father often provided the means through which a coloured woman could attain respectability. As Brody (1998, 54) observes, "By possessing legitimate paternal love, the slave can shift from being property to having property . . . bestowing property becomes a gift of paternal love."

There is some inversion of expectations in *Ti Marie*. Colour does not provide automatic privileges for Eléna. As the darker-skinned of her mother's two girls, she is unlikely to have such a range of opportunities for social climbing as her sister. The penniless white father can bestow only the wealth of a liberal education on his daughter and thus empower her with the "inner spirit" that allows her to be the equal of any free person.

Eléna is encouraged by her mother to have "a special pride" in her mixed race. This is significant. Sherrard (1994, 12) observes, "It is a painful irony that a mother can perpetuate a history of patriarchal, colonizing oppression to ensure her daughter's survival, if not her sanity." Thus, by having Eléna encouraged to embrace both aspects of her racial heritage, Belgrave creates a character who resists oppression. Another strategy employed within the novel is to introduce subtle changes in the traditional pattern of male/female interaction. Physically, Eléna is almost as tall as Barry; he does not tower over her as is customary in popular romance. The closeness in age between them, their similar personality traits and the absence of victimization in their relationship underscore their equality.

## Parody and Characterization of the Male Protagonist

In the romance genre, to make him recognizable a male hero needs a significant proportion of the qualities that define masculinity. Hopkins (1996, 98) defines these as "[hetero]sexual prowess, sexual conquest of women, heading a nuclear family, siring children, physical and material competition with other men, independence, behavioural autonomy, rationality, strict emotional control, aggressiveness, obsession with success and status, a certain way of talking, having buddies rather than intimate friends, etc.". In *Ti Marie*, at nineteen Barry is much younger than the typical male protagonist, who is often a well-established man in his late thirties to forties. His closeness to women, such as his mother, underlines his emotional sensitivity. LaFollette (1996, 121) argues

that "men dominated by . . . standards of masculinity cannot establish relationships as close as can those who are willing to be vulnerable". Thus Barry's
emotional vulnerability presents within the genre possibilities of new levels of
intimacy between men and women.

Significantly, Barry's identification with traditional feminine qualities is
also evident in his lack of power to take charge or control a situation. Despite
his status as a white male of the ruling class, he is powerless against the cru-
elties of slavery. This is seen in his impotence in the face of his great-uncle's
cruelty to his slaves: "His eyes glared fiercely at his uncle. His fists were
clenched. . . . He marched out of the house and walked swiftly down the drive-
way. Not knowing where he was going, he was simply intent on putting
distance between himself and his great-uncle" (Belgrave 1988, 40). His political impotence is counterbalanced by his athleticism, good looks, financial
means and virility, which keep his portrayal from becoming too decidedly
feminine and help to maintain the expectations of the genre.

## Parody: Inversions of Form

The destabilization of form takes place not only in characterization but also
in structural requirements of the genre. One of these is the crucial rescue
scene, which requires the hero to demonstrate his prowess in taking care of
the heroine. In *Ti Marie* this is subverted by another female figure – Yei,
Eléna's mother. She rescues her daughter from a group of Africans while
Barry and his friends hide in the bushes. Belgrave has argued that this lack of
action on Barry's part is consistent with her intention to deconstruct myths
of white supremacy, first through the person of the white man and second
through the use of symbols of his power and authority, such as the gun (Belgrave 1995). This, however, is not convincingly conveyed in the text. Barry
consistently maintains an ideological distance from the mass of Africans in
the novel; he is always sympathetic but does not actively participate in dis-
turbing the status quo.

Another disruption that occurs in the novel is the placement of the con-
summation of the relationship, which in the traditional romance usually comes
at the end of the novel. In *Ti Marie* this exchange takes place before the end.
Brody (1998, 17) notes that there slave society enabled even the " 'darker
skinned' mulatto . . . to become a 'proper' (and perhaps a propertied) lady
provided that providence procured for her proximity to a white gentleman".
In the context of *Ti Marie*, this expectation is not met. Barry returns to England, and Eléna, abandoned and pregnant, chooses respectability through her
marriage to André, a young coloured man. On this point the tension between
parody and genre threatens to destabilize authorial intentions. Belgrave

(1995) argues that Eléna does not choose respectability so much as reject the idealism she has cherished for so long, but given the genre and the context of the times, she seems swallowed up by the same conventions she has opposed.

With respect to its parodic elements, the tour de force of the novel is the third and fourth books, which represent its climax. Gone is much of the stereotypical type presentation. Reality cuts sharply into the discourse. Barry, for example, realizes that he cannot marry Eléna and claim his inheritance in England. There is a growing consciousness among the main characters that their environment is not all fairytale and that "under the brilliance of the tropical sun, subtleties evaporated. To be replaced, however . . . by stark and glaring contradictions" (Belgrave 1988, 171).

## Parody: Problems of Form

There are difficulties in attempts to rework the romance in a counter-discursive environment. Belgrave seems to see formulaic romance as a potential means of managing social tension and promoting cultural stability by incorporating, as Meehan (1999, 110) suggests, new interests into "conventional imaginative structures". Meehan writes specifically about Haiti, where romance is used "to help consolidate an imagined national community by projecting conciliatory narrative closure on a range of disruptive social divisions". Harney (1990, 111), however, believes that the political and economic reality of the majority of citizens mitigates against "racial harmony" and cannot be effectively hidden by the romance.

Belgrave's belief that the romance can provide narrative closure on wounds of the past is steadily undercut by inconsistencies between the humanistic ideals of the main protagonists and the racially stereotypical ways in which characters such as Fist and Antoine are developed. This is the case despite her intention to show respect for the African struggle. Another problem arises out of Barry and Eléna's interracial relationship, which shows the degree to which categories of race are flexible within the capitalist structure of the society, where "race" can be defined not by "[c]ertain physical or biological traits, particularly phenotype (skin color), body structure, and facial features [but] instead the meaning of race shifts according to the power relations among the racial groups" (Marable 1997, 152). Eléna moves through shifts in characterization between "black" and "brown", and the novel ends with her moving into the category of "white" – not in terms of skin colour but in terms of the economic opportunities available to her through marriage. Barry and Eléna's relationship thus flourishes within the established construct of imperial society, and while things will change for her and her children, they will not for those who remain firmly fixed in categories of blackness.

Yet to draw attention solely to the ways in which Belgrave's work apparently colludes with established social practices is to ignore the essential nature of counter-discourse. Robert Young (1996, 148) observes that hybridity "undermines colonial authority because it repeats it differently". Thus the mere act of repeating the history of Trinidad and race relations within the context of the romance from the perspective of another, according to this view, is counter-discursive. Popular romance in a counter-discursive context reveals an ambivalence about who we are, where we live and our place in the world. Yet in order to change the images of ourselves as a colonized people, we must begin by re-visioning ourselves beyond the stereotypes imposed by those who have held civil authority over us and who continue their attempts to define us.

## References

*Adolphus*. 1853. Trinidad: n.p.

Belgrave, Valerie. 1988. *Ti Marie*. London: Heinemann.

———. 1995. Letter to Paula Morgan, 30 June.

———. 1996. Letter to Jane Bryce, 4 August.

Bhatia, Vijay K. 1993. *Analysing Genre: Language Use in Professional Settings*. London: Longman.

Boyce-Davies, Carole. 1994. *Black Women, Writing and Identity*. London: Routledge.

Brodber, Erna. 1982. *Perceptions of Caribbean Women: Towards a Documentation of Stereotypes*. Cavehill, Barbados: ISER, University of the West Indies.

Brody, Jennifer DeVere. 1998. *Impossible Purities: Blackness, Femininity and Victorian Culture*. London: Duke University Press.

Brunt, Rosalind. 1984. "A Career in Love: The Romantic World of Barbara Cartland". In *Popular Fiction and Social Change*, edited by Christopher Pawling, 127–56. London: Macmillan.

Campbell, Jane. 1986. *Mythic Black Fiction: The Transformation of History*. Knoxville: University of Tennessee Press.

Christian-Smith, Linda K. 1998. "Young Women and Their Dream Lovers: Sexuality in Adolescent Fiction". In *The Politics of Women's Bodies: Sexuality, Appearance, Behaviour*, edited by Rose Weitz, 100–111. Oxford: Oxford University Press.

Clatterbaugh, Kenneth. 1996. "Are Men Oppressed?" In *Rethinking Masculinity: Philosophical Explorations in Light of Feminism*, edited by Larry May, Robert Strikwerda and Patrick D. Hopkins, 289–305. Lanham, MA: Rowman and Littlefield.

Collins, Patricia Hill. 1991. *Black Feminist Thought: Knowledge, Consciousness and the Politics of Empowerment*. Vol. 2, *Perspectives on Gender*. New York: Routledge.

Edmondson, Belinda. 1999. "The Caribbean: Myths, Tropes, Discourses". Introduction to *Caribbean Romances: The Politics of Regional Representation*, edited by Belinda Edmondson, 1–10. Charlottesville: University of Virginia.

Fowler, Roger. 1986. *Linguistic Criticism*. Oxford: Oxford University Press.

Geist, Christopher D., and Angela M.S. Nelson. 1992. "From the Plantation to Bel-Air: A Brief History of Black Stereotypes". In *Popular Culture: An Introductory Text*, edited by Jack Nachbar and Kevin Lause, 262–72. Bowling Green, OH: Bowling Green State University Press.

Green, William. 1976. *British Slave Emancipation: The Sugar Colonies and the Great Experiment, 1830–1865*. Oxford: Clarendon Press.

*Hamel, the Obeah Man*. 1827. 2 vols. London: Hunt and Clark.

Harney, Steve. 1990. " 'Men goh respect all o' we': Valerie Belgrave's *Ti Marie* and the Invention of Trinidad". In *World Literature Written in English* 20, no. 2: 110–19.

hooks, bell. 1998. "Selling Hot Pussy: Representations of Black Female Sexuality in the Cultural Marketplace". In *The Politics of Women's Bodies: Sexuality, Appearance and Behaviour*, edited by Rose Weitz, 112–22. Oxford: Oxford University Press.

Hopkins, Patrick. 1996. "Gender Treachery: Homophobia, Masculinity and Threatened Identities". In *Rethinking Masculinity: Philosophical Explorations in Light of Feminism*, edited by Larry May, Robert Strikwerda and Patrick D. Hopkins, 95–115. Lanham, MA: Rowman and Littlefield.

Illouz, Eva. 1997. *Consuming the Romantic Utopia: Love and the Cultural Contradiction of Capitalism*. Berkeley: University of California Press.

Jayawardena, Kumari. 1995. *The White Woman's Other: Western Women and South Asia during British Rule*. New York: Routledge.

Kiremidjian, David. 1985. *A Study of Modern Parody: James Joyce's* Ulysses, *Thomas Mann's* Doctor Faustus. New York: Garland.

LaFollette, Hugh. 1996. "Real Men". In *Rethinking Masculinity: Philosophical Explorations in Light of Feminism*, edited by Larry May, Robert Strikwerda and Patrick D. Hopkins, 119–34. Lanham, MA: Rowman and Littlefield.

Lalla, Barbara. 1996. *Defining Jamaican Fiction: Marronage and the Discourse of Survival*. Tuscaloosa: University of Alabama Press.

Marable, Manning. 1997. "The Black Male: Searching beyond Stereotypes". In *Through the Prism of Difference: Readings in Sex and Gender*, edited by Maxine Baca Zinn, Pierrette Hondagncu-Sotclo and Michael A. Messner, 443–48. Boston: Allyn and Bacon.

*Marly, or, The life of a Planter in Jamaica*. 1828. 2nd ed. Glasgow: Printed for R. Griffin.

Meehan, Kevin. " 'Titid ak pep la se marasa': Jean-Bertrand Aristide and the New National Romance in Haiti". In *Caribbean Romances: The Politics of Regional Representation*, edited by Belinda J. Edmondson, 105–22. Charlottesville: University Press of Virginia, 1999.

Mills, Sara. 1995. *Feminist Stylistics*. London: Routledge.

Nachbar, Jack, and Kevin Lause. 1992. "Getting to Know Us: An Introduction to the Study of Popular Culture: What Is This Stuff That Dreams Are Made Of?" In *Popular Culture: An Introductory Text*, edited by Jack Nachbar and Kevin Lause, 1–35. Bowling Green, OH: Bowling Green State University Press, 1992.

Pratt, Mary. 1992. *Imperial Eyes: Travel Writing and Transculturation*. London: Routledge.

Price, David. 1999. *History Made, History Imagined: Contemporary Literature, Poeisis and the Past*. Urbana: University of Illinois Press.

Rabine, Leslie. 1985. *Reading the Romantic Heroine: Text, History, Ideology*. Ann Arbor: University of Michigan Press.

Reid, Mayne. 1860. *The Maroon*. London: Hurst and Blackett.

Sherrard, Cherene. 1999. "The 'Colonizing?' Mother Figure in Paule Marshalle's *Brown Girl, Brownstones* and Jamaica Kincaid's *The Autobiography of My Mother*". *MaComère* 2: 125–33.

Smith, Faith. 1999. "Beautiful Indians, Troublesome Negroes and Nice White Men: Caribbean Romances and the Invention of Trinidad". In *Caribbean Romances: The Politics of Regional Representation,* edited by Belinda Edmondson, 163–82. Charlottesville: University of Virginia.

Spencer-Strachan, Louise. 1992. *Confronting the Colour Crisis in the Afrikan Diaspora: Emphasis Jamaica*. New York: Afrikan World Info Systems.

Tizard, Barbara, and Ann Phoenix. 1993. *Black, White or Mixed Race? Race and Racism in the Lives of Young People of Mixed Parentage*. London: Routledge.

Walder, Dennis. 1998. *Post-colonial Literatures in English: History, Language, Theory*. Oxford: Blackwell.

Wilkins, William Noy. 1854. *The Slave Son*. London: Chapman and Hall and John Edward Taylor.

Young, Robert. 1996. *White Mythologies: Writing, History and the West*. London: Routledge.

Zinn, Maxine Baca, Pierrette Hondagneu-Sotelo and Michael A. Messner. 1997. *Through the Prism of Difference: Readings in Sex and Gender*. Boston: Allyn and Bacon.

# 7.

# "Culturally Relevant Pedagogy" in the Caribbean

## Traditional Practices and Beliefs in the Science Classroom

SUSAN HERBERT

*An important strand of science education research involves teachers' use of students' indigenous knowledge (traditional knowledge) in helping them to learn science presented in the classroom. This approach can be categorized as "culturally relevant pedagogy" (Ladson-Billings 1995). Within the Caribbean, George (1986, 1995, 1999) and George and Glasgow (1988) were pioneers in research on the use of indigenous knowledge in relation to science education at the secondary level. This body of work provided the stimulus that propelled me to engage in action research on the process of building bridges between students' prior knowledge of traditional practices and beliefs and conventional science concepts within the science classroom. This chapter reports on the inclusion of traditional practices and beliefs as a bridge-building strategy during the enactment of a unit of work titled "Maintaining Health". Two groups of lower secondary students in Trinidad and Tobago participated in the research. The first group of students attended an all-girls urban school. The second group comprised students at a rural co-educational government school. Data were obtained from participant observation of classroom interaction and the students' written and oral responses to the process of bridge-building. The data were analysed using grounded theory methodology. The students' responses to the inclusion of traditional practices and beliefs in the science classroom are discussed.*

## Introduction

During the late 1980s, June George and Joyce Glasgow, two science education researchers employed at the St Augustine and Mona campuses of the University of the West Indies respectively, advocated the use of students' traditional knowledge – referred to as "street science" (George 1986) – in the formal science classroom. The use of "street science" was suggested as a means of increasing the relevance of science curricula with a view towards enhancing science learning. About a decade later, Michael Alleyne, another Caribbean researcher who was working in the field of history of education in Trinidad and Tobago, commented that the curricula of newly independent countries such as Trinidad and Tobago were culturally irrelevant (Alleyne 1996). At the same time, within the international science education community, research which focused on the nexus between cultural heritage and science curriculum was gaining momentum. Accordingly, reports were published on science education research which highlighted the role of indigenous knowledge in helping students to access science concepts (Aikenhead 1996, 2000a; Aikenhead and Jegede 1999).

Influenced by these events, the author of this chapter accepted the challenge to develop a science unit, titled "Maintaining Health", in which aspects of students' cultural heritage (specifically their traditional practices and beliefs in relation to health issues) were included. The use of prior knowledge was identified as a strategy to facilitate students' access to conventional Western science concepts which are presented in the science classroom. The curriculum unit was developed as an action research project which sought to answer this question: how do students respond to the inclusion of traditional practices and beliefs in the formal science classroom setting?

## "Street Science" as Intangible Cultural Heritage

According to UNESCO (2003), the concept of cultural heritage has been modified significantly within recent decades to include what is described as intangible cultural heritage. As stated in the Convention for the Safeguarding of the Intangible Cultural Heritage, "Cultural heritage does not end at monuments and collections of objects. It also includes traditions or living expressions inherited from our ancestors and passed on to our descendants, such as oral traditions . . . social practices . . . knowledge and practices concerning nature and the universe . . ." (UNESCO 2003).

"Street science" is a term used by George (1986) to refer to traditional practices and beliefs of Caribbean people, comprising oral traditions, social practices and knowledge and practices concerning nature. She describes street science as "those social customs and beliefs that deal with the same content areas that are dealt with in conventional science but which sometimes offer different explanations to those offered in conventional science" (1986, 1). Street science can therefore be aptly described as part of the intangible cultural heritage of Caribbean society. Indeed, there is evidence that Caribbean people are influenced by street science despite the predominance of Western science concepts as explanatory tools.

In my experience, the evidence for street science in contemporary life in Trinidad and Tobago is often conveyed orally, in informal discussions. In addition, evidence of the preservation of traditional knowledge in contemporary society is occasionally found in the popular media, such as newspapers. For example, in an article published in the *Trinidad Express*, Rhea-Simone Auguste cited Dr Sophia Ali-Mason as stating, "There are a lot of misconceptions about what causes colds. Some people think they're caused by cold weather. I've heard people say you can catch the cold if you go outside with wet hair. But the truth is, almost all cases of the common cold are caused by viruses." Evidently there are conflicting explanations for the common cold, and these in turn guide practice. For example, the traditional practice in some communities in Trinidad and Tobago that persons "cool off" before bathing to avoid acquiring a cold is related to traditional beliefs about the "heated" human body (Herbert 1999).

The traditional practices and beliefs such as those cited above are often dismissed by medical practitioners. It should be noted that 66 per cent of the street science which George (1986) investigated is not supported by conventional Western scientific principles. However, these practices and beliefs are valued in certain communities and serve as prior knowledge for some children before they are exposed to formal school science.

## Conceptions of Prior Knowledge

Many international researchers have recognized that prior knowledge plays a significant role in learning, and for at least three decades this has become a significant strand of research in science education. The researchers use a wide range of terms to refer to knowledge that is different from the currently accepted Western science concepts and explanations. Among the terms used are "alternative frameworks" (Driver and Easley 1978), "alternative conceptions" (Gilbert and Swift 1895), "untutored beliefs" (Hills 1989), "misconceptions" (Novak 1988), "children's science" (Gilbert, Osborne and Fensham 1982) and "para-scientific culture" (Raw 1979). Gilbert et al. (1982, 627) use the phrase "children's science" to describe "those views of the natural world and the meanings of scientific words held by children before formal teaching". These researchers were generally of the view that formal science teaching should result in conceptual change.

More recently, some researchers have begun to acknowledge, investigate and explicitly honour and respect indigenous knowledge. The terms *traditional ecological knowledge* (TEK) (Snively and Corsiglia 2000) and *indigenous science* (Aikenhead 2006; Ogawa 1995), which are associated with a healthy respect for this knowledge, now appear more frequently in academic publications. For example, TEK is described as an example of indigenous science, which comprises one of the "sciences of the world" (Ogawa 1989, 248).

## Indigenous Science

Ogawa (1995, 588) defines science as "a rational perceiving of reality", and he describes perceiving as "both the action of constructing reality and the construct of reality". Using this framework, he then defines indigenous science as "a culture-dependent collective rational perceiving of reality" (1995, 588). Snively and Corsiglia (2000, 10) remind us that indigenous science includes the knowledge of both indigenous expansionist cultures (for example, the Aztec, Mayan and Mongolian empires) and the home-based knowledge of long-term resident oral peoples (for example, the aboriginal peoples of Africa, the Americas, Asia, Australia, Europe, Micronesia and New Zealand). These researchers posit that this knowledge is constructed in order to make meaning of natural phenomena and to solve problems.

Street science is a Caribbean knowledge base derived primarily from our African and Asian ancestors. Street science, which aims to explain and suggest curative and preventive measures for a wide range of natural phenomena, including health-related issues, can therefore reasonably be described as indigenous science. Yet an analysis of Caribbean science curriculum documents reveals an absence of indigenous science. If such omissions are to be addressed, the work of George (1986, 1995, 1999) and George and Glasgow (1988, 1989) provides a good base from which to start. In this chapter the terms *indigenous science, indigenous knowledge,* and *traditional practices and beliefs* are used interchangeably.

There is a continuum of thought about the use of indigenous knowledge in the science class. There is the view that indigenous knowledge should serve as a bridge to conventional science concepts, and also a view that indigenous science should be valued and respected and not merely act as a bridge to conventional science. For example, McKinley suggests that indigenous knowledge and heritage should be sustained by introducing the "indigenous languages and culture into science education in schools" (2005, 232).

## Bridges and Bridge-Building

A review of the educational literature revealed that the terms *bridges* and *bridge-building* are common metaphors in the discourse on curriculum. They are often used in association with analogies (Dagher 1995; Harrison and Treagust 2006; Treagust 1993), books (Krashen 1998) and models (Gilbert et al. 2000; Matthews 2007; Spencer and Logan 2003) as a means of relating familiar concepts with new concepts, thereby providing opportunities for learning. Since the 1980s the terms *bridges* and *bridge-building* have been adopted by science education researchers (for example, Aikenhead 1996; Allen and Crawley 1998; George 2001; Mittlefehldt 2002) who subscribe to the view that science is a cultural enterprise of the Western world. Allen and Crawley (1998, 112) use the term *bridges* as a metaphor depicting a connection between different world views. They describe a Native American group as "trying to cross the bridge from traditional education to Western education". Mittlefehldt (2002) refers to a need to explore the process of bridging the gap between students' everyday tacit knowledge (TK) and explicit scientific knowledge (ESK) in order to deepen their understanding of science. George (2001) refers to the process of bridging the gap between the cultural context of home and the cultural context of Western science.

As described above, the bridge metaphor has been used to convey a way of thinking about cultural border crossing for some students who reside in either developed or developing countries, as well as for First Nations populations. In sum, from a cultural perspective, learning Western science involves crossing borders and hence requires bridge-building between students' traditional cultures and the culture of science. The discourse on bridging has therefore been extended to include classroom activities which cater explicitly to building bridges between different ways of knowing. Consequently, the idea of a bridge-building strategy that would help students to access conventional science concepts and also respect their prior knowledge was adopted as the conceptual framework for developing the unit of work. In addition to the concept of bridge-building, the literature also provided guidance about culturally relevant pedagogy in relation to student characteristics.

## Science Students: Costa's Framework

Costa (1995) developed a typology of students based on the ease with which they were able to cross the borders between their everyday worlds and the world of science. The categories of students were labelled "Potential Scientists", "Other Smart Kids", "'I Don't Know' Students", "Outsiders" and "Inside Outsiders". In addition, she suggested that the ease with which these categories of students independently cross borders between "worlds" ranges from smooth for Potential Scientists, managed for Other Smart Kids, hazardous for "I Don't Know" Students and virtually impossible for Outsiders. According to Aikenhead and Jegede (1999), the majority of students can be classified into three of Costa's five categories: Other Smart Kids, "I Don't Know" Students and Outsiders. They suggest that students whose worlds are at variance with the "world of school science" may think that science is not relevant to their everyday lives and, as a result, may not be interested in it.

Aikenhead (1996) therefore suggests that teachers adopt an anthropological approach to teaching, in which they act as culture brokers. He further suggests that teachers adopt different roles to cater to the different types of students. For the Other Smart Kids, teachers can assume the role of travel agent. For the other two categories of students, the role of tour guide is suggested. As the metaphors suggest, the essential difference between the roles is that the teacher-as-travel-agent provides less guidance to students who have to cross the borders between their traditional knowledge and conventional science.

## Developing Culturally Relevant Pedagogy

It seemed reasonable to have students engage in "bridge-building" by providing a platform for them to compare the traditional ways of knowing and conventional science. Writers such as Hawkins and Pea (1987), Ogunniyi (1988) and Mittlefehldt (2002) have posited that external criteria, such as similarities in the thinking process among peoples and in the functions and uses of theories, could be used to help students build bridges between different ways of knowing. One example of a similarity in thinking process that is characteristic of both traditional ways of knowing and conventional science is the search for causal explanations. Cobern refers to Kearney's description of causality as a presupposition that guides thinking, and he defines presuppositions as the "concepts, beliefs and values that people share which provide a basic view of the world" (1991, 9).

I therefore sought to employ the bridge-building strategy as a process of facilitating border crossing between the traditional way of knowing and conventional science. Specifically, the bridge-building process was direct comparison of these ways of knowing, in terms of similarities, differences, strengths and weaknesses. Accordingly, students' prior knowledge was introduced explicitly into the lessons and formed the basis for comparison. Furthermore, influenced by Aikenhead (1996), I adopted the role of tour guide and travel agent as I engaged in action research which sought to determine students' responses to the inclusion of traditional practices and beliefs in the science lesson.

## The Research Process

### The Students Involved

Two groups of Form 2 (the second year of secondary schooling) students were the participants in this research. One group, comprising thirty-six students, attended an all-girls denominational school, Parkview Secondary, in the capital city, Port of Spain. The second group of participants – forty-two students – attended a rural co-educational composite school, Seablast Secondary. The Parkview students were twelve to fifteen years old, and the Seablast students were between thirteen and seventeen years old. The general performance of the Parkview students during their Form 1 year had been good: most students had achieved 60 per cent or more on teacher-made tests, and only a minority (four to five) had achieved less than 50 per cent. In contrast, the general performance of the Seablast students on teacher-made tests was below average. The majority of students usually attained less than 50 per cent of the marks, and some performed at levels of 20 per cent or lower.

In Trinidad and Tobago, students aged eleven to thirteen are placed in secondary schools on the basis of their performance on a selection examination. The examination, originally termed the Common Entrance Examination, has since 2001 been known as the Secondary Entrance Assessment. Students who are placed in Parkview Secondary have attained scores within the top 20 per cent of the student population. However, from my fifteen years of experience teaching these students, I have recognized that they are of varying abilities and exhibit varied interest in science presented in the classroom. Based on their performance on teacher-made tests, the Parkview students were classified as representative of four of Costa's (1995) sub-groups: Potential Scientists, Other Smart Kids, "I Don't Know" Students and Outsiders. Seablast students, on the other hand, were representative of Other Smart Kids, "I Don't Know" Students, Outsiders and Inside Outsiders. Taken together, the students at both schools represented the full spectrum of Costa's classification.

### The Unit of Work

A unit of work was designed to use a bridge-building strategy at both Parkview and Seablast. In this study, the unit of work comprised five lessons in which there was explicit comparison of traditional practices and beliefs and conventional science concepts. These lessons were "The Common Cold: Catch Me If You Can", "Cold or Not?", "Cooling-off", "Cooling: A Home Remedy" and "Pimples and the Adolescent". Table 7.1 shows the traditional and conventional science concepts for two lessons.

**Table 7.1** Traditional and Conventional Science Concepts for Health-Related Phenomena

| Lessons | Traditional Principle | Traditional Concept | Conventional Science |
|---|---|---|---|
| The common cold | The common cold occurs when there is a sudden change in body temperature. | Temperature change | Germ theory |
| Cooling-off | "Cooling-off" principle: The "heated" human body should not be exposed suddenly to cold environments. "Cool-off" first. | Conscious control of body temperature | Homeostasis: automatic response from specialized systems |

## Collecting and Analysing the Data

Data were obtained from the classroom sessions that I taught, which were audiotaped and transcribed. In addition, the students' journal entries and my reflections on the lessons were collected. The data were analysed by means of grounded theory methodology in which the processes of open coding, axial coding and selective coding (Strauss and Corbin 1990) were used as the means of data handling.

## Findings

The research question "How do students respond to the inclusion of traditional practices and beliefs in the formal science classroom setting?" is used as the framework for presentation of the findings. The general category "student interest" was induced from analysis of students' classroom behaviours, their written reflections and my reflections and observations.

### Student Interest

The students were keenly interested in the segments of the lessons that related specifically to discussion of traditional practices and beliefs. This interest was demonstrated by behaviours in class such as their participation in class discussions, their spontaneity in responding to questions and comments related to traditional practices and beliefs, and the number of students who voluntarily and spontaneously responded. At Parkview, students asked questions, made suggestions to the teacher, commented on their peers' responses through challenges and evaluations and answered my questions. They were also willing to participate and at times even to dictate my role. Analysis of their written comments also revealed their use of the word "interesting" to describe lessons.

The following verbatim account illustrates students' interest in the lessons, their willingness to share their knowledge of traditional practices and beliefs, and their evaluation of peers' responses. The session was introduced by having students respond to such questions as "How do you catch the common cold?" A table had been drawn on the chalkboard to record students' ideas about the common cold to which they had been exposed in class (the science view) and outside class (the "street science"). In the reporting, students' responses are preceded by the letter S along with a number to distinguish among individual students; T indicates the teacher's remarks.

| | |
|---|---|
| T: | We were talking about the common cold, and many people thought that if they step on the cold floor they will catch cold. So, outside of the classroom, what do you think is said to be the cause of the cold? |
| S1: | When you drink from someone who has the cold. |
| T: | Is that an explanation that is heard outside the class? |
| S2 and others: | No! That's inside the class. |
| S3: | That could be both. Let's put it in both. |
| T: | Yes, S6? |
| S6: | If you have low resistance and go out in the rain. |
| S9: | If you go to bed with wet hair. |
| S10: | When you now get up and you go straight to the bathroom. |
| T: | Okay, straight to the bathroom from bed. Now, what is the explanation that is given in [science] class? In your general science text? I looked at it, so I know it's there. In the general science book, what is said to cause the cold? |
| S5: | Ahm . . . bacteria, viruses. |

There was no shortage of responses from both sites. The students' participation in the discussions was interpreted as empirical evidence of their interest. Furthermore, in addition to discussing traditional explanations of causes of the common cold, the students eagerly shared some preventive measures to avoid its occurrence. For example, they mentioned parents' warnings about "cooling off" and precautions to be taken upon waking. The following excerpt from Seablast illustrates:

| | |
|---|---|
| T: | How many people got advice from their parents about preventing the common cold? |
| S1: | When you get up from sleeping, make sure and put on a slippers, so you won't ketch a cold or stroke. |

T:      Let me hear something else. S2?
S2:     Do not go in the fridge.
S3:     Do not go in the bathroom until you cool off.

In addition to their behaviours in the classroom setting, students' written reflections on the lessons also provided evidence that they were interested in these sessions, and that their interest was maintained beyond Lesson 3. For example, one Seablast student indicated that she was interested in Lesson 4, "Cooling: A Home Remedy", because of its relevance to her everyday life experiences: "It was interesting to me because my grandmother is always talking about 'cooling', and one time . . . someone told me to take a 'cooling' and I didn't have a clue."

## Summary

Generally both sets of students were very animated when provided with opportunities to discuss the traditional practices and beliefs related to the lesson topics. They responded eagerly and positively. They spoke freely and confidently, challenging one another's views during these segments of the lessons. They initiated questions and they commented on my contributions and those of their peers. At both sites the students' spontaneity during these segments often dictated my role. I facilitated the discussion and clarified concepts and/or sought to have students clarify concepts. The students' behaviours, and my role as facilitator, were indicative of their level of interest in the lessons. The students' journal reflections also attested to their general interest in these segments of the lessons, and in a few instances they stated explicitly that their interest derived from the links they had made between what was mentioned in class and their everyday experiences. In other words, some students alluded to the relevance of the science curriculum as one factor that made the science class interesting.

## Discussion

The student participants in this study represented the full spectrum of Costa's (1995) classification, but they all displayed keen interest in the segments of lessons that included traditional practices and beliefs. However, there is very little empirical data on students' responses to this type of science curriculum, so further research is required. Nevertheless, the general interest observed from the students who participated in this study is consistent with the few reports in the literature in which similar curricula have been implemented. For example, Jegede and Okebukola (1991, 282) have reported on the efficacy of the approach in developing positive attitudes towards science. Additionally, Aikenhead (2000b) has reported that one of the advantages of using a cross-cultural science curriculum (one that employs strategies that help students cross the border between traditional or indigenous knowledge and conventional science) is the interest that students display.

Catering for, sparking and maintaining students' interest in the classroom are crucial to the teaching/learning encounter. Student interest establishes an easy and comfortable classroom climate. But according to Dewey ([1900, 1902] 1990) and Herbaert (cited by DeBoer 1991), interest is not the end for which we should strive. There is another important dimension of student interest, which is facilitating the learning of substantive concepts of the lesson. Educational literature suggests that students' affective reactions to the subject matter play an important role in governing their cognitive responses. For example, Dewey states: "Interests are in reality but attitudes toward possible experiences; they are not achievements; their worth is in the leverage they afford, not in the accomplishment they represent" ([1900, 1902] 1990, 193). Supporting this view, Zais warns against reducing the significance of interest and invokes the laws of psychology. He says: "Clearly, interest as a criterion for content selection finds its justification in the laws of educational psychology. To ignore the principle that learning begins with 'wherever the child is' is to risk verbal learning at best, and mental or physical dropping out at worst" (1976, 346).

The unit of work was in fact designed for the specific purpose of assisting students to access Western conventional science, which forms a significant part of the global cultural heritage. These were teacher-centred goals. The students did not have an opportunity to determine the content of the unit, which would have led to its reflecting their own interests. The students' positive response to the inclusion of traditional practices and beliefs within the science lessons was, therefore, a significant outcome.

## Conclusion

DeBoer (1991) reminds us that student interest was firmly established as an education doctrine in the 1920s, and he links interest with motivation to learn. According to Osborne (2003), in much of the work on motivation a distinction is made between individual or intrinsic interest and situational or extrinsic interest. Researchers such as Hidi and Harackiewicz (2000) and Hodson (1998) explain the significance of situational interest, especially in circumstances in which students are disinterested or academically demotivated. Hodson (1998, 71) posits that "situational interest . . . may result in better learning". He says that "high levels of situational interest lead to deeper processing and deployment of metacognitive control strategies". Consequently, there can be cognitive benefits when the curriculum piques the students' interest. It is evident, then, that more research is required on Caribbean students' responses to inclusion of their cultural heritage within formal science curricula. In addition, the cognitive benefits from exposure to culturally relevant pedagogy within the Caribbean – and the role of culturally relevant pedagogy in helping students develop knowledge of and healthy respect for their cultural heritage – should be the subject of future research.

## References

Aikenhead, Glen S. 1996. "Science Education: Border Crossing into the Subculture of Science". *Studies in Science Education* 27: 1–52.

———. 2000a. "Renegotiating the Culture of School Science". In *Improving Science Education*, edited by Robin Millar, John Leach and Jonathan Osborne, 245–64. Buckingham, UK: Open University Press.

———. 2000b. "Stories from the Field: Experiences and Advice from the Rekindling Traditions Team". http://capes.usask.co/ccstu/stories/html (accessed 21 April 2000).

———. 2006. *Science Education for Everyday Life: Evidence-Based Practice*. New York: Teachers College Press.

Aikenhead, Glen S., and Olugbemiro J. Jegede. 1999. "Cross-Cultural Science Education: A Cognitive Explanation of a Cultural Phenomenon". *Journal of Research in Science Teaching* 36, no. 3: 269–87.

Allen, Nancy J., and Frank E. Crawley. 1998. "Voices from the Bridge: Worldview Conflicts of Kickapoo Students of Science". *Journal of Research in Science Teaching* 35 no. 2: 111–32.

Alleyne, Michael H.McD. 1996. *Nationhood from the Schoolbag: A Historical Analysis in Trinidad and Tobago*. Washington, DC: OAS.

Cobern, William W. 1991. *Worldview Theory and Science Education Research*. NARST monograph no. 3. Manhattan, KS: NARST.

Costa, Victoria. 1995. "When Science Is "Another World": Relationships between Worlds of Family, Friends, School, and Science". *Science Education* 79, no. 3: 313–33.

Dagher, Zoubeida R. 1995. "Review of Studies on the Effectiveness of Instructional Analogies in Science Education". *Science Education* 79, no. 3: 295–312.

DeBoer, George E. 1991. *A History of Ideas in Science Education: Implications for Practice*. New York: Teachers College Press.

Dewey, John. [1900, 1902] 1990. *The School and Society and The Child and the Curriculum*. Chicago: University of Chicago Press.

Driver, Rosalind, and Jack Easley. 1978. "Pupils and Paradigms: A Review of Literature Related to Concept Development in Adolescent Science Students". *Studies in Science Education* 5: 61–84.

George, June M. 1986. " 'Street Science' in Trinidad and Tobago: Analysis and Implications for Teaching Conventional Science". Paper presented at the first Regional

Consultation on Science Education Research in Latin America and the Caribbean, Trinidad, February.

———. 1995. "An Analysis of Traditional Practices and Beliefs in a Trinidadian Village to Access the Implications for Science Education". PhD diss., University of the West Indies, St Augustine, Trinidad.

———. 1999. "Indigenous Knowledge as a Component of the School Curriculum". In *What Is Indigenous Knowledge? Voices from the Academy*, edited by Ladislaus Semali and Joe Kincheloe, 79–94. New York: Falmer.

———. 2001. "Culture and Science Education: A Look from the Developing World". http://www.actionbioscience.org/education.george.html?print (accessed 9 November 2010).

George, June, and Joyce Glasgow. 1988. "Street Science and Conventional Science in the West Indies". *Studies in Science Education* 15: 109–18.

———. 1989. "Some Cultural Implications of Teaching towards a Common Syllabi in Science: A Case Study from the Caribbean". *School Science Review* 71, no. 254: 115–23.

Gilbert, John K., and David J. Swift. 1985. "Towards a Lakatosian Analysis of the Piagetian and Alternative Conceptions Research Programs". *Science Education* 69: 681–96.

Gilbert, John K., Carolyn J. Boulter and Roger Elmer. 2000. "Positioning Models in Science Education and in Design and Technology Education". In *Developing Models in Science Education*, edited by John K. Gilbert and Carolyn Boulter, 3–17. Dordrecht, Netherlands: Kluwer.

Gilbert, John K., Roger J. Osborne and Peter J. Fensham. 1982. "Children's Science and Its Consequences for Teaching". *Science Education* 66: 623–33.

Harrison, Allan G., and David. F. Treagust. 2006. "Teaching and Learning with Analogies: Friend or Foe?" In *Metaphor and Analogy in Science Education*, edited by Peter J. Aubusson, Allan G. Harrison and Stephen M. Ritchie, 11–24. Dordrecht, Netherlands: Springer.

Hawkins, Jan, and Roy D. Pea. 1987. "Tools for Bridging the Cultures of Everyday Thinking and Scientific Thinking". *Journal of Research in Science Teaching* 24, no. 4: 291–307.

Herbert, Susan. 1999. "Urban Students' Ideas about the 'Heated' Body: Implications for Science Education". *Caribbean Curriculum* 7, no. 1: 1–20.

Hidi, Suzanne, and Judith M. Harackiewicz. 2000. "Motivating the Academically Unmotivated". *Review of Educational Research* 70, no. 2: 151–79.

Hills, George L.C. 1989. "Students' 'Untutored' Beliefs about Natural Phenomena: Primitive Science or Common Sense?" *Science Education* 73, no. 2: 155–86.

Hodson, Derek. 1998. *Teaching and Learning Science*. Buckingham, UK: Open University Press.

Jegede, Olugbimero, and Peter O.A. Okebukola. 1991. "The Effect of Instruction of Socio-cultural Beliefs Hindering the Learning of Science". *Journal of Research in Science Teaching* 28, no. 3: 275–85.

Krashen, Stephen. 1998. "Bridging Inequity with Books". *Educational Leadership* 55, no. 4: 18–22.

Ladson-Billings, Gloria. 1995. "Toward a Theory of Culturally Relevant Pedagogy". *American Educational Research Journal* 32, no. 3: 465–91.

Matthews, Michael R. 2007. "Models in Science and in Science Education: An Introduction". *Science and Education* 16: 647–52.

McKinley, Elizabeth. 2005. "Locating the Global: Culture, Language and Science Education for Indigenous Students". *International Journal of Science Education* 27, no. 2: 227–41.

Mittlefehldt, Sarah. L. 2002. "Objects in Motion Remain in Motion in the Classroom, but Come to Rest on the Playground: An Analysis of Students' Struggle to Align Everyday Tacit Knowledge with the Explicit World of Science". http://gsewdb.harvard.edu/~t656_web/spring_2002_students/mittlefehldt_sarah_science_lea (accessed 4 April 2008).

Ogawa, Masakata. 1989. "Beyond the Tacit Framework of 'Science' and 'Science Education' among Science Educators". *International Journal of Science Education* 11: 247–50.

———. 1995. "Science Education in a Multiscience Perspective". *Science Education* 79, no. 5: 583–93.

Ogunniyi, Meshach B. 1988. "Adapting Western Science to Traditional African Culture". *International Journal of Science Education* 10, no. 1: 1–9.

Osborne, Jonathan. 2003. "Attitudes towards Science: A Review of the Literature and Its Implications". *International Journal of Science Education* 25, no. 9: 1049–79.

Raw, Isaias. 1979. "Developments in Integrated Science Education in Relation to Nutrition and Health Education". In *New Trends in Integrated Science Teaching*, vol. 5, edited by Judith Reay, 125–29. Paris: UNESCO.

Snively, Gloria, and John Corsiglia. 2000. "Discovering Indigenous Science: Implications for Science Education". *Science Education* 85: 6–34.

Spencer, Sue S., and Kent R. Logan. 2003. "Bridging the Gap: A School-Based Staff Development Model That Bridges the Gap from Research to Practice". *Teacher Education and Special Education* 26, no. 1: 51–62.

Strauss, Anslem, and Juliet Corbin. 1990. *Basics of Qualitative Research*. Newbury Park, CA: Sage.

Treagust, David F. 1993. "The Evolution of an Approach for Using Analogies in Teaching and Learning Science". *Research in Science Education* 23: 293–301.

UNESCO. 2003. Convention for the Safeguarding of the Intangible Cultural Heritage. http://www.unesco.org/culture/ich/index.php?pg=00052 (accessed 15 August 2010).

Zais, Robert S. 1976. *Curriculum: Principles and Foundations*. New York: Harper and Row.

# 8.

# The Role of Proverbs in Caribbean Education

IAN E. ROBERTSON AND BEVERLY-ANNE CARTER

*Globalization, whatever its positive qualities, presents considerable threat to the character and social integrity of small states that do not themselves have a place on the world stage. Such states run the risk of being driven by the economics of globalization to lose their social and cultural identities, as well as their sense of self, as they become increasingly involved in this tantalizing paradigm. Education systems in these countries can best respond to such challenges by increasing the emphasis placed upon more indigenous aspects of their individual cultures. In the cases of essentially orate cultures of the Caribbean, the traditions should be made to play an increasing role in the development of sufficient levels of self-awareness to allow their citizens to face the threats posed with confidence and self-assurance. Caribbean proverbs, sharing as they do a common world view from territory to territory, present an excellent opportunity for ensuring that the store of knowledge based on lived experience and reflecting belief systems and cultural practices from which these societies have evolved is used to avert the threat of a new cultural domination. This chapter examines a range of proverbs for the effectiveness with which they manage to capture and encapsulate the lived experiences of Caribbean people. It also seeks to promote their incorporation into the education systems.*

## Introduction

Perhaps the most significant challenge that the emerging nations of the Caribbean have had to face in their short period of political independence and self-government is that posed by the new global economic world order. Indeed, Sir Shridath Ramphal, former Commonwealth secretary-general and head of the Caribbean negotiating team with European states, opined in 2002 that globalization was in practice not truly global but geographically selective in conferring benefits and opportunities, and that there were many parts of the world economy that the phenomenon had failed to reach. The phenomenon of globalization has reached beyond the limits of its economic bases to make an impact on every area of existence in the modern world (*Daily Nation* 2002, 11). The significance of the input of globalization beyond the simply economic is cause for considerable concern.

Ramphal expressed concern that the territories of the Commonwealth Caribbean appear to have lost their sense of self and of the things that bind them together as they jockey for the less substantial but perhaps more attractive short-term benefits proffered by notions of globalization.

> In our experience, the worst elements of colonialism were at the heart of the divide between rich and poor and we believed that with independence, with freedom would come new opportunities to put aside the iniquities of the colonial system. It turned out that it was not as easy as that. They adjusted too and gave new forms to dominion. Colonialism was overcome but dominion in a deeper sense was not. ("Sadness of a Statesman" 2008, 12)

He continued, in response to the question "Where do you locate the contemporary Caribbean in your global village?"

> That is the biggest area of frustration because for forty or fifty years I had no trouble with that question. We were a small area of the developing world but we were clear-headed. We had an awareness that our contribution did not lie in numbers but that that contribution lay in our capacity to think, cerebrate, develop and sustain a vision, to encourage our colleagues who had the greater clout to pursue a path that would lead to the amelioration of this terrible division, this gap between rich and poor, the elimination of so many elements of the relationship between rich and poor countries that lead to human poverty and destitution within our countries and that poverty is real. . . . I think that we have to recognise that we are small and that to count for anything in the world we haven't got to develop a sense that we matter because we can attract a great many tourists to come and admire our sea and our sand; we have to count by exercising some intellectual leadership that can contribute to sensible and fulfilling global policies. (Ibid., 12, 29)

Interestingly, the education plans of several of the Caribbean territories in the early 1980s reflected many of the concerns necessary for national development. The new draft plan for education in Trinidad and Tobago, for instance, noted that

> The people of Trinidad and Tobago are a unique amalgam of races and cultures who have demonstrated a genius for creativity, tolerance, and good humour. One of the major objectives of our education system must be to develop this creative

genius of our people and to bend it to the task of our uniquely creative minds to the problems and shortcomings of our education system, that solutions best suited to us will be found. . . . Full national independence and identity will be achieved and secured only on the basis of an education system which does not rely on foreign assumptions and references for its existence and growth. The educational revolution which is required is a thorough one, not merely the substitution of a local examination in place of a foreign one nor substitution of tropical architecture, locally produced books and such things in place of foreign equivalents. Every component of the system would require to have, as foundation of its validity, the relevance to the needs of the people it serves. (Trinidad and Tobago 1989)

At the other end of the development spectrum of the Caribbean, Montserrat's government stated that "education policy is based on the belief that education provides indispensable superstructure on which the development of human and material resources of the island must be founded".

That twenty years later the region would appear to have capitulated to the dictates of the new global world order without serious self-examination is justification for the kind of concern expressed by Ramphal above. Such an unfortunate turn of events, within forty years of gaining political independence from the largest colonizer in modern times, is perhaps a reflection of the extent to which these societies appear to have lost sight of what Ramphal called in his acceptance of chancellorship of the University of the West Indies in 1989, "the authentic sources of our own enlightenment". It represents a virtual sacrificing of those aspects of our being that have proven over time to be self-sustaining, on the altars of short-term expediency. The notion of globalization, despite its popular appeal on purely economic grounds, requires for its proper management and effectiveness a high level of self-assurance. Such self-assurance can be born only out of a very positive sense of self and an awareness of how this may facilitate treating with such a complex phenomenon.

Small states like those of the Caribbean must ensure maintenance of a proper balance between economic dictates and the need for a proper sense of self in a world that is driven by the notion of globalization. The peoples of the Caribbean region share a particular social history that is sufficiently different from other communities around the world to have helped shape their own, viable world perspective. Should the dominant states be successful, the products of the historical experiences of these Caribbean states would be lost forever. Such experiences, on the one hand, ought to be considered fundamental parts of global development and should therefore have a pivotal role in the development of truly global strategies. On the other hand, they are necessary for developing an understanding of the Caribbean person. A Guyanese proverb warns: "Snake picknie na know e name til e go a dam" (You do not really know who you are until you become involved with others – and they try to define you).

In summary, the concerns expressed centre on the loss of the self-confidence, or the will, to pursue behaviours that focus on the position and responsibilities of the small island states of the region in the more global context. As a consequence, they show concern about the surrender of initiative to the dictates of the developed world. Finally, there is a suggestion that this is the result of an overeager willingness to play the global game for its short-term benefits, in spite of its predictable longer-term deleterious effects.

## The Role of Education

The position is perhaps the result of the failure of systems of education to seek to inculcate in Caribbean peoples a proper sense of self and a proper awareness of how that self came into being. It is this acute self-awareness that would give Caribbean people a proper understanding of how their own interests may be represented in the new order of thinking. It is therefore to the education systems that we need to return, to insist that all Caribbean peoples develop an awareness of self-sufficiency to deal with the wider world.

The first part of the challenge is to recognize ourselves as having derived understandings and behaviours that have been authenticated in the "school of life". One excellent example of this is a saying of the Macushi Indians of western Guyana: "The sky is the roof of the world, the trees are the pillars that prop the roof. If you cut the pillars the roof will fall." In the context of modern technological sophistication their civilization would be described as simple, yet they appear to understand ecological issues that the world is only now awakening to. These are the sensitivities of what could be regarded as a technologically unsophisticated civilization to as fundamental a truth as ecological balance. Having denuded substantial areas of the world in the quest for development, the developed world is only now awakening to an awareness of the essential truth, which a simple people understood and encapsulated many centuries ago. Even now some powerful interest groups only grudgingly accept this essential truth about our environment, and the need to manage it properly.

One aspect of the problem in the Caribbean is that indigenous traditions, coming as they do from the lived experiences of a largely unlettered population in a young, underdeveloped set of small island states and nations, have little or no purchase in the modern world of high technology and sophisticated science. But there is a Creole proverb that encourages patience while at the same time underscoring the fact that complex structures are built out of simpler forms: "One one dutty build dam" (literally, "Moving earth bit by bit will eventually lead to construction of a dam"). More to the point, a Trinidadian proverb says: "Common sense make before book" – the ultimate statement of faith in the power of wisdom gleaned from life experiences in the real world.

Language is essentially oral, though writing is usually given greater significance. In a general sense, speech is more immediate and direct. It is also true that despite the advantages of writing for preservation over time (though sound is beginning to catch up), in the majority of communication contexts the immediacy of speech is more powerful than delayed access through writing. At any rate, writing demands learned skills and does not readily capture all the nuances of speech. Its usefulness, therefore, for storing the accumulated wisdom conveyed through proverbs is significantly compromised in a scribal world that has little or no faith in the oral.

One of the major contributors to the loss of self-confidence, and of the ability to be assertive in the face of the challenges of globalization, is the failure of the education systems of the region to rely on those very authentic sources to which Ramphal referred. The argument here is that the best way to counter the negative impact of globalization on the Caribbean societies under consideration would be to exploit these self-defining indigenous resources for the purposes of education. That way the traditions would remain familiar and accessible. The wisdom acquired in the school of life would be self-sustaining and self-ensuring.

## The Role of Proverbs in Caribbean Education

This chapter is concerned with the proverbs of the region and their potential for facilitating the education of the Caribbean mind. These proverbs are one subset of a much more comprehensive set of oral traditions that have been the major means of retaining a wide range of the socio-historical experiences of these societies. Within these societies, oral traditions, in particular the music-based ones, are by far the most defining feature of the Caribbean self. Indicative of the power of music traditions are the nicknames of the Jamaican football team (Reggae Boyz) and the Trinidadian football team (Soca Warriors) and the term for the type of cricket that made the West Indies team readily recognized: "calypso cricket". These musical traditions, because they may be quite readily subjected to the more familiar kinds of literary and social analyses, have developed, through the work of icons such as Bob Marley, Mighty Sparrow and Black Stalin, a significance that other aspects of the tradition have not. While grudging acceptance is given to these musical traditions in the higher levels of education systems, little or none is given to the non-musical ones.

Proverbs are not peculiar to the Caribbean societies under consideration here. Indeed, as Allsopp (2004, xvi) notes, "all human cultures on earth develop, store and use them orally". All societies have used proverbs over time to capture the essential wisdom gathered by their members. For the Caribbean, with its history of slavery and indenture along with plantation agriculture, the majority of the population had minimal levels of literacy and education. The consequent linguistic heritage was one in which the creole languages, with their dominant West African (or "Afric", according to Allsopp) world view, developed into the primary means of communication among the vast majority of the populations. These languages came to be regarded as debased forms of the European languages from which the majority of their lexicon may be derived. In conjunction with the fact that creoles are most widely used by the lower socio-economic and other unlettered sections of the populations, this has led the undiscriminating to the conclusion that all things associated with this particular form of expression are debased and lack value. In this context, much of the wisdom of the proverbs is undervalued or even lost. But these societies used their proverbs and sayings to preserve their life lessons. Indeed, the Reverend James Speirs, in the introduction to his *Proverbs of British Guiana*, noted that proverbs were a large part of the normal conversation style of ordinary Guyanese people at that time (Speirs 1902, 1). In other words, "Fly bin getin along before dog ears get sore" – people learned how to be resourceful and survive on the little they had.

In Caribbean societies, proverbs gain their significance from a number of factors. In the first place, they are part of Caribbean oral traditions, a reflection of the nature of these societies, which are essentially oral ones with a relatively recent and thin but increasing overlay of a writing tradition. The proverbs are propagated orally and very few of them have been codified.

There are several ways in which proverbs define Caribbeanness. The first of these is their essential Africanness. Allsopp (2004) argues that this is a direct result of the region's peculiar history, in which large numbers of persons from various areas of West Africa were enslaved in various Caribbean territories. These peoples brought with them the essential world view of the West African, and because the creole languages are a reflex of the Afric input, many Caribbean proverbs have a direct link to one or other West African proverb or oral tradition. Allsopp (2004, xvii) notes that he found the proverb "One finger can('t) ketch louse/flea/bug" occurring in thirteen cases, with creole variants from Guyana, across many anglophone islands and Haiti, to Belize. He also found more than twenty correlates in sub-Saharan African languages.

According to celebrated Nigerian author Chinua Achebe (cited in Young 1980), "Proverbs are the palm-oil with which words are eaten." Their function is to present a lesson in a palatable, though not always pleasant, form.

For the Caribbean, "the proverb represents all those aspects of Caribbean experience which have the potential to enhance the capacity to analyse, evaluate and inform. They are the bedrock of Caribbean critical thought and are expressed in words and images that reflect a Caribbean world view. Consequently, they are readily accessed by the Caribbean person" (Robertson 2004, 4).

There are several ways in which proverbs of the Caribbean help define the essential Caribbean way. The first of these is the ancestral link. This chapter focuses on the Afric link for several reasons. In the first place, among the non-indigenous peoples of the region, the African contribution to the demography of the Caribbean was the earliest and has been the most dominant through time. While there were significant subsequent inputs from India, in particular, and Madeira, the numbers were fewer and restricted to a few territories such as Guyana and Trinidad. These groups no doubt had proverbs as well, but whereas the Afric-derived proverbs found expression in the creole languages, the others were restricted to the respective languages and dialects of their source immigrants. This fact militated against their being integrated into use by the population in general, because the linguistic currency is the creole language. Second, many of the proverbs represent the specific thoughts contained in their West African counterpart. Indeed, it may well be argued that the originals were simply applied where they seemed to fit the new environment in the Caribbean:

1.  If yo(u) no pop ant's belly yo(u) know him hab gut. (Jamaica)
2.  Mash ants soft so yo(u) coud fin(d) (h)e guts. (U.S. Virgin Islands)
3.  Patient man fin(d) fire-ant's guts. (Belize)
4.  When yo(u) tek time for skin ants, yo(u) go see (h)e belly. (Tobago)
5.  Tek time kill ants yo go si i gat. (Krio, Sierra Leone)
6.  If you skin an ant with patience you can see its liver. (Akan, South Ghana)

The various versions of the same proverb are good indicators of the fact that many of the proverbs are generally accessible across the Caribbean. The Sierra Leone and Akan versions of the proverb are reflective of the African ancestral link. In this sense they help point to the common heritage of the region, a heritage that is not shared with most of the regions of the world. This characteristic is central to educating the Caribbean consciousness and to making significant ancestral links. And this proverb is not unique in its spread across the territories of the region.

Many other proverbs are shared across the region, sometimes with a different set of images but more often in identical form. Sometimes they cross the lexically distinct creole varieties.

1.  Cockroach en have place near fowl. (Guyana, Barbados, Jamaica)

2. Wavet pa ni plas douvan poul. (St Lucia)
(It is dangerous for the roach to be in the environment of the domestic fowl.)

1. Laline kuwi tu ju ka wive. (Trinidad French Creole)
2. Moon a run til day a ketch am. (Guyana)
(The moon runs until daylight catches up with it – that is, your deeds will catch up with you eventually.)

Both these proverbs are known in both English- and French-lexicon creoles of the region; the forms represent a replacement of one set of lexical items by another.

In other cases, the same idea is expressed through slightly different images. The roach proverb above may easily be replaced by "Jackass don have place in horse race" (Trinidad). The images are different but the message that one should be sensitive to the natural disadvantage of being in a hostile or unnatural environment is really the same as in the previous cases. The Guyanese proverb "Wa deh a mouth na load" ("That which is in the mouth is not a burden") is readily contrasted with the Jamaican "Jackass cyan too good fuh fetch him own feedin" ("A donkey cannot be above carrying its own food").

This identity and similarity of the proverbs again point to a common world view across the region. This may also be seen as part of the understanding of self that is being promoted here. Even where specific proverbs may not be known in a particular territory, common experiences allow the persons hearing a proverb to be able to interpret it. A proverb such as "Cow na know di use a ii tail til cowfly season" is perhaps not well-known outside Guyana, but the message is transparent to any Caribbean person who was brought up in a rustic environment. Another less known but equally transparent proverb argues, "A respec wa duck gat fo carrion crow make he na-a eat a plate." This proverb also warns that one should be sensitive to the issues of reckless endangerment of self, using the anatomical disadvantage of a duck eating from a plate. It also relies on knowledge that the carrion crow enters the corpse through the anus, which is exposed when the duck is trying to eat.

One further feature of Caribbean proverbs is their selection of images that are part of the environment or the experiences of the average person from these societies. Consider the Guyanese proverb "Never the day canoe bore punt" ("A small wooden dugout is unlikely to be able to damage an iron punt"). The punt is larger; it is constructed of metal; it is used to transport tons of sugarcane. The canoe is a small wooden paddle-boat. The proverb clearly relies on the foreknowledge of the listener to maximize its effectiveness.

Finally, there is a heavy reliance on the use of natural phenomena, in particular the flora and fauna peculiar to the Caribbean.

1. Is only when high wind blow you see fowl drawers/bottom/backside. (Unusual situations will expose things kept in secret.)
2. If yuh blow fiah wid yu mout, ashes sa go a you yeye. (If you promote wrongdoing you might get hurt.)
3. Fowl tread pan ii chicken but ii na-a tread hard. (One shows tenderness and mercy to one's own.)
4. Wattle house gat ears. (One cannot keep a secret in certain situations.)

As has been noted earlier, proverbs encapsulate Caribbean everyday experience. They seek to make available to the members of the community a series of lessons on life in short, highly focused and dramatic ways that make them easily accessed by all members of the community. The following are merely illustrative of the possibilities. Virtually every Caribbean society could identify one or other of its members who came into good times and squandered the advantages. The proverb warns: "Daag gat money he buy butah roas am a fiah" ("A dog gets money, he buys butter and roasts it in the fire"). It speaks to the inappropriate use of resources and cautions against waste.

This proverb chides disrespectful behaviour, especially in the context of being carried away by circumstances: "Happiness make ramgoat jump he mammy" ("Happiness would cause the ram to mate with its mother"). Not only is it an unnatural act but it is also born out of reckless abandon and it flies in the face of family values.

"When shit roll in goat belly, goat think say a strength" ("When waste moves in the intestines it can be mistaken for strength"). This time the proverb cautions against being pompous and overestimating one's own strength, importance or competence, especially since the perception could be based on issues of little substance or worth.

"You eat fowl egg, it sweet, but fowl a feel am" ("You eat the egg of the fowl but the fowl feels the pain"). This proverb relies on the awareness that an egg is the means by which a fowl bears its chicks, the first stage in the succession chain. While it brings pleasure to those who eat it, its eating brings pain to the fowl, both because it is destructive of its produce and also because it gets in the way of future productivity.

"Ungrateful picknie neba see wey he mumma bury" ("An ungrateful offspring will never visit where his parent is buried"). This is another of those proverbs that caution against ingratitude and indicate the need for honouring one's parents. It is a poor man indeed who cannot find a link to his ancestors.

"Sweet orange na-a fall a groun" ("The sweet orange does not usually fall to the ground"). Genuine quality will always be recognized in the end.

"Wen tub na gat hoople ii mus bruk down" ("When a tub has no bands it will fall apart").

"Wen u go fu dig grave, dig two" ("When you decide to dig a grave, dig two"). This time the proverb enjoins one to beware of setting traps for others, as one could easily become ensnared in the same trap.

"If you tek time you guh fine out how waata get a punkin belly" ("If you take time [be careful or cautious] you will find out how water got into the pumpkin"). This is actually more than advice to be patient; it is an indication that the darkest secrets (for example, pregnancy) may be found out.

"Na want a tongue mek cow cyan taak" ("It is not for want of a tongue that the cow cannot speak").

"Is na age wa srimps na gat mek e naa big lakka whale" ("It is not a lack of age that prevents the shrimp from being as huge as a whale").

"Sugar bag na does kill ants" ("The sugar bag does not harm the ant"). Differences in size may not matter in a fine relationship.

## Discussion and Recommendations

The argument being presented here is that a vast and varied store of proverbs is available to each Caribbean society, through either direct acquaintance or the resource of a common world view that renders the unfamiliar ones accessible. The proverbs grow out of the common social history of Caribbean peoples. It has been noted earlier that the proverb is not a unique Caribbean creation and that it serves much the same function worldwide, of encapsulating the accumulated wisdom of society in terms and language peculiar to that society. Caribbean proverbs themselves have a series of common characteristics that are peculiarly Caribbean and therefore demonstrate potential to help the Caribbean person develop a historical perspective of self, and at the same time provide a base from which to interrogate other cultures. They present a unique opportunity to carve out a positive concept of Caribbeanness. They also form the bedrock of productive interaction with other cultures, in particular with those that could be considered natural allies. According to Speirs,

> Those [proverbs] that are peculiar to a people have a special interest for the student, for they tell him something of the character, something of the manners and customs and pursuits, past and present, of the people using them. . . . They are worthy of our careful attention for they contain lessons of wisdom which, if put into practice would diminish evils from which so many particularly suffer, would make us less selfish and more sympathetic and tend to increase the happiness of ourselves and our neighbours. (1902)

It is axiomatic that a proper Caribbean education should ensure that these essential aspects of Caribbean heritage not be downplayed or even omitted altogether from the formal education system. According to Awonini in Agbaje (2005, 49), no successful educational system stands apart from the society that establishes it. Education should be embedded in that society, feeding on its strengths, relying on it for inspiration and nourishment and in turn contributing to opportunities for growth and renewal within the society. The issue is not only one of will. It is also one of understanding and appreciation of the seminal role of these features in the formation of the character of the region and a conviction about the roles they should play in Caribbean education. It is also an issue requiring a more imaginative approach to education, especially the affective aspects that often get ignored, as well as to teaching and learning. Such application cannot be done without a sufficient knowledge base, and if it is to succeed, it must be carefully planned, executed, monitored, evaluated and adjusted.

In order to initiate this use of the traditions, the relevant stakeholders must develop proper knowledge and awareness. The next stage would be to address the pedagogy of proverbs in the Caribbean. Since conscious awareness of oral traditions is not part of the norm for education in the Caribbean, it becomes of strategic importance to develop a cadre of persons who are well enough informed about the oral traditions to be able to do much of the theoretical and other groundwork necessary for arriving at a successful policy and implementation strategy. For this reason it is being suggested here that the place to start is at the tertiary level, both professional and disciplinary, of the education systems. This is where a critical mass of persons sufficiently informed to influence the entire system could be most readily found and developed.

Several options may be considered which could form the basis of a more detailed examination of the issue at hand. A few of them will be given here. The first would be to focus specifically on the oral traditions in general, since the same or similar arguments can be presented for them all. These traditions would include both the musical and the prose, including storytelling, riddles, jokes, sayings and, of course, proverbs. The focus must first be on ensuring that there is sufficient knowledge and understanding for people to appreciate the significance of the traditions, and the need to preserve and even document them, not only as guides for the Caribbean's own operations but also for our interaction with other people the world over. Such a programme would readily fit into any of the creative centres or centres for critical thought in institutions such as the University of the West Indies; full programmes or a significant number of courses could be offered either as a major area of study or as a structured minor.

Alternatively, awareness of the traditions could be treated as a foundation to Caribbean tertiary education. If it were seen as one of the interdisciplinary foundations of education, then information on the traditions could be part of a compulsory core of courses that all tertiary-level students would be required to complete before the awarding of a degree or diploma. In such cases there would be a broad spread over a relatively shallow survey of the traditions, but the awareness so developed would be the foundation on which strengthening could take place in accordance with demands. Yet another possibility would be to integrate oral traditions into the related disciplines of linguistics and communication studies and anthropology. Here there is clearly the additional significance of developing a robust research profile that would allow for greater in-depth study of the traditions.

Finally, the oral traditions could form a very meaningful part of the teaching and learning processes, especially for children who face challenges of learning in the current classroom paradigms. In the Caribbean, students are mainly Creole-speaking and share a common world view, which is sufficiently different from those associated with the processes of education to which they are normally exposed. What is required is a proper examination of the roles which such differences should play in the system of education. At present only the most incidental and grudging regard is given to these concerns. The limitations are linked to the peculiar social history of the region, which precludes their incorporation in a structured way into the education systems.

Students who have been classified as failures in the Caribbean education systems have two main options. The first is to remain in their societies and eke out an existence by relying on much of the accumulated street sense and understanding of things that these traditions encapsulate. Often students who fail in the formal education system manage to do well in life or in education systems outside the region. Many manage the process with a facility that is a serious indictment of the systems themselves. The second option is usually to migrate to the developed societies, where their consciousness of Caribbean selfhood is of marginal significance to success. Again, many succeed. The lack of sensitivity to the potential impact of traditions on learning indicates the limitations of the education system.

## Conclusion

Proverbs and their interpretation require significant higher-order language and comprehension skills. Often the imagery is dense and requires significant processing to get to the message. Unravelling inference, interpreting imagery and developing a sensitivity to the power of the voice are all keys that a Caribbean person requires in order to negotiate the proverbs with success. These are the very skills that students from the region fail to demonstrate within the formal education system, largely because the system assumes an absence of these skills and abilities where they already exist. Rather than use these familiar skills for ensuring transfer to the formal education system, the existing skills are ignored and an attempt is made to develop them *ab ovo*.

The case for the incorporation of oral traditions in general and of proverbs in particular could hardly be more effectively instanced. However, when this matter is finally resolved, the results of paying conscious attention to the defining characteristics of our being and to attempts to understand them and see how they affect our relationships with the remainder of the globe, are bound to be significantly enhanced.

## References

Agbaje, J.B. 2005. "The Place of Yoruba Proverbs in the Understanding of Yoruba Philosophy and Education". *International Journal of African and African American Studies* 1, no. 5 (January): 37–52.

Allsopp, S.R.R. 2004. *A Book of Afric Proverbs.* Kingston: Arawak Press.

Braithwaite, P.A. 1996. *Guyanese Proverbs and Stories.* N.p.

Forde, G. 1988. *Folk Beliefs of Barbados.* Barbados: National Cultural Foundation.

Grannum-Solomon, V. 1999. *Proverbial Wisdom from Guyana.* Pittsburgh: Dorrance.

Robertson, I.E. 2004. "The Role of Proverbs in Developing Critical Thinking Skills in the Caribbean Child". Paper presented at Critical Thinking workshop, University of the West Indies, St Augustine, Trinidad.

"Sadness of a Statesman: Conversations with Sir Shridath Ramphal". 2008. *Trinidad and Tobago Review* 30, no. 10 (6 October): 12.

Seaman, G. 1974. *Not So Cat Walk: The Philosophy of a People and an Era Expressed by Proverbs.* St Croix: G. Seaman.

Speirs, J. 1902. *The Proverbs of British Guiana.* Demerara: Argosy.

Trinidad and Tobago. 1989. *White Paper on Education.* Trinidad and Tobago: Ministry of Education.

Trotman, J. 2006. *The Proverbs of Guyana Explained.* London: Bogle-L'Overture.

Young, C.N. 1980. *Creole Proverbs of Belize.* N.p.: C.N. Young.

# 9.

# Caribbean Languages and Caribbean Linguistics

JO-ANNE S. FERREIRA

*Of the more than one thousand languages of the Americas, at least seventy have survived and are in use to various degrees across the twenty-nine territories of the Caribbean, including the archipelago and continental rimlands. Language situations of the Caribbean are complex, with language users (speakers and signers) managing an interface between and among a variety of heritage languages, each with its own social status and some with both national and official status. Linguistic groupings include indigenous Amerindian, European, Caribbean creole, sign, religious and immigrant languages. The relationships between European-born and Caribbean-born languages are varied, intense and often appear to be problematic, especially in formal education. In addition to the complexity of the living languages and their varieties, there are a number of heritage languages, many of which are in various stages of obsolescence. Caribbean(ist) linguists have been engaged in analysis and documentation of these languages and language situations for several decades, many pioneering work in hitherto neglected areas, with application to a variety of areas. To understand language as an integral and inseparable part of culture is to begin to understand issues of human social and cultural identity. This is the work of linguists in the Caribbean and beyond.*

## Introduction

In the Americas, a region that has suffered very heavy language loss over the past five hundred years, over one thousand living languages are still spoken, a number representing approximately 15 per cent of the world's estimated 6,909 living languages (Lewis 2009). Of these thousand-plus languages in the Americas, using *Ethnologue* criteria, and insofar as languages can be counted accurately, there are at least seventy surviving languages spoken or signed in the twenty-nine territories of the Caribbean.[1] These territories include both the islands of the archipelago and the rimlands of the continent (Allsopp 1996), which includes the non-Iberian linguistic "islands" of Belize, French Guiana, Guyana and Suriname.[2]

A heritage language is often narrowly defined as the ancestral, traditional, ethnic, family, home or first language, usually any language first used in the home other than the official dominant language(s) (see Valdés 2000 and Van Deusen-Scholl 2003; cf. Winer 2005). Such a grouping would usually include the post-emancipation minority languages of the Caribbean – some vital, some obsolescing, all with speakers who display a variety of competence and proficiency. The seventy living and surviving languages of the Caribbean are all the linguistic heritage of the modern Caribbean, whether these languages were used by ancestors of modern Caribbean peoples or have been used in Caribbean homes for generations. Certain languages other than first languages, such as languages belonging to the religious heritage of the region, are also included. Roughly classified according to their chronological appearance in the Caribbean area, Caribbean languages include at least the following (Lewis 2009):

- twenty-three indigenous Amerindian languages – seven Arawakan; ten Carib, including Carib itself; two Tupi; three Mayan; and one isolate, Warao – all spoken in the continental Caribbean.[3] Most of these languages are not bound by post-Columbian borders and are often spoken in more than one political territory (see table 9.1).
- four official European languages: Spanish, French, English and Dutch
- one African language: Kromanti, or Koromanti, an Asante Twi (Akan) language of Ghana, in Jamaica. Saramaccan and Berbice Dutch have especially strong lexical and structural West African components, from Fon(gbe) of Benin and Togo and others, and from Eastern Ijo of Nigeria, respectively.
- at least twenty-three creole languages.[4] fifteen English-lexicon; six French-lexicon, with one official and one national; one Portuguese- or Iberian-lexicon (official); and one Dutch-lexicon, in Guyana (see table 9.2).
- seven post-emancipation immigrant languages: Bhojpuri, Chinese (Hakka and possibly Cantonese), Javanese, Hmong, Arabic, Portuguese and German
- at least nine indigenous sign languages:[5] one in Cuba, one in the Dominican Republic, one in Guyana, one in Puerto Rico, two in Jamaica, two in Suriname, and one in Trinidad and Tobago (cf. Parks and Williams 2011)
- three languages used only as adult-learned second languages (L2s): two religious languages (Lucumi, in Cuba, and Langay, in Haiti) and one trade language (Ndyuka-Trio pidgin, in Suriname).

Figure 9.1 and tables 9.1 and 9.2 summarize the above data.[6]

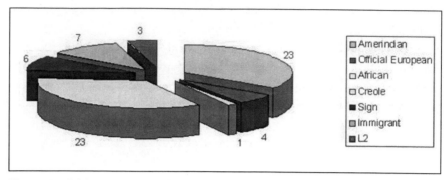

**Figure 9.1** Living languages of the Caribbean

**Table 9.1** Amerindian Languages of Belize and the Guyanas

**Arawakan**

1. Arawak (Lokono)
2. Atorada
3. Garífuna
4. Mapidian (almost extinct)
5. Mawayana (almost extinct)
6. Palikúr
7. Wapishana

**Carib**

1. Akawaio
2. Carib (Kalinha)
3. Macushi
4. Patamona
5. Pemon
6. Waiwai
7. Wayana

**Mayan**

1. Kekchí
2. Mopán Maya
3. Yucatán Maya

**Tupí**

1. Emerillon
2. Wayampi

**Table 9.2** Creole Languages of the Caribbean (Including Belize and the Guyanas)

**English-lexified**

1. Antiguan and Barbudan
2. Aukan
3. Bahamian (closer to the North American varieties than those further south)
4. Belizean
5. Grenadian
6. Guyanese
7. Jamaican (including Maroon Spirit Language, or MSL)
8. Kwinti
9. Samaná
10. Sranan
11. Tobagonian
12. Trinidadian
13. Turks and Caicos
14. Vincentian
15. Virgin Islander

*Note:* The Sea Islands and Afro-Seminole of North America, and San Andrés Islander, Limón, Panamian and Nicaraguan (English creoles of Central America) could also be included. The definition of some varieties, namely, Barbadian (Bajan), Saint-Martin English/Creole – and possibly Trinidadian English/Creole – is still controversial for some linguists. Maroon Spirit Language (MSL), possibly the earliest form of Jamaican, is almost extinct.

**French-lexified**

1. Guadeloupean (and northern Dominican)
2. Guianese (related Amazonian varieties should also be included)
3. Haitian
4. Martiniquan (including Twinidadyen, Grenadian and Venezuelan)
5. St Barth
6. St Lucian and southern Dominican

(Amazonian varieties should also be included, since their origin is West Indian. Some of *Ethnologue*'s categorizations need to be updated.)

**Iberian-lexified**

1. Papiamentu

**Dutch-lexified**

1. Berbice Dutch (recently extinct)

# Standard(ized) Varieties of Official and National Heritage Languages

In total, more than one hundred languages of the Americas have official and/or national status.[7] Together these languages represent almost 10 per cent of the thousand-plus languages of the Americas. Many of these languages with official or national status, particularly the indigenous languages, are still merely national symbols and do not yet fully function at official levels. Compare this to the European Union, with twenty-three fully functional national and official languages out of a total of 239 surviving indigenous European languages, also almost 10 per cent. In the Americas, however, in practice it is European-born non-indigenous languages that continue to function as both official and national languages.

In the Caribbean, six of the seventy surviving languages function in an official capacity. These include Ayisyen/Haitian and Papiamentu, two Caribbean-born languages officialized in 1987 and 2003 respectively, and represent less than 3 per cent of all Caribbean languages, including those originating in Europe. They are listed here in the order of greatest numbers of users to fewest:

- Spanish: twenty-two million speakers in the three territories of the Greater Antilles, Belize and the ABC islands – Aruba, Bonaire and Curaçao
- Haitian, or Ayisyen: more than nine million speakers in Haiti[8]
- English: more than six million speakers in twenty territories, mostly in Caribbean Community (CARICOM) territories and also in Puerto Rico and Sint Maarten
- French: fewer than two million speakers in four territories, including St Barth and Saint-Martin
- Dutch: about half a million speakers in seven territories
- Papiamentu: spoken in Aruba and the Netherlands Antilles

What is known as the English-speaking or anglophone Caribbean might be more usefully described as the English-official Caribbean, that is, areas of the Caribbean in which English functions as an official language but not necessarily as a mother tongue or a vernacular variety used in unofficial and informal contexts (Alleyne 1985). The same applies to the French-speaking or francophone Caribbean and the Dutch-speaking Caribbean, which is even more complex. The Spanish-speaking Caribbean differs, since no creole language varieties are known to exist in these territories (except perhaps Colombia; see below for discussion); it may be referred to as either hispanophone or Spanish-official. Publicly positive attitudes largely favour the official European-born languages, particularly in formal contexts and particularly the non-Caribbean(ized) varieties of these languages. Even Caribbean varieties of European languages, some of which have been spoken in the Caribbean for three to five hundred years, have been subject to internal and international discrimination.

In certain domains, the layman (formally educated or otherwise) has tended to ignore and undervalue both indigenous and creole languages and their users, even if that layman is a native speaker herself. This is so even when covertly positive attitudes towards the indigenous and creole languages do exist. Although Ayisyen and Papiamentu are official languages, they have yet to find complete acceptance among all members of their respective communities. In reaction to this situation, most theoretical Caribbean(ist) linguists have focused largely on creole languages and have been pioneers in the recognition and study of their Afro/Euro origins, development, structure, documentation and analysis (see Alleyne 1980). These linguists, among others, have demonstrated that the term *brokenness* applies neither to the structure of these languages nor to their users, nor to the continuity of their social and linguistic history. Conversely, many scholars have opted not to study the official languages – both their standard(ized) and non-standard(ized) varieties – in the Caribbean context, running the risk of reverse discrimination and leaving the field open to erroneous analysis. Figure 9.2 shows the distribution of official Caribbean languages according to numbers of users, while figure 9.3

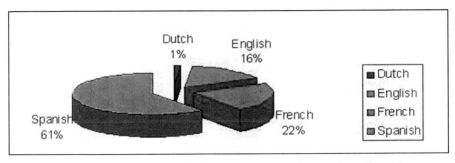

**Figure 9.2** Distribution of official Caribbean languages by number of speakers

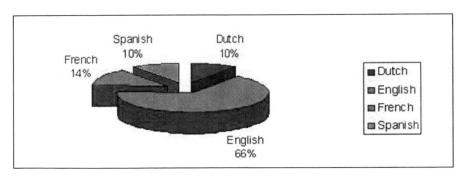

**Figure 9.3** Distribution of Caribbean territories according to official language

shows the distribution of Caribbean territories according to official language.

Language situations of the Caribbean are, like most language situations around the world, quite complex. It is actually difficult to say who is monolingual, monodialectal, bilingual, bidialectal, and so on, in the strictest of terms. In the English- and French-official Caribbean in particular, four language varieties also co-exist (cf. Roberts 2007):

1. standard varieties of official Indo-European languages (often referred to as acrolects or acrolectal varieties[9]);
2. non-standard, vernacular varieties of those European languages, some of which have been called creoles by some, purely on the basis of their Caribbean geographical origins and locations versus their origins and structure;
3. standard varieties of creole languages (Haitian and Papiamentu); and
4. English-lexicon and French-lexicon creoles (with "mesolectal" and "basilectal" varieties).

While creole languages and standardized dialects of European languages are quite different from one another in aspects of phonology and grammar, they each have a number of features that overlap with historic (archaic) and modern non-standardized varieties. The latter have been relatively poorly studied up to the present, at least for English-based varieties, if not for the French-based ones (see Chaudenson 1979).

With regard to native and heritage Caribbean varieties of English, many are at least as old as Early Modern English of the sixteenth to eighteenth centuries, predating varieties of English Creole. This period in the history of English (1500–1700) saw the emergence and standardization of Modern English and its codification by way of grammars and dictionaries, and it also coincides with the English colonization of the Caribbean. Caribbean varieties of English have in fact been spoken natively and written in the region for more than four hundred years, from the early to mid-seventeenth century, although political independence came to the Caribbean only in the mid-twentieth century. Political independence has never been necessarily concomitant with linguistic and literary independence. Caribbean varieties of English, however, can be considered minority vernacular languages in the region.

Contrary to the statements of some scholars on the historical status of Caribbean Englishes, these varieties are not and never have been among the "new Englishes" of the so-called Third Diaspora (cf. Kachru, Kachru and Nelson 2006). Such statements reflect historical inaccuracies. The speakers of English in those "Third Diaspora" countries of Asia, Africa, Europe and South America were and are native speakers of other languages; they were colonized by Britain two centuries after the Caribbean and North America were. As an example of one European-born language, English has been in unbroken continuous usage in certain territories since colonization. The Caribbean was, in fact, the crucible of and in the vanguard of European colonization (some say "civilization") of the Americas (see Roberts 2009).

According to Crystal (1997), Caribbean varieties of English belong to the "inner circle" of English. They have been distinct from modern British English for a long time, some for as long as (or longer than) American English has been distinct from British English. Antiguan and Barbadian English, for example, may have contributed to the development of some varieties of southern US English (Alleyne and Fraser 1989). Others are older than New Zealand English (which is not considered a "new English"), while others are not quite as old. More than four centuries later, the varieties of English in standard use in the Caribbean are separate national varieties, whether formally standardized or not, differing from each other and from non-Caribbean varieties mainly at the levels of phonology (accent) and lexicon (vocabulary). Much descriptive study remains to be done in this area, as well as more language development in the area of prescriptive standardization. At the orthographic level, traditional Commonwealth spelling is still officially preferred and practised throughout CARICOM countries, although personal practice may vary widely because of the influence of high-status and easily accessible North American literature and software.

## Heritage Creole Languages

The very term *creole* has been called into question by linguists such as Alleyne and DeGraff, both of whom have also questioned the view of creoles as exceptional and unique varieties. This is a matter not easily resolved. Using *creole* in the sense of contact languages that are lexically dependent on another language but grammatically independent (Ian Robertson, personal communication), there are almost as many creole languages as there are islands and territories, and possibly more. Much depends on the definition and delineation of different dialects of the creoles. The criterion for counting these varieties as separate entities is usually political (nationality) rather than linguistic (mutual intelligibility). This is also the case for many other languages around the world. One such example is Serbo-Croatian, counted as one language in former Yugoslavia and now counted as more than two varieties, with more than one orthography. The issue of the relatedness of creole language varieties is a matter of ongoing investigation among Caribbean(ist) linguists. Caribbean creole languages include French-lexified varieties, such as Haitian Kreyòl and St Lucian Kwéyòl; Iberian-lexified Papiamentu; English-lexified varieties, such as Antiguan Creole, Belizean Kriol, Jamaican (Creole/Patois), Guyanese

Creolese and Vincentian Creole; and Dutch-lexified Berbice Dutch (now extinct).

In the insular Hispanic Caribbean, unlike the non-Hispanic territories, no known creole languages are spoken. (Palenquero is spoken in the continental Caribbean, namely in Colombia.) French-lexicon creoles (called Patois in many anglophone territories) are spoken in seven insular territories and four continental territories. The former include Dominica, Grenada, Guadeloupe, Haiti, Martinique and St Lucia, all former French territories, and Trinidad. Although Trinidad was not politically colonized by France, it was socioculturally influenced by the French and French Creoles.[10] The four continental territories include French Guiana, Brazil (the state of Amapá), the United States (the state of Louisiana) and Venezuela (two states, through contact with Lesser and some Greater Antilleans). Guyana also has a number of immigrant French Creole-speaking communities of St Lucian origin. International Creole Day – Jounen Kwéyòl Entennasyonal, or Jounen Kwéyòl Toutpatou Asou Latè – began in St Lucia in 1981, and it has been celebrated annually on 28 October since 1983.

For many people in the English-official Caribbean, a variety of English Creole has mother-tongue status and no variety of English (standard or non-standard) functions as the vernacular. Many English Creole speakers, however, may be actively or passively competent in English to varying degrees, and they may therefore be classified as bilinguals or varilinguals (Youssef 1996), or bidialectal, if the Creole variety is closer to English.

Creole varieties are usually still identified by the term *creole*, at least by scholars. The adjectival name of the country is often best suited to designate the so-called creole variety, for example, *Jamaican* (Allsopp 2006). This would be preferred instead of the plethora of terms such as *Jamaican Creole, Jamaican Creole English* or *Jamaican English Creole, Jamaican English-Lexicon Creole, Jamaican English-Lexified Creole, Jamaican English-Lexifier Creole, Jamaican English-Based Creole, Jamaican Patois, Jamaican Patwa*, and so on. This is not an unusual situation, as the naming of languages is largely a political (not a linguistic) problem all around the world.

A name such as *Guyanese English* refers to the English variety (usually standard) of that territory, not to the creole language. National names are problematic in a country such as Trinidad and Tobago, which has two separate territories in its national name and no fewer than three creole languages: Trinidadian French Creole (TFC, or Twinidadyen), Trinidadian English Creole (TrEC, or Trinidadian) and Tobagonian English Creole (TobEC, or Tobagonian). Suriname, on the other hand, has several "creole" languages, each one with its own name and with no reference to the country's name or the term *creole*.

## Extinct and Dying Heritage Languages

Almost two hundred of the languages of the Americas are considered endangered, including four endangered or nearly extinct languages of the Caribbean, all of which may soon join the 170 already-known-to-be-extinct languages. The insular Caribbean archipelago has been described as a linguistic graveyard (Alleyne 2004). As a result of the early extinction of many Amerindian communities, along with long-standing intolerance towards multilingualism in small nation-states, all or most other non-European languages have disappeared. This attitude developed during post-Columbian colonial times. Some creole languages, at least one sign language (Jamaican Country Sign) and most immigrant languages are facing decline and ultimate disappearance. The continental circum-Caribbean and the rest of the Americas face similar issues and challenges, especially with respect to increasingly small and threatened Amerindian communities.

In an effort to recognize and help with the preservation of dying languages, UNESCO established 2008 as the International Year of Languages. International Mother Language Day (IMLD), proclaimed by the General Conference of UNESCO in November 1999, has been observed yearly since February 2000 to promote linguistic and cultural diversity and multilingualism. This initiative emerged from international recognition of Language Movement Day, which has been commemorated in Bangladesh since 1952. Further, the Universal Declaration of Linguistic Rights (known as the Barcelona Declaration) has been in existence since 1996. Until recently, however, this declaration has largely escaped the notice of the Caribbean and its policy-makers: issues of language rights have been ignored in the classroom and the courtroom alike.

The post-emancipation heritage languages that still survive to varying degrees are Bhojpuri (also known as Hindi or Caribbean Hindustani in Trinidad and Suriname), Javanese, Hakka and Yoruba. There were also several Amerindian, European, African, Asian and Caribbean creole languages, many of which are no longer spoken in the region. Some have disappeared altogether, such as Taíno and Island Carib, Yao and other indigenous Amerindian languages (Taylor 1977; see Devonish 2010).[11] Other languages have also all but disappeared in the Caribbean, including colonial European languages such as Danish; African languages such as Ewe-Fon, Hausa and Kikongo; creole languages such as Negerhollands and Skepi Dutch Creole (both Dutch-lexified); and nineteenth-century immigrant languages such as Bengali, Tamil, Telugu, Mandarin, Cantonese, Portuguese, German and Arabic. Of the latter group, German (Plautdietsch,[12] or Mennonite German) continues to be spoken in Belize. Most of these languages, such as Portuguese and Arabic, and to a lesser extent Bhojpuri in Trinidad, are obsolescent and are slowly but surely disappearing, although there has been fresh twentieth- and twenty-first-century input into the Arabic and Chinese communities of Trinidad, for example (cf. Robertson 2010). The majority of their remaining speakers are elderly, bilingual and fluent speakers of their country's official national and vernacular languages. None has young native speakers being born into surviving ethnolinguistic communities, however strongly their lexical influence may persist in creoles and in regional varieties of Dutch, English, French or Spanish.

Two linguistic communities of the Caribbean have been selected by UNESCO as "Masterpieces of the Oral and Intangible Heritage of Humanity". These are the Garífuna of Belize, Guatemala, Honduras and Nicaragua (language, dance and music, proclaimed in 2001) and the Maroons of Moore Town, Jamaica (proclaimed in 2003). In Moore Town, two aspects of the "oral and intangible heritage of humanity" include Kromanti language and culture and the dying English-lexified creole, Maroon spirit language (MSL), which is used only as a second language, or L2. These groups are also on the Representative List of the Intangible Cultural Heritage of Humanity (UNESCO 2008). In the face of the ongoing and, no doubt, permanent destruction of the original (pre- and post-Columbian) linguistic ecology of the Caribbean, the region's endangered languages deserve to be studied, documented and preserved.

## Caribbean(ist) Linguists

Since the nineteenth century, Caribbean languages have attracted a great deal of formal attention, possibly beginning with the work of Trinidadian John Jacob Thomas, in his 1869 *Theory and Practice of Creole Grammar*. Other linguists – Caribbean-born, Caribbean-educated, working in the Caribbean or with a lifelong interest in the Caribbean – have continued to investigate and publish extensively on Caribbean languages. With increasing attention being given to the role and development of language in Caribbean education systems, there have been scholarly contributions to both theoretical and applied linguistics, in the following broad categories:

* language history;
* research into language structure and language contact;
* dictionaries (including onomastics) and grammars, with standardization of vernacular varieties;
* language planning and language policy-making;
* language teaching (Carrington 1976; Craig 1999), including teaching of and in creole languages and language education policies;
* literary linguistics;

- Bible translation;
- speech-language pathology; and
- forensic linguistics.

In support of language study, professional societies convene regularly and publish the findings of their scholars. These include the Society for Caribbean Linguistics, founded in Trinidad and Tobago in 1972 and attached to the University of the West Indies, and Groupe d'études et de recherches en espace créolophone et francophone (now part of the Centre de recherches interdisciplinaires en langues, lettres, arts et sciences humaines), attached to the Université des Antilles et de la Guyane. SIL International (formerly the Summer Institute of Linguistics) has also been active in the Caribbean region, particularly in Belize, St Lucia and Suriname. This latter organization is dedicated to language-based development, and its linguists have assisted in the production of grammars, literacy materials, heritage stories and vernacular Bible translations. The Society for Pidgin and Creole Linguistics, which emerged out of the Society for Caribbean Linguistics in 1988 in the Bahamas and is currently based at the University of the West Indies, Mona, also has an interest in Caribbean languages, but only the creole and pidgin languages.

The research concerns of Caribbean(ist) linguists and linguistics include Caribbean languages of all origins and eras, including indigenous Amerindian languages from the pre-Columbian era and languages of the colonial era, including European, African and Asian to Caribbean creole languages. Several scholars are now moving into the study and documentation of a number of living heritage Caribbean languages, as well as the revitalization of endangered heritage languages. Appendix 9.1 provides a sample list of linguists whose research and publications focus chiefly on languages of the Caribbean. Note that some of these linguists (marked with an asterisk) have studied more than one language grouping.

## Conclusion

Caribbean(ist) linguists have been engaged in analysing and documenting the linguistic heritage of the Caribbean for several decades, many pioneering work in hitherto neglected languages and language situations. These linguistic studies have an immediate application to formal education, language and language education policies, legal issues, sustainable ongoing language and culture development, communication, issues of identity, heritage and ethnicity, nation-building, discrimination and language revitalization. To understand human language as an integral and inseparable part of human culture is to begin to understand human beings and issues of social and cultural identity. This is the work of the linguist in the Caribbean and beyond.

**Appendix 9.1** Some Caribbean(ist) Linguists

| Amerindian Languages | Bhojpuri | Danish | Dutch Creole | English Creole | French Creole | Spanish and Portuguese, including Papiamentu | Yoruba |
|---|---|---|---|---|---|---|---|
| W. Ahlbrinck | A.L. Bosch | Christian Georg Andreas Oldendorp | Silvia Kouwenberg★ | Michael Aceto | Mervyn C. Alleyne★ | Avril Bryan★ | Maureen Warner-Lewis★ |
| Sophie Alby | Surendra Kumar Gambhir | | Ian Robertson★ | Richard Allsopp | Gertrud Aub-Buscher | Marta Dijkhoff | |
| John Peter Bennett | Peggy Mohan | | Robin Sabino | Jacques Arends | Jean Bernabé | Kemlin M. Chin Laurence | |
| A. Biet | Savitri Ram-bissoon Sperl | | | Beryl Bailey | Anngegret Bollée | John Lipski | |
| K.M. Boven | | | | Philip Baker | Lawrence D. Carrington★ | Sylvia Moodie-Kublalsingh | |
| Raymond Breton | | | | Rawwida Baksh-Soodeen | Jean Casimir | David Ortiz | |
| Eliane Camargo | | | | Derek Bickerton | Robert Chaudenson | Yolanda Rivera | |
| Eithne B. Carlin | | | | Frederic G. Cassidy | Pauline Christie★ | | |
| André Cauty | | | | Vincent Cooper | Serge Colot | | |
| Hendrik Courtz | | | | Dennis Craig | Suzanne Comhaire-Sylvain | | |
| Michel Davoust | | | | David De Camp | Raphaël Confiant | | |
| Claudius Henricus de Goeje | | | | Hubert Devonish | Robert Damoiseau | | |
| Sybille de Pury Toumi | | | | Walter Edwards★ | Michel DeGraff | | |
| Janette Forte | | | | Geneviève Escure★ | Yves Dejean | | |
| Laurence Goury | | | | Nicholas Faraclas | David Frank | | |

**Appendix 9.1** Some Caribbean(ist) Linguists (*cont'd*)

| Amerindian Languages | Bhojpuri | Danish | Dutch Creole | English Creole | French Creole | Spanish and Portuguese, including Papiamentu | Yoruba |
|---|---|---|---|---|---|---|---|
| Berend J. Hoff | | | | Kean Gibson★ | László Göbl-Galdí | | |
| Jean-Michel Hoppan | | | | Robert Hall★ | Ralph Ludwig | | |
| Jean La Rose | | | | Ian Hancock★ | Guy Hazaël-Massieux | | |
| Michel Launey | | | | Merle Hodge | Marie-Christine Hazaël-Massieux | | |
| Isabelle Léglise | | | | John Holm | Claire Lefebvre | | |
| Melinda Maxwell | | | | George Huttar★ | Hazel Simmons-McDonald | | |
| Sérgio Meira de Santa Cruz Oliveira | | | | Winford James | Salikoko Mufwene★ | | |
| Jorge Carlos Mosonyi | | | | Ronald Kephart | Hector Poullet | | |
| Marie-France Patte | | | | Barbara Lalla | Pradel Pompilus | | |
| Willem J.A. Pet | | | | Robert B. LePage | Marguerite Saint-Jacques Fauquenoy | | |
| Francesc Queixalós | | | | Bettina Migge★ | Auguste de Saint-Quentin | | |
| Odile Renault-Lescure | | | | Susanne Mühleisen | John Jacob Thomas | | |
| Douglas Taylor★ | | | | Peter Patrick | Pascal Vaillant | | |
| Peter van Baarle | | | | Velma Pollard | Albert Valdman | | |
| Marta Viada | | | | John E. Reinecke | Addison van Name★ | | |

| Amerindian Languages | Bhojpuri | Danish | Dutch Creole | English Creole | French Creole | Spanish and Portuguese, including Papiamentu | Yoruba |
|---|---|---|---|---|---|---|---|
| | | | | John Rickford | Pierre Vernet | | |
| | | | | Peter Roberts★ | | | |
| | | | | Kathryn Shields-Brodber | | | |
| | | | | Jack Sidnell | | | |
| | | | | Alma Simounet | | | |
| | | | | Denis Solomon★ | | | |
| | | | | Jeffrey Williams | | | |
| | | | | Lise Winer★ | | | |
| | | | | Donald C. Winford | | | |
| | | | | Valerie Youssef | | | |

*Note:* The symbol ★ denotes researchers who have studied more than one language grouping.

## Notes

1. The entire area, in fact, is in need of its own linguistic encyclopaedia. The term and region *Caribbean* properly defines the northern Caribbean littoral of Venezuela and Colombia, as well as Panama, Costa Rica, Nicaragua, Honduras and Guatemala, but it has been restricted here to include only the archipelago, Belize and the Guyanas. Full inclusion of these territories would bring the language total up to at least 245, including the 70 mentioned and 178 others.

2. Many of these 177 coastal Caribbean languages are connected to those in Belize and the Guyanas, and also Mexico, El Salvador, Brazil and beyond. The largest number of living Carib and Arawakan languages in any one country today is actually found in Brazil, with at least 12 and 17, respectively. These language families are closely associated with the history of the Caribbean archipelago, which is named after the Caribs. The 177 living languages include 71 that are related to those in the archipelago and the four rimland territories, divided among

the following families: Arawakan (10), Carib (10), Mayan (49) and Tupí (2). The following 106 languages belong to 21 other language families/groupings: Arutani-Sape (2), Barbacoan (3), Chibchan (22), Choco (8), Guahiban (5), Maku (3), Misumalpan (3), Quechuan (3), Salivan (3), Tucanoan (16), Witototan (5), Yanomam (3), language isolates (8), unclassified (5), mixed (1), sign languages (8), English Creole (4), French Creole (1), Spanish Creole (1), Chinese (1) and Indo-Aryan (1). Only a few of these languages are dying; 33 others are already extinct.

3. The Amerindian languages of the Caribbean continent include the following. Those marked with an asterisk are nearly extinct; the letter codes refer to the countries where the languages are spoken, namely, Belize (B), French Guiana (FG), Guyana (G) and Suriname (S). **Arawakan:** Arawak/Lokono (FG, G, S), Atorada (G), Garifuna (B), Mapidian (G), Mawayana (G), Palikúr (FG) and Wapishana (G). **Carib:** Akawaio (G), Akurio★ (S), Carib (FG, G, S), Macushi (G), Patamona (G), Pemon (G), Sikiana★ (S), Trió (S), Waiwai (G) and Wayana (FG, S). **Tupí:** Emerillon (FG) and Wayampi (FG). **Isolate:** Warao (G). **Mayan:** Kekchí, Mopán Maya and Yucatán Maya (all in Belize). Many of the South American languages here are spoken in both Brazil and Venezuela, and many of the Central American are spoken in El Salvador, Guatemala and Mexico.

4. Some linguists use the term *creole* to refer only to people. For those linguists who use it to refer to language(s), the lowercase *creole* is recommended usage for the common noun (and also adjective) referring to the language type in general (either as a socio-historical reference to its genesis or as a typological term, if such is possible). The uppercase *Creole* should be used for the name of a specific language. Thus, "In the study of creole languages . . ." or "This is a characteristic feature of many creoles", but "In Haitian Creole . . ." or "In Haiti, Creole is . . .". The geographic definition of a "creole" language is still highly problematic: there are almost as many as there are national entities. Suriname alone has at least four English-lexified creole languages: Aukan (Ndyuka, also comprising the Aluku, or Boni, and Paramaccan dialects), Kwinti, Saramaccan and Sranan Tongo. The other eleven English-based creoles are Antiguan and Barbudan, Bahamian, Belizean, Grenadian, Guyanese, Jamaican (also spoken in Central America), Tobagonian, Trinidadian, Turks and Caicos, Vincentian and Virgin Islander. (Immigrant varieties now based in North and Central America are not included here.) The six French-lexicon creole varieties include Dominican, French Guianese (including Karipuna and Galibi-Marwono), Guadeloupean (including Marie Galante, St Barth and northern Dominican), Haitian, Martiniquan (including Trinidadian and Grenadian), and St Lucian (Louisianan is not included here). Papiamentu is Iberian-lexified and Berbice Dutch Creole is Dutch-lexified.

5. It is not yet certain when the first indigenous sign language in the Caribbean appeared in deaf communities. The sign languages indigenous to the Caribbean have been subject to influences from indigenous varieties from elsewhere, for example, British Sign Language (BSL), American Sign Language (ASL), French Sign Language (LSF) in French Guiana and Martinique, and Sign Language of the Netherlands (SLN or more usually NGT) in Suriname, Aruba and

Curaçao (cf. Parks and Williams 2011), brought in by missionaries and others. Extensive research into Caribbean sign linguistics is currently underway at the University of the West Indies, Mona and St Augustine campuses, in particular.

6. Other useful charts would include population statistics and maps with identification of border situations.

7. These include Spanish, Portuguese, English, French, Ayisyen, Dutch, Papiamentu, Paraguayan Guaraní, Bolivian Quechua, Bolivian Aymará, Ecuadorean Cofan and all of Peru's ninety-three languages.

8. With regard to French Creole, Ayisyen or Haitian alone is spoken by more than nine million persons in Haiti, plus more overseas, and related varieties are spoken by more than two million people in nine other countries in the Americas, including the United States and Brazil. French-lexified creole varieties are also spoken in Indian Ocean territories; there are similarities but also many differences.

9. In the Caribbean the acrolect is not an external or foreign variety; it is a local or national variety of the prestige language and is not "creolized".

10. French Creoles are Caribbean-born descendants of French-born colonists and immigrants (called *békés* in the French West Indies).

11. However, Arawak languages closely related to Taíno and Island Carib continue to be spoken in Honduras, Belize, Guatemala and Nicaragua (Garífuna, or Black Carib), Venezuela (Paraujano) and Colombia (Wayuu).

12. According to Ethnologue.com (Lewis 2009), the Low Saxon branch of the West Germanic family tree includes ten related languages, Plautdietsch (pdt) being one and Plattdüütsch (nds), or Low German or Low Saxon, which is spoken in Germany and the Netherlands, being another. Plautdietsch is the formal name for Low German/Mennonite German (spoken in Belize, Bolivia, Brazil, Canada, Costa Rica, Germany, Kazakhstan, Mexico, Paraguay and the United States). This is the specific variety brought to the Americas by German Mennonites 150 years ago, and it is not the same as either Plattdüütsch or Plattdeutsch.

## References

Alleyne, M.C. 1980. *Comparative Afro-American*. Ann Arbor, MI: Karoma Press.

———. 1985. *A Linguistic Perspective on the Caribbean*. Washington, DC: Latin American Program, Woodrow Wilson International Center for Scholars.

———. 2004. "Indigenous Languages in the Caribbean". *Society for Caribbean Linguistics Popular Paper* 3 (June).

Alleyne, W., and H. Fraser. 1989. *Barbados-Carolina Connection*. London: Macmillan Caribbean.

Allsopp, S.R.R. 1996. *Dictionary of Caribbean English Usage*. Oxford: Oxford University Press.

———. 2006. "The Case for Afrogenesis". *Society for Caribbean Linguistics Occasional Paper* 33 (July).

Carrington, L. 1976. "Determining Language Education Policy in Caribbean Sociolinguistic Complexes". *International Journal of the Sociology of Language* 8: 27–43.

Chaudenson, R. 1979. *Les creoles français*. Paris: Fernand Nathan.

Craig, D. 1999. *Teaching Language and Literacy: Policies and Procedures for Vernacular Situations*. Georgetown, DC: Education and Development Services.

Crystal, D. 1997. *Cambridge Encyclopedia of the English Language*. Cambridge: Cambridge University Press.

DeGraff, M. 2005. "Linguists' Most Dangerous Myth: The Fallacy of Creole Exceptionalism". *Language in Society* 34: 533–91. http://web.mit.edu/linguistics/people/faculty/degraff/degraff2005fallacy_of_creole_exceptionalism.pdf(accessed November 2010).

Devonish, H.S. 2010. "The Language Heritage of the Caribbean: Linguistic Genocide and Resistance". *Glossa: An Ambilingual Interdisciplinary Journal* 5, no. 1 (March). http://bibliotecavirtualut.suagm.edu/Glossa2/Journal/march2010/The_Language_heritage_of_%20the_caribbean%20.pdf (accessed November 2010).

Kachru, B., Y. Kachru and C. Nelson, eds. 2006. *Handbook of World Englishes*. Oxford: Wiley-Blackwell.

Lewis, M.P., ed. 2009. *Ethnologue: Languages of the World*. 16th ed. Dallas: SIL International. http://www.ethnologue.com/ (accessed May 2010).

Parks, E., and H. Williams. *Sociolinguistic Profiles of Twenty-four Deaf Communities in the Americas*. SIL Electronic Survey Report. Dallas: SIL International, 2011. http://www.sil.org/silesr/2011/silesr2011-036.pdf (accessed 15 January 2012).

Roberts, P.A. 2007. *West Indians and Their Language*. 2nd ed. Cambridge: Cambridge University Press.

———. 2009. *The Roots of Caribbean Identity: Language, Race and Ecology*. Cambridge: Cambridge University Press.

Robertson, I.E. 2010. Language and Language Education Policy. Seamless Education Project Unit. Port of Spain: Government of the Republic of Trinidad and Tobago, Ministry of Education. http://www.moe.gov.tt/national_consultation_primaryschool/ROBERTSON%20I%202010%20Language%20and%20Language%20Education%20Policy.pdf (accessed November 2010).

Taylor, D. 1977. *Languages of the West Indies*. Baltimore: Johns Hopkins University Press.

UNESCO. 2003. *UNESCO Redbook of Endangered Languages*. http://www.tooyoo.l.u-tokyo.ac.jp/archive/RedBook/index.html (accessed May 2009).

———. 2008. "Safeguarding Intangible Cultural Heritage". http://www.unesco.org/culture/ich/ (accessed May 2009).

Universal Declaration of Linguistic Rights Follow-Up Committee. 1998. Universal Declaration of Linguistic Rights. http://www.linguistic-declaration.org/versions/angles.pdf (accessed May 2009).

Valdés, G. 2000. "The Teaching of Heritage Languages: An Introduction for Slavic-Teaching Professionals". In *The Learning and Teaching of Slavic Languages and Cultures*, edited by Olga Kagan and Benjamin Rifkin, 375–403. Bloomington, IN: Slavica.

Van Deusen-Scholl, N. 2003. "Toward a Definition of Heritage Language: Sociopolitical and Pedagogical Considerations". *Journal of Language, Identity and Education* 2, no. 3 (July): 211–30.

Winer, L. 2005. "Indic Lexicon in the English/Creole of Trinidad". *New West Indian Guide* 79, nos. 1–2: 7–30.

Youssef, V. 1996. "Varilingualism: The Competence Underlying Codemixing in Trinidad and Tobago". *Journal of Pidgin and Creole Languages* 11, no. 1: 1–22.

**10.**

# The Role of Libraries in Preserving and Disseminating Caribbean Heritage Materials

## A Case Study of the Alma Jordan Library at the University of the West Indies, St Augustine, Trinidad and Tobago

GERARD H. ROGERS

*Generally, most libraries operate within the context of perceived and clearly artic-ulated roles and functions. These roles and functions are usually associated with the type, size and location of the library in question, and are often expressed as mission statements. In many cases, however, this articulated role is expanded to meet a perceived societal need that has been either inadequately fulfilled or totally unfulfilled in the respective countries/communities in which these libraries exist. In the context of the preservation of cultural heritage materials, this is often the case. In some countries, neither a national library nor a national archive exists. In others, both of these institutions exist but are inadequately equipped to acquire, preserve and facilitate access to heritage materials on a sustained basis. In either scenario, a surrogate library not charged with this responsibility often rises to the occasion and fills the gap. In Trinidad and Tobago, both of these scenarios existed for quite some time, and it is against this backdrop that the librarians at the Alma Jordan Library of the University of the West Indies, St Augustine campus, in Trinidad and Tobago took on the major responsibilities of acquiring, preserving and providing controlled access to Caribbean heritage materials.*

## Introduction

The notion of the library as primarily a repository and a physical location for the dissemination of knowledge and information has been a dominant one for quite some time. As a result of this, librarians came to be considered as gate-keepers of the world's intellectual patrimony. The traditional roles associated with the selection, acquisition, housing and lending of materials attributed to libraries and librarians eventually progressed to include secondary roles. For example, some librarians went on to become reference and subject specialists, specialist cataloguers or systems librarians. Other hybrid roles, such as systems/multimedia librarian or subject specialist/cataloguer would also be thrust upon them, adding to their repertoire of duties. It is not surprising, therefore, that libraries which had developed considerable expertise in collecting, storing and disseminating information could easily subsume the additional responsibility of guardianship of cultural heritage, where necessary. Two of the major roles associated with this task are the preservation and the restoration of historical and cultural heritage materials.

The concept of cultural heritage is a fairly extensive one which has been revised and expanded over time. Consequently, over the years many definitions have been developed in an attempt to encompass cultural heritage in its totality. The definition by UNESCO (2008) aptly illustrates this point: "The term 'cultural heritage' encompasses several main categories of heritage". Under this definition, cultural heritage is broadly divided into two categories: tangible and intangible. For the purposes of this chapter, cultural heritage materials will therefore be taken to mean materials in various formats, such as books, manuscripts, microforms, multimedia, drawings, paintings and other works of art, and other, miscellaneous realia that relate directly or indirectly to the tangible, intangible and natural heritage of Trinidad and Tobago and the wider Caribbean.

## Brief Historical Overview

An examination of the histories of both the public library system of Trinidad and Tobago and the Alma Jordan Library of the University of the West Indies at St Augustine, Trinidad and Tobago (hereafter referred to as UWI StA Library; see figure 10.1), would reveal a certain degree of commonality with regard to the key roles played by these institutions in actively and aggressively collecting and preserving Caribbean heritage materials. In direct response to the lack of a national library and the inadequacies of the National Archives, both these libraries stepped in to fill the gap, and in so doing significantly expanded their primary roles. The main libraries on the sister campuses of the University of the West Indies, in Jamaica (Mona campus) and Barbados (Cave Hill campus), did not need to have the mandate to stand in the gap as national library surrogates, because their respective national library services were established in 1948 and 1906 respectively, much earlier than that of

**Figure 10.1** The Alma Jordan Library (front view), University of the West Indies, St Augustine (courtesy Marketing and Communications Office, University of the West Indies, St Augustine)

Trinidad and Tobago. This chapter, therefore, specifically addresses the contribution of UWI StA Library to the preservation and promotion of unique Caribbean heritage materials. It will briefly examine the library's purposeful, sustained initiatives aimed at enhancing and promoting cultural heritage.

The Caribbean heritage materials at UWI StA Library are a significant component of its West Indiana and Special Collections Division. From the early days of its existence, library administrators recognized the role which its special collections needed to play in the development of Trinidad and Tobago and the wider Caribbean region. In developing societies, the university library is seen as having a role in identifying and preserving a nation's culture through collection development activities, which result in the acquisition of significant collections of national literature and publications (Gakobo 1985, 411). Thus, from its early beginnings, UWI StA Library demonstrated its commitment to collection and preservation of the historical and cultural heritage of the region. The library's recorded history notes that it inherited as its nucleus a small but significant collection of historical texts and manuscripts belonging to the Historical Society of Trinidad and Tobago (Rouse-Jones 2003).

Over the years, infrastructural and other developments continued at both the university and regional levels. Notable gifts continued to be given to the library, numerically and qualitatively propelling West Indiana and Special Collections forward while at the same time incrementally adjusting its role and function. Along with this significant growth came some deliberate strategic planning, as evidenced by two ten-year development plans. Both of these plans took into consideration the need to develop the services of UWI StA Library in the context of the lack of a national library service (Rouse-Jones 2003, 2–3).

During the same developmental period, Caribbean studies featured increasingly in the academic curriculum of the University of the West Indies. As a result, the need for related support materials, and room to house them, became even more critical for UWI StA Library. Consequently, after three expansions to its physical structure from 1970 to 1997, the facilities dedicated to the West Indiana and Special Collections Division were expanded and upgraded. The library continued to acquire additional Caribbean heritage materials – both as gifts and as planned direct purchases. In the process, the papers of a variety of notable Caribbean figures were acquired. These include Derek Walcott, C.L.R. James, Samuel Selvon, Kathleen Warner (Aunty Kay), Eric Roach and so on. Altogether, UWI StA Library currently holds ninety-two special collections, most of which are available for consultation. In addition, bibliographic details can be accessed through the online public access catalogue (OPAC) or the UWI StA Library's website.

**Figure 10.2** Students using the Alma Jordan Library facilities (courtesy Marketing and Communications Office, University of the West Indies, St Augustine)

## The Role of the Library in Preserving Cultural Heritage

In a very passionate keynote address given at the Sofia 2006 conference "Globalization, Digitization, Access and Preservation of Cultural Heritage", Michael Gorman opined that " 'cultural heritage' is a widely used term that refers to all testaments to cultures past and present. It embraces all the works and thoughts made manifest of humans and human societies and groups" (Gorman 2006, 14). In linking this definition to the work of libraries and librarians, Gorman notes that the definition is expanding over time to include new categories. He cites the following significant statement made by UNESCO's Cultural Section to illustrate his point:

> Having at one time referred exclusively to the monumental remains of cultures, heritage as a concept has gradually come to include new categories such as the intangible, ethnographic, or industrial heritage. . . . This is due to the fact that closer attention is now being paid to humankind, the dramatic arts, languages and traditional music, as well as to the informational, spiritual and philosophical systems upon which creations are based. The concept of heritage in our time accordingly is an open one, reflecting living culture every bit as much as that of the past. (Gorman 2006, 15)

In highlighting the vital role of libraries in cultural heritage, the UNESCO Cultural Section goes on to add that "the documentary heritage deposited in libraries and archives constitutes a major part of the collective memory and reflects the diversity of languages, peoples and cultures" (Gorman 2006, 15). In this context, the urgency of preservation and access are underscored, since UNESCO points out that a considerable proportion of the world's documentary heritage is disappearing because of what have been considered "natural causes", such as exposure to heat, light, dust, dampness and acidity. This urgent concern is one of the key driving forces behind UNESCO's Memory of the World project.

To understand the full extent of the current role played by UWI StA Library in the preservation of historical and cultural heritage, one must examine this role against the backdrop of the perceived role of a national library, as well as the articulated role of UWI StA Library itself. As previously noted regarding the glaring need for a national library in a developing country and region, UWI StA Library's management recognized quite early on that it could not simply play the traditional role of an academic library. It would inevitably need to perform some of the functions of a national library. What, then, are the functions of a national library? Cheryl Ann Peltier's very useful survey of the literature as it relates to the Caribbean experience is worthy of mention (Peltier 1995, 20). She draws attention to Humphreys' classic work, which outlines some of the typical functions of a national library and categorizes them broadly as essential, desirable and inessential (Peltier 1995, 17–19). The functions that Humphreys deems *essential* are as follows:

- assembling the outstanding and central collection of a nation's literature,
- providing a centre for legal deposit,
- covering foreign literature,
- publishing the national bibliography,
- acting as the national bibliographic information centre,
- publishing catalogues and
- organizing exhibitions.

Among the functions considered *desirable* are interlibrary lending, collecting and preserving manuscripts and conducting research on library techniques. In the *inessential* category Humphreys lists providing an international exchange service, distributing duplicates, training professionals, providing books for the blind, and assisting other libraries in library techniques and library planning.

Stephney Ferguson, who examines Humphreys' categorization in the Caribbean context, essentially concurs with it but names the third category "convenient" rather than inessential (Peltier 1995, 20–21). Additionally, Ferguson inserts a critical element into the *desirable* category, that of maintaining an oral history and folklore tradition. Peltier, commenting on the significance of Ferguson's inclusion of the oral tradition, cites the work of Cliff Lashley, who mentions the importance of the traditional African folk culture of West Indian societies, which is known to be basically oral in nature. Lashley also notes that the challenge facing librarians is "to identify, collect, preserve and transmit in its variety, form and content 'the total racial memory' especially as it is representative of the African folk traditional culture" (Peltier 1995, 20).

How, then, does UWI StA Library measure up against these standards? As far as both Humphreys' and Ferguson's criteria are concerned, the library performs six of the seven functions considered essential, three of the four functions considered desirable and all of the six functions considered inessential (or convenient) for a national library.

As previously stated, the West Indiana Collection was established at an early stage of the UWI StA Library's development and was initially enhanced and expanded by way of valuable gifts. It should be noted, however, that the expansion of this valuable collection was also due to the deliberate, sustained collection development efforts of the librarians, who exhaustively acquired West Indiana materials published locally, regionally and internationally. This effort included commendable initiatives to fill gaps via repatriation of valuable West Indian documents from institutions overseas, where possible (Rouse-Jones 2003, 5–8).

In addition to establishing the West Indiana and Special Collections, the librarians at UWI StA Library also created comprehensive collection development policies which incorporated guidelines for receipt and treatment of gifts and special collections. Valuable tools and products to assist in scholarly exploitation of the collection were also created. *Derek Walcott: A Bibliography of Published Poems with Dates of Publication and Variant Versions, 1944–1979*; *Gimme Room to Sing: Calypsoes of the Mighty Sparrow, 1958–1993: A Discography*; *A Guide to the Raymond Quevedo Manuscript Collection at the Main Library, the University of the West Indies, St Augustine*; *Spoken History: A Guide to the Materials Collected by the Oral and Pictorial Records Programme (OPReP)*; and *V.S. Naipaul: A Selective Bibliography with Annotations, 1957–1987* are just a few of the tools and products created by librarians at UWI StA.

Displays and exhibitions are regularly organized by the librarians for various purposes, including book launches and the promotion of heritage materials. Some special collections have been digitized to facilitate wider access to their valuable contents. Finally, in terms of meeting the essential criteria for national libraries, UWI StA Library was involved in legal deposits from as early as 1962, right up to 1998, when the legislation was changed. As a legal depository, UWI StA Library was required to receive and securely house one copy of all locally produced copyrighted materials.

Concerning the functions listed in the desirable category for national libraries, UWI StA Library has a long-established interlibrary lending service. This library also has an excellent tradition of manuscript collection and preservation, enabled by the fact that it has an in-house bindery, as well as professional and support staff members specially trained in conservation and preservation techniques. With regard to research, members of the library staff have conducted research on different aspects of library work over the years. UWI StA Library has also fulfilled all the functions listed as inessential criteria for a national library. This includes provision of electronic assistive technologies in 2006 for use by blind and other differently abled students.

In addition to all the criteria listed above, leadership has also been cited as a quality that national libraries are mandated to display (Peltier 1995, 23–24). In a national library setting, such leadership would be manifested in areas such as advocacy, training, provision of services to government departments, membership in statutory bodies and so on. UWI StA Library has been involved in all these areas over the course of its existence, with librarians holding key positions on the executives of local associations, such as the Library Association of Trinidad and Tobago and the Trinidad and Tobago Memory of the World Committee, and membership on statutory boards such as the National Library and Information Systems Authority (NALIS). They have also been actively involved in regional bodies such as the Association of

Caribbean Universities and Regional Institutional Libraries (ACURIL) and the Association of Caribbean Higher Education Administrators (ACHEA).

Apart from the list of functional areas mentioned above, the UWI StA Library has partnered with Erica Williams-Connell, daughter of the late Dr Eric Williams, Trinidad and Tobago's first prime minister, in an historic and significant initiative. Mrs Williams-Connell, to whom the personal library and papers of her father were bequeathed, has partnered with the UWI StA Library in setting up the Eric Williams Memorial Collection. This innovative project is geared towards providing management, preservation and access to a significant collection that is undeniably linked to the national patrimony of Trinidad and Tobago, and the wider Caribbean. This collection, which is on deposit at UWI StA Library, comprises a research library, an archive and a mini museum. The museum depicts aspects of both the life and work of Trinidad and Tobago's first prime minister and includes a reproduction of his study. As part of the agreement with Mrs Williams-Connell, the museum is required to be open to the general public on a regular basis – twice per month on Saturdays for the general public, and on every Friday by prior appointment for schoolchildren. The hosting of this collection and in particular the museum, which transcends the traditional role of a university library, underscores the commitment of UWI StA Library to the preservation and promotion of heritage materials.

In the case of the Williams Collection, and, indeed, all the other special collections held at the library, steps have been taken to ensure that they are kept under strict conditions that enhance their preservation and ensure their protection. Additionally, three collections – the Derek Walcott, Eric Williams Memorial and C.L.R. James collections – have been added to the UNESCO International Memory of the World Register, reflecting their value and importance and the need for them to be preserved for humanity (UNESCO 2005, 5).

Also worthy of special emphasis with regard to the preservation of cultural heritage is UWI StA Library's Oral and Pictorial Records Programme (OPReP). This programme was established in 1981 and is geared towards documentation and preservation of cultural heritage via oral traditions. The programme makes extensive use of audio recordings to document interviews with persons considered to be significant cultural and historical icons in Trinidad and Tobago society, or who would have witnessed important historical events. The unique knowledge, experience and historical memory of these individuals would be lost to posterity without this initiative of the library. (The pictorial aspect of the programme involves collecting photographs of historical importance.) The importance of preserving the oral tradition cannot be overemphasized. Historians are acutely aware that oral sources can provide accounts of events that differ from those found in newspapers and official documents. The oral history data collected by UWI StA Library have the potential to fill information gaps and preserve historical facts about the heritage of Caribbean people.

Librarians who work in the West Indiana and Special Collections Division can develop an in-depth knowledge of the content of the collections through the inventory process. This makes them invaluable allies in exploiting the potential of these collections, which are generally underutilized (Rouse-Jones 2007).

## Use of New Technologies to Disseminate Heritage Materials

The librarians at UWI StA Library are actively exploring the use of new technologies to disseminate information regarding our unique heritage collections. Use of these technologies has also been actively promoted by the library. For example, information regarding most of the library's special collections is currently available via its web page (http://www.mainlib.uwi.tt/divisions/wi/collsp/specialcoll.htm). Additionally, the audiotapes associated with the OPReP collection have all been digitized, and work continues on digitization of the transcripts in order to make the latter accessible online. While the records are generally not yet available to the public, a few samples have been made available for testing purposes. It is anticipated that prior to further dissemination, these records will first be entered into UWISpace, the institutional repository which has been set up by the library's recently constituted Digitization Unit. An OPReP newsletter is also produced, in both hard copy and electronic forms; current and back issues of this newsletter are available online (http://www.mainlib.uwi.tt/divisions/wi/collmain/oprepweb/oprephome.htm).

CARINDEX is another example of a research tool developed by librarians at UWI StA Library specifically to promote Caribbean heritage materials in multiple disciplines. It is an index to the contents of West Indian journals published in the Caribbean region. Its coverage also includes theses, papers presented at conferences, collections of working papers and so on, in the social sciences, humanities, science and technology. This index of more than eight thousand records is soon to be made available to scholars via the Alma Jordan Library's Web portal.

## Conclusions

S.B. Bandara (1979) has made a case for dual-functioning libraries, that is to say, public or academic libraries which also take on the role of national libraries. He points out that at least two features of a university library make it a suitable candidate for this dual purpose. These, he notes, are the "comprehensive collection of national imprints" and "the well-developed organizational framework within which to discharge its duties" (Bandara 1979, 127–43). The UWI StA Library's exhaustive collection of national imprints and its high level of internal organization both support Bandara's assertion, particularly since it has already been performing this dual function unofficially. It should be noted, however, that when a university library takes on the dual role of both university and national library for the short, medium or long term, sustainability becomes a major concern. Functional dichotomy can be a real challenge to dual purpose if a balance is not struck between preservation and access, between primary and adopted roles, and between primary and secondary stakeholders.

A dual-purpose library may face certain challenges that are directly and indirectly associated with its adopted role. These challenges can manifest themselves as space constraints, funding shortfalls, human resource inadequacies or administrative issues. National libraries, like university libraries, are usually "purpose built", and this purpose is reflected in their structural design. A university library that adopts the role of national library over time will probably need to renovate or expand its physical plant in order to effectively carry out a dual function for which it was not originally designed and built. This will especially be likely if the library takes on the task of legal deposits or also acts as a depository for a prolific organization such as the United Nations, as was the case with UWI StA Library. This library, which has grappled with space limitations for decades, has undergone three major structural expansions in order to deal with increases in its book stock, including its special collections. And in addition to increasing the size of its collection, the library has also had to cater to a burgeoning student population that requires additional amenities.

Libraries with growing collections of rare books and manuscripts may also need to create environmentally friendly spaces – such as temperature- and humidity-controlled rooms and acid-free conditions – in order to properly house these valuable, fragile materials. Additionally, if a library decides to preserve a special heritage collection via digitization, microfilming or some other archival process, a considerable amount of funding is required to cover the cost of related staff training and acquisition of specialized equipment. The necessary funding may not be readily available from the existing budget, and therefore will have to be sourced separately. Commitment to the role of a dual-functioning library can also lead to some administrative challenges which may require special concessions or functional accommodations. Such concessions might include introducing special opening hours or times of access, instituting unique or additional security arrangements, installing and using specialized equipment, or even conducting special training for library staff. All these administrative challenges have been encountered by UWI StA Library, and they have been dealt with effectively. The most poignant example of this is public access to and administrative management of the Eric Williams Memorial Collection, which the library has successfully undertaken.

The UWI StA Library can be considered a hybrid or dual-purpose library. Its articulated mission statement and envisioned role is that of an academic library, an institution dedicated to the support of teaching, learning and research at the University of the West Indies, St Augustine campus. However, despite the establishment of a national library in Trinidad and Tobago – NALIS – in 1998, UWI StA Library remains committed to sustaining its deliberate, purposeful efforts at collecting and preserving unique heritage materials of the Caribbean region. The products and services offered by this library attest to this enduring commitment, which definitely transcends the traditional role of an academic library and makes inroads into the realm of a national library – and even a national museum. This role is a vital one in the Caribbean setting.

## References

Bandara, S. 1979. "Can University Libraries Serve the National Library Role in Developing Countries?" *Libri* 29: 127–43.

Gakobo, J. 1985. "The Role of the Special Collection in the Academic Library". *International Library Review* 17: 405–18.

Gorman, Michael. 2006. "The Wrong Path and the Right Path: The Role of Libraries in Access to, and Preservation of, Cultural Heritage". Keynote address presented at "Globalization, Digitization, Access and Preservation of Cultural Heritage" conference, Sofia, Bulgaria, 8 November.

Peltier, Cheryl. 1995. "Meeting the Challenge. Public Libraries as National Libraries: The Caribbean Experience". MLS thesis, University of the West Indies, Mona, Jamaica.

Rouse-Jones, Margaret D. 2003. *Guide to Manuscripts, Special Collections and Other Research Resources for Caribbean Studies at the University of the West Indies, St Augustine Campus Libraries.* St Augustine: University of the West Indies.

———. 2007. "Unveiling Hidden Treasures: An Exploration of Our Caribbean Heritage". Inaugural professorial lecture presented at University of the West Indies, St Augustine campus, Trinidad, 29 November.

UNESCO. 2005. *Safeguarding the Documentary Heritage of Humanity.* Paris: UNESCO.

———. 2008. "Definition of Cultural Heritage". http://portal.unesco.org/culture/en/ev.php-URL_ID=34050&URL_DO=DO_PRINTPAGE&URL_SECTION=201.html (accessed 1 June 2010).

# 11.

# Postcard Images of Trinidad

## The Michael Goldberg Collection

LORRAINE M. NERO

*The images of twentieth-century Trinidad and Tobago are captured on more than five thousand postcards held in the Michael Goldberg Collection at the Alma Jordan Library of the University of the West Indies, St Augustine campus. These cards are source material which can be used to write about aspects of the social and cultural history of the islands. This chapter explores the contents of this collection while highlighting significant pieces and occasions documented on the cards. The accompanying index to the collection provides a subject overview of the contents, and may also be used as an access point for locating these images in the repository.*

## Introduction

The Alma Jordan Library, University of the West Indies, St Augustine campus, is a repository for rare books, manuscripts and special collections covering a wide array of subjects. The collections capture some of the intellectual output of outstanding Caribbean academics; among these holdings are the papers and library of Dr Eric Williams, first prime minister of Trinidad and Tobago, C.L.R. James, pan-Africanist, historian and novelist, and Derek Walcott, writer and Nobel laureate. These three prestigious collections have been placed on the international register of the UNESCO Memory of the World programme.[1] In 2003 the University of the West Indies purchased another significant holding, the Michael Goldberg Collection, which contains albums of postcards primarily from Trinidad and Tobago, as well as souvenir booklets, photographs and glass lantern slides. This collection was accumulated over a ten-year period while Dr Goldberg resided in the United States. A dentist by profession since 1972, Dr Goldberg first visited Trinidad and Tobago in 1976.

His interest in the islands led to his eventual migration from the United States to Trinidad and Tobago in 1998; he worked as a dentist with the non-governmental organization Servol, at its Forres Park Life Centre in south Trinidad.[2] This chapter explores the contents of this collection and highlights significant pieces and occasions documented on the cards. The index to the entire collection, presented in appendix 11.1, provides a subject overview of the contents and may be used as an access point for locating these images in the repository.

## The Goldberg Collection

The Goldberg Collection, which has over five thousand postcards, came to the attention of university officials when an article appeared in a Trinidadian newspaper, the *Sunday Newsday* of 29 April 2002, titled "American Offers Treasured TT Historical Collection for Sale". According to a local publisher, Gerry Besson, who was cited in the article, "these photographs are extremely useful public records . . . since they really show the way we are, and are the only surviving records of what the city and countryside looked like". The significance of the items has also been acknowledged by historian Brinsley Samaroo, who in correspondence dated 15 January 2003 stated that the Goldberg Collection is a "treasure-trove for all those who are interested in our heritage: anthropologists, sociologists, historians and other persons". He encouraged the University of the West Indies to pursue its acquisition.

Once the collection had been purchased, the curators arranged it into seventeen thematic folders and created a temporary hand list to help patrons navigate the resource. The hand list provides general descriptions of each folder and identifies subject areas which have large numbers of cards associated with them. In cases where only one or two cards existed for a particular subject – for example, the 1903 Water Riots in Port of Spain – the list omits mention of that subject. Thus the library team recognized that use of the collection would be better maximized through a more detailed subject index, a marketing strategy for the collection and digitization of the images, which are in the public domain and therefore free from copyright restrictions. The subject index in appendix 11.1 was specifically devised to facilitate cataloguing of the digitized images, since several of the terms refer to Trinidad and Tobago and as such are not available in other thesauri.

Visually, many items in the collection may appear to be duplicates. However, postcards with more or less similar images may be different for several reasons: colour treatment (hand-painted, tinted or black-and-white), captions or lack of captions, divided or undivided backs, handwritten notes, postmarks, textures, borders, or different publishers. The collection spans a period from the late nineteenth century to the close of the twentieth century, with the earliest postmarked card dated 15 July 1893. This card has no image but bears the text "Inland Post Card" and a halfpenny stamp of Queen Victoria of England.

The postmaster-general of Trinidad issued the first set of official prepaid postcards in 1879, to be circulated inland and to foreign destinations at rates of one and one and a half pence respectively. These early postcards were all of a similar design, with a chain-linked motif around the border of the address side. In order to have cards ready for circulation, a run of approximately one thousand cards was printed in Trinidad. This first set of cards, in addition to the chain-linked border, has "Trinidad" stencilled on the address side along with "Foreign" or "Inland Postcard" (Marriot, Medlicott and Ramkissoon 2010). Subsequent cards were issued by the Postal Union later in 1879, and these are identified with the additional text "Postal Union – Union Postale Universelle". The Goldberg Collection contains an unused example of the 1879 Postal Union card.

In September 1894 the British Post Office sponsored legislation for privately produced picture postcards in Britain (Chin Aleong 2003). However, it is unclear when the first image appeared on a postcard of Trinidad and Tobago, although the collection has image postcards dated as early as 1900. Reproduced here (see figure 11.1) is a card dated 31 January 1901, which has a montage of three Port of Spain scenes: an aerial view of Port of Spain, the Colonial Hospital and the Botanical Gardens. It should be noted that the scenes on this 1901 card are in colour. When compared with the bulk of items from around this period, this coloured card may be considered unusual, as many of the early cards in the collection are in black-and-white.

As photography grew in popularity in the early twentieth century, black-and-white prints became the norm and also became the source of many postcard images. Most of the subject areas identified in the collection's index have at least one black-and-white postcard associated with them. In several instances the publishers invested in having the cards enhanced

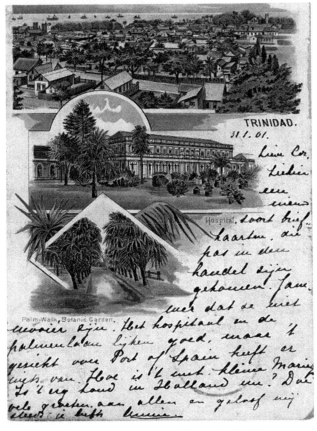

Figure 11.1 Early colour postcard from the Goldberg Collection (courtesy Alma Jordan Library, University of the West Indies, St Augustine)

through hand-painting. It is therefore not unusual to see the same image on several cards but with different colour treatments. This is particularly obvious in the series of cards on East Indian women.

## Historical and Cultural Value of Postcards

Postcards serve an educational function by informing people about other cultures, and this trend has been followed in Trinidad and Tobago. The East Indian community in Trinidad and Tobago provided ample subject material for publishers of cards, and the images seemed to have satisfied consumers, who were fascinated by exotic places and people. Hence, among the early cards (circa 1902 and onwards) are more than one hundred postcards featuring East Indians. The majority of these items present women dressed in traditional wear and adorned with jewellery, particularly large nose rings and hand bracelets, while the most popular images of the East Indian male are of pundits or pundits with their emblems of worship.

On a card postmarked 7 January 1908 sent to Mrs J.W. Hancock, titled "Coolie Woman", the sender echoes the fascination with the exotic appearance of these women by writing: "Lots of picturesque East Indian coolies here note the nose ring" (Folder 1, 8A). In some cases the producer of the card provided a caption as a narrative to the image. The narrative oftentimes indicates the female's ethnicity or profession, for example, cake vendor, milk vendor, fruit seller. There are instances where an image is duplicated but carries different narratives. Figures 11.2 and 11.3 are examples of East Indian women; the subject is the same but the cards are different because they have different colour treatments and captions. One caption reads: "A very rich Coolie Woman – Trinidad B.W.I.", and the other states: "Trinidad. A wealthy Coolie Woman awaiting her husband." On a third iteration of this card, dated 23 February 1907, the sender has erased the word *Coolie* and replaced it with *Indian,* showing that use of the term had already become a source of contestation in the society. This variation of an image also occurs with other subject series.

Many of the photographs from the series of East Indian women and men were taken in photo studios. They were produced by both local and foreign publishers such as Waterman, Stephens and Company, Y de Lima, Muir, and Marshall and Sons, as well as by Peco, a popular publisher from Canada. This means that the final image marketed on the cards as representing the East Indian community would have had several factors affecting its output, such as the circumstances that led to the model's sitting for the photograph, the publisher's thematic emphasis, the editorial process (tinting and other enhancements) and consumer demands. Consequently postcard images

A very rich Coolie Woman.    Trinidad B. W. I.

Trinidad. A wealthy Coolie Woman awaiting her husband.

**Figure 11.2** Image of an East Indian woman
(courtesy Alma Jordan Library, University of the
West Indies, St Augustine)

**Figure 11.3** Image of an East Indian woman
(courtesy Alma Jordan Library, University of the
West Indies, St Augustine)

should be considered along with other sources of documentary heritage when
conducting historical research.

The images of the East Indian community which were captured outside
the studio environment highlight the social life and customs of this group.
In some cases the males are caught in activities such as snake-charming and
smoking, women in the process of food preparation, and both men
and women working in the fields. This community may have been a source
of great fascination because they were a relatively new introduction to the cultural landscape of the West Indies. In Trinidad and Tobago the East Indians
came in 1845, a mere twenty-four years before development of the first
prepaid postcard, which Anzovin and Podell (2000) indicate was issued in
Austria on 1 October 1869.

The Goldberg Collection contains a series of postcards which were used
by business owners to market their products. Based on the variety and number
of these items, one can infer that entrepreneurs took advantage of the popu-

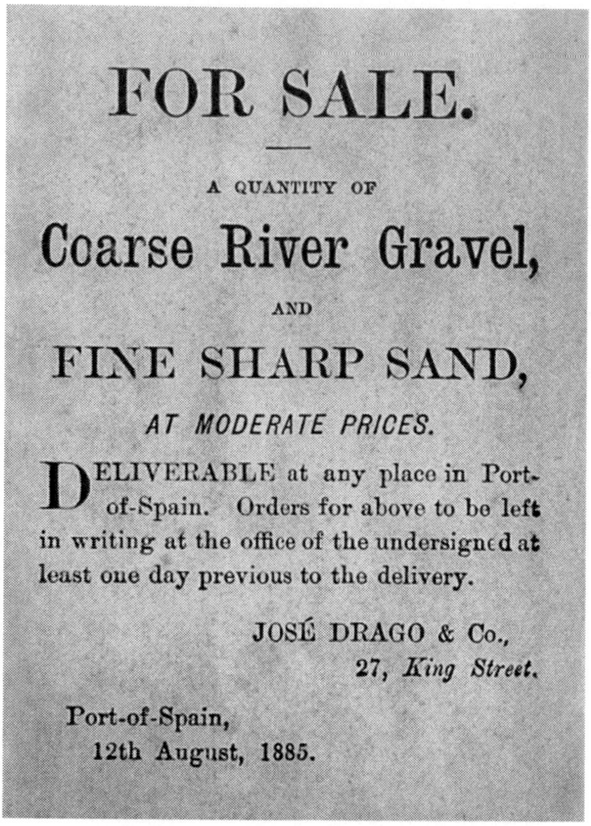

**FOR SALE.**

—

A QUANTITY OF

# Coarse River Gravel,

AND

# FINE SHARP SAND,

## AT MODERATE PRICES.

DELIVERABLE at any place in Port-of-Spain. Orders for above to be left in writing at the office of the undersigned at least one day previous to the delivery.

JOSÉ DRAGO & Co.,
27, *King Street.*

Port-of-Spain,
12th August, 1885.

**Figure 11.4** Nineteenth-century advertising card (courtesy Alma Jordan Library, University of the West Indies, St Augustine)

larity of this medium to reach their clientele. An early example of this type of card is dated 12 August 1885 and advertises the sale of river gravel and sharp sand by Jose Drago and Company (see figure 11.4). Whereas the Jose Drago card is without an image, the bulk of these local business cards are decorated with scenes from Trinidad and Tobago, particularly scenes of Port of Spain and environs, as well as the Pitch Lake. In February 1913 several Trinidadian businessmen patronized inauguration of an air "drop-box" service. Among the companies that participated was the Smith Brothers and Company's Bonanza store, which provided five hundred advertising postcards that included five with a one-dollar claim prize (Wike 1999). The novelty of the airplane drop-box was used as a marketing strategy on another Bonanza card, which had the text "Pay a Flying Visit to the Bonanza" plus images of an aircraft, Brighton Pier, La Brea and Port of Spain.

The use of visual media to create and reinforce stereotypes has been explored in communication studies. The widespread distribution of image postcards contributed to shaping perceptions along with other media such as film. One would also like to suggest that through the images businessmen selected to feature on the cards, and to a lesser extent the text on the cards, the idea was perpetuated of Trinidad and Tobago as an urban centre in the Caribbean. In one such example, the publishing firm Canning and Company advertised its regional significance with the caption: "The largest grocery store in the West Indies" (Folder 3, 87A). Postcards sponsored by business interests outside Trinidad and Tobago are fewer in number in the collection, making it difficult to compare the choices of images by internal and external agencies. However, hoteliers and cruise liners, such as the Hamburg American Line, operating in the Caribbean used postcards as convenient media to lure travellers to the West Indies.

The images on postcards are themselves significant in capturing the visual history of places, but the messages written on the cards add another cultural dimension to the artefacts by giving historical accounts and revealing social attitudes. Such is the case with the cards of the Queen's Park Hotel. The Queen's Park Hotel, which was located next to the Queen's Park Savannah, according to a card caption, was opened to the public on 16 June 1895. It once enjoyed the distinction of being the largest hotel in the West Indies, a piece of information which is stencilled across several cards. The owners of the hotel advertised the facility as the "Riviera of the Caribbean" and provided potential clients with glimpses of the interior such as the dining room, ballroom and kitchen. An unknown writer indicates on the back of a card that it is "The leading hotel of the island where the Duke and Duchess stayed on their honeymoon tour of the island. It faces the Queen's Park Savannah, the island's largest recreation ground" (Folder 7, 64C).

In some cases these Queen's Park Hotel cards were used to impress the intended recipient; writers highlighted the favourable "crowd", the walks to the botanical garden or dining at the restaurant. However, one writer hints at the social environment which may have existed at the time by inscribing on the card: "hotel for white folks only" (Folder 7, 78B). Seemingly casual messages can therefore point researchers towards exploring other cultural dimensions of a subject.

The collection of card images for the Queen's Park Hotel also shows the changing façade of the building and its surroundings. The one-storey structure went through several changes and received a dramatic facelift in the late 1950s, when it became a four-storey building. After the hotel ceased operations, the interior was repurposed for business offices. These Queen's Park Hotel cards can be viewed in conjunction with postcards showing the Queen's Park Savannah to get an appreciation of how the landscape around this savannah changed over the century.

"Every West Indian (British) seems to have a 'Savannah' which really means a large park" – so writes an individual on a 1923 postcard which has an image of a cow grazing in the Queen's Park Savannah (Folder 2, 82A). The writer captures in this general comment some of the significance which the Savannah holds as a cultural and national space for residents of Trinidad and Tobago. It is the largest public recreational park in Port of Spain; the 120-hectare property has been the site of many sporting and social activities, including horse racing and the annual parade of Carnival bands. Since 2006 the Queen's Park Savannah has undergone physical changes with the addition of new structures. Hence these postcards become even more valuable as pictorial records of the evolving landscape.

Some highlights of the postcards in the Savannah series include tramcars, coconut vendors, cattle grazing and horse racing. Writers on some of the cards provide titbits on the use and scenery of the park, for example, "I used to walk and ride here, a good deal many is the gallop I have had across this park"

(Folder7, 80A); "Car line goes around the park – distance 3 miles" (Folder 2, 78A); and "Across the street from the hotel is a large savannah with flowering trees etc. . . ." (Folder 7, 90B). Because of its continuous use and the variety of activities held in the Savannah, the space has become the unofficial national park of Trinidad and Tobago. People have even written to newspaper editors recommending that the space be registered as one of UNESCO's World Heritage Sites (Mycoo 2010).

Surrounding the Savannah are several heritage buildings which have also been featured on postcards. Researchers interested in these buildings and the history of Trinidad and Tobago architecture can also benefit from this archive, as it provides a wide range of buildings constructed in both rural and urban areas. According to Douglas, the glory of the Trinidad-style architecture is in its houses, and he further suggests that their flamboyant and unique styles are reflected in the homes located in the suburbs of Port of Spain: Belmont, Woodbrook and St Clair (Douglas 1996). Representations of these homes from the colonial era are evident in the collection, particularly of the seven historical buildings adjacent to the Queen's Park Savannah. These seven mansions are collectively referred to as the Magnificent Seven – Queen's Royal College, Hayes Court, Roomor, Mille Fleurs, the Roman Catholic archbishop's house, White Hall and Stollmeyer's Castle – and they showcase the intricate and unique architectural features described by Douglas.

The homes of rural families were also photographed, and of special note are the images showing the different styles of tapia houses. A tapia house was made of earth and leaves and its style was influenced by different cultural groups within the Caribbean. There is one card showing the process of applying mortar to the structure (Folder 3, 7B). This series is indeed a complementary resource in tracing the evolution of this rural style of architecture.

The Goldberg Collection also highlights the changes to the city of Port of Spain and its suburbs. One of the prominent physical changes is seen in views of the harbour and lighthouse before the land reclamation project which resulted in extension of the city border. Images of several popular streets and squares are also available; among these is a series on Marine Square, which was renamed Independence Square in 1962 to commemorate the attainment of independence by Trinidad and Tobago. Some of the businesses that operated in Port of Spain during the period are either subject or background images and include firms such as Fogarty's, Millard's, Johnson and Johnson and the Colonial Bank.

The operations of important revenue-generating industries in Trinidad and Tobago outside of Port of Spain are also evident in the collection, particularly the asphalt, sugarcane and cocoa industries. In the early twentieth century, activities related to the asphalt industry occur on more than three hundred cards, including the Pitch Lake, the digging of pitch, processing, refining and shipping from the Brighton Pier. The earliest of these cards is postmarked 1903.

With development came changes to the environment throughout the two islands, and this is visually manifested in the collection. An image of the Churchill-Roosevelt Highway as a two-lane highway, with a single lane of traffic heading west and another heading east, is very valuable, since by 2008 this road had become a six-lane carriage highway. Also of note are a 1944 card showing the rudimentary structure of the monastery at Mount St Benedict and other cards which show the changes that occurred throughout the century. The San Fernando Hill is a landmark in southern Trinidad; it was once covered with lush vegetation, as shown by two postcard images taken before quarrying created the stark limestone hill shown on another card. Flora and fauna which are no longer commonplace can also be seen on the cards, such as massive trees with intricate root patterns, unique fruits and large insects. Popular with publishers among the flora selections were bamboo clumps, cannonball fruits and rope trees.

Postcards functioned as one of the media for photo journalism, informing the world of historic events and places. Within the collection there are two significant sets of cards which served this purpose: the Water Riots of 23 March 1903 and the appearance of a new island off the shore of Trinidad on 3 November 1911. The Water Riots occurred in Port of Spain when the citizenry were protesting plans to introduce a new water ordinance, which was intended to increase the water rates and reduce the water allocation per head. The riots began while the ordinance was being debated in the Legislative Council. One outcome was that several buildings in Port of Spain were destroyed, including the Red House, which functions as the seat of Parliament for Trinidad and Tobago. The postcards show crowds of people surrounding the Red House, the burning building and the shell of the burnt-out structure. These cards are postmarked 1903, demonstrating the speed with which they were produced and circulated.

The second series of cards deal with the mud volcano island which appeared in 1911 off the coast of Chatham, south Trinidad. The black-and-white photographs show the surface of the island. Throughout the modern history of Trinidad, this mud volcano has erupted on several occasions, creating an island which is eventually eroded by the sea. Appearances also occurred in 1928, 1964, 2001 and 2002, with the 1964 instance creating the largest known acreage for the island. The collection has images only of the 1911 appearance.

## Conclusion

The hobby of collecting postcards is referred to as deltiology, a word derived from the Greek word *deltion*, meaning an illustrated tablet or image (Brown 1995). The hobby provides an alternative for persons who are interested in travelling but are unable to do so. For persons who do travel it becomes a photographic record of the places they have been. The result is that postcard images of some places are more widely available than others. This resource has the unique trait of combining images and personal comments which can be used by researchers interested in the social life and customs of Trinidad and Tobago.

One would also like to point to other areas of research, such as the representation of children on postcards; the entertainment industry, including Carnival activities, entertainers and limbo dancing; and rural life. The collection has several cards which show scenes of places outside the major cities; these scenes often show rural and village life and some places that have since developed into urban spaces (for example, San Juan). A few cards highlight villages and other scenery in Tobago, but the majority of the collection is focused on Trinidad. (It is to be noted that other writers have published works on the postcards of some Caribbean islands; these have been included in the bibliography.)

The maintenance of visual archives is an important aspect of preserving Caribbean heritage. In the study of culture, where practitioners investigate various agencies which impact on a particular phenomenon, postcards can be good resources for images and in some cases written commentaries. The subject scope of the Michael Goldberg Collection is quite diverse, as is demonstrated by the index, but more important, it provides images of the social life and customs of Trinidad and Tobago throughout the twentieth century. Samples from the collection which have been digitized by the Alma Jordan Library at the University of the West Indies, St Augustine, are available in the institutional repository UWISpace.

**Appendix 11.1** Subject Index of the Michael Goldberg Collection

| Subject | Folder | Subject | Folder |
|---|---|---|---|
| Airports | 6 | Divers | 2 |
| American Embassy | 5, 6 | Down the Islands | |
| Anglican Bishop's residence | 3 | *See Islands, Trinidad* | |
| Animal drawn transport | 2 | East Indians | 1, 3 |
| Architecture | | Embassy buildings | 5, 6 |
| *See Buildings, Houses* | | Empire Theatre | 6 |
| Asphalt industry | 5 | Entertainers | 1, 2 |
| Badjohn | 1 | Fauna | 9, 14 |
| Balandra | 4, 11 | Fire Station, Port of Spain | 5 |
| Bananas | 11 | Fire Station, San Fernando | 5 |
| Banks | 5, 6 | Fishing | 11, 13 |
| Beaches | 11, 12, 13 | Flora | 8, 9 |
| Blue Basin | 13 | Food preparation | 2 |
| Bocas | | Foods | 14 |
| Botanical Gardens | 3,7, 9 | Fort George | 5 |
| Bridges | 13 | Fruits | 9, 10 |
| Brighton Pier | 4, 5 | Gaspar Grande | 3, 7, 12, 13 |
| Brunswick Square | 3 | Gasparee Caves | 4 |
| Buildings, Port of Spain | 6 | Goat racing | 2 |
| Businesses | 3 | Government buildings | 6 |
| Carnival | 2 | Governor's Residence | 6, 7 |
| Caroni river | 13, 14 | Gulf of Paria | 13, 14 |
| Carrera | 5, 12 | Hamburg American | |
| Caves | 4 | Cruise Line | 3, 14 |
| Cemeteries | 7 | Harbour, Port of Spain | 6, 13 |
| Chacachacare | 6, 12 | Harris Square | 3 |
| Chaguaramas | 11, 13, 14 | Hayes Court | 3 |
| Charcoal burners | 2 | Hosay | 14 |
| Children | 1 | Hospital, Port of Spain | 5 |
| Churches | 6 | Hospital, San Fernando | 5 |
| Churchill Roosevelt Highway | 3, 8 | Hotels | 6 |
| Clubs | 7, 8, 11 | Houses | 3 |
| Coblentz Avenue | 3 | Icacos | 1 |
| Cocoa | 10, 11 | Imperial College of Tropical | |
| Coconuts | 10 | Agriculture | 5, 6 |
| Cocorite | 11 | Islands, Trinidad *See also* | |
| Coffee | | *individual islands* | 12 |
| Columbus monument | 4 | Independence Square | 2, 5 |
| Creoles | 1 | La Basse | 14 |
| Crowds | 2 | Lady Chancellor Hill | 3 |

*Appendix 11.1 continues*

| Subject | Folder | Subject | Folder |
|---|---|---|---|
| Lepers | 1, 2, 4, 7, 12 | —Hart Street | 3 |
| Lighthouses | 6 | —South Quay | 3, 13 |
| Limbo dancers | 2, 13 | Port of Spain Stables | 3 |
| Logging | 2 | Public library | 6 |
| Macqueripe | 12 | Pundits | 1 |
| Manzanilla | 4 | Quarrying | 2 |
| Maps | 13, 14 | Queens Park Hotel | 3, 7 |
| Maracas | 4, 13 | Queens Park Savannah | 2, 3, 9 |
| Maracas Bay | 11 | Queens Royal College | 6 |
| Maraval | 2, 3, 4 | Railroads | 3 |
| Marine Square | 3 | Recipes | 14 |
| Markets | 2 | Red House | 6 |
| Mas (Carnival masquerade) | 2 | Reservoirs | 14 |
| Matura | 4 | Rivers | 13 |
| Mayaro | 2, 11 | Roads | 4 |
| Maypole | 1 | Rural life | 3, 4 |
| Memorial Park | 4 | Saddle Road | 3 |
| Men, East Indian | 1 | St. Anns | 3 |
| Minstrels | 2 | St. Clair | 3 |
| Mora | 3 | St. James | 3 |
| Mosques | 6, 7 | St. James Barracks | |
| Mt. St. Benedict | 2, 7 | *See Police Barracks* | |
| Mud volcanoes | 4 | St. Joseph | 3 |
| Mud Volcano Island | 12, 13 | St. Madeline | 6, 10 |
| Museums | 6 | Steelbands | 2 |
| Nelson Island | | St. Anns | 3 |
| North Coast | 3, 11, 12 | St. Clair | 3 |
| Northern Range | 5 | St. James | 3 |
| Oilfields | 4 | St. James Barracks | |
| Palo Seco | 4 | *See Police Barracks* | |
| Parks | | St. Joseph | 3 |
| Pitch Lake | 5 | St. Madeline | 6, 10 |
| Police | 1 | Salybia | 4 |
| Police Barracks, Port of Spain | 6 | San Fernando | 6 |
| Police Barracks, St. James | 6 | —Harris Promenade | 3, 4 |
| Port of Spain | 3 | —High Street | |
| —Aerial view | 5 | San Fernando | 6 |
| —Broadway | 3 | —Harris Promenade | 3, 4 |
| —Frederick Street | 3 | —High Street | 3 |
| —Hall of Justice | 6 | San Fernando Hill | 3, 4, 14 |

*Appendix 11.1 continues*

**Appendix 11.1** Subject Index of the Michael Goldberg Collection (*cont'd*)

| Subject | Folder | Subject | Folder |
|---|---|---|---|
| San Juan | 4 | **Tobago Index** | |
| Sangre Grande | 4 | | |
| Santa Cruz | 4, 5 | Administration building | 3 |
| Schools | 6 | Arnos Vale | 12 |
| Scouts | 1 | Bacolet | 4, 12 |
| Sea scenery | 13 | Beaches | 12 |
| Snake charming | 2 | Charlotteville | 12 |
| Social life | 2 | Churches | 6 |
| Southern Main Road | 4 | Coconut | 10 |
| Steelbands | 2 | Courland | 12 |
| Stollymeyer Castle | 6 | Crown Point | 12 |
| Sugarcane | 1, 2, 10 | Fort King George | 4, 12 |
| Sunsets | 4, 12 | Harbour | 12 |
| Tapia houses | 1, 2, 3 | Hillsborough | 12 |
| Temples | 6, 7 | Hotels | 7, 13 |
| Tobago | | Houses | 3 |
| Toco | 4 | Kings Bay | 12 |
| Town Hall, Port of Spain | 5 | Lambeau | |
| Town Hall, San Fernando | 5 | Little Tobago | 12 |
| Trams | 3 | Man of War Bay | 12 |
| Trinidad, French influence | 1 | Mt. Irvine | 12 |
| Urban life | 4 | Mt. St. George | 12 |
| Victoria Institute | 5, 6 | Parlatuvier | 12 |
| Waterfalls | 13 | Pembroke | 12 |
| Waterloo | 4 | Pigeon Point | 12 |
| Water Riots, 1903 | 6 | Rockly Bay | 12 |
| White Hall | 5 | Roxborough | 13 |
| Western Main Road | 4 | Rural life | 1, 12 |
| Women, Black | 1 | Scarborough | 3, 13 |
| Women, East Indian | 1 | Scarborough | 13 |
| Woodford Square | 3 | —Carrington Street | 4 |
| YMCA | 6 | —Castries Street | 4 |
| | | —Main Street | 3, 4 |
| | | School children | 1 |
| | | Speyside | 12 |

## Notes

1. The UNESCO Memory of the World programme was established in 1992 to pre-serve and disseminate valuable archival holdings worldwide. The international register lists some of the world's more treasured collections.
2. Biographical information for Dr Michael Goldberg was taken from the website of the Alma Jordan Library at the University of the West Indies' St Augustine campus, www.mainlib.uwi.tt (accessed 23 September 2010).

## References

Anzovin, Steven, and Janet Podell. 2000. *Famous First Facts, International Edition: A Record of First Happenings, Discoveries, and Inventions in World History*. New York: H.W. Wilson.

Brown, Donald R. 1995. "The Institute of American Deltiology: An Emerging Resource". In *Postcards in the Library: An Invaluable Resource*. New York: Haworth.

Chin Aleong, J. 2003. *The Picture Postcards of St Vincent and the Grenadines*. St Anns, Trinidad and Tobago: J. Chin Aleong.

Douglas, Robert. 1996. *Caribbean Heritage: Architecture of the Islands*. Trinidad and Tobago: Darkstream.

Marriot, John, Michael Medlicott and Reuben A. Ramkissoon. 2010. *Trinidad: A Philatelic History to 1913*. Alicante, Spain: British West Indies Study Circle and British Caribbean Philatelic Study Group.

Mycoo, Michelle. 2010. "Savannah as UNESCO World Heritage". Guardian Media. http://guardian.co.tt/commentary/letters/2010/09/18/savannah-unesco-world-heritage-site (accessed 23 September 2010).

Samaroo, Brinsley. 2003. Letter to campus librarian, University of the West Indies, St Augustine campus, 15 January.

Wike, R.G. 1999. *Airmails of Trinidad and Tobago*. Congleton: British West Indies Study Circle.

## Works on Caribbean Postcards

Barbados. 2005. *Postcards in the Collection of the National Library Service*. Bridgetown, Barbados: National Library Service.

Dickinson, Terence A. 2005. *British Guiana Picture Postcards*. Alicante, Spain: British West Indies Study Circle.

Gilmore, John. 1995. *Glimpses of Our Past: A Social History of the Caribbean in Postcards*. Kingston: Ian Randle.

Malone, Shelley Boyd. 1991. *Nostalgic Nassau: Picture Postcards, 1900–1940*. Nassau, Bahamas: Nassau Nostalgia.

Marriott, John B. 1963. *The Philatelic History of Trinidad to 1862*. N.p.: British West Indies Study Circle.

Sabga, Joseph Abdo. 2000. *A Journey of Memories: A Memorable Tour of Trinidad and Tobago Illustrated with Picture Postcards*. Trinidad and Tobago: J.A. Sabga.

*Scarborough, Tobago: Old Postcards*. 2004. Oxford: Jill Aizlewood . . . [et al.].

Zuill, Eldon. 2006. *Bermuda Postcards Revisited: Photographs of an Ever-Changing Landscape*. Hamilton, Bermuda: Print Link.

**Part 2.**

PHILANTHROPY

# 12.

# Audrey Layne Jeffers

## Key to Trinidadian Philanthropic and Social Service Heritage

INNETTE CAMBRIDGE

*The work of the native Caribbean woman Audrey Layne Jeffers and the Coterie of Social Workers of Trinidad and Tobago Inc. stands out among those engaged in the social development of the early twentieth century. Established in 1921, the Coterie developed practical blueprints for many post-independence social support services for Trinidad and Tobago. School feeding and early childhood care programmes, promotion of gender equity, innovative fundraising and various acts of charity have characterized the activities of the Coterie up to the current era. This chapter outlines the heritage of Audrey Jeffers and the Coterie of Social Workers as a forerunner to professional social work practice and the delivery of social services in Trinidad and Tobago.*

## Introduction

In Trinidad and Tobago, social services of the 1800s were organized by the Anglican and Roman Catholic churches. The leadership was dominated by colonial settlers who established residential institutions such as St Mary's Children's Home, St Dominic's, St Michael's Home for Boys and St Jude's Home for Girls. The Scottish philanthropist Bruce Stephens, Bishop Anstey from Bristol, England, and promoters of non-governmental organizations for child welfare and youth left their mark in the early part of the twentieth century.

Formal and structured responses for social welfare were limited. One example was the short-lived League of Social Welfare, which concentrated on regulating and developing social controls for prostitution, liquor abuse, dance-halls and cinemas. Established in 1921, the League was concerned with refor-matories, orphanages, the protection and employment of boys, girls' hostels and prison after-care; soldiers' and sailors' clubs also formed part of the agenda of the male- and expatriate-dominated organization. Other social serv-ice organizations in existence at the time included the Child Welfare League, the Society of St Vincent de Paul of the Roman Catholic Church[1] and Friendly Societies.[2] The Trinidad Field Naturalists, established as a non-governmental organization in 1891, pioneered environmental work during this period.

This situation was in contrast to what was occurring in other parts of the English colonial Caribbean where the state had a more active role in social welfare provision. Before 1900 the English Caribbean colonies had adapta-tions of the Elizabethan Poor Law (1602) for the free poor (Maxwell 2002, 13). Prior to 1834 these benefits would not have been applicable to the major-ity of the population, who were slaves. In Guyana a Poor Relief Act intro-duced in 1839 gave the central government full responsibility for poor relief in that colony (Danns and Scott 1989, 516). In Barbados the Poor Man's Board was set up in 1880 to provide casual relief and the Settlement of the Poor Act of 1897 placed destitute children in almshouses (Edmonds 1973, 229–48).

Bryan (2002, 23–31) details the situation in Jamaica, where both church and state were active in providing health, education and social welfare services for the population. The Anglicans and the Wesleyans established St Hilda's, St Hugh's, St Helena's, York Castle and Wesley High schools. In 1890 the Sis-ters of Mercy began Alpha, an orphanage and industrial school, St Claver's orphanage and St Mary's Industrial School. In 1916 the Roman Catholics founded St Joseph's Hospital. The Salvation Army established a home and school for the blind and men's and women's hostels; they also worked with discharged prisoners. By 1882 the London Charity Organisation Society had established the Kingston and Liguanea Charity Organisation Society, which aimed to eliminate begging and assist the deserving poor through casework.

Trinidad and Tobago did not have as many initiatives on the part of either church or state. The charity organisation societies that existed in Jamaica never developed in Trinidad, nor were there Poor Law almshouses as existed in Bar-bados. The shorter period of British colonization in Trinidad, compared to Jamaica and Barbados, prevented the development of British Poor Law insti-tutions and the pioneering social work of England of the 1800s. Indigenous social support systems of gayap, sousou[3] and family support characterized much of the social safety net of the time.

Within the Trinidadian context, the work of the native Caribbean woman

Audrey Layne Jeffers and the Coterie of Social Workers of Trinidad and Tobago Inc. stood out among initiatives in humanitarianism and social development of the era. Established on 30 April 1921, the Coterie developed practical examples for post-independence services of social support for Trinidad and Tobago. School feeding and early childhood care programmes, promotion of gender equity and various acts of charity have characterized the work of the Coterie up to the present time. The Coterie of Social Workers remains the best-known indigenous local social service to survive from the colonial era into the twenty-first century in Trinidad and Tobago.

Harvey (2001) notes that heritage studies help us to understand the production of identity, power and authority throughout society. An examination of the dominant power structure reveals that persons with the cultural capital to function within colonial society can influence its development. Given a situation of widespread poverty in Trinidad, there was a need for a social welfare response. However, expression of a response in colonial Trinidad had to conform to the dominant philanthropic and social welfare practices in the rest of the anglophone Caribbean. Understanding the heritage of Audrey Jeffers permits an appreciation of her ability to develop social service interventions in a British-dominated colonial era. This chapter outlines the work of Audrey Jeffers and the Coterie of Social Workers as forerunners of social services, voluntary community organizations and social work practice in Trinidad and Tobago by providing an appreciation of the Coterie as a heritage of voluntary social service in a Caribbean context. It also illustrates how the upper-middle-class Anglican heritage of the colonial era influenced the life of a woman whose contribution to Trinidad and Tobago society remains unique into the twenty-first century.

## The Background of Audrey Layne Jeffers

The vision and characteristics of the Coterie of Social Workers are directly linked to the childhood and youth experiences of Audrey Jeffers. Her identity and the authority she wielded in colonial Trinidadian society evolved not only from innate personality characteristics but also from the social environment in which she grew up. Audrey Jeffers (see figure 12.1), whose ancestors were from Barbados and Montserrat, was born on 12 February 1896.[4] Her status as the daughter of a wealthy lawyer with a "small island" heritage,[5] her formal and informal education, a childhood grounding in early-twentieth-century Anglicanism and a very good relationship with her parents predisposed her to take bold steps to develop a self-reliant social service organization capable of adapting to changing needs and evolving social circumstances.

Jeffers was born on Baden-Powell Street in Woodbrook, but national recog-

**Figure 12.1** Audrey Layne Jeffers

nition of her family home belongs to her Sweet Briar Road residence ("Briarsend") in St Clair, an upper-class residential area which serves as home to the Queen's Park Oval, site of international cricket matches, and the great houses Milles Fleurs, Stollmeyer Castle and Queen's Royal College.[6] This milieu provided her with exposure to decision-makers of the era. Discussions with family and visitors to the home would have exposed young Audrey to social issues of the time. Her family's wealth permitted travel, the purchase of books and holiday recreation. Vacations spent "down the islands" or at Toco were a normal part of the family's lifestyle; her father owned properties in both areas. Interaction with immigrant families from the other islands would have broadened her understanding of the Caribbean region.

## Education

In Trinidad Jeffers received her formal education at Tranquillity Intermediate School, the model school of the era. This young woman left the colony in 1914, when she was eighteen years old, returning in 1921 after her training in social science and health in London, England.[7] Her experiences at the National Health Society and Alexander College would have developed an awareness of community social needs. Her informal education and exposure to the First World War must have left an indelible mark on her world view and life choices.

Other informal educational experiences would have included early strains of pan-Africanism.[8] She served with West African soldiers who were part of the war effort; the *Trinidad Guardian* (1998) notes that she organized a West African Soldiers Fund through the West Indian Committee. Another significant influence at the time would have been the women's movement and the struggle for the right of women to vote in 1918. Given her later activities in the political and public life of the country, her younger years in England, in a period of emerging consciousness of women as excluded and underrepresented citizens, must have helped to sow the seeds of the feminism so strongly linked with Audrey Jeffers in her later life.

## Relationship with Her Parents

From all reports, Audrey Jeffers' relationship with her parents may have been the most influential factor in her background that affected her later role in society. She got along well with both parents, who supported her many and varied initiatives for social change. Her mother, Mary Layne Jeffers, set an example of charity and good works. Her father, Henry Israel Jeffers,[9] willingly shared his resources with her, for travel and later for her many projects of social service. This relationship provided Jeffers with a financial base and physical venues from which to initiate some of her early social service projects. Her St Clair home, Briarsend, became the first headquarters for the Coterie and was home to bazaars, concerts and dances for many years.

There is no evidence to indicate that Jeffers did any formal studies in law. Nevertheless, her later interventions in the city council reveal a mind that understood law and legislative change. This heritage, obtained from reading, interacting with people, her parents, her education and travel, provided the cultural capital in the form of knowledge, skills and attitude to develop a self-reliant social service organization and to influence the lives of many women in the early part of the twentieth century, just after the end of the First World War.

## The Coterie of Social Workers of Trinidad and Tobago Inc.

The time following the First World War in Trinidad and Tobago was a period of growing visibility of a conscientious middle class and an expanding intelligentsia. Liberal views gained through travel, education and independent reading were spreading throughout the society. The presence of African-descended professionals and land owners (some from islands such as St Vincent and the Grenadines, Antigua and Barbuda, Barbados and Grenada) was very evident in the society. Audrey Layne Jeffers returned from England into this social environment. With the assistance of other women and her parents, Mary and Henry Israel Jeffers, she began the Coterie of Social Workers in 1921.[10] The vibrancy and visionary characteristics of youth were evident throughout her illustrious career, as demonstrated in her service to her country.

### Formation of the Coterie of Social Workers

Ten to fifteen years before the acknowledgement and subsequent documentation of poverty, malnutrition, housing squalor and lack of representation of women in public affairs by the West Indian Commission in the 1930s, the Coterie of Social Workers had begun to identify these problems within the society and to develop responses to alleviate them. Referring to the first Trinidadian conference on social services, which lasted ten days and was held at Jeffers' parents' "down the islands" holiday resort, Todd (1999) outlines the mood of the new organization in terms of addressing problems of population growth, including the challenge of poverty: "The new organisation would have to be strategists not only for change but also for intervention and coping. The Coterie would have to be involved in a new system for promoting human well-being."

The first objective of the Association was "[t]o cultivate an interest in and to strive to stimulate and promote voluntary social service for the progress and welfare of the community in general with particular reference to women and children, the aged, the needy and the infirm" (Todd 1999, 58). This objective provided the *raison d'être* for subsequent social intervention and action by persons perceived to be a new breed of women in the 1920s. This initiative of starting an association for voluntary social workers preceded the practice of social work by twenty years, and it occurred almost seventy years before professional social work began to be taught in Trinidad and Tobago.

The Coterie created a social space for women to be involved in social change and improvement of the quality of life in the country. As a women's organization of which both the membership and leadership were women of African descent, it allowed a space for feminine self-assertiveness, intellectual development and social intervention to emerge amidst the patriarchal, socially stratified colonial society of the 1920s. Under the leadership of the avowed feminist Audrey Jeffers, the Coterie promoted the rights of women and advocated for improved educational facilities, employment opportunities, social supports and government representation for women. Mills (1968, 8) quotes Jeffers as stating that "the needs of our women have been seriously neglected in the past". Through the Coterie of Social Workers, Jeffers created and maintained a space through which women who wished to could serve and influence society.

## The Programmes of the Coterie

In the 1920s and 1930s novel ideas came from this women's organization. Self-reliance in fundraising and committed voluntary action became the hallmarks of the Coterie's activities. Pioneering community care for persons with disabilities, developing a national response to human need and entering disadvantaged and stigmatized areas to allow for bridging of the social class divide were but some of its strengths. All this occurred prior to establishment of the Social Welfare Department in 1943. Throughout the normal execution of their activities, the Coterie's members encouraged ecumenical worship, thus establishing a pattern for interdenominational Christian worship that has become a norm in Trinidadian society.

## The School Feeding Programme

The work of the Coterie best-known to the Trinidadian public is the school feeding programme. This began in a recognizably structured and sustainable manner with the Port of Spain Breakfast Shed in 1926. Schoolchildren who could afford it could access a balanced cooked midday meal at the subsidized cost of a penny a day, and the meals were free for those who needed them but whose parents were unable to pay. This service depended on regular volunteers such as Elaine Allette to prepare meals and sandwiches for the children. The programme was expanded to include San Fernando, Siparia, Barataria and Tobago. The system of school feeding served as a forerunner and prototype for the national school feeding programme initiated after independence.

The branches of the Coterie that continued to offer school feeding within the national programme soon discovered that the new regulations required adoption of a business approach, as caterers offering meals to schoolchildren are under contract to the state. All suppliers preparing meals for schools are subject to government regulations and audits; they must charge taxes such as the value-added tax (VAT) and also meet labour law requirements. This business model is very different from the days when volunteers frequently cooked the meals themselves to ensure a daily supply of nutritious food for children.

## Community Care for the Disabled

Internationally, "community care" in the form of private residential care homes became a popular form of social-work practice in the late twentieth century. Social care for persons with long-term care needs that can be met outside of hospitals is essential for persons with physical disabilities, the elderly and the mentally challenged. In 1928 the Coterie established the St Mary's Home for Blind Women. The service allowed blind women a certain degree of independence and dignity, long before the passing of legislation and the establishment of policies to support social and economic human rights for all persons, and in particular persons with disabilities.[11]

This institution, which unfortunately closed recently, accepted women who because of their impairment needed care but were unable to live at home. The situation of the St Mary's Home for Blind Women reflects the difficulty that traditional voluntary service organizations have in meeting the challenges of modern standards for communal residences. Difficulties paying staff and the loss of committed volunteers – Coterie members such as Linda Wallace – made it impossible for the Coterie to keep the home functioning.

## Hostels for Working Women

The post–First World War era in Trinidad and Tobago encouraged the emancipation of women. More young women chose to enter the professions of teaching and nursing, while others established a degree of independence as seamstresses, hairdressers and store clerks in Port of Spain. The population viewed with suspicion single women who elected to live independently in the urban capital. Under these circumstances, the Coterie supported the emerging role of economically independent women through the provision of affordable, well-maintained and respectable housing for working women. In 1936 and 1939 respectively, the Anstey Guest House and the Chinnette Alley Centre were established in Port of Spain. In 1938 another hostel, which also served as an administrative centre of the organization, was named "Martha House". Anstey House still offers support to working women, but the Chinnette Alley Centre and Martha House no longer exist.

## Day-Care Centres and Nurseries

Other programmes that served to improve the situation of both women and children were day-care centres/nurseries. In 1940 the first day nursery for children was established at John John. Verna Crichlow, a member of the Coterie at that time, was instrumental in establishing the nursery. At the opening of the John John nursery, Audrey Jeffers stated, "I do not believe many of us here have ever visited the village of John John before. . . . But I'll tell you why we are here. The people here have been forgotten. They need friends and help and this is what we have come to offer" (Mills 1968). The people of John John and the Government of Trinidad and Tobago have since taken over the John John Day Nursery. In addition to this first day-care centre, the Coterie organized other nurseries from their branches in San Fernando and Barataria.

## Celebration of Mother's Day

Audrey Jeffers also introduced the celebration of Mother's Day to Trinidad and Tobago, in 1927. Being very attached to both her parents, she encouraged all of Trinidad and Tobago to recognize the invaluable contributions of mothers to the well-being of their children. The day served as a time to honour mothers, and a Mother of the Year was chosen annually. In celebration of Mother's Day, the Coterie would entertain poor mothers and give them food hampers and clothes. This pattern continues today, with the annual feeding of one hundred mothers on the Saturday after Mother's Day, at Audrey Jeffers House in Port of Spain.

## Community Education

The needs of the era determined the development of some of the Coterie's newer programmes. Examples of more recent activities include a literacy programme for primary and secondary schoolchildren who are unable to read. When necessary, children who attended half-day school under the shift system[12] were supervised during the daytime when they were not at school, thus reducing opportunities for teenage deviance. Maureen Ashby, who pioneered many of these new initiatives, described the new role of the Coterie in the twenty-first century as a focus on feeding and nurturing the mind and the spirit.

Other twenty-first century programmes for women and youth are skills training in garment construction and food preparation and computer literacy classes for the elderly and others needing to adapt to the age of informatics. The Barataria branch has established a senior citizens' centre called the Pearl Gomez James Centre. Different branches periodically support schoolchildren with respect to transportation and school books. Port of Spain and Tacarigua annually celebrate Universal Children's Day; on this occasion, children from custodial institutions are entertained, receive a treat and learn about children's rights.

## Recreation and Entertainment

The Coterie recognized that the poor needed not only tangible help in the form of housing, day care and balanced, well-cooked meals, but also recreation and entertainment. Regular evenings of entertainment for residents of institutions for the elderly, needy children and adolescents were organized by Coterie volunteers. Members of the public were also entertained, at dances, fêtes, luncheons, bazaars and concerts.

Concerts, tea parties, bazaars and cake sales also constituted a key part of the Coterie's regular fundraising activities. These regular projects, which contributed income required for other programmes of social service, included a Palm Sunday concert, a Fête de Noël and a Carnival Monday–night fête. Fête de Nöel, a children's Christmas bazaar, was a forerunner of the many annual Christmas fundraising bazaars that are organized by schools and various community groups today. The Monday-night Carnival fête was unique in its time, as community organizations had not yet understood the potential of Carnival season for income generation. A moonlight excursion through the Gulf was another new experience in the 1930s, while the Palm Sunday concert provided uplifting family entertainment during the Lenten season.

## Advocacy for Women's and Children's Rights

Advocacy work for improved social conditions for women and children formed part of the Coterie's agenda. Audrey Jeffers and other Coterie members sat on various committees and boards that promoted education for girls and women. One intervention to affect the national community was the establishment of a national scholarship to give girls the opportunity of tertiary education.[13] The Coterie's membership also advocated for a youth camp for girls.[14] Jeffers lobbied the government to train persons to work with the disabled, and Lydia Harper, who was the first person trained to work with deaf children, became a committed Coterie member. As a member of the Legislative Council, Jeffers also lobbied for women to be able to join the police force and for store clerks to be allowed to sit when not serving customers. Mavis Griffith, one of the first policewomen, also became a committed Coterie member.

Audrey Jeffers encouraged women to participate in political life so that they could promote beneficial changes for women and children. International and national efforts such as the push for children's rights in the 1960s became part of the Coterie's agenda. So influential was the impact of Jeffers and the Coterie of Social Workers in colonial times that Beryl Patrick-Doyle, a past president of the Coterie, has stated, "Anything concerning women that was a first of its kind at the time could be attributed to Aunt Audrey".[15]

## The Junior Coterie

The Junior Coterie of Social Workers served to initiate adolescents and young adults of the society into voluntary and even professional social work. It provided a safe environment and experiences through which young women could begin serving their communities. Activities of the membership included reading to blind women and organizing Sunday school for the John John Nursery.

Samaroo et al. (2010, 45) note that Zalayhar Hassanali joined the Siparia branch of the Coterie in 1949.[16] The Coterie and the Child Welfare League provided an opportunity for voluntary social service for young Mrs Hassanali, who later became a patron of the organization. Beryl Patrick-Doyle, who became president of the Coterie after the death of Audrey Jeffers, received her early initiation into voluntary social work under the tutelage of Olga Comma Maynard and Mira Austen, also within the context of the Junior Coterie. In 1963 Audrey Jeffers made Patrick-Doyle a Life Member.[17]

One outstanding professional social worker to have benefited from the experience of being a member of the Junior Coterie of Social Workers was Nesta Patrick.[18] According to Joseph (2004), Dr Patrick admired Audrey Jeffers and gained some insights into community service from her working style. Patrick is also a Life Member of the Coterie.

## Ecumenical Action

Ecumenical action occurred even though it was never officially enunciated as one of the objectives of the Coterie. Meetings at the various Coterie activities always began with Christian prayers – the Lord's Prayer and the Prayer of St Francis of Assisi – for early members were Christians of the Anglican, Roman Catholic and Methodist denominations. Given the strong Anglican background of Audrey Jeffers, she felt a need for the Coterie to have regular communal prayers and a period of reflection on the Bible and Christian teachings. The constitution of the Coterie recognizes "the Creator" as well as the importance of service for improving oneself and for nation building.

The Christian calendar was recognized and special programmes for spiritual uplift, such as the Palm Sunday concert and Sunset Talks during the Lenten season,[19] remain on the Coterie's calendar. Todd (1999) notes that prior to Vatican II, when Catholics participating in non-Roman Catholic services could face excommunication, the new women of the Coterie held corporate Communion at St Crispin's Anglican Church in Woodbrook. In this way, interdenominational worship and ecumenism were practised as a normal part of Coterie life.

Audrey Jeffers was a practising Anglican, a regular communicant and participant in communal worship who served in various areas of Anglican church life. One of her initiatives was the Golden Harvest Bazaar at St Crispin's, her parish church. The church's leadership respected her work and the activities of the Coterie. The Anglican Church, through Bishop Anstey, even gave the Coterie a house, known as Anstey House, for use as a women's hostel. Ramkeesoon (1968) describes Jeffers as "a woman to whom Christianity and religion were a way of life, not a mere social façade". She also notes her unceasing support for the Church of England in Trinidad, its priests and the churches in Woodbrook and Toco.[20] Jeffers gave much of her wealth for the use of social services in such a way that the "right hand did not know what the left hand did".[21] Her life reflected in large part the instructions of Jesus to the rich young man.[22]

Audrey Jeffers demonstrated a strong sense of democracy when she was participating in branch or committee meetings, and she always respected the chairperson. She did not allow her headship status to control the decision-making process at either committee or branch level. This tradition has continued within the Coterie into the twenty-first century. Although some perceived her to be domineering, aggressive and self-assertive, persons who knew her well described her as a humble and gracious person with a heart of gold.

## The Philosophy of the Coterie of Social Workers

Members of the organization were motivated by a philosophy of service to those in need in the society. Its motto – "Lift as we climb and give of our best or nothing"[23] – accompanied by an emblem of a woman carrying a child up stairs, served as the inspiration for these activities (see figure 12.2).

This motto provided an idealized interpretation of the purpose and objectives of the Coterie of Social Workers and a guide for members to follow within the organization. The theme "Lift as we climb" implies the need for members to respond to the social stratification of society through their own efforts of climbing and moving upwards, both economically and socially, thus facilitating social improvement and the uplifting of persons of colour in the colonial society. The blue and gold of the emblem – the Coterie's colours – symbolize positive values and aspirations for the members, blue representing the positive and ethereal and gold representing purity and resilience.

**Figure 12.2** Motto and emblem of the Coterie of Social Workers Inc.

The constitution of the Coterie states that the organization is founded on the belief that "[t]he Creator demands our concern for the welfare of one's fellow men". It further acknowledges that talents and abilities, when used by individuals for community service, enhance not only one's own life but also the quality and life of the nation. Voluntary social service based on faith in the Creator is the basis for the Coterie's existence.

## The Administrative Structure of the Coterie

The Coterie developed a national structure coordinated by a national executive and a board consisting of representatives from all the branches. There is an elected president who serves to advance the goals of the Coterie. Presidents have included Elva Thomas, Arlene Hodge-Dipchan, Mrs Donald-Browne and Shirley Hunte. Branches exist in the urban areas of Trinidad – currently in Tacarigua, Siparia, Barataria, San Fernando and Port of Spain – and in Tobago.[24] Within each branch the organizational structure is headed by a chairperson supported by a secretary, a treasurer and committees that focus on specific projects. The site of the national administrative office is Audrey Jeffers House, at 3 Longden Street, Port of Spain; this office accommodates an administrative assistant and, as funds permit, a project coordinator.

Audrey Jeffers served as executive president of the organisation for forty-seven years. Her wealth allowed her to devote her entire adult life to building the Coterie and other women's organizations. After her death, on 24 June 1968, her position was divided between a president (who remained a volunteer) and an executive director. Lystra Charles was the first president after Jeffers and Louise Cambridge the first executive director. These two women were pivotal in ensuring the sustainability of the Coterie of Social Workers after the death of Audrey Jeffers. Many members rallied around the new leadership to ensure continuation of the organization and construction of the headquarters at Longden Street, thus ensuring the survival of the organization into the twenty-first century.

## Volunteer Service

Coterie members maintain various programmes through volunteer service. Members traditionally give of their time and financial and material resources, and they also raise donations from the private sector. This concept of volunteerism has characterized the work of members beginning with Audrey Jeffers, who gave of her personal wealth, time and energy to make the Coterie what it is today. Some of the buildings and land used for the work of the Coterie were Jeffers' own property which she had either inherited or were given to her by her father during his lifetime. Her personal finances supplemented the fundraising activities in order to keep various projects going. Other Coterie members, who still maintain the practice of private, unpublicized donations as part of their fundraising for the different programmes, have copied this pattern. For example, in the aftermath of the 2010 earthquake in Haiti, Coterie members contributed TT$25,000[25] to the Red Cross for use in rebuilding the country.

Time for voluntary social service has become a scarce resource for many women today. Retired persons, assured of their pensions, are best placed to give voluntary service in the Coterie's tradition. The average age of the Coterie's members in the twenty-first century is seventy years, and these women may have lost the visionary ideals and vibrancy of youth that characterized the Coterie for so many decades. In addition, many of the ailments that accompany old age can prevent members from playing as active a role as they did in their youth.

The management and implementation of many of the projects of the organization require full-time hired staff as caretakers, administrators, secretaries and other employees in the school feeding centres, early childhood centres/day nurseries and centres for the elderly. A distinction has to be made between members, who are volunteers committed to the philosophy of the Coterie of Social Workers, on the one hand, and employees, whose situations are subject to labour laws, the National Insurance Scheme (NIS), minimum wages and the Occupational Safety and Health Act (OSHA) on the other hand. The demands placed on branches that have services offering school feeding, nurseries or hostels require a professional, efficient social service with a business orientation.

## A Vision of Women's Involvement in Caribbean Society

Audrey Jeffers' background allowed her a vision that went beyond Trinidad. She pioneered other women's organizations, such as the Caribbean Women's Federation in Guyana, and in 1956 she began the Caribbean Women's Association.[26] These movements influenced women to become involved in the social and political life of their respective countries. Rigsby (2004, vii) notes that in 1959 she spearheaded formation of the first Soroptimist International Club in the English-speaking Caribbean. The aim of this organization is "to strive for Human Rights for all people and to advance the status of women". The programme of the organization consists of education, economic and social development, the environment, health, human rights/advancement of the status of women, and international goodwill and understanding. Soroptomist International has membership in Barbados, Grenada and Jamaica and is co-ordinated by a Caribbean Area Council.

### Participation in Political and Public Life

Audrey Jeffers actively participated in public life. In 1936 she was the first woman to be elected as a member of a city council. Between 1951 and 1956 she was a member of the Legislative Council. Prior to the appointment of women as consuls and ambassadors, she served as honorary consul for Liberia. During her lifetime she and other Coterie members also served on various public and community committees. Her presence in public life contributed to legitimization and normalization of the participation of women in political life.

Following the example of Audrey Jeffers, Verna Crichlow, an active Coterie member, became a member of Parliament for the independent nation of Trinidad and Tobago. Dame Louise Horne, also a member of the Coterie and a nutritionist, accepted the position of independent senator in the new republic.[27] In her maiden speech, Horne promoted the need for a national nutrition programme which, with the blessing of Dr Eric Williams, became the National Nutrition Programme in the 1977 appropriation bill (Horne 2003); the School Nutrition Board later developed from this programme. Audrey Jeffers, Verna Crichlow and Louise Horne have all been recognized for advancing social policy and women's concerns; they also served as forerunners in the involvement of women in the political life of Trinidad and Tobago.

## The Legacy of Audrey Layne Jeffers

Audrey Jeffers left an indelible mark on many women, on the Anglican Church, on the organizations she founded and on the political life of the country.

### The Anglican Church

In the June 2010 issue of the *Anglican Outlook*, Calvin W. Bess, bishop of Trinidad and Tobago, announced "Stalwarts Honoured". The Anglican Diocesan Synod of 2010 endorsed the inclusion of the Most Reverend Arthur Henry Anstey, late bishop of the Diocese of Trinidad and Tobago, and the late Audrey Layne Jeffers in the Trinidad and Tobago Diocesan calendar. This is the first time in the history of Trinidad and Tobago that a national has been so honoured. Her commemoration will be observed annually on 30 April in the Anglican Diocese of Trinidad and Tobago. This unique honour provides an example for other Anglican dioceses in the Caribbean to begin to identify worthy Christians for recognition.

### Social Service Organization

More established aspects of the legacy of Audrey Jeffers include a national organization for addressing social problems of the society. Her approach recognized the need for consultation and problem identification in all social programming. From its inception, the organization identified various areas of human need and devised appropriate policies and programmes. Many poor and needy women and children received the tangible benefits of food, child care, housing and clothing provided by Audrey Jeffers and her group of women.

Through her benevolent and philanthropic endeavours, Jeffers' role in social service innovation in the colonial era was very significant. Many persons of the period, in their roles as grandmothers or grandfathers, uncles or aunties, and godmothers or godfathers (such as Mary Jeffers), quietly helped less fortunate children, especially relatives, to attend school and to obtain lodging and regular meals. These efforts were known only to family or community members. By establishing a social service, the Coterie of Social Workers, Audrey Jeffers provided services based on need to children and women in Trinidad and Tobago. This action made the Coterie the pioneer indigenous voluntary social service organization model for the twin-island state.

## Feminist Inspiration and Action

Lystra Charles, Louise Cambridge, Beryl Patrick-Doyle, Dame Louise Horne and Dr Nesta Patrick are but some of the women who acknowledge the inspirational role of Audrey Jeffers in their lives. And forty years after her death she continues to inspire the young. Sonia Ria Williams, a committed secretary of the Coterie in her early twenties, willingly volunteers her time, skills and resources to the organization. Although not mentioned by name, all the women who served the Coterie over the years in one way or another were influenced by the personality and actions of Audrey Jeffers.

## Reaching the Hearts and Minds of Pre-independence Trinidadians

No appreciation of the pioneering work of Audrey Jeffers and the Coterie of Social Workers would be complete without acknowledging the fond memories the membership and members of society have of the many parties, concerts and bazaars that were such an important part of the social calendar in colonial times. Children of the 1940s and 1950s may recall the annual Fête de Noël with its many colourfully decorated stalls and Santa Claus. Debutantes remember the Christmas parties that served as their coming-out balls. Poor mothers recall the food hampers and entertainment regularly provided as a Mother's Day treat. The Coterie thus provided social services with a difference.

## Recognition by State and Colonial Authorities

The colonial authorities also recognized Jeffers' work. She was a recipient of an MBE (Member of the Order of the British Empire) and an OBE (Officer of the Order of the British Empire) for her contributions to social services (Joseph 2004). In 1937 she received a coronation medal. In 1963 she received a Humanist Certificate for services in community and social work from the Rosicrucian Order (AMORC). In 1969 the Government of Trinidad and

Tobago awarded her a posthumous Chaconia Medal (Gold), and a highway leading west out of Port of Spain was named the Audrey Jeffers Highway.

The *Trinidad Guardian* described her as "The Mother of Social Services". In 1969, at a memorial service after her death, Mayor Hamilton Holder of Port of Spain stated, "it is in this light I commend to all, especially women, the work and memory of Audrey Jeffers". Paraphrasing a quotation from Wordsworth, the mayor described her as "A noblewoman, nobly planned, to warn, to comfort and command". Also in 1969, Fathers O'Loughlin and Metevier of Malick Roman Catholic Church called on people to emulate the shining life of Audrey Jeffers by caring for others.

In many ways Audrey Jeffers demonstrated the difference that one person can make in effecting the evolution of a society. Even though Barbados, Guyana and Jamaica were at the time more advanced than Trinidad in the provision of social services by church and state, there is no evidence of an equivalent woman influencing the development of social services and women's participation in society from the 1920s to the 1940s. Ramkeesoon has recorded that for the Coterie's Silver Jubilee in 1946, an unknown author prepared this poem in honour of Audrey Jeffers:

> Inspired Audrey, you whose work hath shed
> A light and glory round these shores unknown
> Immortal laurels hang about your head
> And living virtues round your heart are grown
> No fame you seek, no hideous mask you wear
> No sword shall pierce the truths for which you stand
> A flaming torch of service you doth bear
> And selfless leadership give to this land.
> (Ramkeesoon 1968)

Thus Audrey Jeffers provided a legacy for women's involvement in social change and the promotion of better conditions for both women and children in Trinidad and Tobago. Both her vision and her work have remained in the hearts and minds of members of the Coterie of Social Workers Inc. who were privileged to have laboured with her. She has provided a rich philanthropic and social service legacy for both voluntary and professional social workers.

# Acknowledgements

The author would like to thank the staff of the National Archives for assistance in sourcing information on the life of Audrey Jeffers. Sincere appreciation is also expressed to the members of the board of 2009–10 and other members of the Coterie who shared information on the life and times of Audrey Jeffers and the Coterie of Social Workers Inc. in the twentieth century.

Interviews were most graciously provided by Beryl Patrick-Doyle, HBM (Humming Bird Medal), past president of the Coterie of Social Workers, 1981–87; Dame Louise Horne, MOM (Medal of Merit, Gold), member and committee chairperson, Coterie of Social Workers; and Dr Nesta Patrick, life member of the Coterie of Social Workers.

## Notes

1. The Society of St Vincent de Paul began in 1857 and may be the oldest voluntary organization in Trinidad and Tobago.
2. Friendly Societies began after emancipation as self-help institutions for ex-slaves.
3. Gayap is a system of community support for planting land and building houses. Sousou is a savings plan of regularly contributing a small sum of money to a group (usually of women) for a period such as six months. After an agreed-upon interval (a month or a week) one member receives the contributions made. This continues until all the members have had a turn receiving all the contributions for the week or month.
4. The *Trinidad Guardian* (1998, 41) states that she was born in 1898.
5. In Trinidad and Tobago, persons who have migrated to the country from neighbouring islands are referred to as "small islanders". Although many of these migrants have been limited to the lower ranks of society, some gave rise to prominent families in the legal, academic and medical professions.
6. Queen's Royal College is a prestigious boys' secondary school which was attended by such notables as V.S. Naipaul (Nobel Prize winner), C.L.R. James (noted author), Eric Williams (first prime minister of Trinidad and Tobago) and Peter Minshall (Carnival band producer).
7. The *Trinidad Guardian* of 9 January 1921 states that Miss Jeffers had obtained a certificate from the National Health Society. Horne (2003) notes that she was a graduate in social sciences from Alexander College in England. The *Guardian* (1998, 41) also states that she left Trinidad for England in 1913, at the age of fifteen, to study social science and returned home in 1920.
8. Henry Sylvester Williams was a Trinidadian who was organizing such meetings in the early 1900s. It is very likely that Ms Jeffers was exposed to the small community of West Indians in England at the time, and the early ideas of pan-Africanism.
9. Her father was a successful lawyer who owned many properties in the Port of Spain area.
10. The term *coterie* means an exclusive group of people who meet for a common interest.

11. The Universal Declaration of Human Rights was signed in 1948. The Convention on the Rights of Disabled Persons was ratified by the General Assembly of the United Nations in 2006.

12. From the 1970s up until the twenty-first century, there existed a shift system for some secondary schools. One school operated in the mornings, from seven a.m. to noon, while in the afternoon, from one to five p.m., another school used the same building.

13. In an era when there were five to ten national scholarships for sixth-formers completing Senior Cambridge, boys won all the scholarships. This contrasts with current patterns, where girls regularly surpass boys in academic excellence.

14. One camp was developed for girls, at El Dorado.

15. This statement was made during the author's interview with Mrs Patrick-Doyle.

16. Zalayhar Hassanali, née Mohommed, married Noor Hassanali, a past president of the Republic of Trinidad and Tobago. She is well-recognized for her community activities and support for women and children.

17. Life members are persons who have served the organization with distinction and commit themselves to life membership in the organization. They play an important role in maintaining the institutional memory of the organization.

18. In 2001 Nesta Patrick was the first Trinidadian social worker to receive an honorary doctorate from the University of the West Indies. She has also received the following honours: Caribbean Award in Mental Retardation (1978); Government of Trinidad and Tobago Public Service Medal (Gold) for Community Services (1979); Principal of the Year (1979); Caribbean Women's Association Award (1982); *Trinidad Express* Individual of the Year (1982); CARICOM Award for Women (1984); and Henry Sylvester Williams Award from the Emancipation Support Committee (2000).

19. Sunset Talks are prayer sessions and discussions reflecting Biblical themes. They take place late in the afternoon during Lent.

20. St Crispin's church is located in Woodbrook and Jeffers's country house was in Toco.

21. Beryl Patrick-Doyle stated that her mother, Mrs Patrick, used this expression to describe much of the charity of the Jeffers family, in particular Audrey Jeffers, at the time.

22. "Jesus answered, 'If you want to be perfect, go, sell your possessions and give to the poor, and you will have treasure in heaven. Then come and follow me' " (Matthew 19:21).

23. The "Lift as we climb" part was inspired by the motto of the National Association of Colored Women's Clubs, formed in 1896 in the United States.

24. The Point Fortin branch no longer exists.

25. One Trinidad and Tobago dollar (TT) is worth 16 cents in US currency, making the donation worth approximately US$4,000.

26. These two organizations are no longer functioning.

27. In 1976 Trinidad and Tobago moved from a constitutional monarchy, in which the British sovereign is represented by a governor general, to a republic with a president as the head of state.

# References

"Audrey Jeffers". 1998. *Trinidad Guardian*, 1 August, 41. http://www.nalis.gov.tt/Biog raphy%5CAudreyJeffers.html (accessed 21 January 2008).

"Audrey Jeffers' Coronation Chair Given to the City". 1969. *Trinidad Guardian*, 25 June, 9.

Bess, Calvin W. 2010. "Stalwarts Honoured". *The Anglican Outlook* 187 (June): 5.

Bryan, Patrick. 1990. *Philanthropy and Social Welfare in Jamaica.* Kingston: Institute of Social and Economic Research, University of the West Indies.

Coterie of Social Workers of Trinidad and Tobago Inc. N.d. "The Constitution of the Coterie of Social Workers Inc.".

———. 1991. "The 70th Anniversary, 1921–91".

Danns, George, and Nerberne Scott. 1989. "Social Welfare in Guyana". In *New Directions in Caribbean Social Policy: Conference Proceedings*. St Augustine: Department of Sociology, University of the West Indies.

Edmonds, J. 1973. "Child Care and Family Services in Barbados". *Social and Economic Studies* 22, no. 2: 229–48.

"From Our Files: Fifty Years Ago". 1981. *Trinidad Guardian*, 23 June, 9.

Harvey, David C. 2001. "Heritage Pasts and Heritage Presents: Temporality, Meaning and the Scope of Heritage Studies". *International Journal of Heritage Studies* 7, no. 4 (December): 319–38.

Horne, Louise. 2003. *The Evolution of Modern Trinidad and Tobago.* Trinidad: Enaith's Printing.

Joseph, Fitzroy Gregory. 2004. *The Life of Nesta Bonaparte Patrick: A Truly Caribbean Woman.* St Augustine: School of Continuing Studies, University of the West Indies.

"League of Social Welfare". 1921. *Trinidad Guardian*, 21 January, 12.

"Louise Cambridge – A Life Worthy of Emulation: Coterie Confers a Rare Honour". 1981. *Trinidad Guardian*, 20 July, 14.

Maxwell, John. 2002. "The Evolution of Social Welfare Services and Social Work in the English Speaking Caribbean". *Caribbean Journal of Social Work* 1 (March): 11–31.

Maynard, Olga Comma. 1971. *The Briarend Pattern: The Story of Audrey Jeffers O.B.E. and the Coterie of Social Workers.* Port of Spain: Busby's Printerie.

Mills, Therese. 1968. "Women in Charge of Everything: This Was Audrey's Prescription for Efficiency". *Sunday Guardian,* 28 June, 8.

"Miss Audrey Jeffers Dies, 70". 1968. *Trinidad Guardian*, 25 June, 2.

Ramkesoon, Gemma. 1968. "A Tribute to Audrey Jeffers". *Trinidad Guardian,* 1 July, 8.

Rigsby, Lorna. 2004. *Extolling the Dignity of Service: 45 Years of Soroptimism.* Port of Spain: Soroptimist International of Port of Spain.

Ryan, Selwyn. 1991. *Social and Occupational Stratification in Contemporary Trinidad and Tobago.* St Augustine: Institute of Social and Economic Research, University of the West Indies.

Samaroo, B., Y. Teelucksingh, and K. Ramchand. 2010. *Zalayhar: Life of a First Lady.* Port of Spain: Naparima Association for Past Students and Scotia Bank Trinidad and Tobago Foundation.

"Success of Miss A. Jeffers". 1921. *Trinidad Guardian*, 9 January, 8.

Todd, Neila. 1999. *The Legacy of the Coterie of Social Workers.* N.p.: Coterie of Social Workers Inc.

Tribute to the "Mother of Social Services". 1969. *Trinidad Guardian*, 25 June, 9.

# 13.

# West Indian Patriot in West Africa

## A Study of George James Christian of Dominica and the Gold Coast

MARGARET D. ROUSE-JONES AND ESTELLE M. APPIAH

*This chapter examines a little-known case of reverse migration to West Africa in the early decades of the twentieth century. George James Christian of Dominica, in the Windward Caribbean, went to London to study law in the 1890s. On completion of his legal training in 1902, he migrated to the Gold Coast (now Ghana) and became a prominent lawyer there until his death in 1940. Christian is an important figure among the small group of West Indian professionals who emigrated to the Gold Coast in the early twentieth century. In examining Christian's life, several questions relating to his experiences will be considered. How did this teacher from Dominica at the turn of the century become a prominent lawyer, Liberian consul and member of the Legislative Council of the Gold Coast? The chapter will give an insight into the lifestyle attained by Christian and the issues which concerned him. In particular, it will show that, notwithstanding the fact that Christian chose to leave his home to return to Africa, he remained loyal to his West Indian heritage. The data will also shed some light on the wider group of Caribbean migrants who relocated from the Caribbean to an African nation and made an impact there. The unveiling of the details of the lives of these migrants, who can be seen as heroes, is of importance for identity and nation building in the Caribbean.*

## Introduction

Historically, migration has been central in the formation of Caribbean societies. One writer has pointed out that "by definition, islands look out as well as are looked in at".[1] Descendants of the African slaves who were transported to the Caribbean islands in the fifteenth to eighteenth centuries have moved to other parts of the globe in various migration movements. The idea of emigration to Africa by descendants of slaves dates back to the African slave trade itself. In those early years the movement was a sporadic affair, but after emancipation came to the slaves, back-to-Africa schemes quickly appeared.[2]

In her documentation of the Caribbean migration experience, Elizabeth Thomas-Hope has commented generally on the role which the experience of slavery played in shaping migratory patterns.[3] She also identified the role of education as a means of mobility in the class structure and an important factor for acquiring a profession and improving one's social status. A foreign education was considered to be of particular value, and indeed, long before higher education was available to nationals of the English-speaking Caribbean within the home region, it was available to them in the 'mother country', the United Kingdom.

This chapter examines a little-known case of reverse migration in the early decades of the twentieth century, of a Caribbean student who went from London 'back to Africa'. George James Christian of Dominica, in the Windward Caribbean, went to London to study law in the 1890s. On completion of his legal training in 1902, he migrated to the Gold Coast (now Ghana) and became a prominent lawyer there, remaining until his death in 1940. What were the sociocultural implications surrounding this case of reverse migration from the Caribbean to West Africa? Here was a descendant of enslaved Africans who consciously decided to return to the home of his ancestors. What cultural heritage had he internalized from his West Indian birth and upbringing? *Heritage* in this context refers to traditions, social practices, rituals, festive events and the "wealth of knowledge and skills that is transmitted . . . from one generation to the next".[4] Christian was an important figure among the small group of West Indian professionals who went to the Gold Coast at that time. The unveiling of the details of his life is of importance for identity and nation building, both in Dominica and in the wider Caribbean.

## Early Years

George James Christian, who was born in Dominica on 23 February 1869, was the son of a migrant, and he was introduced to the idea of migration at a young age. His father, also named George James Christian, was an Antiguan solicitor who had moved to Dominica. The younger Christian returned to Antigua to be educated at the Mico Training College, after which he returned to Dominica and served as a schoolteacher there.[5] At the Mico College he was no doubt influenced by one of his teachers, Charles Farquhar, who subsequently served as a priest in Guinea. As was evident at this stage in his life,

Christian was very conscious of the experience of enslaved Africans and his African heritage.[6]

It is therefore not surprising that when Christian subsequently left Dominica again in 1899, to study law at Gray's Inn, London,[7] he became involved in the African Association, which was founded in 1897 by Henry Sylvester Williams, a fellow student from Trinidad. Williams had been planning for the famous first Pan-African Conference at least a year before Christian arrived in London. Christian not only attended the conference in 1900 but participated actively, leading a discussion on the theme "Organized Plunder and Human Progress Have Made of Our Race Their Battlefield". Christian's contribution to the conference was a "wide-ranging survey of conditions in Africa" which clearly demonstrated that he had knowledge and understanding not only of the atrocities of slavery but also of the continued domination and exploitation of African states by the colonization process.

It is reported that the overseas delegates to the conference left behind "those like Williams and Christian who had to complete their studies".[8] In the wake of the conference, a permanent Pan-African Association was formed, into which the African Association was subsumed. Christian, who served as treasurer of the association,[9] spent another two years completing his law studies. He was called to the bar on 11 June 1902[10] and went directly to the Gold Coast fairly soon afterwards.

What are the factors that led Christian to migrate to the Gold Coast when he had completed his law studies at Gray's Inn? Initially, before he was called to the bar, he had applied for a "legal appointment in the colonies" but was advised that he could not be considered for such a position without experience as a "practising barrister".[11] However, as Christian himself indicated, he "had some idea of coming to Africa as [his] home". Therefore, when he had completed his studies at Gray's Inn, on the night of when he was called to the bar,[12] he summoned the courage to ask Sir Philip Crampton Smyley, who was serving in Sierra Leone at the time, where in Africa he would recommend. Smyley had replied: "Well, I would not advise you to go to the Gambia, Sierra Leone is overcrowded, Nigeria I know nothing about, but if you are worth your salt, try your luck on the Gold Coast."[13] Years later, Christian acknowledged that he owed a debt of gratitude to Smyley for having given him this advice.[14]

Christian's arrival in the Gold Coast presented some challenges but he quickly surmounted them; a year after his arrival he established a legal firm. He became a "concessions" lawyer for the gold-mining industry and had a successful private practice in both Sekondi and Tarkwa.[15] Christian was a very astute lawyer who had developed a reputation as early as 1903. He was involved in the famous Essiamuah murder case, which ended with acquittal of the accused; Christian was congratulated in the media for his able defence.[16]

An analysis of Christian's career development, interests and activities in the Gold Coast clearly demonstrates that his purpose for migrating was not only betterment of himself. His was a conscious attempt to use his skills and abilities for the advancement of Gold Coast society in general and also in his particular area of expertise. There is no doubt that he was an extremely successful lawyer. One of his outstanding achievements as a legal luminary in the Gold Coast was the prominent role he played in opening up the Ashanti region to legal practitioners. He served as counsel in the famous trial of Benjamin Knowles, who had been convicted of the murder of his wife and sentenced to death after trial in Ashanti without a jury. The appeal was heard in the Privy Council, and after intense consideration of the Ashanti Administration Ordinance, the conviction was overturned.[17] His concern for mankind at every level of society led him to defend many poor persons free of charge.[18] He maintained good relations with everyone, "both Europeans and Africans", and he was in no way discriminatory in the help he gave to all.[19]

Christian also served as the Liberian consul for thirty years, a position he acquired through his personal friendship[20] with Edwin Barclay, who was secretary of state and then president of Liberia in 1931. In this capacity Christian was responsible for the welfare of local Liberians, many of whom worked on ships which frequented the Sekondi seaport.[21]

Alongside his legal career, he became increasingly involved in the political life of the community. Christian served on the Sekondi town council from 1911 to 1915 and from 1920 to 1926.[22] In 1927 a constitutional change granting the Town of Sekondi representation in the Legislative Council required that candidates meet strict criteria in order to qualify for nomination.[23] The conditions of the Municipal Corporations Ordinance meant that municipal members of the Legislative Council could now be elected. Initially, Christian's efforts to be nominated and elected were unsuccessful. However, with time he gained acceptance, and in 1930 he was elected as a municipal member of the Legislative Council.[24] He was re-elected to the position on two occasions and served continuously as a member until his death in 1940.[25]

Throughout his terms in the Legislative Council, his contributions to the discussions were wide-ranging. In 1930–31 he drew attention to the inadequate education facilities in Takoradi and the reduced establishment of medical staff in the western province and raised the question of the role of pathologists as the final court of appeal in the instance of a doubtful medical diagnosis. He commented on the absence of experimental stations in the colony and suggested ways in which funds might be channelled to educate the populace in the cultivation of various products. In one contribution he referred to having visited Trinidad and questioned whether the Imperial College [sic], to which the Gold Coast government had paid thousands of pounds, was meeting the manpower needs of the Gold Coast in the area of agriculture. He also shared his views on the building of a railway line for the Northern Territories and the economic benefits of erecting permanent pillars for that line.[26] He argued strongly on issues of direct taxation, protection for the mining industry and the introduction of income tax. He also drew attention to the well-known evils which beset foreign sailors landing from ships at Takoradi and enquired whether a sailors' home could not be established. This brief survey of his performance in the Legislative Council gives a clear indication that his experience and training permitted him to make valid contributions on a wide range of subjects. It also demonstrates his commitment and contribution to the Gold Coast society which he had made his home.

Christian's decision to become a Freemason, very soon after his arrival in the Gold Coast, was in furtherance of a tradition which had been passed on to him from his father, who had introduced him to the Oddfellows organization almost a decade before he left Dominica.[27] The Oddfellows, like the Freemasons, were a fraternal organization, and many men joined both.[28] When Christian was in London, he was initiated into the 2nd Middlesex Artillery Lodge in 1901. He was responsible for founding the St George Lodge No. 3851, in Sekondi in 1918, and also for encouraging the spread of freemasonry in Kumasi and Cape Coast in 1921.[29] Other West Indians in the Gold Coast with whom Christian associated – Clarence E.M. Abbensetts and Robert E. Dick – were also initiated into the Sekondi Lodge.[30] His contribution to its development, welfare and improvement was recognized in 1937 with his appointment to the Grand Lodge and Supreme Grand Chapter ranks and presentation of a silver salver.[31]

Despite having settled in the Gold Coast and established his home and family there, Christian did not forget or neglect the West Indian home and family he had left behind. When he left to go to England, he had three Dominican-born children, Peter, Clara and Maude. In the Gold Coast he fathered several other children. It is evident from his dealings with his children that Christian's upbringing and experience in the West Indies had taught him the value of education as an agent of social mobility. Not only did he ensure that all his children received the best possible education, he continuously instilled in them the importance of having a worthwhile career as a means of self-advancement and attaining a better standard of living.[32] Most of the children were educated in England and for the most part they went on to lead successful lives, making a valuable contribution to society.

For example, two of his Dominica-born children went on to higher education. Peter, who studied dentistry at Howard University, returned to

Dominica and practised there until his death. Peter did visit his father in Sekondi on at least one occasion and spent time with some of his African-born siblings.[33] His daughter Maude Mary trained as a state registered nurse and midwife in England, then joined her father in the Gold Coast and worked as a nurse in the hospital in Sekondi;[34] unfortunately she died of black-water fever. Among the African-born children, Sarah trained as a nurse and later worked at Achimota School in Accra; Angela trained as a teacher in England and taught in both Ghana and England before joining the Ministry of Foreign Affairs, where she gave distinguished service;[35] and Essi became the first woman to be called to the Ghana bar. Christian's son Howard was also a barrister, and Ferdinand and Edward became a radiologist and a medical doctor, respectively.[36]

In his response to the death of his daughter Maude Mary, Christian also showed that he thought it important that the Gold Coast community be reminded of her West Indian heritage. He was deeply affected by her death and established a memorial fund in her name to provide equipment for the maternity ward of the African Hospital at Sekondi. A bronze plate – inscribed "These rooms were furnished to perpetuate the memory of Maude Mary Christian, a midwife and native of Dominica, British West Indies and a benefactor to this institution. Born 24-12-1899; Died 28-6-1933" – still serves as a reminder of Maude Mary Christian's Caribbean heritage.[37]

## African/West Indian Links

The presence of other West Indians in the Gold Coast provided a framework within which Christian could further maintain his cultural traditions and forge a sense of community. At the time of Christian's arrival in 1902, while he was still without accommodations, another West Indian, Lenard Muss, who had heard about him "by accident", befriended him.[38] One year after his arrival in the Gold Coast, in 1903, he established a legal firm, Messrs Christian and Leung, with Francis Stanislaus Leung from British Guiana.[39]

Very few official statistics on the size of the West Indian community in the Gold Coast are available. However, a 1931 census document indicates that there were 3,182 non-Africans in the Gold Coast, of whom twenty were West Indians: seventeen males and three females.[40] Another source has identified three "legal practitioners" and six of the thirteen "African" medical practitioners in the Gold Coast in 1937 as West Indians.[41] Fortunately, the oral data, combined with scattered references throughout correspondence in the papers left by Christian, have shed more light on this small community of West Indians who settled in the Gold Coast in the first quarter of the twentieth century. There was an engine fitter who worked for the railway department in Sekondi from 1908 to 1924,[42] as well as an assistant commissioner of police from Barbados, working in Kumasi, Ashanti, in the 1920s.[43] Among Christian's circle of friends and associates were two other lawyers, from British Guiana and Trinidad,[44] four medical doctors, from Trinidad, St Lucia and British Guiana,[45] and a sanitary inspector who had come from Trinidad in 1910 and subsequently was responsible for the training of public health officers in the Gold Coast and other West African countries.[46]

There were also two St Lucians, George Joseph Francois and George Stanley Lewis, the eldest of the five Lewis brothers. Francois, who had left St Lucia to join the British army, had come to the Gold Coast at the end of the First World War on the invitation of Franz Dove, a lawyer from Sierra Leone who was a businessman in Accra. Together they started the Anglo-African Corporation, which was involved in the export of cocoa. Both Francois and Dove were friends of Christian.[47] Lewis, the last surviving West Indian to have settled in the Gold Coast in the twentieth century, came there in 1929 at the invitation of Francois. He reportedly met Christian at Dove's house in 1930.[48] Lewis worked in the cocoa-farming industry in Sohum in the eastern region for seventeen years; when disease spelt the demise of the cocoa industry in the late 1940s, he moved to the capital, Accra. In 1950 he established Lewis and Company, which went on to become one of the leading non-European commercial firms in Ghana. He was also an active member of his church and made outstanding contributions as a community leader until his death, at the age of ninety-three, in 1999.[49]

Christian's home in Sekondi, which was named Dominica House, was an obvious constant reminder of his West Indian heritage. Described as a "mini castle" by one of his sons, Dominica House was architecturally a unique edifice. It was designed by a black American architect named Chapelle and was built of imported timber from Canada.[50] Interestingly, Christian also acquired properties in Dominica, one of which was named Sekondi House, which he bought for his Dominica-born son, Peter.[51] In this way his descendants in the West Indies would be reminded of their ancestor who had returned to the Gold Coast. On his death Peter bequeathed the house to his African-born brothers Howard, Ferdinand and Edward.[52]

Christian played a major role in creating a West Indian community in the Gold Coast by organizing periodic gatherings of his West Indian colleagues and friends. During the Christmas and Easter holidays, Dominica House was the venue for many annual gatherings of the West Indian community in Sekondi and the surrounding areas. Christian himself, describing one such gathering in a letter to his son Peter, reported that "on New year's Day the West Indian clan gathers at Dominica House and bring joy and happy recollections of home and distant ones".[53] It is reported that "those who couldn't fit in Dominica House were accommodated at [a] beautiful bungalow on the farm", situated between Sekondi and Takoradi.[54] Lewis, who attended an Old Year's Night gathering in 1931, made reference to a large room which was used as a billiard room and as a sitting room when entertaining. Lewis also reported that other members of the West Indian community hosted similar gatherings during other holiday periods. Lewis, who had outlived all his West Indian peers in the Gold Coast, noted that very few ever brought wives with them, and they therefore married local women. They also seldom returned to the West Indies. Lewis was of the view that the gatherings did much to knit together the small group of West Indians.[55]

The evidence, both written and oral, suggests that as a group, the West Indian community in the Gold Coast was homogeneous, providing services, social life and support to one another. Christian played a significant leadership role in the group. He obviously used his professional expertise for the benefit of individual members when the need arose. He was also pivotal in establishing and maintaining a sense of community among the West Indians, using his social networks and his material resources to full advantage in this regard.

Christian himself died while still serving on the Legislative Council and is buried alongside his daughter Maude in the European Cemetery in Sekondi. The inscription on his tombstone, which is also a reminder of his West Indian antecedents, reads as follows: "In ever loving memory of George James Christian of Roseau, Dominica, British West Indies, Barrister at Law, who died at Sekondi, April 17, 1940."[56]

## Conclusions

Gordon Rohlehr's definition of "a sense of heritage" as "the shadow and substance of passing and current lifestyles, as well as the inter-linkages between them" is applicable to George James Christian's experience as a West Indian who made the Gold Coast his home.[57] He could be considered a West Indian patriot on account of his positive and supportive attitude to his homeland; his identification with other West Indians in the Gold Coast; the activities and values which he continued to practise; his symbolic acts to remind himself of his homeland; and other expressions of his West Indian heritage. At the same time, however, he could also be described as a pan-Africanist. He was involved with the early pan-Africanists and attended the first conference in London in 1900; he was knowledgeable about Africa and fulfilled his desire to make his home there. Indeed, the fact that Christian's life can be interrogated is directly as a result of his "sense of heritage". This was expressed in his clear understanding of the importance of documenting his experience while it was happening and passing on the information to the next generation, who subsequently ensured that his papers were made available for the use of scholars and researchers in the Caribbean.[58]

This brief biography has given a glimpse of the life of George James Christian and, to a lesser extent, has shed some light on the group of West Indians who migrated to the Gold Coast in the early twentieth century. There is no doubt that he was an important figure among them. Many were professionals and they made a significant contribution to the development of the society. A study of their lives and contributions would be of importance to researchers and students of history and other social science disciplines, both in Ghana and in the Caribbean.

Diaspora studies are becoming increasingly relevant in the era of globalization. The unveiling of the details of the lives of these migrants, who must be seen as heroes in the Caribbean, is of importance for identity- and nation-building in these emerging societies. As scholars and researchers continue to explore the phenomena of migration, pan-Africanism, the Caribbean diaspora, heritage studies and other related areas of research and study, it is hoped that additional collections and source materials will become available. In this way, the story of others like Christian who have been hidden from history will find their place in the mosaic of the black Atlantic world.

## Notes

1. Mary Chamberlain, *Caribbean Migration: Globalised Identities* (London: Routledge, 1998), 4.

2. Edwin S. Redkey, *Black Exodus: Black Nationalist and Back-to-Africa Movements, 1890–1910* (New Haven: Yale University Press, 1969), 17–23.

3. Elizabeth Thomas-Hope, "Globalisation and the Development of a Caribbean Migration Culture", in *Caribbean Migration: Globalised Identities*, ed. Mary Chamberlain (London: Routledge, 1998), 188–91.

4. UNESCO, Convention for the Safeguarding of the Intangible Cultural Heritage, http://www.unesco.org/culture/ich/en/convention/, 2003 (accessed 5 November 2010).

5. "Hon. George James Christian, Defender of Poor Criminals, Passes Away at Sekondi", *African Morning Post*, 19 April 1940, 1; correspondence between Geo. J. Christian and Sherriff M. Bowers [and Chas W. Farquhar], Roseau, Dominica, 29 March 1890, George James Christian Papers [GJC Papers], Alma Jordan Library, University of the West Indies, St Augustine, folder 49.

6. See, for example, the exchange of correspondence between Christian and Bowers (and Farquhar), Roseau, Dominica, 29 March 1890, GJC Papers, folder 49. Also from the GJC Papers, see also correspondence between Christian and the son of his roommate, Rev. Joseph O. Bowers, fifty years later: Joseph O. Bowers,

SVD, to Mr Christian, 21 March 1940, folder 50; [Christian to Bowers], 6 April 1940, folder 64; Christian to Rev. Charles W. Farquhar, All Saints Parsonage, Conakry, Guinea, 29 October 1924, folder 18.

7.  Gray's Inn Admissions and Calls Register, 1625–1945, Gray's Inn, London.

8.  Owen Charles Mathurin, *Henry Sylvester Williams and the Origins of the Pan-African Movement, 1969–1911* (Westport, CT: Greenwood, 1976), 35, 67, 74.

9.  George Christian to secretary, Pan-African Association, 15 September 1900, GJC Papers, folder 33.

10. Gray's Inn Admissions and Calls Register, 1625–1945.

11. E. Marsh, Colonial Office, Downing Street, to George James Christian, 21 June 1901, GJC Papers, folder 32.

12. Essi Matilda Forster (Christian's daughter), interview by Estelle Appiah, Accra, Ghana, 13 June 1992, Oral and Pictorial Records Programme (OPReP) Collection, Alma Jordan Library, University of the West Indies, St Augustine.

13. Speech by Christian on the occasion of a farewell function for Chief Justice Sir Philip Crampton Smyley, GJC Papers, folder 23.

14. George James Christian to Horace Douglas, 21 August 1929, GJC Papers, folder 119.

15. Forster, interview.

16. *Gold Coast Leader,* 21 March 1903, 2.

17. Benjamin Knowles and the King on Appeal from the Chief Commissioner's Court of Ashanti (Eastern Province), House of Lords and Privy Council (1930): 366–77. See also "George Christian Laid to Rest", [Sekondi *Spectator Daily*], 21 April [1940].

18. "Hon. George James Christian", 1–2.

19. "Justice Strother-Stewart and Crown Counsel Ainsley Speak Highly of Late Barrister Christian", *Daily Echo,* 24 April 1940.

20. Forster, interview.

21. Raymond Leslie Buell, *Liberia: A Century of Survival, 1847–1947* (Philadelphia: University of Pennsylvania Press, 1947), 36.

22. "Hon. George James Christian", 1.

23. Frederick Gordon Guggisberg, *The Gold Coast. A Review of the Events of 1920–1926 and the Prospects of 1927–1928* ( Accra, Ghana: N.p., 1927), 7.

24. *Gold Coast Gazette,* 4 October 1930, 1786.

25. Colonial secretary's motion expressing regret at the death of the Honourable George James Christian, Legislative Council Debates 1940: 1 October 1940, 5, National Archives of Ghana, Accra.

26. Minutes of the Legislative Council and Sessional Papers 1930–31: 9–16; ibid. 1931–32: 16; Legislative Council Debates 1932–33: 127–34 and 214–20.

27. Geo. J. Christian to [Charles Farquhar], Dominica, 29 March 1890, GJC Papers, folder 49.

28. Mark A. Tabbert, "Masonic Papers: The Odd Fellows", http://www.freemasons-freemasonry.com/tabbert5.html, 2003 (accessed 5 November 2010).

29. [Christian] to Worshipful Master, St George's Lodge, Sekondi, 30 May 1927, GJC Papers, folder 71, 4; "Hon. George James Christian", 2.

30. St George's Lodge (Secondee) No 3851, For private circulation only [front cover]: C.W. Tachie-Menson, *Brief History of the St George's (Seccondee) Lodge No. 3851 of Ancient, Free and Accepted Masons, English Constitution 1918–1939* (Sekondi: Hope Press, 31 March 1939), 12, 16–17, 41, GJC Papers, folder 32.

31. St George (Seccondee) Lodge No. 3851, Citation to George James Christian . . . on appointment to Grand Lodge and Supreme Grand Chapter Ranks, presented 11 December 1937, GJC Papers, folder 153.

32. See, for example, [Christian] to Mrs Leung, 1 October 1927. Mrs. Leung was the guardian of his children while they were in England, and she was asked to emphasize to them the importance that they should "each qualify in some calling", which would make them self-supportive. GJC Papers, folder 10.

33. Estelle Appiah, interview by Margaret D. Rouse-Jones, London, England, 9 July 1991, OPReP Collection; Forster, interview.

34. Appiah, interview.

35. "Biography of the Late Angela Christian", in "Burial and Thanksgiving Mass for the Late Angela Christian . . . Sunday, 18 March 2000" [booklet], 5–7.

36. Ferdinand Francisco Christian, interview by Estelle Appiah, Accra, Ghana, 19 April 1992, OPReP Collection.

37. The authors visited Ghana and photographed the graves of Christian and his daughter in 1994.

38. George James Christian to Mr Broadhurst, vice-consul for Liberia, 5 January 1940, GJC Papers, folder 70.

39. *Gold Coast Leader*, 31 March 1903, 2.

40. A.W. Cardinall, "Non-African Population", in *The Gold Coast, 1931: A Review of Conditions in the Gold Coast in 1931 as Compared with Those of 1921, Based on Figures and Facts Collected by the Chief Census Officer of 1931, Together with a Historical, Ethnographical and Sociological Survey of the People of That Country* (N.p., 1931), 255.

41. Gold Coast (government), *The Gold Coast Handbook, 1937* (N.p., 1937), 402, 32–46, 42–56.

42. George J. Christian to Frank J. Ribeiro, colonial secretary, 14 January 1925.

43. Correspondence between Christian and Walter and Eve Callender, 16 October 1927 to 6 January 1928, GJC Papers, folder 54.

44. George Stanley Lewis, interview by Estelle Appiah, Accra, Ghana, 24 June 1992, OPReP Collection.

45. Ferdinand Christian, interview.

46. Dr Ralph Hoyte Jr, interview by Margaret Rouse-Jones and Estelle Appiah, Trinidad and Tobago, 28 June 2005, OPReP Collection.

47. Edward Francois, interview by Margaret D. Rouse-Jones, Accra, Ghana, 14 August 2007, OPReP Collection.

48. Forster, interview; Appiah, interview.

49. "Biography of the Late George Stanley Lewis" and "A Tribute to the Late Mr Stanley Lewis", in "Burial and Thanksgiving Service for the Life of George Stanley Lewis, Friday, 14 January 2000" [booklet], 4–5, 8–9, GJC Papers, folder 19.

50. Ferdinand Christian, interview.

51. Chrissie Burke, interview by Margaret D. Rouse-Jones, Roseau, Dominica, August 1993, OPReP Collection.

52. Supreme Court of the Windward Islands and Leeward Islands, Colony of Dominica, Probate, 29 November 1945: Last Will and Testament of Peter Charles Christian, 5 April 1945, GJC Papers, folder 50.

53. [Christian] to Dr Peter Christian, 15 January 1938, GJC Papers, folder 83.

54. Ferdinand Christian, interview.

55. Lewis, interview.

56. The authors visited the European Cemetery in Sekondi in 1994 and photographed the graves of Christian and his daughter Maude Mary.

57. Gordon Rohlehr, "National Heritage Library: Catalyst for Sovereignty and Literacy", in *Transgression, Transitions, Transformation: Essays in Caribbean Culture* (San Juan, Trinidad and Tobago: Lexicon, 2007), 386.

58. The George James Christian Papers were donated to the University of the West Indies, St Augustine, and officially handed over by his granddaughter Estelle Appiah in a ceremony at the main library on 22 June 2005.

# Part 3.

# THE NATURAL ENVIRONMENT AND PLANT USES

# 14.

# Caribbean People and the Sea

JUDITH GOBIN

*The Caribbean by its very name conjures up images of blue-green seas, sunshine, warm golden sand and an abundance of tourists. Its beauty is surely reflected in its natural environment, not least in the coastal zones and their associated marine areas. Coastal environments reflect this idyllic beauty while at the same time supporting an incredible diversity of marine flora and fauna. Caribbean coastal zones possess a number of natural resources, which include coral reefs, seagrasses, mangroves, intertidal ecosystems and beaches. The economic, ecological and social importance of these systems stems primarily from their goods, services and attributes. This chapter describes the inextricable link between Caribbean people and the seas, especially in terms of their traditional uses. It also identifies some of the human activities which have a significant impact on our heritage and the traditional uses associated with the sea.*

## Introduction

The Caribbean Sea, at approximately 2.5 million square kilometres in area, is the second-largest sea in the world (McGinley 2008); its name is derived from that of the Carib people, who were early inhabitants of the region. The Caribbean is generally defined by the island arc that extends from Trinidad and Tobago in the south to Cuba, Hispaniola, Jamaica, Puerto Rico and the Bahamas in the north; it includes the islands of the Lesser and Greater Antilles as well as the continental territories bordering the sea (Belize, Costa Rica, Nicaragua, Honduras, Guatemala, etc.). The sea will be discussed here within the broader definition of *coastal zone*, that is, the land/water interface where aquatic and terrestrial ecosystems co-exist.

Caribbean coastal zones possess natural resources that provide a wide range of goods and services which fuel economic growth and development in the individual territories. These resources include coral reefs, seagrass beds, mangroves, intertidal ecosystems, beaches, sand dune systems and the proximal coastal and marine waters. The Caribbean region is complex not only in terms of its ecosystems and species diversity but also in its historical, political and cultural richness. It is this complexity which contributes to the variety of benefits that Caribbean people derive from the sea.

## The Sea and Associated Ecosystems

Coastal and marine areas in the shallower waters of the Caribbean are highly productive, as they are associated with coral reefs, mangrove swamps, coastal lagoons, estuaries and seagrasses.

In the Caribbean, coral reefs provide fish (both for food and ornamental); shellfish, such as lobsters, crabs and conchs; pharmaceuticals from sea fans and sponges; black corals used for jewellery; and skeletal materials also often used in ornaments and jewellery. Coral reefs are the basis of coastal fisheries,

**Figure 14.1** The exposed reef flat at Salybia Bay, Trinidad (photo courtesy L. Beddoe)

providing food and shelter for both finfish and shellfish. Of the more than 300 reef species, an estimated 180 species are landed for human consumption (Towle and Towle 1991). Coral reefs are also a major tourist attraction, part of the multi-million-dollar industry in the region. The annual value of services provided by Caribbean coral reefs is an estimated 3.1 to 4.6 billion US dollars (Burke and Maidens 2004). In these respects, coral reefs are very important for both subsistence and economic development to Caribbean coastal communities as well as their wider economies.

Seagrasses such as *Thalassia testudinum* (turtle grass) and *Zostera marina* (eel grass) occur throughout the Caribbean, increasing the biodiversity of coastal waters. They provide grazing and foraging meadows for a variety of fauna which includes turtles (*Chelonia mydas*), manatees (*Trichechus manatus*), snappers (Lutjanidae family), parrotfish and grunts (Scaridae family), commercially important species of queen conchs *(Strombus gigas)*, lobsters (*Panulirus argus*) and the edible sea urchin (*Tripneustes esculentus*). They also absorb carbon dioxide ($CO_2$) from coastal waters and convert it into organic matter, while their decomposition contributes large amounts of detrital food material to offshore ecosystems. Seagrasses are often undervalued for the contribution they make to key services of marine areas, such as fisheries and tourism (Agard, Cropper and Garcia 2007).

In the Caribbean, mangrove swamps and coastal lagoons provide goods such as construction materials and firewood; fishery, molluscan and crustacean resources (finfish, shellfish and crabs); and wildlife resources such as birds and reptiles. Mangroves also provide recreational and educational opportunities in addition to being important tourist attractions. Their beneficial attributes include increasing the biodiversity of coastal waters and providing unique scenic landscapes that have considerable aesthetic value.

## Sea, Sand and Recreation

The original inhabitants of the islands – the Ortoiroid, Casimiroid, Saladoid, Barrancoid, Troumassoid, Island Carib, Ostoinoid and Taíno peoples (Reid 2009) – traversed the seas in dugout canoes to colonize islands or in search of food and trading goods, as well as in another, more advanced type of watercraft, "a Carib skeg design" (Callaghan 2007). Reid (2009, 110) describes "this ability of pre-colonial peoples to adapt and to travel by sea over relatively long distances using their knowledge of sea currents and trade winds" as indicative of their adeptness at boat building and marine navigation. Columbus's travels, constituting an important period in our maritime history, were also facilitated by ocean currents and trade winds associated with the Caribbean Sea.

After Columbus arrived in the Caribbean in 1493, claiming some islands for Spain, Spanish ships continued the search for treasures of gold and land. The Caribbean Sea then became the main route of Spanish expeditions and the site where many Spanish ships and convoys were attacked by navigators of rival powers. The pirates included British, French, Dutch and Danish rivals (Honychurch 1995), who also settled in the colonies. Later, during the seventeenth century, another plundering group of buccaneers – comprising shipwrecked sailors and escaped prisoners and indentured servants – also roamed the Caribbean seas. These tough sea rovers wandered from island to island plundering vessels and towns.

Notwithstanding our rich history, traditionally the attractiveness of the islands of the Caribbean to tourists has largely been their relaxed pace of life, scenic beauty and beautiful sandy beaches shaded by palm trees. In this respect, contemporary recreational sailing and yachting have grown into a multimillion-dollar industry. Yachts of all sizes converge on the islands of the Caribbean annually: for example, in 2009 St Lucia had 31,997 such visits, Grenada 4,083, Antigua 3,671, and Trinidad and Tobago 1,262 (St Lucia 2010; Grenada 2010; Antigua and Barbuda 2008; Trinidad and Tobago 2010).

Most of the Caribbean islands have numerous beaches, with Antigua and Barbuda boasting of "one beach for every day of the year", a total of 365; these include Barbuda's distinctive pink sand beaches at Palmetto Point. In addition to the beautiful beaches, other traditional seaside activities enjoyed by tourists and locals include camping and beach outings, or "limes". In Tobago Buccoo Beach is a long, narrow white sand beach protected by the world-famous Buccoo Reef. At Negril in Jamaica lies the widest and most breathtaking stretch of the renowned Seven-Mile Beach. Barbados possesses mile-long beaches of white sand; one of these, Crane Beach, was rated "one of the ten best beaches in the world" by the television show *Lifestyles of the Rich and Famous*. A very popular recreational and tourism activity which has developed in many territories is watching marine turtles lay their eggs on the beaches. The leatherback turtle (*Dermochelys coriacea*) is classified as critically endangered by the World Conservation Union (IUCN), and two of the largest nesting populations, numbering more than six thousand animals each, occur in Costa Rica and in Trinidad and Tobago.

A variety of water sports is also associated with the Caribbean Sea, such as snorkelling, water-skiing, jet-skiing, sailing, kayaking and scuba diving. Many of the islands have annual boat-racing events with considerable international participation. These include the Classic Yacht Regatta and Stanford Sailing Week in Antigua and Barbuda, the Angostura Classic in Trinidad and Tobago, the Sailing Festival in Grenada and the Easter Regatta in Carriacou.

Tourism is the fastest-growing economic activity in the Caribbean, with a US$28.4 million contribution to the gross domestic product (Agard et al. 2007), US$2.4 million towards employment, alleviation of poverty and associated foreign exchange earnings. The tourist industry therefore contributes significantly to the overall well-being of Caribbean people.

## Fish and Other Seafood

Fisheries have always been a source of livelihood and sustenance for the people of the Caribbean, contributing to food security, poverty alleviation, employment, foreign exchange earnings and development of rural and coastal communities (Agard et al. 2007). In fact, earlier Caribbean peoples (the Ortoiroids and Casimiroids of the Archaic period) are well-known to have been shellfish consumers, having left evidence in shell collections and artefacts made with pieces of shell (Reid 2009). Today fish is the staple protein in many Caribbean coastal communities, with per capita consumption hovering around fifteen kilograms per year (Agard et al. 2007).

Capture fisheries in the Caribbean include subsistence fisheries (catches are consumed by the local community), artisanal or small commercial operations, and industrial fishing using sophisticated vessels and modern technology. Catches from coral reefs amount to ten tonnes per square kilometre per year (Burke and Maidens 2004) and include species of snapper, grouper (Serranidae family), jack (Carangidae) and the less valuable parrotfish and surgeonfish (Acanthuridae). The shell fishery comprises conchs and lobsters, both associated with seagrasses and corals, and shrimp, which are typical of muddy coastal sediments. The fishing industry employs hundreds of thousands of people in both stable full-time and part-time jobs. This includes more than 200,000 fishers and about 100,000 workers associated with the processing and marketing of fishery products (Agard et al. 2007).

The Caribbean has some of the best saltwater fishing grounds in the world, which makes sport fishing a popular component of the tourism industry, particularly in Grenada, Antigua, Barbados, Tobago, Bahamas and the Dominican Republic. It is a prime destination for deep-sea fishing for bluefish (Pomatomidae family), swordfish (Xiphiidae), shark (Selachimorpha), marlin and other billfish (Istiophoridae). Fly-fishing and angling target barracuda (Sphyraenidae), bonefish (Albulidae), kingfish (Scomberomoridae), tarpon (Megalopidae), grouper and snappers. Many game-fishing tournaments are held in the Caribbean, and often world records (as designated by the International Game Fishing Association) have been achieved. The most recent record-breaker was a fifteen-year-old Trinidadian, Sean Mendonca, off Charlotteville, Tobago, in April 2008. He is now the new IGFA "Male Junior

Atlantic Blue Marlin World Record Holder", having landed an 890-pound (404 kg) blue marlin (Southern Caribbean Bill Fish Circuit 2010).

A variety of non-fish foods are also harvested from the Caribbean Sea. Marine algal species such as *Euchema isiforme, Gelidium serrulatum* and *Gracilaria* species (sea moss) are harvested from the sea in St Lucia, Trinidad and Tobago and Grenada. The dried algae are used to produce agar, a gelling agent, which in turn is used in a variety of products in addition to being sold as a packaged drink. The eggs (roe) of sea urchins are a high-value product in St Lucia and throughout the French Caribbean. In most of the other islands, bivalves such as oysters (*Crassostrea rhizophorae*) are commonly found in mangrove swamps, while mussels, or mok (*Mytilus edulis*), are found in coastal estuarine muds. Chitons (Polyplacophora family) – or pacro, as they are known in Trinidad – and the green mussel (*Perna viridis*) can be found attached to coastal rocky substrates. These seafood delicacies are eagerly harvested for their supposed aphrodisiac properties.

## Seafood Festivals

The Caribbean's oceanic surroundings continue to provide a diversity of seafood, including large game fish such as mahi-mahi (Delphinidae family), marlin and grouper, red snapper, mackerel (Scombridae) and "flying fish" (Exocoetidae), which is typical of the cuisine of Barbados. Conchs (*Strombus* species), spiny lobsters (Palinuridae family), sea urchins (*Tripneustes* species) and crabs (brachyurans) are plentiful and can be prepared in a variety of delicious ways.

Appreciation of the sea and its products is reflected in many traditional Caribbean seafood festivals, which are popular with both locals and tourists. The Oistins Festival in Barbados during the Easter weekend promotes the fishing community by allowing members to display "crafts of their trade". It typically involves a Friday-night fish fry at which a variety of fish are prepared in various ways. The festival includes music, dancing and water sports. Similarly, in St Lucia, the "original fish fry", which started in the village of Gros Islet, has now extended to other villages such as Dennery and Anse La Raye. In many of the Caribbean islands, including Grenada, Trinidad, St Lucia and Jamaica, the birth date of the patron saint of fishermen, Saint Peter, is celebrated on 29 June. The celebration starts with a religious service, followed by festivities accompanied by specially prepared fish dishes and other foods, music, dancing and revelry. Kingston, Jamaica, has an annual Old Harbour Fish and Bammy Festival, where an assortment of foods is served, including fresh fish in many different styles, accompanied by traditional cassava cakes, called bammies. As is typical of the rest of the Caribbean, there is lively music, dancing and entertainment, accompanied by dancing and singing competitions. In Grenada "Gouyave Fish Friday" is similarly celebrated with street festivities and a variety of seafood dishes. These festivals offer visitors a chance to sample some of the Caribbean's finest seafood, as well as other local delicacies.

## Religious Festivals and the Sea

Caribbean peoples, by virtue of their ethnic and cultural diversity, embrace a number of religions. Many of these have traditionally engaged in symbolic spiritual practices relating to the "powers" of the sea. There are many Hindu seaside practices which have strong spiritual symbolism, for example, the Kartik Snan in Trinidad, where Hindus bathe in the sea to be "cleansed" as the Indians do in the Ganges. Ganesh Jayanti is another Hindu spiritual ceremony, during which clay murtis (figurines) of Lord Ganesh are taken to the sea to be cleansed.

For Indian Arrival Day (30 May) there is a re-enactment of the arrival of the *Fatel Razack*, the first ship that brought East Indians to Trinidad, and its landing at Moruga. Settlement Day is similarly celebrated in Belize on 19 November by the Garifunas, who arrive on shore in traditional dugout canoes.

The Muslim ceremony of Hosay in Trinidad and Tobago commemorates the martyrdom of Muhammad's grandson Hussein with the symbolic building of *tadjahs*, replicas of his tomb. After four days of celebration the tadjahs are dragged to the sea, where they are destroyed. Also in Trinidad and Tobago, Yoruba worshippers of the goddess Osun perform one of their symbolic services in coastal areas where "a river meets the sea", for example, at Manzanilla. Food is offered to the sea in recognition of its "good waters" and its cleansing properties. The Shouter Baptists of Trinidad and Tobago conduct baptisms by immersing celebrants in the sea so that they are "born again". In Belize, the ceremonial Dugu feast of the Garifunas involves preparing offerings for ancestral spirits which are subsequently released into the sea.

## Other Caribbean Marine Resources

The coastal and marine areas continue to provide the peoples of the region with important economic resources such as oil and gas. Only three countries in the Caribbean region have significant oil and gas reserves: Trinidad and Tobago, Cuba and Suriname. In 2006 these three states had a combined 1.85 billion barrels of proven crude oil reserves and 29.9 trillion cubic feet of proven natural gas reserves (*Oil and Gas Journal* 2006). It is not uncommon to see rigs, gas flares and oil and gas boats dotting the Caribbean waters.

The Caribbean is one of the main exporters of live ornamental fish for the aquarium pet trade, which is a multimillion-dollar industry in the United States. More recently, other non-food goods such as marine sponges, jellyfish, red algae and corals have played an important role in the field of medicine. Natural products are being extracted from Caribbean species for use as pharmaceuticals, drugs and other manufactured chemical products. At the Cave Hill campus of the University of West Indies in Barbados, Professor W. Tinto, a natural products chemist, is actively researching bioactive compounds which he has extracted from Caribbean octocorals and sponges.

## Threats to Resources

A variety of activities which tend to permanently alter ecosystems such as mangroves and coral reefs pose serious threats to Caribbean coastal resources. These include pollution and contamination from industrial, urban and agricultural activities as well as coastal infrastructural developments. In many territories – for example, St Vincent, Tobago and Grenada – mining and built coastal developments have led to loss of beaches and other proximal coastal resources. The leatherback turtles' nesting habitat is being threatened both by these anthropogenic activities and by natural erosion, which often results in loss of their eggs (figure 14.2).

While pollution and increased oceanic temperatures have played a role in reducing some fisheries, scientists agree that overfishing on a vast scale is the

**Figure 14.2**
Leatherback turtle (*Dermochelys coriacea*) eggs exposed by natural erosion on the beach at Matura, Trinidad (photo courtesy D. Rousseau)

primary culprit (Dayton, Thrush and Coleman 2002; Pauly et al. 1998). Overharvesting has led to the decline of wild stocks of some species, for example, the white sea urchin (*Tripneustes ventricosus*) and its roe in St Lucia, Barbados, the Tobago cays and the French islands, and the humpback whale (*Megaptera novaeangliae*) in the Lesser Antillean waters.

Gardener and colleagues (2003) suggest that since 1980, mangrove areas in the Caribbean have decreased by about 1 per cent per year and have lost about 413,000 hectares, while Caribbean coral reefs have lost approximately 80 per cent of their living coral over the past twenty years, with some declines of more than 50 per cent. Our fragile resources are additionally threatened by hurricanes, storms and global climate change.

## Future of the Caribbean Sea and Its Resource Utilization

It is very difficult to isolate a specific cause for the changes in our coastal resources, since they are often a result of a combination of factors. For example, deleterious impacts on a mangrove swamp will affect coastal water quality as well as life in adjacent coral reefs and/or seagrass beds. Additionally, human impacts on Caribbean environments tend to be significant because of high population densities, poverty and the absence of adequate sanitation facilities in many islands. It is these negative impacts which compromise the resource values of ecosystems by directly and indirectly affecting the ability of particular resources to sustainably produce goods and services.

Figure 14.3 Michelle Cazabon's MPhil research project (University of the West Indies, St Augustine) aims to determine the status and distribution of the hawksbill turtle (*Eretmochelys imbricata*) and green turtle (*Chelonia mydas*) in Tobago (photo courtesy L. Beddoe).

Many Caribbean territories are already applying management strategies in an attempt to address these issues. Current initiatives include an integrated approach to management of coastal and marine resources. In this regard, the Integrated Watershed and Coastal Areas Management/Global Environment Fund project, the Caribbean Monitoring Productivity project and others are making significant contributions. Biodiversity, conservation and protection, sustainable tourism, reductions in land-based pollution, integration of environmental considerations into physical planning, Marine Protected Area management and community-based management are among the region's key strategies. Regional turtle conservation/protection projects in Costa Rica, Barbados, St Kitts and Trinidad have already begun to yield positive results. The coastal village of Matura in Trinidad presents an exemplary success story; conservation and protection measures there include participatory management on the part of the local community. Additionally, coastal environmental protection has increased with the introduction of new domestic legislation in some islands. These include, for example, the Coastal Zone Management acts of Barbados (1998) and Belize (revised 2000) for overall coastal zone management and protection. Some territories, such as Jamaica, Barbados, St Lucia, the Bahamas, Trinidad and Belize, have become signatories to key international legislation such as the Ramsar Convention for the protection of wetlands and the Convention on Biological Diversity.

The lives of Caribbean people are inextricably linked to the sea, with its blue-green warmth running through their veins. It is therefore imperative that we significantly increase our efforts to protect this integral part of our heritage so that future generations can also enjoy its tremendous benefits.

## Acknowledgements

I thank Shari Fitzpatrick for all her assistance in the collection and collation of research material and Alana Jute for her assistance with some additional material. Lee Ann Beddoe and Dani Rousseau are gratefully acknowledged for the use of their photos.

## References

Agard, J., A. Cropper and K. Garcia, eds. 2007. "Caribbean Sea Ecosystem Assessment (CARSEA)". Special issue, *Caribbean Marine Studies* (August).

Antigua and Barbuda. "Cruise and Yacht Vessel Arrivals by Month 2008". Ministry of Tourism and Civil Aviation. http://www.tourismantiguabarbuda.gov.ag/tourism_programs/pdf/statistics/arrivals_by_sea_cruise_2008.pdf (accessed November 2010).

Burke, L., and J. Maidens, eds. 2004. *Reefs at Risk in the Caribbean.* Washington, DC: World Resources Institute. http://pdf.wri.org/reefs_caribbean_full.pdf (accessed June 2008).

Callaghan, Richard T. 2007. "Survival of a Traditional Carib Watercraft Design Element". In *Proceedings of the 21st Congress of the International Association for Caribbean Archaeology*, edited by Basil Reid, Henry Petitjean Roget and Antonio Curet, 739–46. St Augustine: School of Continuing Studies, University of the West Indies.

Dayton, P.K., S. Thrush and F. Coleman. 2002. *Ecological Effects of Fishing in Marine Ecosystems of the United States.* Arlington, VA: Pew Oceans Commission.

Food and Agriculture Organization of the United Nations (FAO). 1997. *The State of the World Fisheries and Aquaculture, 1996.* Rome: FAO Fisheries Department.

Gardener, T.A., I.M. Cote, J.A. Gill, A. Grant and A.R. Watkinson. 2003. "Long-Term Regionwide Declines in Caribbean Corals". *Science* 301: 958–60.

Grenada. "Tourism Statistics". http://www.grenadagrenadines.com/images/uploads/Tourism_statics_2 010.pdf (accessed November 2010).

Honychurch, L. 1995. *The Caribbean People*, vol. 2. Cheltenham, UK: Nelson Thornes.

McGinley, Mark, ed. "Caribbean Sea Large Marine Ecosystem". In *Encyclopedia of Earth*, edited by Cutler J. Cleveland. Washington, DC: Environmental Information Coalition, National Council for Science and the Environment. http://www.eoearth.org/article/Caribbean_Sea_large_marine_ecosystem (accessed November 2010).

Miloslavich, P., and E. Klein, eds. 2005. *Caribbean Marine Biodiversity: The Known and Unknown.* Lancaster, PA: DEStech Publications.

*Oil and Gas Journal.* 2006. http://www.ogj.com/resourcecenter/ (accessed June 2008).

Pauly, D., V. Christensen, J. Dalsgaard, R. Froese and F. Torres Jr. 1998. "Fishing Down Marine Food Webs". *Science* 279: 860–63.

Reid, Basil. 2009. *Myths and Realities of Caribbean History.* Tuscaloosa: University of Alabama Press.

St Lucia. 2010. "Economic and Social Review 2009". http://www.stlucia.gov.lc/docs/EconomicReview2009.pdf (accessed November 2010).

Southern Caribbean Bill Fish Circuit. 2010. "Pre Tournament Press Statement from the Trinidad and Tobago Game Fishing Association 2010". http://www.billfishcircuit.com/tournaments2010/ttgfa2010.htm (accessed June 2010).

Towle, E.L., and J.A. Towle, eds. 1991. "Environmental Agenda for the 1990s". St Michael, Barbados: Caribbean Conservation Association.

Trinidad and Tobago. http://www.tourism.gov.tt/ (accessed November 2010).

# 15.

# Natural History of Trinidad and Tobago

COURTENAY ROOKS AND GREGOR BARCLAY

*Trinidad and Tobago offers the world a unique heritage of neotropical South American and Caribbean flora and fauna, including more than 460 bird species, amongst the greatest diversity of any island on Earth. More than two thousand species of plants grow on these tiny islands, in a wide range of habitats that include brackish to freshwater wetlands, rainforests, elfin woodlands, coral reefs and dynamic coasts. This diverse heritage of life is threatened by unplanned industrial growth, mining and poor waste disposal, which have caused water pollution, heavy metal poisoning and coral reef damage. Urban sprawl and agriculture have caused habitat loss and fragmentation. Legislation to protect the environment has not prevented illegal excavation or forestry, and squatters have invaded all of the sanctuaries and most forest reserves. Live capture for the caged-bird trade has drastically reduced the number of birds, including the moriche oriole and the saffron finch. However, while the scarlet ibis, the white-tailed sabrewing hummingbird and the endemic Trinidad piping guan (pawi) are endangered, their populations are increasing because of their ecotourism value. Also, community ecotourism efforts have reduced poaching of the endangered leatherback turtle, demonstrating that ecotourism and other conservation efforts can be effective tools for preserving our wildlife heritage.*

## Introduction

This chapter describes the roles played by geography, climate and geological history in creating the natural heritage of Trinidad and Tobago (see figures 15.1 and 15.2), specifically its flora and fauna. Maintenance of habitats, with

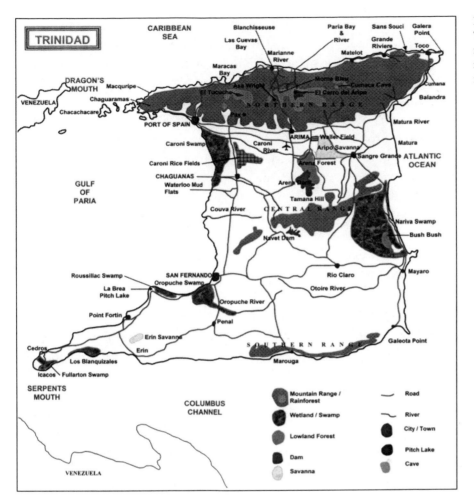

**Figure 15.1** Map of Trinidad, showing natural features, major roads and inhabited areas

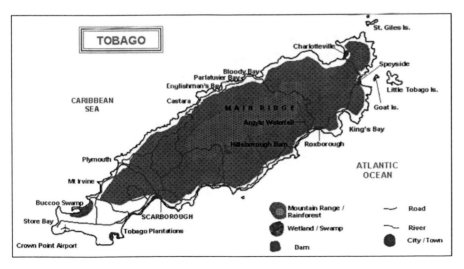

**Figure 15.2** Map of Tobago, showing natural features, major roads and inhabited areas

221

their attendant communities of diverse species, is required to conserve this heritage in the face of urbanization, agricultural practices, illegal logging and other pressures. As a general principle, biodiversity increases with the size of an ecosystem, which is why, for example, the Nariva Swamp in Trinidad and the Forest Reserve in Tobago are so special. Their size permits a very much greater variety of habitats and ecological niches for organisms to occupy than afforded by, for example, Cleaver Woods, on the outskirts of Arima, or the Blue Basin waterfall in Diego Martin, both of which have charms of their own but are very small in comparison.

The natural history of Trinidad and Tobago results from a fascinating mix of features and events that is as diverse as it is dynamic, producing the southern Caribbean's most biologically interesting islands. Briefly, Trinidad and Tobago is a combination of South American continental and Caribbean island ecosystems. The country sits on both northern and southern migratory bird routes, and its extensive habitats are crowded onto two small islands washed by both the Caribbean Sea and Atlantic Ocean. These marine ecosystems are in turn particularly nutrient-rich because they are fed by the Amazon, Essequibo and Orinoco rivers, yet nutrient-poor enough to host some of the Caribbean's most diverse reef systems. Trinidad and Tobago's natural history is inherently linked to its biodiversity. It defines everything from tiny liverworts to giant silk cotton trees, from coral polyps to the reefs they build – everything is diverse and frequently surprising. Kenny (2000, 2008) wrote prolifically on the plants, the wildlife and especially the biodiversity of Trinidad and Tobago.

## Geography

The biodiversity of Trinidad and Tobago, given the influence of elevation on habitats and niches, is strongly influenced by its geography. North Trinidad is dominated by the Northern Range, which is the most eastern outlier of the South American Andes (Liddle 1928). It is made mostly of metamorphic rock about 150 million years old, with small formations of calcium carbonate. At just over 900 metres it is not very tall, but it remains a very rugged range. The range was created by the Caribbean Plate as it pushed eastwards across the northern edge of the South American Plate, shearing off the top of the Andes and then being cut up by the erosive powers of many small, fast-flowing rivers. Trinidad and Tobago's most well-known mountain, El Tucuche, is found here. However, the highest peak in the country is not El Tucuche but El Cerro del Aripo, which at 940 metres above sea level is three metres taller.

Moving south, the mountains level out into the Caroni Plains, where deposition from the continent resulted in the sandy/clay soils that dominate the rest of Trinidad. The undulating hills of the Central Range rise out of the plains, and together with the Southern Plains and the Southern Range they form an assortment of closely spaced geological features with distinct geographies. Anaparima Hill – Amerindian for "single hill" and of mystical significance to the people of the First Nations – otherwise known as San Fernando Hill, is a solitary Cretaceous projection in a Tertiary rock plain. Tamana Hill is more obviously an ancient and massive coral reef, emphasizing the geological diversity of this region. The Southern Range, which is really made up of steeply rolling hills rather than mountains, hugs the south coast. It is commonly believed that Trinidad got its name from Columbus's sighting of the Trinity Hills, as in this quotation from Washington Irving cited by de Verteuil (1884):

> "On the 31st of July," says Washington Irving in his life of Columbus, "there was not above one cask of water remaining in each ship, when about mid-day a mariner at the mast-head beheld the summit of three mountains rising above the horizon, and gave the joyful cry of Land! As the ships drew nearer, it was seen that these three mountains were united at the base. Columbus had determined to give the first land he should meet the name of the Trinity. The appearance of these three mountains united into one, struck him as a singular coincidence; and, with a solemn feeling of devotion, he gave the island the name of 'La Trinidad,' which it bears at the present day."

However, it is difficult to see these three distinct hills from the Columbus Channel, where the explorer would have been. It is more likely that what he saw were the Northern, Central and Southern Ranges from off the east coast, since on clear days in July and August these are a common sight. Scattered throughout the three ranges are seemingly random pockets of calcium carbonate outcrops. Tamana has whole mountains made of this material. These small karst systems drain quickly, tending to dry out the vegetation above, and also erode beneath, creating cave systems in both the Northern Range and Tamana Hill.

Geologically, Tobago is more related to Aruba, Bonaire and Curaçao than it is to Trinidad. It comprises mainly two features: the calcium carbonate plateau of southwest Tobago's lowlands and the volcanically influenced Main Ridge, which makes up the northern three-quarters of the island. The highest point in Tobago is the 550-metre Pigeon Peak, near Speyside.

## Climate

Climate is the other major factor shaping Trinidad and Tobago's natural history. At just over ten degrees north of the equator, the country's climate is tropical and the temperature changes very little annually. The two islands host substantial mountain ranges that both enhance tropical weather systems and create convection rainfall, which increases with altitude. Because of the islands' location, between the Atlantic Ocean and the Caribbean Sea just off the South American continent, rains come from several sources. The northeast trade winds have a major effect on the republic because they are responsible for the pattern of rainfall, in general making the islands' east coasts somewhat wet, the central portions the wettest, and the west coasts the driest areas. Two other major sources of precipitation are the Intertropical Convergence Zone and tropical waves and depressions as they move across the Atlantic into the Caribbean.

While officially south of the hurricane belt, Trinidad has on occasion experienced hurricanes. Prime examples are Flora in 1963, which was one of the Caribbean's deadliest storms – the death toll was more than seven thousand – and Emily in 2005. The feeder bands of storms and hurricanes can deposit metres of water in a day. In the past they have caused damage even worse than direct hits, such as the effects of Tomas on Trinidad and Tobago in October 2010.

## Geological History

Within recent geological history, Trinidad and Tobago was connected to the South American continent by land bridges resulting from repeated ice ages over the past 100,000 years. During the cooler periods, sea levels were much lower, since so much of Earth's water was locked up in massive glaciers far away. This explains the South American flora and fauna of the twin-island republic. According to Comeau (1991), the last land bridge would have been present during the height of the most recent glaciation, about eighteen thousand years ago. Tobago was connected to Trinidad by a land bridge until at least fourteen thousand years ago, and the final separation between Trinidad and South America occurred at the beginning of the Holocene epoch, about fifteen hundred years ago (Kenny 2000).

## Habitats

This combination of elevations, history and climate has conspired to bless Trinidad and Tobago with a diverse range of habitats. The most obvious residents of the terrestrial habitats are, of course, the plants. Systematic description of the plant life began in the early nineteenth century with superintendents of the Royal Botanic Gardens – notably Herman Crüger, who contributed an "Outline of the Flora of Trinidad" to de Verteuil (1884) – collecting and organizing specimens that led to the establishment of its herbarium. Of the published work on plant life that followed, Beard (1946) was a standout; his treatise on forest habitats listed more than 300 tree species in Trinidad and more than 160 in Tobago. More recently, Quensel and Farrell (2005) have written an engaging and well-illustrated text on the forest habitats of Trinadad and Tobago and the trees native to them. The chief characteristics of the more significant habitats are as follows.

The summits of Trinidad's highest mountains, El Cerro del Aripo and El Tucuche, are home to Elfin Woodland, which is continuously wet. This forest is affected by dense cloud cover that douses the plants with more than four metres of rain annually while starving them of sunshine. This combination of circumstances effectively reduces the tree canopy to less than ten metres high, while rain-loving plants flourish, including epiphytes, ferns, mosses and palms. While the constant cloud cover at these summits often hides memorable views, the forest, shrouded in soaking clouds, makes for some of the island's most primordial scenes.

At altitudes below 900 metres is found Upper Montane Rain Forest, which is also very wet and cool; the tallest trees gain a height of only about twenty-five metres, and palms and ferns are common. Interestingly, both the tallest palms (species of *Euterpe*) and the short palms (species of *Genoma* and *Prestoea*) occur at the higher locations. The most abundant and fecund rainforest, the Lower Montane Rain Forest, is found between 750 metres and 150 metres above sea level. This habitat occurs in all of Trinidad's ranges and in Tobago's Main Ridge, where the tallest emergent trees can reach heights of more than fifty metres, with canopies beginning at twenty-five metres. This is possibly the most biodiverse habitat, with a range of both lowland and highland characteristics, and almost every species of forest flora and fauna has found residence here at one time or another. Climbing bamboo (*Arthrostylidium* species) is found in all habitats above 600 metres. This bamboo is notable for its tendency to grow across trails, often clogging them. The leaves are annoyingly sharp and the stems are very flexible and tough, making it very difficult to cutlass through.

The lower elevations are dominated by Seasonal Evergreen Forests and Wetlands. The Seasonal Evergreen Forest is similar to Lower Montane Rain Forests but includes taller and more deciduous species because it is influenced by an annual dry season, which these species tolerate. The dominant tree species are crappo (*Carapa guianensis*) and guatecare (*Eshweilera subglandulosa*). Several plants are common in the Lower Montane Rain Forests and Seasonal Evergreen Forests, including chaconia (*Warsewiczia coccinea*), the national flower. Its conspicuous "flower" is really a double row of bright scarlet petaloid sepals. Epiphytes are common in both forest types, including aroids, bromeliads, climbers, ferns, lianas and orchids. Some of these plants compete with the trees for light, in particular the climbers and lianas, which can interfere with the growth of trees and, when abundant, damage them. Also found in these habitats is the peach palm (*Bactris gasipaes*), commonly called pewa in Trinidad and Tobago, which has edible fruit and is distinctive because its trunk is festooned with long, sharp needle-like bracts.

At the lowest elevations, often in coastal areas, are Semi-evergreen Seasonal Forests, which host the largest trees. Of note here are kapok (*Ceiba pentandra*) near Marouga Bouffe and sandbox (*Hura crepitans*) in Bush Bush, a part of the Nariva Swamp. The diversity of species in this forest is readily affected by the dry season, and depending on its location and soil type, different tree species may dominate. In the Northern Range, the forests can look similar to the Seasonal Evergreen Forest, whereas south of the Northern Range, bois mulatre (*Pentaclethra macroloba*) may dominate. In both types of seasonal forests the dry season is marked by spectacular displays of blossoms of the yellow poui (*Tabebuia serratifolia*) and black poui (*T. rufescens*).

There are many types of wetlands in Trinidad and Tobago. In the savannas of Aripo and Erin are found many plant species which because of their adaptations are unique to these habitats. Marsh Forest and Palm Marsh Forest are probably the least well-known type of wetlands, with Mangrove Swamp being the most well known. The Caroni Swamp in Trinidad is its largest brackish wetland system; Nariva in Trinidad is the largest freshwater wetland and the most biodiverse. The Buccoo Swamp in Tobago is of critical importance, as it has a symbiotic relationship with the island's famous Buccoo Reef.

However, habitats do not stop at the seashore. Tobago hosts a wide variety of reef systems, from fringing reefs such as those in Speyside to barrier reefs such as Buccoo Reef. Trinidad has far fewer reefs, with a barrier reef at Salybia Bay and finger-coral reefs scattered along the north coast. The reef systems in the Gulf of Paria were largely destroyed by the US military during the Second World War, when they dredged the coral to use as aggregate for construction. Skirting the west coast wetlands are many large tidal mudflats that hundreds of thousands of birds rely upon as feeding grounds.

## Wildlife

While Trinidad and Tobago's fauna is basically South American, both islands are routes for migratory birds from the northern and southern hemispheres, some of which have started to nest in the country, such as the southern lapwing (*Vanellus chilensis*). This means that Trinidad and Tobago's list of bird species continues to rise, from 434 just fifteen years ago to currently more than 460. Extreme weather events, such as storms and floods, divert migratory birds off course, adding to the twin-island republic's total bird list but not to the diversity of resident nesting birds. Regular flooding of the Orinoco Delta has the potential to resupply and add new species to enrich the country's biodiversity. When this massive river floods, it carries along floating reeds, branches and other debris. Small fauna such as snakes, insects and frogs ride on this flotsam, which can wash up on Trinidad's beaches, where they become new residents.

## Diversity of Species in Trinidad and Tobago

- more than 260 species of breeding birds
- more than 150 migratory bird species from North and South America
- more than 50 accidental migrant bird species
- more than 600 species of butterflies
- more than 190 species of orchids
- more than 100 mammals, of which about 60 are bats
- more than 100 reptiles and amphibians
- more than 2,500 species of flowering plants

## Insects and Arthropods

Terrestrial habitats host innumerable insects, including leaf-cutting ants, wasps, moths, bees and soldier ants, that have intricate and important relationships with the forest as predators, pollinators, recyclers and food. A favourite with visitors are the butterflies, some of which are simply spectacular, for example, the fast-flying king shoemaker (*Prepona demophon*), the bamboo page (*Philathria dido*), the king page (*Papilio cresphontes*), the yellows (*Phoebis* species) with their sulphur dabs of colour, the dashing red of the flambeaus (*Agraulis* species) and the blue emperor (*Morpho peleides*) with its blue laser-light show. Mention should also be made of the arachnids, or spiders. The most notable for their size are the golden silk spiders (*Tetragnathidae* species) and tarantulas (*Theraphosidae* species); both may be found in various habitats, except for the wettest of forests.

## Crabs

Crabs are also an important part of local fauna. The seashore and wetlands host the blue-backed crab (*Cardisoma guanhumi*), most celebrated for the part it plays in Tobago's world-famous crab races and delicious curried crab and dumpling. The hairy or swamp crab (*Ucides cordatus*), a delicacy mostly in Indian communities, can be found in swamps. People living in the mountains will be familiar with the mountain or manicou crab (*Eudaniela garmani*), for which groups of locals can be seen hunting during and immediately after heavy rains. Mudflats host tiny fiddler crabs (*Uca* species) waving their massive claws. Their displays lead them to their becoming food for herons (Ardeidae family), ibis (Threskiornithidae family) and other large shorebirds; this makes the fiddler crab a key species in wetland food webs.

## Mammals

The larger South American mammals, including jaguars (*Panthera onca*), tapirs (*Tapirus terrestris*) and the giant anteater (*Myrmecophaga tridactyla*), are missing from the forests, but even without them the mammalian fauna are diverse (Emmons 1997). Five species are regularly hunted: the diurnal, vegetarian agouti (*Dasypus agouti*); the nocturnal, vegetarian and closely related lappe or paca (*Agouti paca*); the nocturnal, mainly carnivorous tattoo or nine-banded armadillo (*Dasypus novemcinctus*); the diurnal, vegetarian collared peccary, also known as quenk or wild hog (*Tayassu tajacu*); and the crepuscular, vegetarian red-brocket deer (*Mazama americana*). The forests host a variety of other interesting species; the otter (*Lutra endris*) and its cousin the tyra (*Eira barbara*) are often called "high-woods dogs" because of their dog-like bark. The ocelot (*Felis pardalis*), a predator of a variety of wildlife, is locally endangered and threatened worldwide. Trees host several mammals with prehensile tails, including the opossum, or manicou (*Didelpihs marsupialis*), which is also heavily hunted; the porcupine (*Coendou prehensilis*); the three-toed anteater (*Tamandua longicaudata*); and two monkeys, the red howler (*Alouatta seniculus*) – the Americas' loudest mammal – and the white-fronted capuchin (*Cebus albifrons*).

## Birds

Trinidad and Tobago is well-known for its wide variety of species and its sheer numbers of birds; the standard text on their identification and habits is ffrench (2004). The spectacular scarlet ibis (*Eudocimus ruber*) is the national bird of the island of Trinidad and can be found in the west coast wetlands. The cocrico, or rufous-vented chachalaca (*Ortalis ruficauda*), is present throughout Tobago and is that island's national bird. Some truly strange birds also reside in Trinidad and Tobago. For example, the devilbird, or oilbird (*Steatornis caripensis*), is a rare, cave-dwelling species that uses echolocation to navigate – one of very few species of bird to do so. It feeds on palm fruits, the oils of which can make the chick weigh as much as double the weight of its parents. The bearded bellbird (*Procnias averano*) uses an unusually loud *bonk* call to mark its territory and attract females. The barred antshrike (*Thamnophilus doliatus*) – described as a zebra in pyjamas – and the spotted tody-flycatcher

(*Todirostrum maculatum*) can both eat a third of their weight in insects daily.

With twenty-two species of tanagers, twenty-five of wood warblers, seventeen of hummingbirds and ten of parrots and macaws, there is no shortage of brilliant colour and character among the local avian fauna. Trogons (*Trogonidae* species) and manakins (*Pipridaes* species) are notable for their vivid colours and distinctive behaviour. Trogons are violet, green, blue, yellow and red, and they have a habit of taking acid baths in azteca ant nests. Male manakins execute snappy and elaborate whizzing, buzzing, moonwalking, cartwheeling dances while dressed in blue, red, gold, black and white as they try to impress the picky (and camouflaged) females.

## Reptiles and Amphibians

The reptiles and amphibians of Trinidad and Tobago are also of South American origin, and they form a diverse group (Boos 1991; Murphy 1997). The three biggest snakes cause the most fear. One of the world's largest snakes, and certainly the king of constriction, is the huile (pronounced *wheel*), or anaconda (*Eunectes murinus gigas*). It is the apex predator of the freshwater wetlands of central and south Trinidad; stories abound of dogs, pigs and even cows being devoured by anacondas. The beauty of the pink and black diamond scaling of the bushmaster (*Lachensis muta muta*) is unrivalled. This snake's venom is deadly, but fortunately it tends to be docile. Legends of its attaining lengths of five metres or more are probably just that, but it does grow to just under four metres, making it the longest member of its family. The arboreal tropical rat snake, or tigre (*Spilotes pullatus pullatus*), which may reach a length of three metres, also elicits a strong response from people; however, stories of it chasing people all around forests are again pure fantasy. The snake that evokes the most fear, and for good reason, is the fer-de-lance, also known as lance-head viper or mapepire balsain (*Bothrops altrox*), which is known for delivering the most venomous of snakebites not only in Trinidad but also in much of South and Central America. The young of this snake are among the most common, since the mother can give birth to up to fifty live young, but they are preyed upon by many animals, including the crapaud, or marine toad (*Bufo marinus*), which is itself poisonous, the poison being stored in large parotid glands on the sides of its head.

The night air is alive with the songs of many frogs, including the rolling call of tree frogs (*Hyla* species) and the chirping of the *Manophryne* species. The frog that is most prized by local naturalists is the golden tree frog (*Phyllodytes auratus*), which is endemic to Trinidad. It can be found living in bromeliads on mountains at elevations above 600 metres – a very restricted habitat. Certainly if these areas become warm and dry because of climate change, this species, which is already listed on the International Union for Conservation of Nature UCN Red List as Critically Endangered, may disappear altogether.

Zandolies (*Ameiva ameiva*), a common garden and forest lizard known for its speed, faces no threat of disappearing anytime soon. However, the iguana (*Iguana iguana*) and the matt, or golden tegu (*Tupinambis teguxin*), both appear on hunters' menus; their futures are less certain. Several geckos call Trinidad and Tobago home, the best-known being the wood slave (*Thecadactylus rapicauda*), while one of the showiest is *Gonatodes ceciliae* with its yellow, orange, red and black head. Five species of sea turtle are known to breed in Trinidad and Tobago; the most commonly seen is the leatherback turtle (*Dermochelys coriacea*), followed by the hawksbill turtle (*Eretmochelys imbricata*), the green turtle (*Chelonia mydas*), the loggerhead turtle (*Caretta caretta*) and finally the least common, which is the olive ridley (*Lepidochelys olivacea*). All of these turtles are on the IUCN Red List, as they are considered to be endangered.

## Conservation and Ecotourism

Conservation on these islands started in Tobago with the declaration of the Main Ridge as a protected area. The Main Ridge forms the spine of the legally protected Tobago Forest Reserve, which was established in 1776. Forest reserves have been created throughout history, but the Tobago Forest Reserve was the first to encompass its own watershed, making it unique. It is reported that this reserve was one of the first, if not the first official act of conservation by humans.

This was followed by formation of the Trinidad and Tobago Field Naturalists' Club in 1891. While the club's intent was to cultivate an interest in natural history rather than conservation, its membership has included many of Trinidad and Tobago's most vociferous conservationists. This in turn has led to the fact that almost every conservation-based non-governmental organization in Trinidad and Tobago has been started by a Trinidad and Tobago Field Naturalists' Club member, by members' actions or by action of the club itself. The list is impressive: the University of the West Indies Biological Society, Environment Tobago, the Asa Wright Nature Centre, the Point-a-Pierre Wildfowl Trust, the Council of Presidents of the Environment, the Caribbean Forest Conservation Association and Nature Seekers, amongst others. Added to this list are government organizations such as the Emperor Valley Zoo, the Institute of Marine Affairs and the Forestry Division, all of which have been influenced by the Trinidad and Tobago Field Naturalists' Club.

Ecotourism has had a major effect on conservation in Trinidad and Tobago.

It actually began in the hills of the Arima Valley, with the purchase of the Spring Hill Estate in 1967. It was then transformed into the Asa Wright Nature Centre, named after its former owner. The centre spent many years operating at a loss but reversed this by encouraging naturalists and birders to visit the centre for a fee, beginning in the early 1970s. Hence the owners of the Asa Wright Nature Centre ventured into the business of ecotourism before there was a name for it.

## Conservation of Birds

Trinidad and Tobago is host to only one endemic bird: the pawi, or Trinidad piping guan (*Pipile pipile*), which is listed as Critically Endangered on the IUCN Red List and is of Immediate Conservation Priority in the Cracid Specialist Group action plan. Hunting and loss of habitat have threatened its survival, with its range being reduced from most of the Northern and Central Ranges and possibly even the Southern Range. Just one population remains, confined to a part of the Northern Range in northeast Trinidad. In response to this alarming situation, the Forestry Division and community groups started the "We Pawi" programme in the mid-1990s. The programme's organizers used the "We Pawi" name, supported by education programmes and educational literature, to evoke an emotional response of national pride in the pawi, and this resulted in a serious decline in pawi hunting. Burgeoning ecotourism activities, specifically bird tours, have engendered a greater sense of its value and pride in this bird. In 2004 the Pawi Study Group was formed to bring together individuals and groups that were interested in the pawi and in actively promoting its conservation. Scientists, including Professor John Cooper and Kerrie Naranjit, lent their expertise to community-based organizations including the Guardian Wildlife Fund, Nature Seekers and the Grande Riviere Nature Tour Guides Association, which are continuing study and conservation of the pawi through local communities.

Another case of an endangered bird's being saved concerns Tobago's white-tailed sabrewing (*Campylopterus ensipennis*), which was thought to have been extirpated from the Montane Rain Forests of the Main Ridge for some two decades following Hurricane Flora in 1963. Recently it has been making a marvellous comeback, resulting from the birding ecotourism industry and the fact that its habitat lies within the protected area of Tobago's Main Ridge. The reappearance of the sabrewing is of great importance, since its only other population is in Venezuela, where numbers are rapidly diminishing because of habitat destruction. Hence, Tobago may soon host the world's only wild population, and there are no known captive ones.

The scarlet ibis (*Eudocimus ruber*) population collapsed in the mid-1980s, with numbers dropping from an estimated 100,000 to about 2,500, mainly because of aggressive hunting and habitat loss in the west coast wetlands. The bird has made a substantial comeback since the destruction of Caroni Swamp, its main habitat, was halted in the same decade. Ecotourism in the swamp has enabled many visitors to appreciate this bird's beauty and its tenuous situation, also converting the hearts and minds of many locals. It is exciting to see that a selling point for real estate in Roussillac, Trinidad, is that many scarlet ibises can now be seen there.

But the scarlet ibis was not alone in its need for intervention. By the early 1970s, other populations of wildfowl, including the black-bellied whistling-duck (*Dendrocygna autumnalis*) and the fulvous whistling-duck (*D. bicolor*), had matched its fate for the same reasons. This prompted a conservation effort in the form of the Point-a-Pierre Wildfowl Trust, which was established in 1967 to breed wildfowl and other wetland-dwelling species, including the blue-and-yellow macaw (*Ara ararauna*), to be raised and released into the wild. Macaws had been extirpated from their natural home range by the 1970s through capture for the caged-bird trade. The captive breeding programme was successful from the start. However, once released, the birds were shot by hunters; they were subsequently released only at the trust property. Working with the Forestry Division and others, the trust has now released breeding pairs of blue-and-yellow macaws in Bush Bush. It is understood that there has been a commendable 50 per cent success rate of released pairs surviving to reproduce.

The caged-bird trade requires special mention because it has been the most significant cause of population loss by birds in Trinidad and Tobago. Without quick action, the population plunge of the macaws will be followed by four seedeaters – the grey (*Sporophila intermedia*), variable (*S. americana*), yellow-bellied (*S. nigricollis*) and ruddy-breasted (*S. minuta*); two seed finches, the large-billed (*Oryzoborus crassirostris*) and the lesser (*O. angolensis*); the saffron finch (*Sicalis flaveola*); the yellow-crowned parrot (*Amazona ochrocephala*); and the moriche oriole (*Icterus chrysocephalus*). These birds were originally rated Somewhat Common to Very Common; all are now rated Very Rare or Thought to Be Extirpated. The Forestry Division has tried to curb this lucrative and illegal business, but because of understaffing and underfunding it has enjoyed only limited success. A possible solution is the further development of ecotourism, in which the birds are seen as more valuable and more beautiful in the wild than in a cage.

White-fronted capuchin and red howler monkeys were once found through-out Trinidad, but mass die-offs in the 1960s and 1970s from yellow fever restricted their populations to the central and southern forests. However, vac-cination of the human population, conservation efforts and ecotourism have resulted in both monkey species making a comeback in all of their ranges. They have recently been seen in the Matura Wildlife Reserve and on El Tucuche, and are easier still to find in Bush Bush and Chaguaramas.

Traditionally the agouti, lappe, armadillo, collared peccary, red-brocket deer and other mammals were hunted for food and for some extra cash, but recently this has increased significantly because of the rapidly increasing value of "wild meat". As in many other countries, wild-caught game is seen as not only healthier to eat but also excellent for providing strength and virility. Hunting has evolved from an activity for only some villagers and rich folk to a growing industry. This has devastated natural wildlife populations, since hunting has expanded beyond traditional prey to include caimans (*Caiman crocodiles*), iguanas (*Iguana iguana*), doves (Columbidae family) and many more animals. Again, a possible solution to this apparent epidemic is eco-tourism, because live wildlife is much more valuable than dead game.

## Conservation of the Leatherback Turtle

The odyssey of leatherback turtle conservation started with a visit by the Trinidad and Tobago Field Naturalists' Club in the late 1960s to Matura Beach, where they witnessed a ghastly scene: enormous leatherbacks lying on the beach in various stages of decay, having been hacked apart for their meat. This horrific discovery led to research on turtle-nesting behaviour by Profes-sor Peter Bacon, beginning in the late 1960s, supported by the University of the West Indies and the Trinidad and Tobago Field Naturalists' Club. This study was used in 1975 to strengthen laws protecting the turtles, although little was done to enforce the laws. A video featuring the turtles' plight was aired on local television in Trinidad and Tobago, and it incited Matura resi-dents to become actively involved in turtle conservation. In 1990 this led to the formation of Nature Seekers. Nature Seekers forged a very difficult path to success as it battled the government, friends, family and even environmen-talists. Single-minded perseverance led to internationally acclaimed success, and this victory for leatherback turtle conservation has now been repeated in Grande Riviere, Fishing Pond and Tobago. This is an excellent example of what can be achieved in effective conservation of the natural history of

Trinidad and Tobago through concerted action at both the community and national levels.

## Conclusion

Conservation of Trinidad and Tobago's natural heritage can be improved if a number of things occur. Current laws that protect watersheds and sensitive habitats will be effective only if they are enforced. Further development of legislation must include participation from all stakeholders; most critical are rural communities with whom partnerships exist for conservation through habitat and wildlife management, and ecotourism. This includes protection of keystone species – species upon which many others depend in various ecosystems – and of flagship species such as the leatherback turtle and the scarlet ibis, which are vulnerable, charismatic or otherwise popular, and likewise bring protection to ecosystems when they themselves are protected.

Ecotourism in Trinidad and Tobago can become even more valuable and ethical if the associated accommodation providers, tour operators and their travel packages do not leave energy and cultural footprints with impacts more deleterious than the benefits they are perceived to bring. Unmanaged ecotourism can attract hordes of visitors from wealthy countries to delicate and remote areas – too often located in developing countries – destroying more than they are protecting.

But most of all, everyone, from all strata of society, must come to appreciate and value their own natural heritage rather than simply taking it for granted, paying only scant notice if, for example, a forest is destroyed by fire or by illegal logging. While public awareness campaigns have a role to play, continued education, both in the classroom and in the field, about wildlife and habitat conservation in Trinidad and Tobago, beginning at the primary school level, is the most cost-effective way to achieve long-lasting changes.

## References

Beard, John S. 1946. *The Natural Vegetation of Trinidad*. Oxford: Oxford University Press.

Boos, Hans E.A. 2001. *The Snakes of Trinidad and Tobago*. College Station: Texas A&M University Press.

Comeau, Paul L. 1991. "Geological Events Influencing Natural Vegetation in Trinidad". *Living World: Journal of the Trinidad and Tobago Field Naturalists' Club*: 29–38.

Comeau, Paul L., L. Guy, E. Heesterman and C. Hull. 1992. *The Trinidad and Tobago*

*Field Naturalists' Club Trail Guide.* Port of Spain: Trinidad and Tobago Field Naturalists' Club.

de Verteuil, Louis A.A. 1884. *Trinidad: Its Geography, Natural Resources, Administration, Present Condition and Prospects.* 2nd ed. London: Cassell.

Emmons, Louise H. 1997. *Neotropical Rainforest Mammals: A Field Guide.* Chicago: University of Chicago Press.

ffrench, Richard A. 2004. *Birds of Trinidad and Tobago.* Oxford: Macmillan Education.

Kenny, Julian S. 2000. *Views from the Ridge: Exploring the Natural History of Trinidad and Tobago.* Port of Spain: Prospect Press.

_____. S. 2008. *The Biological Diversity of Trinidad and Tobago: A Naturalist's Notes.* Port of Spain: Prospect Press.

Liddle, Ralph A. 1928. *The Geology of Venezuela and Trinidad.* Fort Worth, TX: J.P. MacGowan.

Murphy, John C. 1997. *Reptiles and Amphibians of Trinidad and Tobago.* Malabar, FL: Krieger.

Quesnel, Victor, and F. Farrell. 2005. *Native Trees of Trinidad and Tobago.* Port of Spain: TTFNC.

# 16.

# Medicinal Plants of Trinidad and Tobago

GREGOR BARCLAY

*Medicinal use of plants began in Trinidad and Tobago with the first inhabitants, Amerindians from northeast South America, at least seven thousand years ago. Their indigenous treatments were supplemented by European explorers and settlers, starting in the fifteenth century, then by slaves from Africa and later by indentured labourers from India and Southeast Asia. Urbanization, accompanied by increasing dependence on prescription drugs, threatens to marginalize the traditional pharmacopeia, but acceptance of herbal and other forms of alternative medicine continues to grow. A review of the literature revealed a total of 338 different plant species with reputed medicinal properties now growing in Trinidad and Tobago. Strategies for maximizing the potential of indigenous medical treatments include biochemical screening of plants, protection of traditional knowledge and ongoing education and promotion of herbal cures.*

## Introduction

Herbal remedies associated with traditional health care, a synergy of "Medicine meeting the Humanities" (Andermann 1996), are a significant part of drug therapy in Trinidad and Tobago. Traditional medical practices stem from Caribbean creole culture and the heritage of its African, Asian, European and South American Indian peoples. The history of medicinal plant use in Trinidad and Tobago began when Amerindian immigrants arrived some seven thousand years ago from South America. Written records of medicinal use of plants by Amerindians date from the end of the fifteenth century, with the arrival of Christopher Columbus in the Caribbean; at that time the Amerindian population of Trinidad and Tobago was about ten to forty thousand.

The Amerindian pharmacopeia included a number of plants familiar to us today. Sanderson (2005) describes the cultivation and medicinal uses of sweet potato (*Ipomea batatas*) as well as of cassava (*Manihot esculanta*) and arrowroot (*Maranta arundinaceae*) by the Amerindians. They used a poultice of mashed arrowroot rhizome to draw the poison from poisoned-arrow wounds. The plant may have gotten its name from this use, or perhaps it is derived from *aru-aru*, Amerindian for "meal of meals". Other plants with medicinal uses that were grown by Amerindians include mammee apple (*Mammea americana*), tobacco (*Nicotiana tabacum*), avocado (*Persea americana*), annatto (*Bixa orellana*), calabash (*Cresecentia cujute*), white sapote (*Casimiroa edulis*), black sapote (*Diospyros digyna*), hog plum (*Spondias mombin*), bottle gourd (*Lagenaria siceraria*) and cohoba (*Piptadenia peregrine*), which they used to make an hallucinogenic snuff (Newsom 1993, in Lans 2007).

According to de Verteuil (1858) the Amerindian population dwindled over time, declining from just 2,032 in 1783 to 1,082 in 1798, and only 689 were left in 1830. He estimated that between two and three hundred remained in 1858, and explained the reasons for this decline as follows:

> It is highly probable that many [sought] a refuge and home in the virgin forests of Venezuela; but I also coincide in opinion with some judicious observers, who trace the approximate extinction of these tribes to the marked preference manifested by the Indian women towards the negroes and the whites, by whom they were kindly treated, whilst they were regarded by their husbands, of kindred race, more as slaves and beasts of burden, than as equals or companions. As a consequence of those connections, there exists at present, in the colony, a certain number of individuals of Indian descent, but of mixed blood.

Mingling of Amerindians with the Spanish, British and Africans created a distinct people, known as cocoa panyols (derived from *español*), who lived and worked on the cocoa plantations of Trinidad's Northern Range, especially in the Caura Valley (Saunders 2005). The cocoa panyols have been in decline since the early twentieth century; many of those remaining live at the Lopinot cocoa estate. However, their culture persists in the popular music and dance of parang and in other Hispanic cultural practices brought to Trinidad and Tobago, which include religious-based beliefs about plant uses (Lans 2008), mainly from Venezuela.

De Verteuil noted that all of the Amerindians in Trinidad and Tobago had adopted the Spanish language and customs, notably *dolce far niente* – Italian for "sweet doing nothing". The Spanish consolidated the Amerindians at the mission of Santa Rosa de Arima, a 534-hectare estate that the British preserved after Trinidad and Tobago was ceded to them in 1802. However, when Governor Woodford died in 1828, his successors did not maintain the system of Spanish governance. The mission was effectively terminated in the 1840s and the Amerindians lost ownership of their lands (Moodie-Kublalsingh 1994, in Forte 2003), apparently illegally. Today the Amerindian people are represented by the Santa Rosa Carib Community of Arima. They are a fount of knowledge about indigenous medical treatments in Trinidad and Tobago.

## Heritage of the Names of Medicinal Plants

The history of some medicinal plants used in Trinidad and Tobago is reflected in their names. For example, the scientific name for aloes, *Aloe barbadensis* (one of a number of taxonomic synonyms for *A. vera*), is said to have originated in the practice of Jesuit clergy of sending plants to Jamaica and Barbados, then under Spanish rule (Pickersgill 2005). Seeds of Amerindian plants were also sent to Europe to be grown in monastery gardens, notably of the genus *Capsicum* (which includes both sweet and hot pepper species), perhaps the reason for the spread of this plant across Europe.

For some species, common names refer to local uses, which can create confusion but reveal some interesting relationships. For example, children learning to walk have their feet and knees rubbed with leaves of *Xiphidium caeruleum* (Wong 1976) or are given an infusion of its red berries, so the local name of this plant is walk-fast. *Trimezia martinicensis* (syn. *Neomarica longifolia*), a member of the Haemodoraceae (bloodwort) family, is one of a few plants known locally as dragon's blood. Its grated red rhizome is used to treat women's menstrual problems (Wong 1976). The red colour results from the presence of phenylphenalenones and related compounds, the chemotaxonomic markers of this family. A name more widely used for this plant species, which is native to South America but now occurs wild throughout the tropics of the New World and elsewhere as a houseplant, is walking iris. This name arose for a quite different reason than that of walk-fast. *T. martinicensis* reproduces vegetatively by above-ground stolons, with plantlets taking root along them at more or less uniform step-like intervals from the host plant, hence its common name.

A more everyday example of the intricacies of common names is arrowroot, which can be any species of *Maranta*, a genus of mostly large herbaceous perennials of the family Marantaceae. As a food, "arrowroot" is often used to describe the easily digestible starch obtained from the rhizomes of *Maranta arundinaceae*, the so-called real, or West Indian, arrowroot. But other plants produce similar starches, including East Indian arrowroot – species of *Curcuma*, chiefly *C. angustifolia*, of the Zingiberaceae (ginger) family, native to central India; Queensland arrowroot (*Canna edulis*, family Cannaceae); and Brazilian arrowroot (*Manihot esculenta*), or tapioca, of the Euphorbiaceae (spurge) family. In fact, Brazilian arrowroot, more commonly known as cassava, is the chief source of commercial arrowroot starch.

None of these plants should be confused with species of *Sagittaria* (family Alismataceae), which are sometimes called "arrowhead" and used as root vegetables. What is more, there are at least four other plants that yield starch copiously enough to be named arrowroot. Perhaps the oddest one is Florida arrowroot, or sago palm (*Cycas revoluta*), which is neither a member of the palm family nor indeed a flowering plant at all, but a member of the relictual Cycadaceae, a major plant group of the Mesozoic era now listed as endangered worldwide. Finally, *C. revoluta* is not to be confused with *Metroxylon sagu*, the true sago palm; it is notable for its trunk, which when mature is rich in starch that is a staple food mainly in eastern Indonesia and Papua New Guinea.

## The Doctrine of Signatures

The doctrine of signatures is frequently associated with medicinal plant use. It dates back through Nicholas Culpeper's herbal of 1652 to the works of Theophrastus in the fourth century BCE; it is also found in traditional beliefs in Africa, China, South America and India that originated earlier still. The doctrine prescribes the treatment of like with like, holding that if a part of a plant resembles part of the human body which needs medicinal treatment, or if it has a characteristic similar to the malady's, such as its colour, it can be used to treat that part or that illness. It is in this spirit that cat's claw (*Macfedyena unguis-cati*), which is distinguished by trifid tendrils with sharply hooked tips resembling claws, arising in its leaf axils, and the liana monkey ladder (*Bauhinia cumanensis*), which has spiralling woody stems, are used in Trinidad and Tobago for treating snakebite. Decoctions of the red mature wood of the latter plant, as well as of the red flowers of cooper hook (*Brownea latifolia*) and the rhizome of dragon's blood (mentioned above), are used for treating women's menstrual problems.

Tiny and delicate liverworts grow along the constantly wet, shaded and undisturbed margins of woodland streams, especially in the Northern Range of Trinidad and in the Tobago Forest Reserve. They acquired their unseemly common name from *wort*, the Anglo-Saxon name for "plant", and *liver*, referring to the shape of the vegetative part of *Marchantia* and similar species. Hepatophyta, the Latin name for the liverwort division (which consists of something like eight thousand species worldwide) means "liver plant". Belief that this beautiful yet unlikely toxic plant might actually be good for the liver, just because of its shape, remained strong enough that it remained in use in Europe until the nineteenth century to treat liver diseases.

# Literature on Medicinal Plants of Trinidad and Tobago

A number of authors have contributed to the body of knowledge on medicinal uses of plants in Trinidad and Tobago. In 1966 and 1967 Wong (1976) collected more than nine hundred individual recipes for local remedies, using 186 plant species, from seventy informants living in Blanchisseuse, a village of about nine hundred people (1960 census) on the north coast. The village is wedged between forest-covered mountain slopes and the sea, with the nearest town some forty kilometres away by a narrow, twisting road. At the time of the study there was no electricity, running water or sewage system, and no full-time physician. A nurse at a government-run infirmary provided basic health care and dispensed non-prescription drugs. Notably, Blanchisseuse lacked any "bush doctors", or specialists in folk medicine, apparently an anomaly for a village in this country. Hence knowledge of medicinal treatments resided with the people, as a living cultural practice. They grew their own medicinal plants or collected them as weeds or from the dense forest crowding around the village. The majority of the adults were bilingual, speaking both English and French Creole. The latter is a dialect of French, and a version of patois specific to Trinidad, that infused the locally used names for medicinal plants, all but four of which were patois (Wong 1976).[1]

Mahabir (2008), using information from thirty-six East Indian informants in various parts of Trinidad (none of them living near Blanchisseuse), described the medicinal and other uses of sixty-three plants. Notably, fifty-one of the species described by Mahabir are not described by Wong, indicating how geographical and cultural differences can affect which plants are used medicinally. Mahabir includes the transcript of an engaging interview with one informant who refers to twenty-five species alone, revealing how indigenous knowledge of plants should form part of a continuously updated archive.

The theme of Lans's comprehensive book *Creole Remedies of Trinidad and Tobago* (2007) is ethno-veterinary medicine. However, she also includes information on 189 plants, of which at least 40 per cent were introduced species, that are used medicinally by people. She discusses the interdisciplinary discipline of anthropology – which she refers to as soft science – versus Western science as hard science, and explains the development of folkloric medical practice in Trinidad and Tobago. She refers to the collection of treatments, which resulted from combining local and introduced plants with local Amerindian and introduced immigrant knowledge, as creolized folk medicine, using case studies as examples.

Seaforth (2007) offers a frank and opinionated assessment, based on thorough scientific inquiry, of the major traditional claims associated with nutritional and medicinal uses of fifty-seven plants that figure in the folklore of the

**Table 16.1** Complete List of Medicinal Plants of Trinidad and Tobago as Cited by Lans (2007), Mahabir (2008), Seaforth (1991, 2007) and Wong (1976)

| | | |
|---|---|---|
| Abelmoschus esculentus | A. caramabola | C. nocturnum |
| A. moschatus | Azadirachta indica | Chamaesyce hirta |
| Abrus precatorius | Bambusa vulgaris | Chaptalia nutans |
| Acalypha wilkesiana | Barleria lupulina | Chenopodium ambrosioides |
| Acnistus arborescens | Basella alba | Chromolaena odorata |
| Achyranthes indica | Bauhinia cumanensis | Chrysobalanus icaco |
| Acrocomia aculeata | B. excise | Cinnamomum verum |
| Adenanthera pavonia | Begonia humilis | Cissampelos pareira |
| Aegle marmelos | Bidens cynapiifolia | Cissus sicyoides |
| Aframomum melegueta | B. pilosa | C. verticillata |
| Ageratum conyzoides | Bixa orellana | Citharexylum spinosum |
| Allium cepa | Blighia sapida | Citrillus lanatus |
| A. sativum | Bontia daphnoides | Citrus aurantifolia |
| Aloe barbadensis | Borreria verticillata | C. aurantium |
| A. vera | Brassica chinensis | C. limonia |
| Alternanthera philoxeroides | Brownea latifolia | C. nobilis |
| A. sessilis | Bryophyllum pinnatum | C. paradisi |
| Amanas comosus | Cajanus cajan | C. sinensis |
| Amaranthus dubius | Caladium bicolor | Clusia rosea |
| Ambrosia cumanensis | Calendula officinalis | Coccinea grandis |
| Amomum melegueta | Calotropis gigantea | Coccoloba uvifera |
| Anacardium occidentale | Cannabis sativa | Cocos nucifera |
| Ananas comosus | Capraria biflora | Codonanthe crassifolia |
| Andira inermis | Capsicum frutescens | Coffea arabica |
| Andrographis paniculata | Carapa guianensis | Cola nitida |
| Annona muricata | Cardionspermum microcarpum | Coleus aromaticus |
| Antigonon leptopus | Carica papaya | Colocasia esculenta |
| Apium graveolens | Cassia alata | Colubrina arborescens |
| Areca catechu | C. fruticosa | Commelina elegans |
| Aristolochia rugosa | C. occidentalis | Commelina sp. |
| A. tribolata | Catharanthus roseus | Cordia curassavica |
| Artemisia absinthium | Cecropia peltata | Cordyline terminalis |
| Artocarpus altilis | Cedrela odorata | Costus cylindricus |
| A. heterophyllous | Ceiba pentrada | C. scaber |
| A. lakoocha | C. rosea | Crescentia cujete |
| Asclepias curassavica | Centropogon cornutus | Crotalaria incana |
| Averrhoa bilimbi | Cestrum latifolium | C. retusa |

*Table 16.1 continues*

**Table 16.1** Complete List of Medicinal Plants of Trinidad and Tobago as Cited by Lans by Lans (2007), Mahabir (2008), Seaforth (1991, 2007) and Wong (1976) (*cont'd*)

| | | |
|---|---|---|
| *Croton flavens* | *E. thymifolia* | *Lepianthes peltata* |
| *C. gossypifolius* | *Euterpe oleracae* | *Lippia mircomera* |
| *Cucumis anguria* | *Ficus benjamina* | *L. alba* |
| *Cucurbita pepo* | *F. nymphaeaefolia* | *Lisianthus chelonoides* |
| *Curcuma domestica/longa* | *F. religiosa* | *Luffa acutangula* |
| *Cuscuta americana* | *Flemingia strobilifera* | *L. aegyptiaca/cylindrica* |
| *Cymbopogon citratus* | *Fleurya aestuans* | *L. operculata* |
| *Cynodon dactylon* | *Furcraea agavephylla* | *Lycopersicum esculentum* |
| *Cyperus rotundus* | *Gomphrena globosa* | *Lygodium volubile* |
| *Datura metel* | *Gossypium hirsutum* | *Malachra alceifolia* |
| *D. stramonium* | *Gossypium* sp. | *Maliphigia glabra* |
| *Dendropanax arboreus* | *Gouania polygama* | *Mammea americana* |
| *Desmodium adscendens* | *Gracilaria* sp. | *Mangifera indica* |
| *D. canum* | *Guarania spinulosa* | *Manihot esculenta* |
| *Dillenia indica* | *Heliotropium indicum* | *Manilkara/Achras sapota* |
| *Dioscorea alata* | *Hibiscus rosa-sinensis* | *Maranta arundinacea* |
| *Dipteryx odorata* | *H. sabdariffa* | *Matelea viridiflora* |
| *Dorstenia contrajerva* | *Hippobroma longiflora* | *Microtea debilis* |
| *Doxantha unguis-cati* | *Hylocereus lemairei* | *Mikania micrantha* |
| *Dracontium foecundum* | *Hymenocallis tubiflora* | *Mimosa pudica* |
| *Eclipta alba* | *Hyptis atrorubens* | *Momordica charantia* |
| *E. prostrate* | *H. capitata* | *Monstera dubia* |
| *Elettaria cardamomum* | *H. suaveolens* | *Morinda citrifolia* |
| *Eleusine indica* | *Ipomea batatas* | *Moringa oleifera* |
| *Eleutherine bulbosa* | *I. aquatica* | *Morus alba* |
| *Enicostema verticillatum* | *Iresine herbstii* | *Mucuna pruriens* |
| *Entada polystachya* | *Jatropha curcas* | *Murraya keonigii* |
| *Ervatamia divavicata* | *J. gossypifolia* | *Musa paradisiaca* |
| *Eryngium foetidum* | *Justica pectoralis* | *M. p.* var. *sapientum* |
| *Erythrina pallida* | *J. secunda* | *Myristica fragrans* |
| *Eupatorium inulaefolium* | *Kalanchoe pinnata* | *Myrospermum frutescens* |
| *E. macrophyllum* | *Lablab niger* | *Nasturtium officinale* |
| *E. odoratum* | *Lagenaria siceraria* | *Nerium oleander* |
| *E. triplinerve* | *Lantana camara* | *Neurolaena lobota* |
| *Euphorbia hirta* | *Laportea aestuans* | *Nicotiana tabacum* |
| *E. neriifolia* | *Lawsonia inermis* | *Nopalea cochenillifera* |
| *E. oerstediana* | *Leonotis nepataefolia* | *Ocimum americanum* |

*Table 16.1 continues*

**Table 16.1** Complete List of Medicinal Plants of Trinidad and Tobago as Cited by Lans by Lans (2007), Mahabir (2008), Seaforth (1991, 2007) and Wong (1976) (*cont'd*)

| | | |
|---|---|---|
| *O. campechianum* | *P. nigrum* | *Sechium edule* |
| *O. gratissimum* | *Pitcairnia integrifolia* | *Senna alata* |
| *O. micranthum* | *Pithocellobium unguis-cati* | *S. occidentalis* |
| *O. sanctum* | *Pityrogramma calomelanos* | *Sesamum indicum* |
| *Oryza sativa* | *Plantago major* | *Sida acuta* |
| *Ottonia ovata* | *Pluchea odorata* | *Siparuna guianensis* |
| *Panicum maximum* | *P. symphytifolia* | *Solanum americanum* |
| *Parinari campestris* | *Plumeria rubra* | *S. melongene* |
| *Parthenium hysterophorus* | *Pogostemon cablin* | *S. nigrum* var. *americanum* |
| *Paspalum conjugatum* | *P. heyneanus* | *Spiranthes acaulis* |
| *Passiflora virgatum* | *Portulaca oleracea* | *Spondias cytherea* |
| *P. edulis* | *P. pilosa* | *S. mombin* |
| *P. foetida* | *Pothomorphe peltata* | *Stachytarpheta cayennensis* |
| *P. lauriflolia* | *Pouteria sapota* | *S. jamaicensis* |
| *P. quadrangularis* | *Pseudelephantopus spicatus* | *Syngonium podophyllum* |
| *P. suberosa* | *Psidium guajava* | *Syzygium cumini* |
| *Pelargonium zonale* | *Pueraria phaseoloides* | *Tagetes patula* |
| *Peperomia emarginella* | *Punica granatum* | *Tournefortia hirsutissima* |
| *P. pellucida* | *Rauvolfia ligustrina* | *Trichosanthes cucumerina* |
| *P. rotundifolia* | *Renealmia alpinia* | *Trimezia martinicensis* |
| *Persea americana* | *R. exaltata* | *Triumfetta lapula* |
| *Petiveria alliacea* | *Richeria grandis* | *Urena lobata* |
| *Phaseolus mungo* | *Ricinus communis* | *U. sinuate* |
| *Philodendron latifolium* | *Rolandra fruticosa* | *Vernonia scorpioides* |
| *Phoradendron piperoides* | *Rorippa nasturtium aquaticam* | *Vetiveria zizanioides* |
| *Phthirusa adunca* | *Rosmarinus officinalis* | *Vitex trifolia* |
| *Phyllanthus amarus* | *Roupala montana* | *Wedelia trilobata* |
| *P. niruri* | *Ruellia tuberosa* | *Xanthosoma brasiliense* |
| *P. urinaria* | *Ruta graveolens* | *X. undipes* |
| *Physalis angulata* | *Saccharum officinarum* | *Xiphidium caeruleum* |
| *Pilea microphylla* | *S. barberi/sinese* | *Zea mays* |
| *P. dioica* | *Salvia occidentalis* | *Zingiber officinale* |
| *Pimenta racemosa* | *Sambucus intermedia* | *Ziziphus mauritiana* |
| *Piper betle* | *S. simpsonii* | |
| *P. hispidum* | *Sansevieria guineensis* | |
| *P. marginatum* | *S. thyrsiflora* | |
| *P. m.* var. *catalpaefolium* | *Scoparia dulcis* | |

Caribbean. He includes the key active constituents and health and nutritional values, as well as warnings entailed by their use. While his coverage is not limited to Trinidad and Tobago, all of the plants he describes grow here and are part of its medicinal plant heritage. Information from an earlier work (Seaforth 1991) is incorporated to bring the total plants investigated to seventy-two species.

Together, Lans, Mahabir, Seaforth and Wong list a total of 338 different species (table 16.1). The inventory in table 16.1 has been compiled as a working document subject to continual amendment. Taxonomic names can provide more convenience than rigor, hence the appearance of plants with two or more Latin binomials, which results from their being classified differently by different taxonomists for a myriad of reasons. Then again, the taxonomic organization of organisms is not meant to be immutable: it will change with time. Since only some plants were cited by more than one author, more medicinal plants must exist in Trinidad and Tobago than appear on the list (gleaned from a total of 510 citations); otherwise the overlap between each author's citations would have been much greater.

This prompts the question "How many plants in Trinidad and Tobago have medicinal properties?" There seems to be no useful estimate for this country, and few exist for others. In any case, such statistics are of little absolute value when considered in relation to the programmes of some countries to actively introduce medicinal plants. For example, the National Institute of Medicinal Materials in Vietnam (2006) has reported that its introduction of some three hundred new species boosted the national total to 3,948 known species of medicinal plants, 52 species of medicinal algae, 408 species of medicinal animals and even 75 medicinal minerals.

Introduction of medicinal plants to a new area carries the same risk as introducing any other species – plant or animal. The visitor might take up permanent residency and become a nuisance if the environment is favourable and it has a competitive advantage. For example, fifty-four species listed in table 16.1 are identified as invasive weeds of various levels of severity by the SEPCC (Southeast Pest Control Council of the United States), which covers Florida and seven nearby states. Some of these species are surprising, such as *Cajanus cajan* (pigeon pea), a staple legume of the tropics that now thrives in a few counties in Florida. *Catharanthus roseus* (rose periwinkle), endemic to Madagascar and the source of a cancer drug, as explained later in this chapter, also appears. Both of these species probably escaped from gardens.

## The Concept of Balance in Traditional Treatments

All of the medicinal plants and diseases described to Wong (1976) by the inhabitants of Blanchisseuse were classified as being either "hot" or "cold". These are Hippocratic principles, traditions of medical practice brought from the Spanish colonies, which include wet and dry, raw and cooked, sweet and sour – all are contrasting qualities. According to this belief, imbalance creates disease; it is not advisable to, for example, eat cold food when one is hot or, as claimed in Trinidad and Tobago, iron clothes and defrost the refrigerator on the same day. In Amerindian folkloric tradition, a hot or "heating" treatment was given for a cold ailment to obtain balance, and thus a potential cure. Lans (2007) meticulously discusses the concept of balancing symptoms with treatments, which appears also in Aztec and other beliefs, in her account of ethno-medicinal creolization. Clement et al. (2011) surveyed 450 households in rural Trinidad, finding that the concept remains alive today. Forty-four species were used for cooling (mostly cat's claw [*Macfedyena unguis-cati*], verven [*Stachytarpheta jamaicensis*], candle bush [*Piper tuberculatum*], caraile [*Momordica charantia*] and shiny bush [*Peperomia pellucida*]), while twenty-eight species (mostly lemon grass [*Cymbopogon citratus*] and jackass-bitters [*Neurolaena lobata*]) were used for fever. Interestingly, the World Health Organization's definition of health, which has not been amended since 1948, is "a state of complete physical, mental and social well-being and not merely the absence of disease or infirmity", which conjures up nothing if not balance.

The Ayurvedic tradition, an ancient Hindu system of healing practised by many millions in the Indian subcontinent, began as an organized system of medicine with texts written in Sanskrit in about 1500 BCE, but its roots extended many millennia earlier still. Ayurvedic medicine was brought to Trinidad and Tobago by indentured labourers from India more than a century and a half ago. It holds that

> Everything in the universe (living or not) is joined together, everyone contains elements that can be found in the universe, we are born in a state of balance within ourselves and in relation to the universe, and this balance is upset by the processes of life. Disruptions can be physical, emotional, spiritual, alone or in combination. Imbalance weakens the body and makes us prone to disease. Health will be good if our interaction with the environment is effective and wholesome. *Disease arises when a person is out of harmony with the universe.* [This is a paraphrase of the description given in one form or another by many sources.]

That final sentence is most important. Variations of it appear in both Native American folklore (Creighton University Medical Center) and Taoism (True Tao), which echo the Ayurvedic approach to medical treatment in seeing the patient as a whole being within the cosmos, not as an isolated collection of symptoms. Ayurvedic medicine mirrors indigenous Amerindian ways in that disease is thought to occur because of an imbalance which can be restored by corrective holistic treatment.

But Western medicine continues to update itself while the Ayurvedic tradition has remained embedded in the past. Consider this quotation from Dash and Junius (1983) about the Ayurvedic approach, which they, like others, set out as being at once holistic yet scientific, and somehow parallel to Western medicine:

> In order to gain admission to the Faculty of Medicine at the University of Taxila [Taxashilā Institute, Ahmedabad, India], aspiring students were put to test [sic]. They were sent to a nearby forest with the instruction to bring all those plant species not possessing medicinal properties. Most of the students returned with a number of species. Only Jīvaka returned without a single plant and told the gate keeper (Examiner) that he could not find a single non-medicinal plant. About Jīvaka many stories describing his keen sense of observation are reported.

While Jīvaka may have had a keen sense of observation, a conservative estimate of the number of extant flowering plants alone is 235,000 species (Raven, Evert and Eichhorn 2005), a tall order for any pharmacopeia to encompass. If the Ayurvedic considers all plants to be medicinal, it is a complex system indeed. There are around eight thousand Ayurvedic recipes – still a lot – and most blend many plant and other ingredients, making it difficult to discover which might have what function. Heavy metals are present in a significant number of Ayurvedic medications, among them arsenic, cadmium, lead and mercury, creating potentially lethal remedies (Ernst 2002; Saper et al. 2004). However, given the recent publicity generated about the heavy metal content of its medications, this issue will likely be addressed and corrected.[2]

## Cautions about Medicinal Plant Use

There can be serious risks to be considered when using traditional remedies. *Ephedra*, a relictual plant without flowers or typical-looking leaves, has been used in traditional Chinese medicine for five thousand years to treat asthma, hay fever and the common cold, and Native Americans and Mormon pioneers drank it as a tea. Its constituents, ephedrine and pseudoephedrine, were used until recently in weight-loss pills and other non-prescription dietary supplements, but side effects included hyperthermia, irregular heartbeat, seizures, heart attack, stroke and death. The US Food and Drug Administration (FDA) consequentially banned the use of *Ephedra* in 2004.

A few years ago, imported noni juice, made from the fruit of *Morinda citrifolia* – local names include spirit fruit, pain bush and pain killer (Winer 2009) – was sold for hundreds of dollars per litre in local pharmacies. Wild health claims on the Internet and from multilevel marketers made such exorbitant prices possible. One imaginative salesman told me that there were five thousand species of noni while offering to sell an extract of the only effective species. I had to tell him, "Sorry, but that is not true." In fact, *M. citrifolia* is one of only about eighty species in the genus *Morinda*. Its family, the Rubiaceae, gives us coffee, ixora and gardenia (such as *G. jasminoides*). Quinine, an early remedy for malaria, is extracted from *Cinchona officinalis*, from the same family.

It came to public attention in the midst of the noni juice hype that *M. citrifolia* trees were growing along the northeast coast in the vicinity of Toco, and soon afterwards the fruit appeared in grocery stores for a few dollars a pound. Strangely enough, the Amerindian use for the plant (which probably originated in Southeast Asia) involved the leaves (Honychurch 1986), not the fruit, which has a loathsome smell and taste. While some continue to drink the juice, it has yet to demonstrate any clinically valid health benefits whatsoever, and there are documented cases of its causing liver damage and hyperkalemia. On the other hand, legitimate claims regarding the medical effectiveness of folk medicines should be taken seriously. Farnsworth (1988) found that 74 per cent of the claims made for traditional treatments in the United States, ascribed to 119 plants containing different and specific active chemicals, were borne out by the pharmaceutical uses of chemicals extracted from those plants.

## Conclusion: The Need to Unlock the Potential of Medicinal Plants

Efforts directed towards screening plants for new drugs are supplementing traditional knowledge. The anticancer drug paclitaxel, first called Taxol, was originally isolated in 1967 from the bark of the Pacific yew, *Taxus brevifolia*, a plant used medicinally by American Indians. While it can now be more readily obtained from other plants, paclitaxel is usually synthesized directly in the laboratory. Vincristine, a drug important for the treatment of childhood leukemia, was isolated in 1958 from Madagascan periwinkle, *Catharanthus roseus*. It was first sold by Eli Lilly and Company in the United States in 1963, just five years after a crude extract of the plant was screened and found to show anti-tumour activity.

Such advances have been facilitated by the advent of online information sources such as Purdue University's Aromatic and Medicinal Plants Index

(AMPI) and the Natural Products Alert (NPA) relational database. A recent result of intensive screening of and research on properties of plants in Trinidad is the report by Seaforth and Tikasingh (2008), who thoroughly studied the chemical, pharmacological and other characteristics of twenty species with medicinal and other uses with an eye to industrial development. Worldwide, traditional knowledge is being freely appropriated by others; it cannot resist continued biopiracy unless existing intellectual property systems are rewritten to safeguard it. Sapp (2006) concludes that private contracts are preferable to patents or treaties, which have not been successful at protecting traditional knowledge or providing compensation for it. She suggests that specific traditional-knowledge legislation, if accompanied by multilateral enforcement and a comprehensive database or other type of information management, would be another way to protect it.

Efforts are ongoing by groups mandated to document and carry out research on medicinal plants in the Caribbean. One such organization is the Programa de investigación científica aplicada de plantas medicinales (Traditional Medicine in the Islands, or TRAMIL), which has published a herbal pharmacopoeia for the Caribbean. Guided by the principle "knowledge should go back to its source", TRAMIL works mainly in the French- and Spanish-speaking Caribbean to authenticate traditional Caribbean medicine, and with low-income families who are for the most part dependent on home remedies. TRAMIL has also published a book for the illiterate, which uses illustrations to describe the proper use of herbs. Another group is the Caribbean Association of Researchers and Herbal Practitioners (CARAPA), which hosts an annual Symposium on Herbal Medicine and is gaining recognition and support from the Government of Trinidad and Tobago. Its mission is to provide a scientific rationale for the traditional uses of plants, to assist in information exchange, to train local people in the proper use of herbs and to aid the formation of a self-sustaining herbal industry that produces safe, affordable products.

## Notes

1. French botanical heritage became concentrated in Blanchisseuse – in a country that was never ruled by France – as a result of serendipitous events. Social and political unrest in France, a prelude to the French Revolution, was affecting life in its colonies during the late eighteenth century. Many planters and their slaves in the French territories, especially Martinique, took advantage of the *cédula de población* published by the king of Spain in 1783, which invited any Catholic subject of a monarch friendly to the Spanish crown to move to Trinidad and Tobago.

The newcomers had such an influence on society in this British colony that patois became the predominant language of the working population. Over time the dialect became stigmatized as broken French and hence marginalized, but it is still spoken in other villages as well, including Avocat, Bourg Mulatress, Brasso Seco, La Lune, Morne La Coix, Paramin and Toco. It can be heard in such turns of phrase as "it have", used instead of "there is".

2. The US National Institutes of Health maintains an excellent website about research being done on the Ayurvedic tradition and other forms of complementary and alternative medicine, through the National Center for Complementary and Alternative Medicine.

# References

Andermann, Anne. 1996. "Physicians, Fads, and Pharmaceuticals: A History of Aspirin". http://www.med.mcgill.ca/mjm/issues/v02n02/aspirin.html#anchor131 6276 (accessed 21 August 2011).

Aromatic and Medicinal Plants Index (AMPI). n.d. http://www.hort.purdue.edu/new crop/med-aro/toc.html (accessed 21 August 2011).

Caribbean Association of Researchers and Herbal Practitioners (CARAPA). http:// medplant.icimod.org/index.php?name=Web_Links&req=viewlinkd etails&lid=28 (accessed 21 August 2011).

Clement, Yuri, Y.S. Baksh-Comeau, R. Ragoo and C. Seaforth. 2011. "Cooling It with Herbs". *UWI Today*, 29 October, 8–9.

Creighton University Medical Center. 2010. "Indian Theories of Medicine". *Complementary and Alternative Medicine*. http://altmed.creighton.edu/americanindian med/theories.htm (accessed 21 August 2011).

Dash, Vaidya B., and Acarya M. M. Junius. 1983. *A Handbook of Ayurveda*. New Delhi: Concept Publishing.

Ernst, Edzard. 2002. "Heavy Metals in Traditional Indian Remedies". *European Journal of Clinical Pharmacology* 57, no. 12 (February): 891–96.

Farnsworth, Norman R. 1988. "Screening Plants for New Medicines". In *Biodiversity*, edited by Edward O. Wilson, 83–97. Washington, DC: National Academy Press.

Forte, Maximilian C. 2003. "How the Amerindians of Arima Lost Their Lands". *Issues in Caribbean Amerindian Studies*. http://www.centrelink.org/landreport.html (accessed 21 August 2011).

Honychurch, Penelope N. 1986. *Caribbean Wild Plants and Their Uses*. Oxford: Macmillan.

Lans, Cheryl. 2007. *Creole Remedies of Trinidad and Tobago*. N.p.: C. Lans.

———. 2008. "Behaving Like a Warao". Society for Caribbean Studies prize-winning essay. N.p.: C. Lans.

Mahabir, Kumar. 2008. *Medicinal and Edible Plants Used by East Indians of Trinidad and Tobago*. Trinidad: Chakra.

National Center for Complementary and Alternative Medicine. n.d. http://nccam .nih.gov/health/ayurveda/ (accessed 27 September 2010).

National Institute of Medicinal Materials. 2006. http://www.vienduoclieu.org.vn/vien duoclieu/page.asp?id=154 (accessed 21 August 2011).

Pickersgill, Barbara. 2005. "Spices". In *The Cultural History of Plants*, edited by Ghillean Prance and Mark Nesbitt, 153–72. New York: Routledge.

Raven, Peter H., R.F. Evert and S.E. Eichhorn. 2005. *Biology of Plants*. New York: W.H. Freeman.

Sanderson, Helen. 2005. "Roots and Tubers". In *The Cultural History of Plants*, edited by Ghillean Prance and Mark Nesbitt, 61–76. New York: Routledge.

Saper, R.B., S.N. Kales, J. Paquin, M.J. Burns, D.M. Eisenberg, R.B. Davis and R.S. Phillips. 2004. "Heavy Metal Content of Ayurvedic Herbal Medicine Products". *Journal of the American Medical Association* 292, no. 23 (December): 2868–73.

Sapp, H.A. 2006. "Monopolizing Medical Methods: The Debate over Patent Rights for Indigenous Peoples". *Temple Journal of Science, Technology and Environmental Law* 25, no. 2 (Fall): 191–212.

Saunders, Nicholas J. 2005. *The Peoples of the Caribbean: An Encyclopaedia of Archaeology and Traditional Culture*. Oxford: ABC-CLIO.

Seaforth, Compton. 1991. *Natural Products in Caribbean Folk Medicine*. Kingston: University of the West Indies Press.

———. 2007. *Caribbean Herbs and Nutritional Supplements*. St Augustine: University of Trinidad and Tobago.

Seaforth, Compton, and T. Tikasingh. 2008. "A Study for the Development of a Handbook of Selected Caribbean Herbs for Industry". Technical Centre for Agricultural and Rural Cooperation (TCA). http://www.anancy.org (accessed 21 August 2011).

Southeast Pest Control Council. n.d. http://www.se-eppc.org/index.cfm (accessed 21 August 2011).

TRAMIL. "Program of Applied Research to Popular Medicine in the Caribbean". http://www.funredes.org/endacaribe/traducciones/tramil.html (accessed 21 August 2011).

TrueTao.org. n.d. "Taoism". http://www.taoism.net (accessed 21 August 2011).

University of Illinois at Chicago Program for Collaborative Research in the Pharmaceutical Sciences. NAPRALERT. http://www.napralert.org/ (accessed 21 August 2011).

Verteuil, Louis A.A. de. 1858. *Trinidad: Its Geography, Natural Resources, Administration, Present Condition and Prospects*. London: Ward and Lock.

Winer, L. 2009. *Dictionary of the English/Creole of Trinidad and Tobago*. Montreal: McGill-Queen's University Press.

Wong, W.Y.Y. 1976. "Some Folk Medicinal Plants from Trinidad". *Economic Botany* 30, no. 2: 103–42.

# 17.

# Caribbean Food Plants

LAURA B. ROBERTS-NKRUMAH

------

*The Caribbean is a relatively small region with a wide range of native food plants, several of which have become important staples and agricultural commodities internationally. This chapter provides an overview of the genetic heritage of food plants that were used by the first peoples of the Caribbean and the factors that resulted in the change to their status that started with European colonization. The current status and nutritional value of these crops, as well as the main dishes in which they are utilized, are described. The implications of neglect of this aspect of the Caribbean heritage are discussed within the context of food and nutrition security for the region.*

## Introduction

The Caribbean consists of an archipelago of islands extending from the Bahamas in the north, at 24° 5′ north, 76° west, to Trinidad in the south, at 11° north, 61° west. In spite of the dominating effect of the sea on the climate within this small tropical space, several different microclimates and a range of vegetation exist. The biodiversity of this flora has provided the region with many plant species suitable for human food; this variety was extended further by domesticated crop species introduced from Mexico and Central and South America by the early peoples who migrated from these circum-Caribbean areas to the Caribbean. This chapter focuses on indigenous food crops and those introduced through such migrations, mainly in the pre-Columbian era, as a genetic resource that is an integral aspect of Caribbean heritage. The status of their contribution to the food supply in the region from pre-Colombian times is outlined, and some important historical factors that influence current levels of production and consumption are described. Finally, the relationship between the status of our food plant resources and of food security and human health within the region is discussed.

## Caribbean Food Plants

Food plants comprise a very valuable component of the genetic diversity of the flora of the Caribbean, both in terms of the number of genera and the number of species and intra-specific variations. Many of these food plants originated and were domesticated in different parts of this archipelago, while others were imported by the earliest peoples of the region (table 17.1). These plants, some of which were already being cultivated as crops before Europeans' arrival, constitute a significant food resource through their nutritional content, representation in every major food group, and suitability for a wide range of food uses in Caribbean cuisine as they include starchy crops, legumes, vegetables, fruits, industrial crops that are consumed only as processed products, beverage crops, and condiments and spices. The discussion that follows considers the status of these crops and the extent to which their food potential has been recognized and developed in the course of the region's history, and the implications for its food and nutrition security.

## Historical Status of Indigenous Food Crops

### Pre-Columbian Status

During the Archaic period, which extended from 5000 to 200 BCE, the first migrants and earliest Caribbean peoples, the Ortoroids and Casimiroids, though primarily hunter-gatherers, practised some forms of cultivation (Keegan 2000). Archaeological evidence exists that maize (*Zea mays*), manioc or cassava (*Manihot esculenta*), sweet potato (*Ipomoea batatas*) and beans (*Phaseolus* spp.) were processed (Pagán Jiménez and Rodríguez Ramos 2007; Reid 2009). The later Saladoid peoples, so named for their pottery with its characteristic red and white markings, migrated downstream along the banks of the Orinoco River in Venezuela and from the coastal areas of the Guianas, moving northward through the Lesser Antilles as far as Puerto Rico. They established inland riverine settlements and extensive gardens from which they harvested manioc, their main staple, and other crops. Remnants of griddles suggest that they processed the cassava (Keegan 2000). Cassava was important in the diet as a major source of carbohydrates for energy. Since its protein content is low, they relied on animals for that nutrient; they migrated to coastal areas and utilized marine animals when the terrestrial sources were depleted.

**Table 17.1** Caribbean Food Plants: Nutritional Composition and Use

| Names (Common, Scientific and Botanical Family); Origin[*] | Major Nutrients/100 g[**] | Major Dishes[***] |
|---|---|---|
| **CEREAL CROPS**<br>Maize/corn (*Zea mays*, Graminaceae); origin: Mexico | Cornmeal – 353 kcal, carb. – 71.5 g, protein – 9.3 g, DF3 – 11 g | Boiled or roasted cobs, cornmeal porridge, dumplings, coo-coo, fungi, arepas, pastelles, jug-jug |
| **ROOT CROPS**<br>Cassava/manioc/yuca (*Manihot esculenta*, Euphorbiceae); origin: Mexico and Central America (CA) | Fresh root, cooked – 120 kcal; carb.2 – 27g; potassium 690 mg | Farine, porridge, cassava bread/bammie, pone, cassareep |
| Sweet potato (*Ipomoea batatas*, Convulvulaceae); origin: Tropical America (TA) | Fresh tuber, cooked[3] – 103 kcal; carb. – 24.3 g; vitamin A – 2182 RE4 | Pudding, pone, baked sweet potatoes, ingredient in soups, chips |
| Yams – Cush-cush (*Dioscorea. trifida*, Dioscoreaceae); origin: Northern SA | Fresh root, cooked – 116 kcal; carb. – 27.6 g; potassium – 670 mg | Roasted yam, grilled yam, ingredient in soups, riced yams, yam balls, foofoo, salad, pie |
| Tannia, yautia, cocoyam (*Xanthosoma sagittifolium*, Araceae); origin: TA. | Fresh root, raw – 133 kcal; carb. – 31 g | Fritters, pudding, riced, grilled or fried tannia, pie, ingredient in soups, salad |
| Arrowroot (*Maranta arundinacea*, Marantaceae); origin: Northern SA, Lesser Antilles | Flour – 340 kcal; carb. – 85 g | Porridge, blancmange, thickening agent in sauces, soups, ice cream |
| Topi tambu/lleren (*Calathea allouia*, Marantaceae); origin: West Indies and Northern SA | | Boiled tubers served with a savoury dip, curried topi tambu, salad, ingredient in soup |
| **LEGUMES**<br>Ground nuts, peanuts (*Arachis hypogaea*, Leguminosae); Origin: SA. | Raw seeds with skin, dried – 567 kcal; fat – 49.2 g; carb. – 16.2 g; protein – 25.7 g; potassium – 717 mg; niacin – 13.8 mg | Roasted nuts salted or unsalted, nut cake or peanut brittle, peanut punch |

*Table 17.1 continues*

**Table 17.1** Caribbean Food Plants: Nutritional Composition and Use (*cont'd*)

| Names (Common, Scientific and Botanical Family); Origin* | Major Nutrients/100 g** | Major Dishes*** |
|---|---|---|
| **LEGUMES** (*cont'd*) Common beans, red/kidney beans, black beans (*Phaseolus vulgaris*, Leguminosae); Lima beans (*P. lunatus*, Leguminosae); origin: Mexico and CA | Red/kidney beans whole seeds, dry, raw – 337 kcal; carb. – 61.3 g; protein – 22.5 g; DF – 10.4 g | Red peas and rice, red peas soup, lima bean and oxtail |
| **VEGETABLES** Vegetable amaranths, bhagi, callaloo, spinach (*Amaranthus* spp., Amaranthaceae); origin: CA and Mexico | Raw – protein – 2.5 g; calcium – 215 mg; potassium – 611 mg; iron – 2.3 mg; vitamin A – 292 RE | Steamed calaloo/bhagi, pepper-pot soup, bhagi and rice |
| Pumpkin (*Cucurbita maxima, C. moshata*, Cucurbitaceae); orign: TA. | Raw – potassium – 340 mg; vitamin A – 160 RE | Steamed pumpkin, curried pumpkin, pumpkin soup, pudding, custard, fritters |
| Heart of palm (cabbage palm – *Roystonea oleracea*; pewah, peach palm – *Bactris gasipaes*, Palmae/Arecaceae); origin: Trinidad, TA | 47.6 kcal; carb. – 5.2 g; protein – 1.5 g; calcium – 42.4 mg; potassium – 193.6 mg | Heart of palm steamed, salad |
| **FRUITS** Grapefruit (*Citrus paradisi*, Rutaceae); origin: West Indies, probably Barbados | 30 kcal; potassium – 129 mg; vitamin C – 38 mg | Concentrate, juice, drink, fresh fruit, fruit salad |
| Avocado (*Persea americana*, Lauraceae); origin: Mexico and CA | 161 kcal; fat – 15.3 g; protein – 2.0 g; potassium – 599 mg | Salad, guacamole |
| Pineapple (*Ananas cosmosus*; Bromeliaceae); origin: SA | 49 kcal; carb. – 12.4 g; potassium – 113 mg | Concentrate, juice, drink, pina colada, fresh fruit, fruit salad, pizza topping, pie filling, jams, jellies, ice cream |

*Table 17.1 continues*

**Table 17.1** Caribbean Food Plants: Nutritional Composition and Use (*cont'd*)

| Names (Common, Scientific and Botanical Family); Origin[*] | Major Nutrients/100 g[**] | Major Dishes[***] |
|---|---|---|
| **FRUITS** (*cont'd*) | | |
| Papaya, pawpaw (*Carica papaya*, Caricaceae); origin: Mexico and CA | 39 kcal; carb. – 9.8 g; potassium – 257 mg; vitamin A – 201 RE | Fruit salad, nectar, juice; immature fruit – steamed, pawpaw balls, pepper sauce |
| Passion fruit (*Passiflora edulis* var. *flavicarpa*, Barbadine; *P. quadrangularis*, Passifloraceae); origin: SA | 97 kcal; carb. 23.4 g; protein – 2.2 g; potassium – 200 mg; vitamin A – 201 RE | Nectar, drink, ice cream |
| Guava (*Psidium guajava*; Myrtaceae); origin: TA. | 51 kcal; carb. – 11.9 g; potassium – 284 mg; vitamin A – 79 RE; vitamin C – 184 mg | Jam, jelly, cheese, nectar, juice |
| West Indian/Barbados cherry (*Malphigia glabra*, Malphigiaceae); origin: West Indies, Northern SA | 32 kcal; carb. – 7.7 g; potassium – 145 mg; vitamin A – 77 RE; vitamin C – 1677 mg | Nectar, drink |
| Cashew (*Anacardium occidentale*, Anacardiaceae); origin: TA | Apple – 46 kcal; carb. – 11.6 g; vitamin A – 40 RE; vitamin C – 219 mg | Jam, drink |
| | Whole seeds, dry – 561 kcal; fat – 45.7 g; carb. – 27.9 g; protein – 17.2 g; iron – 3.8 mg; potassium – 464 mg | Roasted nuts |
| Guinep (*Melicoccus bijugatus*, Sapindaceae); origin: TA. | 59 kcal, carb. – 19.9 g | Fresh |
| Soursop (*Annona muricata*, Annonaceae) | 66 kcal; carb. – 16.8 g; potassium – 278 mg | Punch, nectar, drink, ice cream |
| Sugar apple (*A. squamosa*, Annonaceae), custard apple (*A. reticulata*, Annonaceae); origin: CA, SA and West Indies. | | Fresh fruit |

*Table 17.1 continues*

**Table 17.1** Caribbean Food Plants: Nutritional Composition and Use (*cont'd*)

| Names (Common, Scientific and Botanical Family); Origin* | Major Nutrients/100 g** | Major Dishes*** |
|---|---|---|
| **FRUITS** (*cont'd*)<br><br>Sapodilla (*Manilkara achras*, Sapotaceae), balata (*M. bidentata*, Sapotaceae), caimite/starapple (*Chrysophyllum cainito*, Sapotaceae), mammy sapote (*Calocarpum sapota*, Sapotaceae); origin: CA, Mexico, Trinidad and SA | Sapodilla: 83 kcal; carb. – 20 g; potassium – 193 mg<br>Caimite: 68 kcal; carb. 14.5 | Fresh fruit |
| Mammey apple (*Mammea americana*, Guttiferae); origin: West Indies and TA | 51 kcal, carb. – 12.5 g | Jam, jelly |
| Jamaica plum (*Spondias purpurea*, Anacardiaceae), chili plum (*S. lutea*, Anacardiaceae), hog plum (*S. mombin*, Anacardiaceae); origin: TA | | Drink |
| **INDUSTRIAL CROPS**<br><br>Cocoa (*Theobroma cacao*, Sterculiaceae); origin: CA, SA, Trinidad | | Chocolate, cocoa/chocolate drinks |
| **BEVERAGE CROPS**<br><br>Mauby (*Colubrina arborescens* or *C. elliptica*, Rhamnaceae); origin: West Indies and TA | | Fresh drink, fermented drink |
| Seamoss (*Gracilaria* spp., Rhodophyta); origin: West Indies | | Punch with milk, drink |
| **CONDIMENTS AND SPICES**<br><br>Hot pepper (*Capsicum frutescens*, Solanaceae); origin: Peru, Mexico | | Pepper sauce, condiment in jerk seasoning and chutney |
| Sweet pepper (*C. annum*, Solanaceae); origin: Peru, Mexico | | Salads |

*Table 17.1 continues*

**Table 17.1** Caribbean Food Plants: Nutritional Composition and Use (*cont'd*)

| Names (Common, Scientific and Botanical Family); Origin[*] | Major Nutrients/100 g[**] | Major Dishes[***] |
|---|---|---|
| **CONDIMENTS AND SPICES** | | |
| Pimento (*Pimenta dioica*, Myrtaceae), bay (*P. racemosa*, Myrtaceae); origin: Jamaica | | Used in pickles, escoveitch fish, ketchup, pimento dram |
| Roucou/annatto (*Bixa orellana*, Bixaceae); origin: West Indies and TA | | Annatto oil |
| Vanilla (*Vanilla fragrans*, Orchidaceae); origin: CA and the West Indies | | Essence used in baked goods, drinks, ice cream |
| Tonka bean (*Dipteryx odorata*, Leguminosae); origin: SA | | Grated seed added to baked goods |

*Notes:*

[1]DF = dietary fibre

[2]Carb. = carbohydrate

[3] Varieties with ddep yellow flesh, cooked in skin

[4]RE = retinol equivalents

*Sources:*

[*]    Purseglove 1974.

[**]    Caribbean Food and Nutrition Institute 1998.

[***]    Benghiat 1985; Ortiz 1995; Parkinson 1999; Wood 1973.

The Taínos, who evolved from earlier groups in the Caribbean and occupied the Greater Antilles, cultivated large gardens of 1 to 2 hectares which they called *conucos*, in which they planted cassava, sweet potatoes, yautia or tannia (*Xanthosoma sagittifolium*), topi tambo (*Calathea allouia*), beans, peanuts (*Arachis hypogaea*), cucurbits (*Cucurbita* spp.) and chile peppers (*Capsicum frutescens*). Fruit trees, including guava (*Psidium guajava*), soursop (*Annona muricata*), mammee apple (*Mammea americana*), chenette (*Meliococcus bijugatus*) and cocoplum (*Chrysobalanus icaco*), were also cultivated. Their production system was partly based on "slash and burn" agriculture, in which cultivated plots were abandoned when their fertility could no longer support the food needs of the group or family (Keegan 2000). After a fallow period of several years, during which fertility was restored, cultivation could be undertaken again.

Among the Taínos cassava was the main crop, with both the sweet and bitter types being grown. The tubers of the sweet types contain low levels of cyanogenic glycosides, which form toxic prussic acid; they must be harvested soon after maturity to prevent deterioration in eating quality. The bitter types contain higher levels of these toxins, which must be destroyed before consumption. This was achieved by exposing the flesh of the tubers to air, first by grating, then by squeezing to remove as much liquid as possible. The resulting cassava meal was then baked on a griddle to make a flatbread or toasted to make farine, in which form it could be stored for long periods. The liquid that was removed was called casareep, which was used as a preservative by boiling it over several days and adding meat to the pot at intervals; it was also used to make a beer. Processing bitter cassava and baking the meal on griddles seems to have been practised since the Archaic period. However, the main method of food preparation the Taínos used for roots and vegetables was boiling, while fruits were eaten fresh. Maize was of secondary importance at this time and was consumed mainly as roasted whole cobs (Keegan 2000).

## European Influence on the Status of Indigenous Crops

When the Spanish arrived in the Caribbean in 1492, they found indigenous people whose diet was varied, with several plant sources of energy, protein, and other nutrients. Protein needs were supplemented further by hunting. Also, a mixture of crops with varying maturity periods ensured that there was a constant supply of food. The arrival of European colonists – first the Spanish, then the British, French and Dutch – brought far-reaching changes to both the economic and social landscape and to the flora and fauna of the Caribbean, which completely disrupted the lifestyles and the livelihoods of the Taínos.

Initially the Taínos supplied food and labour to the Spanish as tribute. But, with few exceptions, the indigenous crops were not sustained, because of serious decline of the Taíno population due to war, disease caused by new pathogens to which they had no resistance, and abuse of their labour in the search for gold by the Spanish. Also, the cattle and pigs imported as protein sources for the Europeans were allowed to roam freely to forage, and in so doing they destroyed many of the Taínos' gardens (Keegan 2000).

One of the few crops that became important to the colonists was cassava, the source of cassava bread. Keegan (2000) cites other authors who describe cassava bread as "the bread of conquest". This was not a new role for the food: cassava meal could be stored for long periods, and the bread made from it had facilitated long-distance travel and wars of expansion by the early natives. It similarly sustained the European colonists during their conquest of the Caribbean and Latin America. This was not necessarily by choice, but rather an acceptance of the reality that bread made from wheat was less suited to sustaining life during long expeditions in this part of the world. But although the Portuguese and Dutch during their colonization of Brazil adopted indigenous foods and subsistence systems, the British and French colonists in the Caribbean showed little similar inclination. Their preference for their own foods was so strong that they attempted to import temperate food plants to the Caribbean. Though most of these failed to thrive, it did not deter eventual transformation of the biodiversity of the region and assertion of a preference for foreign foods that ultimately relegated the indigenous food plants to the status of minor crops.

No other plant so affected the Caribbean landscape as sugarcane (*Saccharum officinarum*), which was imported from Asia to produce sugar to satisfy the growing demand in Western Europe. Many of the remaining Taínos were enslaved for production of this crop, and when their numbers dwindled, Africans were enslaved and imported to supply the needed labour. Therefore, from the sixteenth century onwards there was an acceleration of the steep decline in the production of indigenous food crops that had started earlier. Among the major contributing factors was the clearance of large tracts of forest and cultivated areas for sugarcane production. Among the British planters, especially those in the flatter islands of Barbados, Antigua and St Kitts, which were cultivated only for sugarcane, little thought was given to food production, even for maintaining the enslaved labour force. Instead, imported food supplies such as cornmeal, wheat flour and salted meat and fish from the American colonies and Britain were strongly preferred to local food production (Sheridan 1976). The importation of corn products is noteworthy because it indicates that corn was not an important crop locally.

Another factor was that in territories such as Jamaica and St Vincent, the

Africans were expected to supplement their meagre rations of imported food with food crops familiar to them. These were introduced from Africa and included yams (*Dioscorea alata, D. rotundata* and *D. cayanensis*), plantains (*Musa* spp.) and akee (*Blighia sapida*). The enslaved were allowed to cultivate these crops in hilly areas that were of marginal quality for sugarcane production. Besides cocoyam (*Xanthosoma sagittifolium*) and sweet potato, they also grew cassava, which they had learnt to process thorough contact with the Taínos. Higman (2008) cites early writers who indicated that even the English planters in Jamaica ate cassava as a bread during the seventeenth century; by the eighteenth century a cassava cake – a precursor to the bammy – was being sold at local markets by the enslaved Africans.

The cocoyam was said to be preferred to yam or cassava, even though the tubers were less palatable, because they produced a higher yield with less care, had edible leaves and offered the common advantage of extended harvest of the tubers, which were eaten boiled or roasted. According to Higman (2008), although it stored poorly, sweet potato was regarded favourably by the Europeans because it was perceived as having a superior taste, was easy to digest and nourishing and was thought to have aphrodisiacal properties. Thus the Africans became custodians of the indigenous crops through recognition of their food value and acquisition of knowledge of their agronomy, processing technologies and methods of use. As the Taínos had done before them, they cultivated these crops both in nearby kitchen gardens and in distant provision grounds.

Nevertheless, the planters' overall attitude to the provision grounds where some indigenous crops survived was negative, especially during periods when sugar prices were high. All labour had to be devoted to sugarcane production for the greatest profit. Only when it became uneconomical to purchase food for the labour force, or when it became almost impossible to obtain regular supplies of imported food, was local food production encouraged. Supplies of imported food were cut off during the American War of Independence; hurricanes and droughts during the 1770s and 1780s destroyed the provision grounds, thereby exacerbating the food shortage and contributing to tremendous loss of life. Increasing competition with other sugar producers led to declining prices, so even after trade resumed with the former North American colony and continuing into the early nineteenth century, it became increasingly uneconomical to purchase imported food for the labour force (Sheridan 1976). It was these circumstances that forced legislation requiring a portion of all plantations to be used for food-crop cultivation, partly to meet the prescribed standards for rations for the labour force (Tobin 1999).

Although the legal requirements were not always observed, the provision grounds continued to be cultivated and eventually became a significant domestic food source. The local white population also benefited from supplies from the provision grounds – which were sold at Sunday markets – since they were the only available fresh foods. Tobin (1999) cites Mrs. A.C. Carmichael, a sugarcane planter's wife who frequented the markets; she noted, among the produce on sale, the presence of the indigenous cassava, sweet potato, corn, pumpkin (*Cucurbita maxima, C. moshata*), vegetable amaranths (*Amaranthus* spp.), legumes, peppers, pineapples (*Ananas cosmosus*) and arrowroot (*Maranta arundinacea*) and cassava starches. Corn was also grown, to feed pigs and poultry which were sold at the market. Many of these items were ingredients in the "negro pot", as various soups were called that were frequently prepared for the planters' families. Nevertheless, provision grounds were not universally encouraged. Even when profits from sugarcane production were declining, it was still important to the planters to maintain control over the labour force, and some sought to do so by controlling the supply of food. The sense of importance and independence that the provision grounds and the Sunday markets gave the Africans must have challenged this advantage. Where provision grounds were encouraged by planters, they were used as evidence that slavery was not as bad as it was being made out to be by the abolitionists, because even the enslaved were thriving financially (Tobin 1999).

Another factor emerged which militated against the indigenous food crops' regaining their prominence. This was the importation of many plant species from colonies in Asia, Africa and the Pacific, especially during the eighteenth century, in the search for other crops of possible economic importance and also for an easy food source. Breadfruit (*Artocarpus altilis*) was imported to fill the latter role because of the previously described food crises of the 1770s and 1780s. Besides sugarcane, other transplanted crops that eventually gained significance in the Caribbean included banana (*Musa* spp.), coffee (*Coffea arabica*), citrus (*Citrus* spp.) and other fruit crops such as mango (*Mangifera indica*). While this was not a one-way flow of germplasm – the colonists also distributed the region's germplasm to other areas of the world (Powell 1976) – the net effect was diminution of the significance of indigenous biodiversity as a food source.

During this period, indigenous crops and food ways were also preserved by the small populations of Amerindian descendants that remained in some territories. Within the English-speaking Caribbean, they were represented by the Carib descendants of Dominica and the Garifuna, a mixed Carib and African ethnic group that originated in St Vincent and was later forced to migrate to Belize (then British Honduras) and Honduras. While both groups were exposed to the newly introduced crops, and to European and other influences on the preparation of indigenous foods, they also retained the practice of cultivating and methods of use of some of the native food plants.

## The Post-Emancipation Period

The period after emancipation of the enslaved people was marked by two major developments that influenced the future status of indigenous crops in the Caribbean. In spite of the legacy of the previous period that had established social distinctions and, consequently, preferences for crops and foods, a peasantry consisting primarily of emancipated Africans emerged and expanded production of the crops grown on the provision grounds (Marshall 1985). This not only served the purpose of developing a local food-crop sector within the economy but also preserved the remaining indigenous crops as an integral part of the region's food system. This peasantry was critical to sustaining the local population as sugarcane production declined and new export crops developed (Marshall 1985). Officially, however, production of local food crops was still not supported because it drew labour away from sugarcane; it gained support from the colonial governments only during periods of food shortage, when campaigns were mounted to encourage food production. This interest was not sustained when better economic circumstances prevailed, because of the preference for foreign foods and the stigma attached to local foods, especially the root crops, or ground provisions, as they had come to be known. In his book *The Middle Passage*, V.S. Naipaul describes the contempt in which Trinidadians held Grenadians because they ate ground provisions.

The second major development was the emergence of cocoa (*Theobroma cacao*), a plant indigenous to tropical America, as a major export crop. According to Purseglove (1974) it was cultivated from ancient times by the Amerindians of Central America, who held it in high esteem as a food for the gods. This status may have arisen from its consumption by persons of higher rank, as a thick beverage made by mixing the roasted and pounded beans with maize and pepper. The Spanish, who preferred to consume the ground beans mixed with sugar and vanilla (*Vanilla fragrans*), made it into chocolate and initiated the trade to Europe. Cocoa germplasm initially consisted of two strains: Criollo, from Central America, and Forastero, from the Amazon region. Both were brought to Trinidad (Criollo first, by the Spanish in 1525), where they hybridized to produce Trinitario, a strain that combined the best characteristics of the two parent groups: fine flavour and hardiness (Purseglove 1974). This permitted development of the cocoa industry in Trinidad, which was a leading exporter up to 1920. Cocoa transformed the local society because it was cultivated on much smaller holdings than sugarcane, so many more producers were able to participate and earn wealth.

Cocoa was the first indigenous crop to enjoy serious research attention. The Imperial College of Tropical Agriculture (ICTA), the forerunner of the

Faculty of Agriculture at the University of the West Indies, was founded in 1922 in Trinidad and became the first and foremost institution in the world for cocoa research and postgraduate training in tropical agriculture. Also, a board was established to regulate the industry, including production and all aspects of marketing the beans, in the same manner as the boards for the sugar and banana industries; the cocoa industry is still controlled by a board today. New, improved cocoa material was distributed to other territories, such as Grenada and St Lucia, expanding cocoa production for export throughout the region.

## The Current Status of Food Crops

### Starchy Crops

The starchy crops include cereal grains, tubers and rhizomes that are grown to supply energy from carbohydrates, primarily starch. Maize is the third most important cereal internationally after wheat and rice and is comparable to both as a source of energy. It also supplies appreciable quantities of protein and minerals and surpasses wheat and rice in vitamin A content (CFNI 1998). Within the Caribbean, maize is second to rice in both production (538,342 tonnes)[1] and consumption (17.51 kg per capita per year),[2] with Cuba and Haiti being the major producers. It is available fresh, processed as cornmeal, corn flakes, canned whole kernels and creamed corn, and as cornstarch. Maize is consumed at all main meals and in a variety of favourite dishes (see table 17.1). Snack foods such as tortillas and corn curls are popular, although chili bibi, or sansam – a traditional African snack prepared by mixing roasted and pounded corn grains with sugar – is less well-known today. The main dishes reflect Amerindian, African, European and modern North American influences.

Cassava and sweet potatoes are the major root crops produced (893,184 and 538,671 tonnes, respectively) and consumed (18.98 and 16.64 kg per capita per year) in the Caribbean, and among tropical root crops they rank first and second in international production. Within the region, most production is undertaken on small farms, and fresh tubers are available at local markets. Cassava roots are prepared by boiling, or they may be grated and made into several traditional dishes (see table 17.1). More modern uses include tapioca starch, a food extender, and fried chips are more evident. Cassareep is still used to preserve cooked meat in the popular Guyanese dish pepperpot.

Yams (*Dioscorea* spp.) rank third in production among root crops internationally and in the Caribbean. However, cush-cush, the only yam species native to the New World, is not widely cultivated in the region, although its small (15 to 20 cm long) tubers with white, cream, yellow or purple flesh are appreciated for their sweet flavour and soft texture. Tannia is an aroid and related to dasheen (also called taro or cocoyam; *Colocasia esculenta* var. *esculenta*) and eddoes (*C. esculenta* var. *antiquorum*), which are also grown as starchy tubers in the region, but more tannia is produced (215,344 tonnes). Tannia is available as fresh tubers and is consumed boiled or fried. Another minor root crop is topi tambo, which is produced in a very few countries that include Trinidad and Tobago. The small (2 to 5 cm long) tubers grow in a clump; when cooked they have a crisp texture and nutty flavour. All the root crops with the exception of topi tambo are consumed at main meals. Boiling as a preparation method predominates, while the more time-consuming roasting and preparation of meal have declined.

The key factor that has determined the current status of starchy crops in the Caribbean, especially the root tubers, is that during the colonial era these crops were not important for export; therefore their cultivation and improvement were not encouraged. The situation was different for maize, which was being produced in North America for human and livestock consumption and on which international research was being conducted at the Centro internacional de mejoramiento de maíz y trigo (CIMMYT) in Mexico beginning in 1943 (Morris 2002). When the food potential of cassava and sweet potato was recognized elsewhere, similar internationally funded research began at the International Institute for Tropical Agriculture (IITA), which was established in 1967 in Nigeria (IITA 2007). Eventually research also began within the Caribbean, at ministries of agriculture and regional research institutions, to address constraints to availability and consumption. Improved production, post-harvest management and processing technologies were sought for problems such as low yields, seasonality, lack of convenience forms and the presence of anti-nutritional constituents such as cyanogenic glycosides (University of Puerto Rico 2002). These efforts have been directed mainly towards cassava, sweet potato, introduced yams and, to a much less extent, tannia. Cushcush and topi tambo have not benefited from these improvements. Germplasm collections for cassava, sweet potato and yams, consisting of both traditional local selections and imported accessions, are held by the University of the West Indies at St Augustine, Trinidad and Tobago, but much larger collections exist in the Spanish-speaking countries. These crops are considered non-traditional or minor export crops.

In its rhizomes, or underground stems, the arrowroot plant produces a fine-grained, highly digestible starch that is very useful in the diets of infants and convalescents. Because of its high viscosity it is also widely used as an extender to thicken soups and in ketchup. Arrowroot starch was a major export of St Vincent from 1900 to 1965 (Purseglove 1974). The industry has since declined but is being revived, since the demand for high-quality starch remains. Although little research has been undertaken to improve production of this crop, its importance in St Vincent is recognized by an annual Arrow-root Festival, held during the May harvest period.

## Legumes and Vegetables

Peanuts are not a major legume in the region, and consumption is heavily reliant on imports. Production is undertaken by small farmers, and the major producing countries are Haiti, Cuba and Jamaica. The highly nutritious shelled or baked-in-shell nuts are among the most popular snacks in the region, consumed daily as a rich source of protein, energy – because of their high fat content – and dietary fibre. Nutcakes and peanut brittle are traditional sweetmeats that were developed by the African population. Imported peanut butter is much consumed, and its use in stews and soups may be of both Amerindian and African origin (Parkinson 1999). Varietal trials have been undertaken to develop the region's peanut production (CARDI 2005).

A variety of common beans are consumed, ranging in colour from white to black. Black beans are highly favoured in the Spanish-speaking Caribbean and, along with rice, are the basis of the Cuban national dish, Moros y Cristianos. Red or kidney beans are more popular elsewhere; in Jamaica they are used in a very popular dish, rice and peas (Parkinson 1999). Beans are a relatively cheap source of protein and other important nutrients, and when combined with rice they provide a complete amino acid profile. They are consumed widely on a daily basis at main meals. While most dried beans are imported, both immature pods and dried beans are also produced locally. They are commonly small-farmer crops, and production is highest in Cuba, the Dominican Republic and Haiti. Significant research has been conducted on cultural aspects of bean production, its genetics and diseases throughout the region, especially in Cuba and Puerto Rico, where germplasm collections are held.

Vegetable amaranths (*Amaranthus* spp.), better known as bhagi, callaloo or spinach, are a highly appreciated and cheap source of important minerals, vitamins and proteins and are eaten at all main meals. They much exceed green leafy vegetables of temperate origin, such as lettuce, in nutritional value; however, because of their calcium oxalate crystal content, persons with health problems such as kidney stones should avoid consuming large quantities. Several types are available in the region, differing in plant height, leaf size and vein colour, degree of succulence, flavour and nutritional content. The fast-growing plant is cultivated by small farmers and is available year-round as fresh bundles of green shoots. Small quantities are exported outside the region. Research has been undertaken on varietal evaluation, agronomic assessment and pest control for improved production. Since the amaranths can also be weeds in other crops, investigations have been conducted on their allelopathic effects, their role as carriers of viruses and methods of control (Martin, Ruberté and Meitzner 1998).

Pumpkin remains an important vegetable crop in the region, and among all the vegetables in Puerto Rico it is the second highest in revenue generation. Selections of traditional varieties are cultivated by small farmers. The University of Puerto Rico has conducted research on several areas of improvement, including growth habit, and a semi-bushy type, 'Taina Dorada', has been developed. 'Bodles Globe', an improved type with good flesh colour and culinary properties, has been developed in Jamaica; it is favoured for the export market because of its shape (University of Puerto Rico 2002).

The original "heart of palm", a high-priced delicacy, is the enclosed apical bud of the cabbage palm tree (*Roystonea oleracea*). The tender bud is consumed steamed and in salads. The tree is destroyed during harvesting of the bud, so the pewah, or peach palm (*Bactris gasipaes*), which regenerates naturally by suckers, is a better species for commercial production, because younger trees or suckers replace the harvested ones. Production in the region is not widespread; traditionally, as in Trinidad, pewah trees are grown mainly for their starchy fruits, which are consumed as a snack. A major constraint to production are the long, sharp spines along the stems of the plants. Heart of palm is usually available as an imported canned product. Production was attempted in Jamaica during the 1980s, and currently it is a major non-traditional export crop from Guyana, a CARICOM country on the South American mainland.

It is clear that the indigenous legumes and vegetable crops possess considerable potential to contribute to regional food supply. The high nutritional value of cassava leaves and those of other root crops is virtually unexploited compared with elsewhere in the tropics. They remain largely underdeveloped because, in most of the Caribbean, the major impetus for development of these crops is their export potential.

## Fruits

It is thought that grapefruit arose in the West Indies, possibly in Barbados, as a mutation from pumelo or from a hybrid of pumelo (*Citrus grandis*) and orange (*C. sinensis*), both being close relatives of Asian origin (Purseglove 1974). Grapefruit is second only to the orange in the international citrus fruit trade, and it is the most important Caribbean fruit. Cuba and the Dominican Republic are major producers and exporters. 'Ortanique' and 'Ugli', hybrids of orange and tangerine (*C. reticulata*) and grapefruit and tangerine, respectively, were developed in Jamaica (Higman 2008), which is also a major producer and exporter. Citrus fruits provide appreciable quantities of vitamin C and other important nutrients such as bioflavonoids. Production is undertaken by enterprises of all sizes, with the level of technology being higher on larger farms. Production, processing, marketing and research of these fruits are coordinated and controlled by citrus growers' associations and state organizations. Grapefruit, 'Ortanique' and 'Ugli' are available as fresh fruit, juices and concentrates. The major threat to production in the region is the citrus tristeza virus (CTV), and new orchards are being established on CTV-resistant rootstocks.

Avocado (*Persea americana*) germplasm consists of three races: Mexican, Guatemalan and West Indian (Purseglove 1974). Within the Caribbean it is mainly the West Indian race, which is well adapted to the prevailing high-temperature conditions of most of the region, that is grown, with the highest production in Cuba and the Dominican Republic. The fruit is a good energy source because of its fat content; traditionally it is consumed at meals more as a vegetable in salads than as a dessert or snack, as with other fruits. It is exported from several territories.

Pineapple (*Ananas cosmosus*) and papaya (*Carica papaya*) are also among the Caribbean fruits that have become well-established on the international market. Apart from the nutrients they supply, they are valued for their enzymatic properties, which are especially effective for protein digestion. Both crops are grown throughout the region on farms of various sizes. Most pineapple and papaya production occurs in the Dominican Republic, Cuba and Jamaica, and among the pineapple cultivars, 'Antigua Black' and 'Sugar Loaf' were developed in the Caribbean. These fruits are available fresh and are also processed into a range of value-added products (see table 17.1).

Of less commercial importance are fruits such as passion fruit (*Passiflora edulis* var. *flavicarpa*), barbadine (*P. quadrangularis*), guava, West Indian cherry (*Malphigia glabra*), cashew (*Anacardium occidentale*), genip or chenette, soursop and sapodilla (*Manilkara achras*). These all supply significant levels of nutrients, with some fruits being particularly outstanding; for example, the cashew nut, which is a true fruit, provides high levels of energy, protein and potassium, whereas West Indian cherry is one of the best natural sources of vitamin C. Exports of fresh fruit to regional markets is limited, and commercial production is small-scale. With the exception of passion fruit, guava, West Indian cherry and imported cashew nuts, processing is generally limited to the cottage level.

The Jamaica plum (*Spondias purpurea*) and chili-plum (*S. lutea*) are probably better known and more utilized than hog-plum (*S. mombin*), mammee apple, mamee-sapote (*Calocarpum sapota*), caimite (*Chrysophyllum cainito*) and balata (*Manilkara bidentata*) because the relatively small plum trees are easily accommodated in backyards, whereas the trees of the other fruits are much taller and tend to occur in forested areas. While limited quantities of fresh fruit are available for sale, commercial production and processing of this last group of indigenous fruits are uncommon. All these fruits are extensively appreciated for their unique flavours, but many young persons do not know them. This lack of familiarity and, apparently, lower levels of consumption than in the past are due largely to declining tree populations and hence availability, especially in residential areas.

The picture that emerges among the fruits is that, with the exception of grapefruit, introduced fruits such as banana and mango have assumed more importance in the Caribbean than the indigenous species or those of tropical American origin. Within the latter group, only those fruits that are exported internationally have been developed and have organized industries. Others considered to have this potential have been included in agricultural diversification efforts. Research effort is needed to remove production and utilization constraints, such as low supplies for processing, pests and inadequate post-harvest handling. A wide range of fruit germplasm is held in Costa Rica, but except for efforts in Cuba (with guava), the Dominican Republic (with avocado) and Martinique and Guadeloupe (with pineapples), relatively limited attention is paid to the critical area of germplasm conservation in the Caribbean.

## Industrial Crops

Fine-flavoured cocoa based on the Trinitario clones is produced mainly in Trinidad and Tobago, and also in Grenada, St Lucia and Jamaica. The quality of Trinitario cocoa attracts the highest prices on the world market; it is used to manufacture expensive dark chocolates. The beans from the Forastero type, grown mainly in West Africa, produce the less expensive bulk cocoa that is processed into milk chocolates, cocoa butter and cocoa/chocolate drinks. These cheaper cocoa products, but not the dark chocolates, are available throughout the region, and chocolate balls or blocks from which the traditional hot chocolate drink is made can be found at local markets.

In all exporting countries of the Caribbean, the cocoa industry is regulated by a board which plays a key role in the production and marketing of the cocoa beans. Current production and exports from Trinidad and Tobago are a mere fraction of their 1920s levels because of disease and loss of the labour force required for cultivation and processing of quality cocoa. Small quantities of cocoa are also exported by other Caribbean countries. True to its imperial mandate, the ICTA facilitated the growth and development of cocoa industries in other parts of the British Empire that eventually became much larger cocoa producers and exporters than the Caribbean. One enduring legacy of that institution in the region, however, is that Trinidad and Tobago has been designated an international cocoa germplasm repository, and germplasm is distributed to support research on cocoa improvement worldwide. This is the result of significant efforts by the ICTA and one of its successors, the Cocoa Research Unit (CRU) of the University of the West Indies, in collaboration with the ministry of agriculture in Trinidad, in germplasm collection, breeding and selection of improved clonal material. The work at the CRU on developing germplasm descriptors, disease control and flavour quality is ongoing. Currently efforts are being made to revive the regional industry, with increased funding for research, better financial support and prices to boost production, new approaches to marketing to secure a better international market share and prices, and plans to embark upon chocolate manufacturing.

## Beverage Crops

Mauby is a drink with a bitter aftertaste. It is made by boiling the bark of the tree *Colubrina arborescens* (*C. elliptica*) with spices to which sugar and essence – typically aniseed (*Pimpinella anisum*) – are added, and it is served cold. Dried bark, concentrated syrups to which only water has to be added, and a carbonated drink, Mauby Fizz, are locally available; limited amounts are exported. Mauby trees are not cultivated in commercial plots, so the bark is collected from trees growing on farms or in forested areas. Research has been conducted on the chemical constituents, fermentation and preservation of mauby (Graham and Chaparro 1982; Burke 1991).

Sea-moss or Irish moss (*Gracilaria* spp.) refers to both the dried sea plants and the drink made from them. Traditionally the plants are collected in shallow water at the coastline and dried until ready for use. The dried plants are boiled in water with spices until they dissolve into a gel. When cooled, sugar and milk (which are optional) are added; the resulting drink is highly regarded for its nutritional value. Sea-moss is available as dried plants, as a gel and as prepared drinks. Overharvesting of natural stocks has decreased supplies, but commercial production has been undertaken in both St Lucia and Barbados (Smith 1986; St Hill 1986). Haiti, however, is a larger and cheaper producer. While most sea-moss processing is small-scale, Benjo's is a medium-scale producer in Dominica that produces a range of sea-moss-based drinks for the local and regional markets. Unlike citrus and cocoa, which are major beverage crops, and in common with most of the minor crops, mauby and sea-moss are still consumed primarily by the local market and their potential is relatively untapped.

## Condiments and Spices

Both hot and sweet pepper (*Capsicum frutescens, C. annum*) are major condiments in Caribbean cooking, with the hot pepper in particular being used to flavour many dishes, including jerked meats, curries and souse. Several different pepper varieties, varying in pungency, size, shape and colour, are recognized, including the 'Scotch Bonnet' variety of Jamaica and the 'West Indian Red'. Traditionally, hot and sweet peppers were cultivated commercially by small farmers for local markets; however, recently hot peppers have been promoted as a non-traditional export crop with much potential, and in several English-speaking Caribbean territories it is a priority crop for development. Accordingly, research has been conducted on the breeding and selection of superior types such as 'CARDI Red' and 'Caribbean CARDI Green', improvement of agronomic techniques and post-harvest management for export (CARDI 2008). In the Spanish-speaking countries there has been research on both hot and sweet peppers.

Pimento (*Pimenta dioica*) is associated mostly with Jamaican cuisine (see table 17.1). This flavouring, which is said to have the combined flavour of spice, clove and nutmeg, is the dried berries of the pimento tree that grows throughout the island. Dried pimento berries are sold locally. There is little information within the region on overseas markets for the berries, production levels or research to improve aspects of production and processing. The bay (*P. racemosa*), a related species, is grown for its aromatic leaves, especially in Dominica, where small farmers tend bay trees in pure stands or intercropped. Bay leaves have been used traditionally as a spice in hot drinks, and they are distilled to produce bay rum.

Roucou (*Bixa orellano*) is a traditional food flavouring and colourant throughout the Caribbean region. For example, it is used to impart a yellow colour to confectionery, cheese and butter, and it has also been used in butter made from buffalo milk in Cuba (Ortega Fleitas et al. 1996). The demand for roucou as a natural food additive is growing internationally. There is little evidence of research on this product in the region, in contrast to work being done in Latin America.

Vanilla is a very expensive food flavouring used for sweet dishes, baked products and drinks. The extract is derived from the pods of a vine that grows on trees. Because of its expense, it has been significantly replaced by synthetic substances. The seeds of the tonka bean (*Dipteryx odorata*) fruit, for example, yield an extract that is very similar to vanilla. The trees grow uncultivated in Trinidad, and very small quantities of seeds are usually available for sale locally. Generally, with the exception of pepper, and to a lesser extent pimento and bay, little is being done to develop the commercial potential of indigenous condiments and spices.

## Implications for Food and Nutrition Security in the Caribbean

From the preceding discussion it is clear that, with few exceptions, the indigenous food crops of the Caribbean have been relatively neglected. With a food import bill of almost US$4 billion, the Caribbean is the most food-insecure region in tropical America. This situation is made even more pathetic by the region's natural endowment of food resources and points to the policies regarding agriculture and food that have shaped the region's development. The most glaring policy error is the disconnect between agriculture and food, which has ensured that agriculture has not become a vehicle for development, but rather for underdevelopment, through its dominant focus on production of primary products for international markets. This is a legacy of the colonial era that continues to persist, even though the need for a new paradigm has been underscored repeatedly by the region's several periods of economic downturn.

The critical lesson learnt by the Maroons of Jamaica and, elsewhere in the region, African proto-peasants and the small entrepreneurial farmers of the post-emancipation and World War periods, is that food security is the foundation of true independence, a concept which has not yet been fully appreciated. In the post-independence period, especially in the English-speaking Caribbean, levels of root crop consumption declined drastically, primarily because of a preference for imported white potatoes and cereals and the traditional stigma against root crops – referred to colloquially as "blue" (slave) food.

Since food prices began to increase in 2008, governments in the Caribbean have placed domestic agriculture higher on the national and regional agendas, and campaigns are being mounted to encourage the consumption of local foods. In some cases – for example, in Jamaica in 2010 – food import bills have been slashed; in that same year, the rate of inflation in Trinidad and Tobago reached its highest level in twenty-seven years, mostly because of food prices. There is grave concern throughout the region about the potential impact of both natural disasters and increasing demand from China and India on access to food and on food prices worldwide. Farmers are once again being encouraged to grow more root crops, especially cassava, and various value-added products are being explored and made available on the market. While these efforts are necessary and must be encouraged, they are often too late to be as effective as desired.

The inadequacy of research and development work to support expanded production and utilization is one major deficiency, while the issue of consumer tastes and preferences, particularly among youth, is another. In countries outside the region, to which several of these crops have been introduced and have thrived, research has been undertaken to address these issues. The information and insight gained from such research provide a valuable starting point for developing these crops to make a sustainable and substantial contribution to food security in the Caribbean.

The prevalence of nutrition-related diseases such as diabetes mellitus, hypertension, cancer and various allergies create an additional imperative for increasing the content of indigenous food crops in the diet of the Caribbean. During the period of slavery, malnutrition due to over-reliance on inadequate supplies of poor-quality imported food was a key contributor to ill health and death (Pilcher 2000). Furthermore, overconsumption of salt (used as a preservative) led to death from hypertension-related dropsy, and the food was often of no nutritional benefit because of its significant deterioration. Pilcher cites Kiple as noting

> shortages of most important vitamins, as well as calcium and iron. The most serious problems resulted from deficiencies of vitamin $B_1$ (thiamine) and $B_3$ (niacin). Slaves subsisting on white rice were at risk of developing beriberi, a thiamine-deficiency disease that takes two distinct forms. Both wet beriberi, with symptoms including swelling of the limbs and cardiac failure, and dry beriberi, characterized by muscular deterioration and paraplegia, were common to the Caribbean under the names "dropsy" and mal d'estomach. Corn rations, meanwhile, led to pellagra, a niacin-deficiency disease that caused dermatitis, dysentery, dementia, and death. (Pilcher 2000)

Kiple also reported the prevalence of night blindness due to vitamin A deficiency and scurvy and festering sores and wounds due to vitamin C deficiency, which were also related to calcium and iron deficiencies. The toll on infants was particularly severe, since they were frequently born underweight, and mortality rates were high because of poor nutrition.

On the other hand, it was noted that enslaved Africans who produced their own food had a better diet and were healthier, and in territories such as the Bahamas, where sugarcane production did not dominate, they were taller. Pilcher (2000) notes that in the Caribbean the population of enslaved Africans had to be maintained by regular importation of new labour because reproductive rates were low. This was in large measure because of poor nutrition, and doctors recommended to planters that they encourage provision grounds for the cultivation of food crops, including indigenous crops, to increase the birth rate among enslaved women.

In the post-emancipation era, nutrition-related diseases still prevailed, primarily because of continued reliance on imported food, much of it in highly processed forms that came to be preferred to freshly prepared food. Even though most territories have become independent, nutrition-related lifestyle diseases continue to debilitate a high percentage of the population, affecting their productivity, quality of life and longevity. Naipaul notes in *The Middle Passage*, "To be modern is to ignore local products and to use those advertised in American magazines" (1978, 48). The more powerful and pervasive television and Internet advertising now available have undoubtedly reinforced this centuries-old psychological disposition towards foreign tastes. But perhaps it might also prove a crucial ally in changing people's taste patterns.

## Conclusion

The Caribbean's rich biodiversity in food plants made major contributions to the diets of the indigenous people, early settlers and migrants to the region, and through their distribution they play a similar role, providing agricultural incomes in many parts of the tropical world. This contribution has been especially strong in the case of the starchy crops, cocoa and some of the fruits. In the Greater Antilles, while land and population size account for higher levels of production and consumption of these crops, research and germplasm conservation activities suggest that they generally enjoy a higher status than elsewhere in the region. Within the English-speaking Caribbean, the only species that are still considered important are primarily those that have secured extra-regional export markets. Most food plants are underutilized even though they offer significant potential for future development based on their nutritional value and adaptation to prevailing environmental conditions. However, there is need for improved consumer awareness of these benefits in order to create market demand, and for research to develop appropriate production systems and value-added products. Urgent attention to these issues is required, without which the indigenous food plants – an important Caribbean heritage and a critical resource for development of the region – could be lost.

## Notes

1. FAO production data for 2006.
2. FAO consumption data for 2003.

## References

Benghiat, N. 1985. *Traditional Jamaican Cookery*. Middlesex, UK: Penguin Books.

Burke, M.A. L. 1991. *Preliminary Studies on the Extraction of Water-Soluble Components from the Bark of the Tree* Colubrina arborescens *(or* Colubrina elliptica*)"*. MPhil thesis, University of the West Indies, St Augustine, Trinidad and Tobago.

CARDI (Caribbean Agricultural Research and Development Institute). 2008. *Annual Report 2005*. http://www.cardi.org/publications/annualreports/2005/2005annualre port.pdf (accessed 1 July 2008).

CFNI (Caribbean Food and Nutrition Institute). 1998. *Food Composition Tables for Use in the English-Speaking Caribbean*. 2nd ed. Kingston: Caribbean Food and Nutrition Institute and Pan American Health Organization.

FAO (United Nations Food and Agriculture Organization). 2011. FAOSTAT: "Crops". http://faostat.fao.org/site/567/default.aspx#ancor (accessed 1 July 2008).

———. 2011. FAOSTAT: "Food Balance Sheets". http://faostat.fao.org/site/368/ default.aspx#ancor (accessed 1 July 2008).

Graham, H.D., and M. Chaparro. 1982. "Preservation of Mabi by Chemical and Physical Means (Fermented Drink Made from the Bark of the Mabi Tree, *Colubrina elliptica*, Pasteurization, Sodium Benzoate)". *Journal of Agriculture of the University of Puerto Rico* 66, no. 2: 89–98.

Higman, B.W. 2008. *Jamaican Food: History, Biology, Culture*. Kingston: University of the West Indies Press.

Inter-American Institute for Cooperation on Agriculture. 1996. "Potential Development of Minor Fruit Crops of Trinidad and Tobago". Workshop held at University of the West Indies, St Augustine, Trinidad, 25–26 October 1995. Port of Spain: Inter-American Institute for Cooperation on Agriculture.

IITA (International Institute for Tropical Agriculture). 2007. *Annual Report*. http:// www.iita.org (accessed 1 July 2008).

Janick, J., and R.E. Paull, eds. 2008. *Encyclopedia of Fruits and Nuts*. Oxfordshire, UK: CAB International.

Keegan, W.F. 2000. "The Caribbean, Including Northern South America and Lowland Central America: Early History". In *The Cambridge World History of Food*, edited by K.F. Kiple and K.C. Ornelas. Cambridge: Cambridge University Press. http://www.credoreference.com/entry/cupfood/v_d_3_the_caribbean_including_ northern_south_america_and_lowland_central_america_early_history (accessed 8 October 2010).

Marshall, W.K. 1985. "Peasant Development in the West Indies since 1838". In *Rural Development in the Caribbean*, edited by P.I. Gomes. Kingston: Heinemann Educational (Caribbean).

Martin, F.W., R.M. Ruberté and L.S. Meitzner. 1998. *Edible Leaves of the Tropics*. 3rd ed. North Fort Myers, FL: Education Concern for Hunger Organization.

Morris, M.L. 2002. *Impacts of International Maize Breeding Research in Developing Countries, 1966–1998*. Mexico: Centro internacional de mejoramiento de maíz y trigo.

Naipaul, V.S. 1978. *The Middle Passage: Impressions of Five Societies – British, French and Dutch – in the West Indies and South America*. Harmondsworth, UK: Penguin.

Ortega Fleitas, O., J. Camejo Corrales, M. Otero and M. Fonseca. 1996. "Colourants in Buffalo Butter Processing 1: Use of *Bixa orellana*". *Alimentaria (España)* 34, no. 273: 47–49.

Ortiz, E.L. 1995. *The Complete Book of Caribbean Cooking*. Edison, NJ: Castle Books.

Pagán Jiménez, J.R., and R. Rodríguez Ramos. 2007. "Sobre el origen de la agricultura en Las Antillas". In *Proceedings of the Twenty-first Congress of the International Association for Caribbean Archaeology*, edited by B. Reid, H.P.J. Roget and A. Curet, vol. 1, 252–59. St Augustine: School of Continuing Studies, University of the West Indies.

Parkinson, R. 1999. *Culinaria: The Caribbean, a Culinary Discovery*. Köln, Germany: Könemann.

Pilcher, J.M. 2000. "The Caribbean from 1492 to the Present". In *The Cambridge World History of Food*, edited by K.F. Kiple and K.C. Ornelas. Cambridge: Cambridge University Press. http://www.credoreference.com/entry/cupfood/v_d_4_the_caribbean_from_1492_to_the_present (accessed 8 October 2010).

Powell, D. 1977. "The Voyage of the Plant Nursery H.M.S. *Providence*, 1791–1793". *Economic Botany* 31: 387–431.

Purseglove, J.W. 1974. *Tropical Crops: Monocotyledons*. London: Longman Group, ELBS.

Reid, B.A. 2009. *Myths and Realities of Caribbean History*. Tuscaloosa: University of Alabama Press.

Sheridan, R.B. 1976. "The Crisis of Slave Subsistence in the British West Indies during and after the American Revolution". *William and Mary Quarterly*, 3rd ser., 33, no. 4: 615–41.

Smith, A., 1986. "Seamoss Farming in St. Lucia: From Myth to Reality". *Caribbean Conservation News (Barbados)* 4, no. 6: 7–8.

St Hill, C.A. 1986. *Mariculture of Seamoss in Barbados*. MPhil thesis, University of the West Indies, Cave Hill, Barbados.

Tobin, B.F. 1999. " 'And There Raise Yams': Slaves' Gardens in the Writings of West Indian Plantocrats". *Eighteenth-Century Life* 23, no. 2: 164–79.

University of Puerto Rico. 2002. *Annual Report of Accomplishments and Results*. Mayaguez: Agricultural Experiment Station, College of Agricultural Sciences. http://www.reeis.usda.gov/web/areera/AES.PR.report.2002.pdf (accessed 1 July 2008).

Wood, B. 1973. *Caribbean Fruits and Vegetables: Selected Recipes*. London: Longman Caribbean.

**Part 4.**

LAND TENURE AND BUILT HERITAGE

# 18.

# Valuing Our "Family Land" Heritage

CHARISSE GRIFFITH-CHARLES AND SUNIL LALLOO

*The "family land" form of communal tenure is an important part of our Caribbean heritage. Its significance lies in its historical, economic and social value as well as in its positive impacts on environmental and governance issues. These values can be examined to support a case for retaining this form of tenure instead of attempting to eradicate it in favour of the assumed benefits of individualized and formally documented tenure. Conflicting views exist on the desirability and value of communal tenure generally, and on family land as practised in the Caribbean, but examples of its value as a tenure form and its sustainability in the face of pressure abound, as it continues to exist in many countries of the Caribbean. Despite a well-structured and efficient programme to formally register individual parcels in St Lucia during the 1980s, for example, family land continues to exist to the present day. In Tobago, governance structures on family land are also still intact. The tenure form, therefore, unquestionably has significant value as a part of our heritage.*

## Introduction

The land tenure system known as "family land" is part of our Caribbean heritage, deriving from a collective cultural response to a shared social and economic history of conquest, colonization and slavery. This heritage, like many vestiges of our cultural past, is under assault from economic, political and legal challenges, from modernization of thought, societal structures and technology, and from globalization of markets and movement. As with most cultural artefacts, the question is whether this facet of our heritage should be preserved or allowed to become a footnote in history books. The answer to this question usually lies in assigning a value to the artefact, whether that value be economic, social or aesthetic, amongst other labels under which value is ascribed. The greater this assigned value, the stronger the motivation to protect the artefact from harm. This investigation documents the various perspectives on family land that could help to determine a value, and thus decide whether the tenure form should be supported against the onslaught of destructive elements or left to its natural demise.

## Defining *Family Land*

Land tenure is the way in which land is held, as defined by the legal structures, formal or informal, that determine the rights, restrictions and responsibilities attached to the holding of the land. Land tenure is a relationship between the landholder and others in respect to the use of the land (Ting and Williamson 1999; Furubotn and Pejovich 1972). There can be no land tenure, therefore, without some form of negotiation between the holder of the land and others in the community, whether such negotiation is silent or spoken, documented or undocumented, formal or informal. Family land is a subset of the communal tenure forms found in many societies where a group of persons holds the land collectively and where the tenure is not only a negotiated relationship among the members of the group but also between the group and the society. The term *family land*, however, makes reference to the fact that membership in this particular communal group is determined by membership in a family, howsoever this family may be defined by the family itself.

At its simplest level, family land can be defined as land held communally by a group, the members of which are related through some common descent line, where each member of the group holds some level of rights to the land. It is often defined legally as co-ownership in undivided shares by the descendants of the original purchaser or group of purchasers. This definition not only generalizes the origin of the current family land tenure situation and negates other forms of original acquisition, such as settlement or conquest, but also gives the impression that a formal legal framework underpins the informal procedures of family land governance. This impression leads to the idea that family land developed as a passive, uneducated interaction with the formal legal system and not, as is more likely, as an active, thoughtful response to restrictive formal institutions that sought to insert barriers between the society and the land.

Concerning a Barbados case study, Greenfield opines that family land emerged from the English law itself, where he asserts that "this system of tenure is found not only to be in complete harmony with the law, but it is actually based upon it. The present system of family land . . . will be shown to have been an application by the rural folk of certain principles of the English common law of an earlier period" (1960, 166). James (2001), however, believes that if family land reflects formal law, it has more in common with corporate law than laws of survivorship, as the land does not so much bequeath to the heirs of the individual members as it does to the surviving corporate members of the family group. This analogous relationship of family land structures with legal concepts may, however, be coincidental, as similar communal tenure forms occur elsewhere in the world where tribal, clan and other group relationships define membership. Family land, therefore, is an extant tenure form in the Caribbean that is governed by a complex of dynamic customary laws together with procedures similar to formal legal structures, where land is transferred through succession to the subsequent family group in undivided, inalienable shares.

## Historical Value

As an example of the origins of family land, in British Guiana, subsequent to the abolition of slavery in 1834, ex-slaves contributed to a common fund with which they bought large estates and subdivided them in relation to the level of contribution (Hall 1982). Land ownership through collective efforts was a survival strategy for the peasant classes. Colonial institutions in many of the Caribbean countries provided mechanisms to restrict access to land by the former slaves, by inflating prices or by selling large, unaffordable estates. The growth of small farming and land ownership by families depended on three factors: (1) the availability of land, (2) the ability to pay the price of such land, and (3) the desire to become independent of wage labour (Hall 1982). Since plantations existed primarily on flat lands, peasant farming was most common on mountainous, marginal lands.

The recourse of the ex-slave family unit, and by extension the peasantry in this era, is highlighted by Brereton, who notes that in the families' strategies for economic autonomy "family and community goals were frequently given priority over individual enhancement . . . the survival and welfare of the family group were probably paramount for most of the freed people in the unsettled aftermath of August 1st, 1838" (1999, 92). The ex-slaves therefore found economic and social strength in community efforts and achievements, and this philosophy was expressed in the emergence of family land as a preferred form of land tenure.

The debate on the origin of family land in the Caribbean is pointed out by Espeut (1992), who segregates the viewpoints of the region's academia into two lines of thought. The first suggests African origin while the second implies its emergence from land scarcity and oppression derived from the plantation economy and the post-emancipation era. Family land, nevertheless, has been found in almost all of the Caribbean jurisdictions, including Jamaica, Antigua, Nevis, Montserrat, Dominica, St Lucia, St Vincent, Grenada, Bequia, the British Virgin Islands, St John, Barbados, and Trinidad and Tobago (Besson 1984). As far as a pan-Caribbean experience is concerned, it is commonplace to accept that one of the very few things every jurisdiction has in common is African roots. Clarke (1957), for example, attributes the origin of the family land system to African culture, in particular to Ashanti customs. Espeut (1992) challenges Clarke's theory and disputes the genesis of family land purely from African cultural heritage. Smith (1956), in his Carriacou case study, noted that legal tenure was converted to customary tenure when members of the black section acquired land and passed it down through the generations.

Family land is therefore of historical value, as it reflects a shared history of the region and a complex evolution within similar environments. This value cannot be quantified but is of great importance and significance. Its value is further reflected in the sentimental links that current family land members have with the ancestral holders of the land, a perception that is described in the following sections as part of the social value of family land. It is a shared heritage that unites many countries of the Caribbean. In preserving the tenure form, we preserve our heritage and our links to our ancestors.

## Economic Value

Land, because of its increasing scarcity in the face of increasing populations and decreasing resource yields as a result of overexploitation, is escalating in economic value. It is also necessary as a factor of production, alongside labour, capital and entrepreneurship, for any productive activity. In the management of land, policymakers often face difficulty in deciding on best-practice models to control the use of land so that it yields its maximum economic potential. Such models incorporate existing land rights, and such rights form the basis of comprehensive and complete land administration systems that best support land management decisions. Individualized tenure is thought to support the establishment and growth of land markets by increasing objective, documentary security of tenure and providing collateral for credit access, thus encouraging investment in the land. Current standard economic models therefore impose individualized tenure systems on communal tenure. Vibrant land markets inject energy into the economy and also support development (Barnes and Griffith-Charles 2007; Feder and Noronha 1987; Feder et al. 1988). In many of the countries of the Caribbean, therefore, land titling and registration programmes are being proposed and effected in an attempt to individualize tenure, establish and invigorate land markets, and encourage investment and development on land.

Communal land tenure, however, also originated to serve an economic role by providing subjective security of tenure to its claimants as well as preventing the successors of titles from ever becoming landless. Subjective security of tenure is the confidence landholders feel that their use and occupation of the land will not be challenged. Even if this perception of security is unsupported by objective or documentary tenure, such as a title certificate, it encourages the user to plough resources into the land. This maximizing of effort leads to individual economic growth and, by extension, economic growth of the society at large. In countries such as St Lucia and Jamaica, where family land holdings are usually in rural, agricultural landscapes, access to family land provides a source of income and sustenance. This economic role is also seen in Espeut's case study, where he notes that one of the main functions of family land is to "provide support for those who don't mek it" (1992, 77).

Dujon (1997) gives an account of how family land provides for agricultural development by referring to a case study in the rural district of Micoud, St Lucia. Young farmers, she explains, use the family land to accumulate capital to purchase private holdings. Retaining an unused share in family land allows the farmer to avoid becoming an economic burden on the state should a market collapse prevent him from being able to retain his individually owned holding. Individually owned parcels go on the land market easily, as opposed to family land parcels, which are difficult, if not impossible, to sell. In a regional environment where agricultural land markets are underdeveloped and fragile, and insurance against market impacts is non-existent, family land provides a cushion against poverty. While individualized title, being fungible, is more economically viable than family land, family land provides an economic buffer against poverty. The imposition of individualized tenure over informal communal tenure has been shown to result in landlessness for those not experienced in the activities of the land market.

Family land is, therefore, of economic value, especially to the poorer members of the family group. Besides providing an economic cushion and a refuge for members of the group who experience temporary economic setbacks, it provides a means to earn an income or at least subsistence. This is also of economic benefit to the state, as otherwise the state will have to provide for the individual. As land escalates in value, therefore, the value of our heritage increases with it and is preserved for posterity.

## Social Value

Family land also has a symbolic social role to play. Besson clarifies this thought thus: "the short term economic aspects of such land (family land) are subordinated to its long-term symbolic role. For the land serves primarily as a symbol of personhood, prestige, security, and freedom for descendants of former slaves in the face of plantation-engendered land scarcity. It also provides for a symbol of their family lines" (1987, 14–15). This symbolic role provides social cohesion and a feeling of belonging to the members of the family land group. This can best explain why members retain their links to the group by nominally holding on to a share in the land interests, in spite of the lack of economic benefit derived from ownership of a minuscule portion of rights to the family land.

The persistence of family land can be illustrated in the case of St Lucia, which undertook a comprehensive systematic land registration and titling project (LRTP) in the 1980s. One of the objectives of this project was to eradicate the family land situation, which was considered to be restricting the land market. The second objective was to provide documentary security of tenure to landholders. Despite this attempt to deal effectively with the problem through titling and registration, research has shown that in 2004 levels of family land had not changed significantly in the communities sampled (Griffith-Charles 2004). The combined research of Griffith-Charles (2004) and Stanfield (1988) shows that in the community of Micoud the incidence of family land increased between the years 1987 and 2004, while in Babonneau the change was not statistically significant (table 18.1; see figure 18.1 for their locations). This is an important finding in that it corroborates the statement made by Smith (1956) that customary tenure displaces formal tenure. However, Espeut (1992) is of the view that while formal tenure tends to revert to customary tenure, some customary tenure becomes individualized so that the net effect is nil. This indicates a need for family land tenure to coexist with individualized tenure.

Table 18.1 Incidence of Family Land Parcels in Babonneau and Micoud, St Lucia, 1987 and 2004

| | 1987 | | | | 2004 | | | |
| | Number | | Per Cent | | Number | | Per Cent | |
| Type of Ownership | Bab. | Mic. | Bab. | Mic. | Bab. | Mic. | Bab. | Mic. |
|---|---|---|---|---|---|---|---|---|
| Individual | 41 | 9 | 57.7 | 22.0 | 17 | 13 | 56.7 | 43.3 |
| In common (husband and wife) | 14 | 18 | 19.7 | 43.9 | 6 | 5 | 20.0 | 16.7 |
| Family land | 16 | 14 | 22.5 | 34.1 | 7 | 12 | 23.3 | 40.0 |
| Totals | 71 | 41 | 100 | 100 | 30 | 30 | 100 | 100 |

*Note:* Bab. = Babonneau; Mic. = Micoud

*Sources:* Griffith-Charles 2005; source for 1987 data, Stanfield 1988.

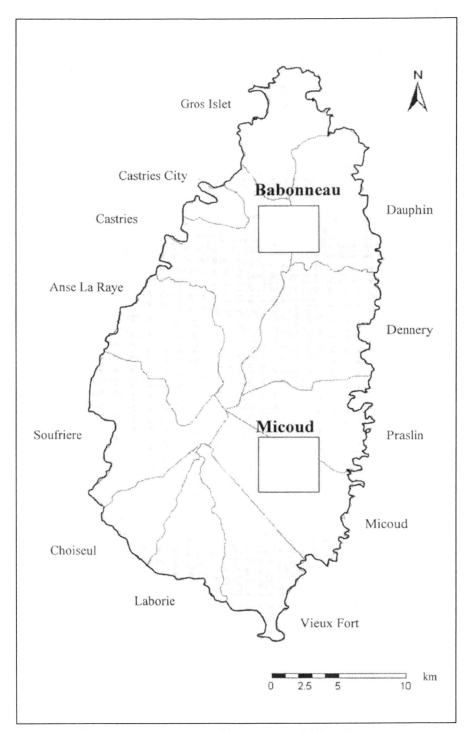

**Figure 18.1** St Lucia, showing locations of Babonneau and Micoud

**Table 18.2** Family Land Ownership in Tobago

| Parish | Number of Claimants/Owners | | | | | | |
| --- | --- | --- | --- | --- | --- | --- | --- |
| | 1 | | 2 | | ≥ 3 | | |
| | Number | Per Cent | Number | Per Cent | Number | Per Cent | Total |
| St David | 32 | 33 | 28 | 29 | 37 | 38 | 97 |
| St John | 33 | 36 | 18 | 20 | 41 | 44 | 92 |

Persistence in family land tenure was also reflected in a Tobago survey conducted by the authors. In the areas sampled, family land, as determined by percentages of parcels with three or more owners, was calculated at 38 to 44 per cent in the parishes of St David and St John, as indicated in table 18.2.

Perceptions of security of tenure can be high on family land because the occupants feel safe in the knowledge that a large community acknowledges and supports their claim to use of the land. The social value of the family land, therefore, goes far beyond the economic domain and can be used to ensure strong community behaviours. To eradicate family land by either individualizing or disposing of it denies both our social heritage and people's sense of family and generational interconnectedness.

## Governance Value

Among the distinguishing characteristics of family land are the manner in which land is passed down through the generations and whether heirs exercise their rights to land from both their mother's and father's inheritances – in other words, through bilateral, or cognatic, descent – or from only one line of inheritance, or unilateral descent. If the principle of transferring land rights undivided to all heirs is practised, then even after a few generations there would be numerous claimants to one limited parcel of land (Davenport 1961). Davenport and Solien (1959) both insist that restrictions must be imposed on cognatic descent procedures of family land in order to prevent ultimate dispersion of the property into unusable portions. Espeut (1992), in his study of the parish of St Thomas, Jamaica, found restrictions in cognatic descent due mainly to voluntary non-use of land and conflicts that arose within the extended family circle, which he refers to as "crab antics". Natural restrictions include voluntary non-use, migration (both rural-to-urban and abroad), marriage and affluence.

Besson (1984) denies any type of restriction. Her writings indicate a belief that family land is inherited by all of the heirs, regardless of absenteeism, generation or distant relations with the current occupiers of the land. She further explains that all heirs retain inalienable rights to the land, resulting in a staggering number of claimants to one parcel. She feels that her argument is supported by evidence of wasteful land use under family land governance, throughout the Caribbean, resulting from the numerous claims of absentee heirs. Governance procedures within the group allow management of the use and occupation of the land. Conflicting needs and desires for use and occupation increase as the group expands, but these demands are still managed within the group.

In recent studies on Tobago family land undertaken by the authors and Felix (see Felix 2007; Griffith-Charles 2006, 2008), all the groups surveyed could indicate a person or persons who had been given responsibility for management of the land. These individuals, together with established rules and procedures, prevented or reduced conflict and dealt with day-to-day management of the use of the land. Thirty-nine per cent of those managers were the most educated of the group, while 44 per cent were the eldest of the group. Governance structures appear to emerge organically with very little conflict or question in most cases, and with an abiding respect for order. While conflict will occur in any group, the governance procedures provide for negotiation and consensus to assist in maintaining a united community. The existence of these self-imposed governance structures is of considerable benefit to state structures that find themselves overburdened and under-resourced in their land management responsibilities.

## Environmental Value

As a natural resource, land is limited, and misuse of land leads to several ramifications, as clearly outlined by Otsuka and Place: "When rising populations put pressure on land and other resources, the result – in the absence of technological and institutional innovations – is poverty and unsustainable use of natural resources" (2001, 1). The policies, legislation and land administration schemes of many regional state governments are designed to promote optimal use of land in order to prevent its being kept idle by absentee landlords. Sometimes land speculation occurs, without the owner's inputs, where it is anticipated that surrounding development trends will create an artificial increase in the value of the land. Underuse of lands can therefore occur on both individualized and communally held lands.

Clarke (1953) asserts that family land is wasteful and underused, especially in the rural environment. However, it is through such underutilization that

**Figure 18.2**
Tenure as a predic-
tor of parcel size
(Griffith-Charles
2004)

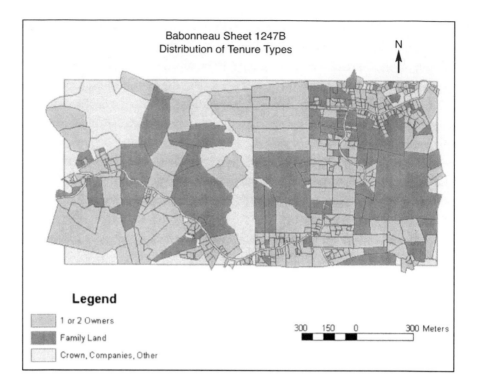

environmental sustainability can be achieved. Both Freyfogle (2002) and Oestereich (2000) hold the view that sustainable land management is best practised at larger scales: managers in charge of governance of a family's land holdings would base their decisions on the family's extended time frame – its future generations – rather than on individual needs. Additionally, boundaries within family land holdings can be temporary so that subdivision, especially for agricultural or temporary shelter purposes, need not necessarily lead to fragmentation in the way that formal subdivision would. In fact, family land tenure was found statistically to be a predictor of large parcel size in rural St Lucia, as shown in figure 18.2, which shows parcels in the peri-urban environment by tenure type (Griffith-Charles 2004).

It is clear that environmental management is of value to state land management institutions. If this is being provided by family land groups, then these activities support the activities of the state.

## Productive Value

In arguments for or against the sustainability of family land tenure, current land use trends on family land must be considered. The level of productivity of such lands has been discussed in the family land debate. Espeut (1992) supports the view that family land restricts development, particularly rural agricultural development. Family land discourages investment where occupants are unsure of their ability to restrict or exclude other family members from their holding. Family land cannot be used to access credit for supporting increased investment in the land. Family land cannot be bought and sold easily without agreement of all the members, which is in most cases impossible to achieve. Other researchers, such as Momsen (1972), Finkel (1971) and Platteau (1990), support such findings in their own case studies on communal land tenure.

However, not all writers agree that family land is intrinsically wasteful. For example, Crichlow (1994) declares that because of the nature of the historical origins of family land as compared to non-family land, non-family land tends to be more arable. The original family land occupants would have had to settle for the poorer, marginal land in their contestation for space, and these were the lands that were bequeathed to succeeding generations. These confounding factors would need to be considered in any analytical comparison of productivity between family land and non-family land. Despite the low quality of the land, Crichlow found that in St Lucia 18 per cent of freehold land is cultivated as opposed to 39 per cent of family land. Her evidence conflicts with those previously cited, suggesting that family land is not in itself a hindrance to agricultural development. In all likelihood, factors unrelated to family land may have contributed to the low level of productivity identified by other researchers (Crichlow 1994). Blustain (1981) also supports such findings in his Jamaican case study.

It can be argued, however, that despite the economically restrictive disadvantages of family land that negatively affect its productivity, family land has a number of social advantages that counterbalance these negatives. Individuals on family land feel sufficiently secure to invest their energies in development of the land, knowing that their rights are supported by the group. Significant expenditure of effort and development can therefore occur with the knowledge that their individual input is valued and respected by other members of the group.

There is, therefore, evidence to indicate that family land is unproductive. The lack of productivity, however, may not be because of the tenure system but because the land is less arable or because there is a lack of credit to invest in increasing productivity and use of technology. Crichlow (1994) correctly asserts that, in order to determine whether or not family land inhibits rural or agricultural development, a concise comparison must be done with family land agricultural production vis-à-vis production of lands held under individual titles. Dujon's (1997) work complements Crichlow's findings by contesting that family land is not in itself a hindrance to development, agricultural or otherwise.

## Conclusion

The evidence suggests that the family land communal tenure system, in the form practised in the Caribbean, originated in the post-emancipation era as a response by ex-slaves to institutionally imposed land scarcity and oppression in the plantation economy. Its origin can be variously ascribed to African forms of communal tenure and existing legal concepts. The tenure system persists in contemporary society; several researchers attempt to explain this persistence by saying that the reasons for its inception (namely, restricted access to land and lack of documentary security of tenure) still exist today. Family land provides land access for the rural poor and prevents less fortunate family members from becoming landless.

Family land is part of our heritage, since it owes its genesis to our colonial history. For this reason it should be supported as a means of retaining its cohesiveness that both unites and strengthens families and communities. Family land has economic value for all members, but primarily for individuals in the Caribbean who fall into dire financial straits. These individuals would have somewhere to return, relieving the state of having to provide for them. Family land has social value, providing a sense of belonging to members of the family group; even if they travel internationally they will retain a symbolic claim to their land rights back home. Family land also has environmental value, allowing land to remain unused where there is not an urgent need for development. The land can be subdivided for use for a fixed period and then reconfigured at a later time, without the fragmentation becoming permanent. The system even has value in demonstrating workable and resilient governance principles that could be emulated by the state. Despite its disadvantages, family land has distinct advantages that create a worthwhile place where communal tenure can exist alongside individualized tenure. While it may be difficult to quantify and compare the various values intrinsic to family land in solely monetary terms, this tenure form should be acknowledged and supported as part of our rich Caribbean heritage.

## Acknowledgements

The support of the University of the West Indies Research and Publications Fund for the authors' survey on family land in Tobago is gratefully acknowledged.

# References

Barnes, G., and C. Griffith-Charles. 2007. "Assessing the Formal Land Market and Deformalization of Property in St Lucia". *Land Use Policy* 24, no. 2: 494–501.

Besson, J. 1984. "Family Land and Caribbean Society: Toward an Ethnography of Afro-Caribbean Peasantries". In *Perspectives on Caribbean Regional Identity*, edited by E.M. Hope, 57–83. Liverpool: Centre of Latin American Studies, University of Liverpool.

———. 1987. "Family Land as a Model for Martha Brae's New History: Culture Building in an Afro-Caribbean Village". In *Afro-Caribbean Villages in Historical Perspective*, edited by Charles V. Carnegie. Kingston: African-Caribbean Institute of Jamaica.

Blustain, Harvey. 1981. "Customary Land Tenure in Rural Jamaica: Implications for Development". In *Strategies for Organization of Small Farm Agriculture in Jamaica*, edited by Harvey Blustain and Elsie LeFranc, 47–65. Kingston: Institute of Social and Economic Research, University of the West Indies.

Brereton, B. 1999. "Family Strategies, Gender and the Shift to Wage Labour in the British Caribbean". In *The Colonial Caribbean in Transition: Essays of Post-emancipation Social and Cultural History*, edited by B. Brereton and K.A. Yelvington, 77–107. Gainesville: University Press of Florida.

Carnegie, C. 1987 "Is Family Land an Institution?" In *Afro-Caribbean Villages in Historical Perspecive*, edited by Charles Carnegie, 83–99. Kingston: African-Caribbean Institute of Jamaica.

Clarke, E. 1953. "Land Tenure and the Family in Four Communities in Jamaica". *Social and Economic Studies* 1, no. 4: 81–118.

———. 1957. *My Mother Who Fathered Me: A Study of the Family in Three Selected Communities in Jamaica*. London: Allen and Unwin.

Crichlow, M.A. 1994. "An Alternative Approach to Family Land Tenure in the Anglophone Caribbean: The Case of St. Lucia". *New West Indian Guide* 68, nos. 1–2: 77–99.

Davenport, W. 1961 "The Family System of Jamaica". *Social and Economic Studies* 10, no. 4: 420–54.

Dujon, V. 1995. *National Actors against World Market Pressures: Communal Property and Agricultural Development in the Caribbean*. Madison: University of Wisconsin Press.

———. 1997. *Communal Property and Land Markets: Agricultural Development Policy in St. Lucia*. Portland: Portland State University.

Espeut, P. 1992. "Land Reform and the Family Land Debate: Reflections on Jamaica". In *Plantation Economy, Land Reform and the Peasantry in a Historical Perspective: Jamaica, 1838–1980*, edited by Claus Stolberg and Swithin Wilmot, 69–84. Kingston: Friedrich Ebert Stiftung.

Feder, G., and R. Noronha. 1987. "Land Rights Systems and Agricultural Development in Sub-Saharan Africa". *World Bank Research Observer* 2, no. 2: 143–69.

Feder, G., T. Onchan, Y. Chalamwong and C. Hongladaron. 1988. *Land Policies and Farm Productivity in Thailand*. Baltimore: Johns Hopkins University Press.

Felix, A. 2007. "Family Land Governance Procedures in Tobago". BSc project report, Surveying and Land Information Programme, University of the West Indies, St Augustine.

Finkel, H.J. 1971. "Patterns of Land Tenure in the Leeward and Windward Islands and Their Relevance to Problems in Agricultural Development in the West Indies". In *Peoples and Cultures of the Caribbean*, edited by M. Horowitz. 291–304. New York: Natural History Press.

Freyfogle, E.T. 2002. "The Tragedy of Fragmentation". *Valparaiso Law Review* 36, no. 2: 307–37.

Furubotn, E., and S. Pejovich. 1972. "Property Rights and Economic Theory: A Survey of Recent Literature". *Journal of Economic Literature* 10, no. 4: 1137–62.

Greenfield, S.M. 1960. "Land Tenure and Transmission in Rural Barbados". *Anthropological Quarterly* 33: 165–76.

Griffith-Charles, C. 2004. "The Impact of Land Titling on Land Transaction Activity and Registration System Sustainability: A Case Study of St. Lucia". PhD diss., Geomatics Program, University of Florida.

———. 2006. "The Persistence of Family Land in the Caribbean". *Proceedings of the 2006 Meeting of the Latin American Studies Association, San Juan, Puerto Rico, March 15–18, 2006*.

———. 2008. "The Implications of SDI Development to the Family Land Communal Tenure Structure in Trinidad and Tobago". *Proceedings of GSDI 10: The Tenth Annual Conference for Geospatial Data Infrastructure, 25–29 February 2008*.

Hall, D. 1982. *The Caribbean Experience: An Historical Survey, 1450–1960*. Kingston: Heinemann Education.

James, R.W. 2001. "Land Tenure: Tradition and Change". *Caribbean Law Review* 11, no. 2 (December): 163–77.

Momsen, J. 1972. "Land Tenure as a Barrier to Agricultural Innovation: The Case Study of St Lucia". *Proceedings of the Seventh West Indian Agricultural Economics Conference, Grand Anse, Grenada*.

Oestereich, J. 2000. "Land and Property Rights: Some Remarks on Basic Concepts and General Perspectives". *Habitat International* 24: 221–30.

Otsuka, K., and F. Place. 2001. *Land Tenure and Natural Resource Management: A Comparative Study of Agrarian Communities in Asia and Africa*. Washington, DC: International Food Policy Research Institute.

Platteau, J. 1990. "Land Reform and Structural Adjustment in Sub-Saharan Africa: Controversies and Guidelines". Report prepared for the United Nations Food and Agricultural Organization (FAO).

Smith, M. 1956. "The Transformation of Land Rights by Transmission in Carriacou". *Social and Economic Studies* 5, no. 2: 103–38.

Solien, N. 1959. "The Non Unilineal Descent Group in the Caribbean and Central America". *American Anthropologist* 61, no. 4: 578–83.

Stanfield, D. 1988. "Theoretical and Methodological Framework". In *Land Registration, Tenure Security, and Agricultural Development in St. Lucia: A Research Report*. Vol. 1, *Overview of Land Tenure Patterns and Effects of the Land Registration and Titling Project*, 1–20. Madison: Land Tenure Center, University of Wisconsin-Madison.

Ting, L., and I. Williamson. 1999. "Land Administration and Cadastral Trends: The Impact of the Changing Humankind-Land Relationship and Major Global Drivers". *Proceedings of International Conference on Land Tenure and Cadastral Infrastructures for Sustainable Development*. Melbourne, Australia: UN-FIG.

# 19.

# The Evolution of a Townscape

## "Archi-scapes" and "Archi-facts" in Port Antonio, Jamaica

ELIZABETH PIGOU-DENNIS

*This chapter develops in greater detail themes related to the evolution of the town-scape of Port Antonio, Jamaica, which were first presented at the WAC Inter-Congress in May 2007. The primary vehicle for analysis is the image – in the form of a reproduced print, extant postcards and contemporary photographs by the author. Each image captures a particular "moment" in the spatial inscription of "archi-scapes", which refers to the totality of landscape and built form, as well as of "archi-facts", which refers to specific architectural entities. Via the vantage points of these images, interpretations are offered with regard both to the actual features of the evolving townscape that are represented and to ways in which the images and the townscape serve as enactments and re-enactments of particular ideologies and agendas with respect to colonization, creolization and contemporary collective memory. The emphasis is on the complexity of this space, which is a reposi-tory of disjunctures, erasures and interventions with roots in both the local condi-tion and the global movements of people, commodities and ideas.*

## Introduction

The title of this chapter is somewhat ambitious. However, the intention is not to create a full urban history of Port Antonio but rather to sketch the contours of development of the "footprint" of this town on the northeast coast of Jamaica. The nature of the sources used produces an outcome at the bound-aries of architectural history, urban history and geography. The main sources are four images: one a print of a circa 1830 landscape painting of Port Antonio; two postcards by the lithographer A. Duperly and Son, dating to about the turn of the twentieth century; and a black-and-white photograph in the 1899 Tomson album. These images serve as proxies for the reality of Port Antonio's historic landscape. They assist in our ability to reconstruct the materiality of a past townscape and to interpret those objects that remain in the contemporary townscape as "architectural heritage". However, as images, they cannot be interpreted entirely on face value; as modes of representation, they reflect particular social and cultural attitudes on the part of their authors, and their audience.

## History of Port Antonio

As a space with a documented identity, Port Antonio dates to the sixteenth century, during the period of Spanish occupation. The chronicle of Oviedo, written in 1535, mentions the existence of Puerto de Anton as a good harbour (Padron 2003), and the port played a significant part in the Spanish island economy from 1523. The site was also documented on a 1609 Mercator map (Portland Parish Council 2000, 3-1). There is no image available for the Spanish period of Port Antonio's existence.

An early reference to the town is found in the John Taylor manuscript of 1687 (Buisseret 2008). The English conquest of Jamaica in 1655 created new complexities for Port Antonio, its hinterland and its mountain environs. This took the form of clashes between the plantation economy of the English and the resistance movement of Africans and Taínos who had fled Spanish and English slavery. The Maroons settled in the Blue Mountains. Known as the Windward Maroons, their settlements were well established by the 1680s, and were so successful in their contestation of the resources and spaces of the plantation economy that by 1730 the English governor established military barracks at Port Antonio (Portland Parish Council 2000, 3-2). The parish of Portland was formed in 1723, comprising parts of the earlier parishes of St George and St Thomas-in-the-East (Portland Parish Council 2000, 3-5; Senior 2003, 391–92).

During the eighteenth century, Port Antonio's fortunes were tied to the development of the plantation economy, at the peak of which there were twenty-nine sugar estates (Portland Parish Council 2000, 3-3). The nineteenth century was dominated by the emancipation of the slaves, the subsequent decline of the sugar industry – only four sugar estates remained in operation by the 1850s (Portland Parish Council 2000, 3-3) – the rise of the peasant economy and emergence of the banana plantation and export economy. The significance of the port activities of the town fluctuated, from the early plantation area through the decline after emancipation and a revival under the auspices of the banana trade after the 1870s. The monopolistic hold of the United Fruit Company, while it proved detrimental to the interests of smallholders, nevertheless provided a basis for economic expansion through to the 1930s, and it had the spinoff benefit of engendering a tourist industry in Port Antonio. Hurricanes and disease wreaked havoc on the banana industry, however, and after the 1930s the trade declined severely.

However, during the 1940s and 1950s the town thrived on the Hollywood tropical mystique created by frequent visits and property acquisitions by movie idols of the time (Portland Parish Council 2000, 3-5–6; Senior 2003, 391–92). The heyday of film star visits and banana prosperity has now passed, but the town has sought in recent years to revive its reputation as a tourist venue, mainly through a new marina, which was completed in 2000; the development of nature trails and Maroon history trails; and the operations of hotels in the vicinity of the town such as DeMontevin Lodge, Jamaica Palace and Goblin Hill Hotel and Villas. The town remains outside the large-scale tourist developments of the North Coast, mainly because of its location – reached via steep and winding mountain roads, often gutted with potholes – as well as its not being a major cruise ship destination. Perhaps because of this, Port Antonio has retained an Old World charm, visible in its walkable scale and the presence of several historic structures. Added to this is its postcard-quality tropical environment, situated between the Caribbean Sea and the Blue Mountains and surrounded by lush vegetation.

## Evolution of a Townscape

What does the above brief historical survey have to do with the evolution of a townscape? This is a question which will be answered via the images mentioned above. The earliest image known to the author is one by J.B. Kidd, from circa 1830, reproduced on the cover of the development plan for Portland in 2000 (figure 19.1). Painting from a vantage point on the nearby hillside, the artist draws the eye of the viewer towards the horizon of the sea and sky. The peculiar formation of the Titchfield promontory, between the east and west harbours (where Fort George was located) is evident, with the main part of the town being nestled close to its east coast and quite lushly vegetated.

The painting is in the tradition of Romantic landscape paintings, depicting real "scapes" yet with a sensibility which idealized relationships and meanings. For instance, in Kidd's depiction there is an air of peace, calm and contentment in the muted natural hues and soft light, and most especially in the idyllic lingering of two black figures in the right foreground. The African-Jamaican rural persona is captured in the basket, the headdress, the cotta and provisions on the head of the female figure. Who were these figures, if the painting is

**Figure 19.1** Port Antonio, J.B. Kidd, circa 1830 (lithograph from original painting, "J.B. Kidd", plate 10, courtesy National Library of Jamaica)

indeed from 1830? Free blacks? Whoever they were intended to be, they are located at the nexus of urban–rural realities, fitted with agricultural props that seem destined for the marketplace of the town. Their presence in the scape embodied by the painting locates the scene as creole and tropical, as do the goats grazing on the hillside, the palm trees and the distinctive timber rendering of creole Georgian architecture.

## Architecture

Architecturally, the structures which are represented all feature the close-cropped, steeply pitched hip roof which evolved in Jamaica and elsewhere in the British Caribbean. This roof type was deemed most resilient in the context of heavy rainfall and hurricane-force winds. Indeed, the steep pitch bears a resemblance to the constructions of not only traditional English architecture but also of both the Taínos and certain West African groups (Watts 1990; Schreckenbach 1983; Kliment 2007). The prevalence of two-storey structures in the painting suggests a combination of mercantile and domestic usages, a common element of many pre-modern urban typologies. At street level the typical façade opened to form colonnaded arcades, creating a threshold between the public space of the street and the enclosure afforded by the building. This made the life of the pedestrian more endurable in an environment where shade was of premium value, and it also enhanced the quality of life in the building's interior by admitting breezes (Segre 2001).

The buildings are closely clustered together, with hints of vertical and horizontal street axes forming a grid, which was spared from a severe appearance by the interspersed trees and open spaces. The main structures on Titchfield Hill are the military barracks on the edge of the promontory, facing the open sea. The salient qualities of this early-nineteenth-century view of the Port Antonio townscape are its tiny scale – only about fifty main structures are discernible – its immersion in a wider dual seascape and countryscape, and its virtually uniform creole timber architecture. This architecture borrowed not only from Taíno and West African traditions in its roof design but also from the English Georgian sense of symmetry and proportion of elevations and building massing.

## Postcards and Photograph

These two postcard images are quite different from the landscape painting discussed above. The history of the postcard specifically in the Caribbean has been ably dealt with by John Gilmore (Gilmore 1995). The earliest British government-issued postcards date to 1870, while the first privately printed cards were authorized after 1894 (Gilmore 1995, vi). The divided-back postcard with one side entirely devoted to a picture came into use after 1902, and both these postcards may be dated approximately by their divided-back feature. They were published by the local firm A. Duperly and Son, based in Kingston.

The postcard was a modern aspect of mass production and consumption. Some aspects of the landscape painting tradition are carried over into postcard views, which direct the eye to a sweeping perception of an entire townscape against a background of mountains or sea. There is an emphasis on the idyllic – the placid or static – in that the cards appear to have been retouched to eliminate people and any signs of busy activity. There is also an emphasis on civic monuments, especially in a postcard titled "Greetings from Jamaica, Town of Port Antonio", where the courthouse, built in 1895, and Christ Church, built in 1840, are clearly visible. Very clear in this postcard are the characteristics of the tropical creole Georgian town. The predominant materials appear to be timber and shingles, and the predominant features hipped and gabled roofs, with colonnaded covered arcades at street level. The electrification of the town is evident in the utility poles. The curvilinear configuration of the main road, following the shoreline of East Harbour, is evident. The vantage point of this view is from the direction of Titchfield Hill, looking

**Figure 19.2** Port Antonio, 1899 (postcard, Tomson Album, courtesy National Library of Jamaica)

towards the mountains. Port Antonio is seen nestled at the foot of the hills and residences are apparent on the slopes directly above the town.

The photograph depicting Port Antonio from the 1899 Tomson album (figure 19.2) is very similar in vantage point to the coloured postcard image. The courthouse is not included in the composition of the photograph; however, it shows architectural details at closer range and with greater clarity. Thus, in the foreground, the significant element of louvered cooler boxes over the windows, which created shade and cooled interiors, is plainly visible. Vertically sliding sash windows as well as windows which pivot outward are also evident, and the construction materials are plain to see, with timber and brick being predominant.

## Titchfield Hotel

The visual agenda of the second postcard is apparent from the caption, which reads "Port Antonio showing Titchfield Hotel". The Titchfield Hotel, built in 1897, is the subject of several postcards and was sometimes photographed in a more dominant position (see figure 19.3). However, this particular view

serves to draw attention to the fact that the hotel overlooks the west harbour, capturing both the tropical allure of the Caribbean Sea and its proximity to the small-town urban context of Port Antonio. The courthouse is clearly evident in the middle ground, and overall the town appears to be more dense than the 1830 landscape painting depicted. Expansion is very evident on Titchfield Hill, where a number of residences have been constructed. Titchfield School, originally founded in 1785, appears to be located on the promontory.

**Figure 19.3** Titchfield Hotel, Port Antonio (postcard, collection of Elizabeth Pigou-Dennis)

## Discussion

The discussion above has focused on what I have termed *archi-scapes*. It has endeavoured to describe the main features of the town as depicted in key images of the nineteenth and early twentieth centuries. The town is a composite of its resources, topography and built environment and the people who inhabited its spaces. The scope of this chapter does not cover a description of the personalities who inhabited the town and their daily activities. It does, however, attempt to "read" certain kinds of intentions from the evidence of these images and the secondary sources which also inform this present project. A number of issues arise to reflect on. It is interesting to note that while Kidd, during the period of slavery (1830), includes a few idyllic-looking rural blacks, the twentieth-century postcards avoid the issue of people altogether. Gilmore (1995) considers that, for the most part, the historic postcards of the Caribbean "present a complacent, upper-class view of things" (1995, ix). Although used internally, they were intended primarily for an external audience: white, metropolitan and American or British. Perhaps post-emancipation issues of race, colour and class were too complex for the postcard printing press. Perhaps the location itself, as a scape of structures which had somehow fallen into place within a luxurious landscape for tourist consumption, held visual and emotional appeal.

As an archi-scape, Port Antonio, as featured in these postcard images, is depicted as an assemblage of urban elements which is both continuous and disjunct. There is an obvious linearity that must exist to facilitate streets as "voids" for mobility and permeability, in contrast to the masses of the built forms. Yet there is a softer, curvilinear aspect to the town as it is moulded against the coastline and its ruptures and enfolded within the surrounding hillsides. No postcard image could encompass all the key vantage points of the town. To appear "centred", the image would have to include the courthouse, which was the major monumental structure of the coastal segment of the town. Either the image must face towards the east, to capture that other icon of urbanity, Christ Church – which, sited on a small hill, was actually the dominant structure in the urban hierarchy – or it must be constructed facing west, to capture Titchfield Hill and the hotel. The point is that the images are fabrications, creating two-dimensional "mini-worlds" on paper. Yet it is clear that the townscape definitely evolved between 1830 and the early 1900s. The key generator was economic reorganization after emancipation, particularly through the banana and tourist industries, which gave rise to local capacity to erect modest monuments in the form of Christ Church, the courthouse, the Titchfield Hotel and DeMontevin Lodge, as well as a cohesive body of commercial and residential buildings.

The visual evidence of the painting, postcard and photographic record is corroborated by descriptive text of the late nineteenth century which states that the town was "built among irregular eminences which never allow one to perceive it as a whole" (Moore and Johnson 2000, 142). The key assemblages of buildings are also mentioned, such as the fort, the courthouse, other public buildings and the town's main landmark, the parish church.

## Christ Church

The title of this chapter coins the term *archi-facts,* with reference to specific examples of urban architecture. Each archi-fact may be interpreted within its own spatial bandwidth, so to speak, somewhat segregated from the entire townscape; thus the story of a specific building may be told. The spatial "bandwidth" may become very complex, encompassing close relationships with external building precedents or an external architect and interweaving with an architectural history which goes beyond the confines of the local. Christ Church (figure 19.4) will be briefly discussed in this regard.

Arguably the most significant landmark in contemporary Port Antonio in terms of its siting, Christ Church was constructed in 1840, having been designed by the English architect Annesley Voysey. It was extensively repaired

**Figure 19.4** Christ Church, Port Antonio (photograph, courtesy Donnette Zacca)

after a 1903 hurricane (Senior 2003, 110). In terms of architectural style, it is Romanesque revival (Senior 2003, 110), which was popular in mid-nineteenth-century America and England and other European countries. The style imitates aspects of eleventh- and twelfth-century Romanesque – or in England, Norman – architecture. These elements include heavy masonry construction, use of the round arch and barrel vault, buttresses, aisle arcades, and central square, round or polygonal towers. Ornamentation consists of surface articulation of brick and stone courses, as well as designs derived from nature and rendered in stone or in stained glass (LaChuisa 2002).

This single archi-fact is capable of summoning up a complex tapestry of cultural transfers and meanings which transforms Port Antonio from a small coastal town in a western hemisphere tropical colony to a participant in a global flow of persons, ideas and materialization of built forms. Romanesque revival architecture has a rather intriguing history, beginning in Germany with a text by architect and theorist Heinrich Hübsch published in 1828, titled *In What Style Should We Build?* (Lewis 2004). This was a burning question in European architectural theory during the nineteenth and early twentieth centuries as architects grappled with the legacies of traditions in architectural materials and expressions set against the imperatives of modernization and industrialization. Rival ideological positions became attached to the canon of Classical architectural orders and to the "revolt" posed by Gothic Revivalism and the Romanticism of the Arts and Crafts movement (Hearn 2003). Resolution to these questions came in the form of the Modern movement of the early twentieth century, which served to generate another round of critique and innovation later in the century. However, within this melee of searching and questioning, Romanesque revival architecture, with its subdued version of classical detailing, its structural integrity and its low-key ornamentation, is deemed by Curran to have played a significant role in the movement towards more abstract forms of architectural representation and the interest in functionalism and structuralism that served as a prelude to Modernism (Lewis 2004).

At the time of writing this chapter, the full details surrounding the church's architect, Annesley Voysey, had not been ascertained. He is listed in the *Biographical Dictionary of British Architects, 1600–1840* (Colvin 2008, 1077) and mention is made of his design of Christ Church, a fact also cited on a tablet erected in his honour in the church. While there are to date no available documents which give clues to the ideas of Christ Church's architect or make comparisons with any of his other works, it is clear that the church meets the criteria for designation as Romanesque revival, with its very distinctive central tower, recessed rounded arches, heavy masonry walls, buttresses and stained glass at the altar end. For the roofing and roof supports, timber trussing was used instead of stone vaulting and ribbing, but this was within the range of medieval-inspired roof technologies. Porter (2006) supplies the information that the materials used were bricks and local limestone.

## Globalization

Even this brief discussion of the implications of Christ Church within a broad context of architectural history serves to highlight the nature of the globalization that was possible long before the era of air travel, cable television and high-speed Internet. The colonial enterprise facilitated the movement of technologies and building typologies: in Jamaica during the nineteenth century, innovative structures such as the 1801–2 iron bridge over the Rio Cobre at Spanish Town (Francis Brown and Francis 2005), the Naval Hospital of 1817 at Port Royal (Cox and Cox 1999) and the temporary pavilion for the 1891 Great Exhibition in Kingston (Tortello 2007, 151–52) became part of its varied landscapes/townscapes.

Indeed, although it is in contemporary discourse quite a buzzword, globalization as a process has a long history; in terms of the linkages between the "Old World" and the "New World", it may be traced to the advent of Columbus in Taíno territory. His accidental encounter with a supposed Orient unleashed a transatlantic frenzy of depopulation, emigration, enforced migration, servitude and movement of crops, labour and capital in the most complex system of economic organization that the world had ever known. The ethics of the system, on the points of indigenous peoples' rights and treating humans as chattel, were certainly questionable, yet it laid the platform for the next phase of globalization: the Industrial Revolution, which would spur the nineteenth-century colonial expansion of European nations into Africa and Asia. The multiple influences of colonization, creolization and industrialization, within the context of a general North–South organization of exploiting and exploited countries respectively, carried within its cultural blueprint flows of building technologies, architectural ideas and materials. Port Antonio was by no means immune to these influences.

## Conclusion

The scope of this chapter does not permit detailed discussion of other significant structures in Port Antonio, such as the courthouse, DeMontevin Lodge, the old railway station or the Titchfield Hotel. Each tells a story of the paradoxical borderlessness of architectural expression in combination with the distinctive ways in which specific structures fit into a local context. The courthouse combines Georgian proportions in brick with cast-iron galleries; DeMontevin Lodge displays a Victorian sensibility, also with cast-iron details; the railway station utilizes cast-iron elements; and the Titchfield Hotel combines a subdued abstraction in masonry with a wraparound verandah element suited to the tropics.

Interestingly, cast iron is a recurrent element in a number of these structures. This is in itself a fantastic story with modern roots in the English Industrial Revolution. Although there was some limited pre-modern use of cast iron, it was industrial processes using the steam engine which made possible the mass production and export of cast-iron building components. Exemplified by the grand accomplishments of the Crystal Palace, the Eiffel Tower and the cast-iron structures of New York, New Orleans, Port-au-Prince, Fort de France, Port of Spain, Melbourne and other cities, cast iron was the material of innovative architecture prior to the widespread use of steel and the early-twentieth-century Modernist aesthetic of abstraction, which eliminated extraneous details and ornaments. While the nineteenth-century architects on the whole did not eschew ornamentation, they ushered in modernity with its capacity for mass production and distribution. Cast-iron balconies, brackets, fretwork, columns and frames were mass-produced, catalogued and exported around the world. Thus Port Antonio, participating in a global North–South economy that favoured bananas and luxury vacations, was able to incorporate within its nineteenth-century archi-scape local icons of global modernity.

## References

Buisseret, David, ed. 2008. *Jamaica in 1687: The Taylor Manuscript at the National Library of Jamaica.* Kingston: University of the West Indies Press.

Colvin, Howard. 2008. *A Biographical Dictionary of British Architects, 1600–1840*, 4th ed. New Haven: Yale University Press.

Cox, Oliver, and Jean Cox. 1999. *Naval Hospitals of Port Royal, Jamaica.* Caribbean Architectural Monographs Series no. 1. Kingston: University of Technology, Jamaica.

Curran, Kathleen. 2003. *The Romanesque Revival: Religion, Politics and Transnational Exchange.* Philadelphia: Pennsylvania University Press.

Francis Brown, Suzanne, and Peter Francis. 2005. *The Old Iron Bridge: Spanish Town, Jamaica.* Caribbean Architectural Monograph Series no. 2. Kingston: University of Technology, Jamaica.

Gilmore, John. 1995. *Glimpses of Our Past: A Social History of the Caribbean in Postcards.* Kingston: Ian Randle.

Grosz, Elizabeth. 2001. *Architecture from the Outside.* Cambridge, MA: MIT Press.

Hearn, Fil. 2003. *Ideas That Shaped Buildings.* Cambridge, MA: MIT Press.

Kliment, Stephen A. 2007. "Discovering African Identity in African-American Architecture: Part 1". *AIA Architect*. http://www.aia.org/aiaarchitect/thisweek2007/0803/0803arc_face_full.cfm (accessed 20 August 2011).

LaChuisa, Chuck. 2002. "Buffalo Architecture and History: Romanesque Revival". http://www.buffaloah.com/a/arch/rom/index.html (accessed 20 August 2011).

Lewis, Michael J. 2004. Review of *The Romanesque Revival: Religion, Politics and Transnational Exchange,* by Kathleen Curran. Institute for Sacred Architecture. http://www.sacredarchitecture.org/pubs/saj/books/romanesque_revival.php.

Moore, Brian, and Michele A. Johnson. 2000. *The Land We Live In: Jamaica in 1890.* Kingston: Department of History, University of the West Indies.

Morales Padron, Francisco. 2003. *Spanish Jamaica*, translated by Patrick Bryan. Kingston: Ian Randle.

Pigou-Dennis, Elizabeth. 2002. "Hyperspace/Hypertext: The Crossings, Loops and Links of Port Antonio, Jamaica". *Southern Crossings: Proceedings of the Sixth Australasian Urban History/Planning History Conference*, 513–24. Auckland, NZ: University of Auckland.

———. 2006. "Spatial Responses of the African Diaspora in Jamaica: Focus on Rastafarian Architecture". In *Diasporic Africa*, edited by Michael A. Gomez, 147–70. New York: New York University Press.

Porter, Anthony R.D. 2006. *Bricks and Stones from the Past.* Kingston: University of the West Indies Press.

Portland Parish Council et al. 2000. *The Parish of Portland: A Sustainable Development Plan.* N.p.

Schreckenbach, Hannah. 1983. "Traditional Building Methods in Northern [Southern] Ghana". In *Construction Technologies for a Developing Country*, 21–72. Eschborn, Germany: GTZ Publications. http://www.arcghana.org/traditionalarch.htm.

Segre, Roberto. 2001. "Architecture and City in the Caribbean". In *Tropical Architecture*, edited by Alexander Tzonis, Liane Lefaivre and Bruno Stagno, 113–53. London: Wiley-Academy.

Senior, Olive. 2003. *Encyclopedia of Jamaican Heritage.* Kingston: Twin Guinep.

Tortello, Rebecca. 2007. *Pieces of the Past.* Kingston: Ian Randle.

Watts, David. 1990. *The West Indies: Patterns of Development, Culture and Environmental Change since 1492.* Cambridge: Cambridge University Press.

# 20.

# Geology and the Preservation of Historic Buildings

## Cracking in the Walls of the Citadel, Brimstone Hill Fortress, St Kitts

BRENT WILSON

*Buildings of international cultural importance, even though placed on the UNESCO World Heritage List and cared for by local personnel, are not immune to decay. The walls of the citadel at Brimstone Hill Fortress, St Kitts, West Indies, have been known to be cracking for at least thirty years. The fortress is situated on a volcanic dome in a tectonically active area, and it has in the past been assumed that the cracks were seismic in origin. However, other possible explanations for development of the two main orthogonal cracks include leaching of rubble infill, from which the fortress is constructed; soil creep, weakening the foundations; and dissolution of limestone beneath the volcanic dome. It is recommended that the geological settings of all buildings on the World Heritage List be surveyed to help ensure that our global heritage endures well into the future.*

## Introduction

Sites of cultural importance are placed on the UNESCO World Heritage List, which includes both natural features such as the Victoria Falls, Zimbabwe, and buildings as diverse as Salzburg city centre, Austria, and the mosque at Bagerhat, Bangladesh (the list is available at http://whc.unesco.org/pg .cfm?cid=31). Natural deterioration of the listed buildings is occurring from a variety of causes. For example, the Leaning Tower at Piazza del Duomo, Pisa, Italy, is sinking into marshy soil, while many mud-brick buildings in the two-thousand-year-old city of Bam, Iran, were destroyed during an earthquake on 27 December 2004.

Such buildings are a major part of mankind's heritage. Once irreparably damaged, they will be lost to future generations. The upkeep of listed sites, however, is frequently left to local organizations, some of which have only scant resources. This chapter describes one example of a World Heritage site in the Caribbean region, the fortress at Brimstone Hill, St Kitts (17° 17′ north, 62° 45′ west; figures 20.1 and 20.2), which is currently deteriorating and for which only meagre funds are available to cover the cost of repairs. That this is one of only two sites in the Lesser Antilles included on the UNESCO list (the other comprises the volcanic Pitons, St Lucia) underscores its importance to our regional heritage. The ongoing development of cracks 1 to 3 centimetres wide in the citadel walls is causing unease to the curators, the Brimstone Hill National Park Society (BHNPS). This chapter presents hypotheses concerning the origin of the cracks, in the hope that, armed with such knowledge, the BHNPS will be able to focus its skimpy assets in an effective manner.

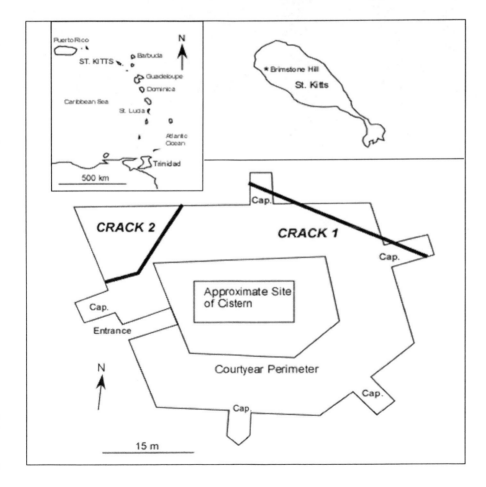

**Figure 20.1**
**A.** Location of St Kitt's, Caribbean Sea. **B.** Location of Brimstone Hill Fortress. **C.** Outline plan of citadel, Brimstone Hill Fortress, showing location of caponiers ("Cap."), approximate location of cistern and locations of Cracks 1 and 2.

**Figure 20.2** The citadel at Brimstone Hill Fortress, looking west from Monkey Hill, showing the only pointed caponier. The arches in the foreground indicate the infantry officers' quarters, and the wooden buildings comprise the visitors' centre. The slopes below the citadel were graded during construction to ensure an unobstructed line of fire.

## Geological Background

Brimstone Hill Fortress is perched atop a volcanic dome in a tectonically active area, the hill consisting of a mass of hypersthene andesite that covers 0.35 square kilometres, is 240 metres high and lies only about 100 metres from the south-western shore of St Kitts (Martin-Kaye 1959). When it erupted, the dome dragged up slabs of Plio-Pleistocene coral-filled limestone approximately 3 metres thick; they now dip outwards about 45 degrees on the south and west sides of the hill and are locally stained with hematite from fumarole activity. These fumaroles may still be active: the name Brimstone Hill refers to the smell of hydrogen sulphide associated with hot spring activity. Baker (1969) cites a radiocarbon age of 44,000 + 1,200 years BP for the limestone.

The corals forming the bulk of the limestone are broken and chaotically arranged, suggesting that they did not comprise a coral reef but rather were storm rubble, perhaps deposited in a back-reef environment (see Blanchon, Jones and Kalbfleisch 1997; Meyer et al. 2003). Foraminiferal microfossils in the limestone comprise predominantly *Amphistegina gibbosa* d'Orbigny, 1839, which typically lives on coral reefs (Rose and Lidz 1977) and is easily transported to form almost monospecific lag deposits in high-energy areas (Bandy 1964; Li et al. 1997; Wilson 1999).

The fortress walls are constructed from andesite quarried from Brimstone Hill; the window frames and cornices are decorated with two types of types of limestone: grey, massive and hard, with millimetre-scale veins of calcite, and fossiliferous, which is pinkish and less resistant. Local lore has it that the limestone was imported from the neighbouring island of Antigua. However, this seems unlikely, given the proximity of limestone outcrops around Brimstone Hill. The mortar in the walls, prepared in a large limekiln at the base of Brimstone Hill, contains many coral fragments that may have come from the rock or been brought from the nearby shore.

## Historical Background

Brimstone Hill Fortress is the largest of many military fortifications built during the turbulent colonial history of the Lesser Antilles island arc between 1650 and 1850. During this period British and French forces repeatedly invaded some islands (Hubbard 1996). The fortress, built for defence by the British using slave labour, is so large it has been called "the Gibraltar of the West Indies" (Hubbard 2003). It was constructed over a hundred-year period beginning in 1690, expanded in the late eighteenth century, effectively abandoned in the mid-nineteenth century and renovated as a tourist attraction in the 1930s and 1940s (Armony 2004). Its cultural value is such that it was added to the UNESCO World Heritage List in 1999.

The Brimstone Hill Fortress National Park Society, which administers the site, has become concerned about cracks that are developing in the walls of caponiers – protected passageways with gun ports that radiate outwards from the main fortification – on the north and east sides of the citadel. Some cracks were recently patched with cement that has also fractured, indicating that the cracks are widening. The society has only limited funds for monitoring the cracks, and none for their repair.

## "Seismic Cracks"?

There are two main cracks in the Citadel. Crack 1 trends 100 degrees and affects both the northeast part of the body of the citadel and a caponier on the north side (figure 20.3). Crack 2, which is generally orthogonal to Crack 1, trends approximately 10 degrees and affects the body of the citadel only (figure 20.4). In addition, there are many minor cracks.

The Brimstone Hill Fortress National Park Society has in the past presumed that all cracks in the citadel are seismic in origin, although evidence of this is slight. Furthermore, they draw a distinction between what they term "seismic cracks" and "step cracks", although the distinction is not clear. It would appear that in "seismic cracks" the fracture traverses the andesite blocks, presumably exploiting areas where the rock is weaker than the mortar; in "step cracks" the fracturing affects the less resistant mortar between the blocks of andesite or limestone, giving a fracture that in profile resembles a flight of stairs. However, several fractures have been noted that have a "seismic crack" profile in one area and a "step crack" profile in another. It is therefore

**Figure 20.3** Crack 1, affecting the roof of the main citadel and, in the background, the caponier on the north side.

**Figure 20.4** Crack 2, on the west side of the citadel.

suggested here that, until there is incontrovertible evidence that earth tremors created any of the cracks, use of the term *seismic crack* is unwarranted.

The only evidence that any of the cracks is of seismic origin is anecdotal – some staff suggest that they formed in 1974 during an earthquake of unknown magnitude that was centred northwest of Antigua, about 60 kilometres east of St Kitts. However, this must be viewed with caution. The author is not aware of any structural surveys prior to 1974 that might have noted incipient cracking. And Richard Robertson, of the Seismic Research Unit, University of the West Indies, St Augustine, Trinidad, has stated: "There are no other reports of damage on St Kitts from the 1974 tremor" (personal communication). Other tremors have affected St Kitts, however. In 1843 an earthquake of unknown magnitude centred between Antigua and Guadeloupe caused considerable destruction in all the islands from Saba to Dominica, as well as nearly two thousand deaths, mainly in Guadeloupe. A major tremor in 1955 destroyed Gingerland High School on Nevis, the neighbouring island about 5 kilometres southeast of St Kitts, and would undoubtedly have affected Brimstone Hill. Baker (1969) notes that small earth tremors in 1959 triggered a major landslip in the summit crater on Mount Misery, St Kitts.

It is possible that the cracks developed from the cumulative effects of a series of tremors over the past few centuries. However, the Seismic Research Unit of the University of the West Indies in Trinidad has a monitoring station on Brimstone Hill, and it has not recorded any recent microseismic activity that might explain the continued widening of the cracks (Richard Robertson, personal communication). It is therefore suggested that the cracking may be due to other causes entirely, of which three possibilities are outlined below.

In view of the BHNPS's limited funds, low-cost methods were sought to allow them to monitor crack propagation. The easiest and most durable proved to be nails, placed at the apices of a right-angled triangle, hammered at known distances into the walls around some of the cracks (figure 20.5). The BHNPS is currently using Vernier callipers to measure any change in distance between the centres of the nail heads.

**Figure 20.5** Three nails (arrows) placed at the apices of a right-angled triangle for monitoring crack propagation in the caponier on the north side of the citadel.

## Leaching of Infill

Folk wisdom has it that, because Brimstone Hill Fortress stands on the summit of a volcanic dome, its foundations must be on solid bedrock. However, this assumption is false. The floors of two caponiers recently excavated for renovation were each found to comprise an upstanding knob of andesite about a metre in diameter surrounded by an infill of rubble. It therefore seems probable that the irregular distribution of the five caponiers (figure 20.1) was dictated not by the whim of the designer but by the pre-existing distribution of upstanding knolls of andesite. Some indication of the original form of the knolls is seen on nearby Monkey Hill, which was the site of the governor's house within the fortress (Kate Orchard, Brimstone Hill Fortress National Park Society, personal communication): a knoll approximately 4 metres high can be seen west of the artificially flattened top of the hill. It has not proven possible, however, to discern the bedrock–infill boundary using ground-penetrating radar (David Rollinson, personal communication, 2004). This may be because of limited density contrasts between the bedrock and the infill.

The steep grassed slopes flanking the east wall of the citadel are underlain by a soil that contains angular blocks of limestone and andesite, and are presumed to be manmade. That these slopes and the caponier floors are largely floored by infill prompts the question, What would be the consequences if the remainder of the fortress was similarly underlain by infill? The centre of the citadel is built over a cistern – an underground reservoir that stores rainwater draining from the citadel roofs and courtyard. The precise dimensions of the cistern are not known, and it is not clear whether it was excavated into the volcanic dome (an arduous process, though this could have been the source of some rock used to build the fort) or whether it comprises walls built on a bedrock floor and surrounded by rubble infill. The latter construction would explain why water is leaching from the walls at some places around the citadel. In turn, this leaching may have dissolved limestone in the infill, weakening its structure, and redistributed fine grains in it, causing stresses responsible for the cracks.

## Soil Creep

The foundations of some caponiers, at least, and possibly much of the remainder of the citadel, are apparently not firmly anchored on bedrock, but built on soil and regolith, so it is likely that soil creep may be inducing stresses by removing support for the foundation. Soil creep, an ongoing process whereby soil particles migrate downslope under the influence of gravity, usually occurs at a rate of a few millimetres per year, though this increases where vegetation is thin and rainfall is high. No slopes are immune to soil creep, and such gentle deformation would not be detected by the seismometer situated on the hill. However, there is other evidence of soil creep: trees which normally grow upright develop a characteristic curvature on creeping slopes, and there are many J-shaped trees on the northern slopes below the citadel.

## Limestone Dissolution

St Kitts is one of three volcanic islands occupying the St Eustatius Bank (Martin-Kaye 1969), the others being Nevis and St Eustatius. Limestone is apparently widespread on this bank: much of St Eustatius is flanked by a raised carapace of limestone, and Hutton (1968) and Hutton and Nockolds (1978) recorded blocks of limestone in the conglomerate on Saddle Hill, Nevis. The limestone flanking Brimstone Hill may underlie much of the west of St Kitts. Robinson (1996) invoked dissolution of limestone to explain the formation of collapse holes near Dieppe Bay Town, about 2 kilometres northeast of Brimstone Hill. Thus it is possible that limestone underlies northern and eastern Brimstone Hill, that dissolution of the rock is causing the volcanic dome to settle, and that stresses induced by this are responsible for the cracks. However, this explanation seems less likely than soil creep, as movement of the dome – should it be frequent – would be detected by the seismometer located on the hill.

## Conclusion

Brimstone Hill Fortress, St Kitts, is one of only two sites in the Lesser Antilles included in the UNESCO World Heritage List. The fabric of the citadel is cracking, but the cause of the cracks is not clear. Earth tremors may be implicated, but examination of the fortress's structure suggests several other causes. Monitoring of crack propagation has been started to help structural engineers suggest measures to mitigate the problem. It is recommended that the geological settings of all buildings included on the World Heritage List be surveyed as part of efforts to ensure that our global heritage endures well into the future.

## Acknowledgements

Thanks are due to Larry Armony (Brimstone Hill National Park Society, St Kitts), David Rollinson (historic buildings specialist, Nevis) and Professor Richard Dawe

(University of the West Indies, Trinidad) for discussions. Partial funding of this paper was provided by the Research and Publications Fund of the University of the West Indies.

## References

Armony, L. 2004. "The Mighty Brimstone Hill". *LIAT Islander* 66: 38–39.

Baker, P.E. 1969. "The Geological History of Mt. Misery Volcano, St. Kitts, West Indies". *Institute of Geological Sciences, Overseas Geology and Mineral Resources* 10: 207–30.

Bandy, O.L. 1964. "Foraminiferal Biofacies in Sediments of the Gulf of Batabano, Cuba, and Their Geological Significance". *American Association of Petroleum Geologists Bulletin* 48: 1666–79.

Blanchon, P., B. Jones and W. Kalbfleisch. 1997. "Anatomy of a Fringing Reef around Grand Cayman: Storm Rubble, Not Coral Framework". *Journal of Sedimentary Research* 67: 1–16.

Hubbard, V. 1996. *Swords, Ships and Sugar: A History of Nevis to 1900*, 4th ed. Corvallis, OR: Premiere Editions International.

———. 2003. *History of St Kitts: The Sweet Trade*. Northampton, MA: Interlink.

Hutton, C.O. 1968. "The Mineralogy and Petrology of Nevis, Leeward Islands, British West Indies". In *Transactions of the Fourth Caribbean Geological Conference, Trinidad, 1965*, 383–88.

Hutton, C.O., and S.R. Nockolds. 1978. *The Petrology of Nevis, Leeward Islands, West Indies*. Institute of Geological Sciences, Overseas Geology and Mineral Resources, series 52. London: HM Stationery Office.

Li, C., B. Jones and P. Blanchon. 1997. "Lagoon-Shelf Sediment Exchange by Storms: Evidence from Foraminiferal Assemblages, East Coast of Grand Cayman, British West Indies". *Journal of Sedimentary Research* 67: 17–25.

Martin-Kaye, P.H.A. 1959. *Reports on the Geology of the Leeward and British Virgin Islands*. St Lucia: Voice Publishing.

———. 1969. "A Summary of the Geology of the Lesser Antilles". *Institute of Geological Sciences, Overseas Geology and Mineral Resources* 10: 172–206.

Meyer, D., J. Bries, B. Greenstein and A. Debrot. 2003. "Preservation of *In Situ* Reef Framework in Regions of Low Hurricane Frequency: Pleistocene of Curaçao and Bonaire, Southern Caribbean". *Lethaia* 36: 273–86.

Robinson, E. 1996. "Report on a Visit Made to Examine Collapse Features in Northern St Kitts". Report prepared for NEMA, St Kitts. Department of Geography and Geology, University of the West Indies, Kingston.

Rose, P.R., and B. Lidz. 1977. *Diagnostic Foraminiferal Assemblages of Shallow-Water Modern Environments: South Florida and the Bahamas. Sedimenta*, series 4.

Wilson, B. 1999. "The Origin of Sediments in and around the Redoubt". In " '. . . the old stone fortt at Newcastle . . .': The Redoubt, Nevis, Eastern Caribbean", edited by Elaine Morris. *Post-Medieval Archaeology* 33: 194–221.

# 21.

# Exploring Caribbean Industrial Heritage

ALLISON C.B. DOLLAND AND CLEMENT K. SANKAT

*The industrial heritage of Barbados, Jamaica, Guyana, and Trinidad and Tobago consists of material and intangible elements of industrial culture created by our past and present economic activities. The manifestations of this heritage can shed light on not only the socio-economic history of the region but also developments in civil, mechanical, chemical, electrical, mining and naval engineering. The related artefacts are imbued with spiritual, emotional and symbolic values which are critical to cultural identity and national pride. In the territories under review, preservation of this type of heritage has been for the most part incidental to overall efforts to preserve regional heritage and has not constituted a priority in and of itself. To ensure that the fragments of our industrial past and the realities of our industrial present are analysed, documented and where possible preserved, industrial heritage must be given special attention. Combined efforts of the stakeholders must be directed at formulating a clear agenda and a framework for maximizing available intellectual, financial and human resources. As societal awareness of the importance of industrial heritage grows, so too will the success of preservation initiatives.*

## Introduction

Heritage is our legacy from the past, what we live with today and what we pass on to future generations. Our industrial heritage is the ensemble of industrial exploitation elements generated by our past and present economic activities. Tangible manifestations of this heritage are scattered throughout the region – in buildings and machinery, workshops, mills and factories, wells and mines, sites for processing, refining and manufacturing, and warehouses. They are also found in places where energy is generated, transmitted and used, in transport and communications infrastructure and in complex water processing and distribution systems, as well as in structures associated with social activities, including religious worship and education. These manifestations are of historical, archaeological, technological, social, architectural and/or scientific value. Imbued with spiritual, emotional and symbolic values which are critical to cultural identity and national pride, they may also have aesthetic value resulting from the quality of their architecture, design or planning (International Committee for the Conservation of the Industrial Heritage 2003).

This chapter briefly explores some of the early manifestations of the industrial heritage of Barbados, Jamaica, Guyana, and Trinidad and Tobago. It underscores the importance of identifying, documenting, promoting and preserving this heritage and examines the success of such initiatives to date. Strategies designed to strengthen these efforts are subsequently suggested.

## Agro-industry: The Early Years

European colonization of the Caribbean was begun by Spain in the 1490s, with England, France, Spain and the Netherlands subsequently establishing a presence throughout the region. Because of their significant income-generation potential, Caribbean territories were of immediate economic interest to the Europeans. This resulted in widespread conflict between rival European colonizers seeking to establish dominance. The industrial heritage of the region finds its genesis in the development of the economic potential of these colonial possessions.

### Sugar and Rum

Initially, tobacco, cocoa and cotton, and other crops, were cultivated in the region, although sugar production soon became the dominant economic activity. By 1700 the English planters in Barbados, Jamaica and the Leewards were supplying close to half of the sugar consumed in western Europe (Dunn 2000). The sugar industry and its allied rum production represent some of the earliest manifestations of industrial activity on these islands. Successive generations of Caribbean sugar planters were both farmers and manufacturers (Satchell 2002a). Securing significant returns on investment required knowledge of the cane plant, climate and soil, as well as the technical expertise required to manage a factory complex. The primary components of this complex were the mill, trash house, boiling house, curing house, distillery and artisan workshop (Satchell and Roper 2007).

**Figure 21.1**
Morgan Lewis Mill
(1727), Barbados
(photo by A. Dol-
land, 2008)

Some of the most common vestiges of the industrial heritage born of the Caribbean sugar industry are mills. Well-known ones include the restored Morgan Lewis Mill (1727) in Barbados, the Hogg Island Windmill in Guyana and the Ironshore Windmill Tower in Jamaica. Equally popular with tourists are the mighty waterwheels that powered some of the sugar production facilities, such as those in Arnos Vale (1857) in Tobago; Tryall (1790), Drax Hall, Maima-Seville Heritage Park, Columbus Park and Martha Brae in Jamaica; and Diego Martin in Trinidad. In Jamaica, several fine examples of aqueducts can also be found. These include the Papine-Mona Aqueduct (1758), located on the compound where the Mona campus of the University of the West Indies now stands, and Bushy Park Aqueduct (1760–80), both of which exemplify building techniques of eighteenth-century Jamaica.

The rum distilleries constitute another integral element of sugar-based industrial heritage. Traditionally, Caribbean governments, as well as private individuals and corporate citizens, have provided both locals and visitors with an opportunity to experience this heritage first-hand. The Mount Gay Rum Estate (1703) and St Nicholas Abbey (1658) in Barbados, Jamaica's Appleton Rum Estate and Distillery (1749), the Demerara Rum Heritage Centre

Figure 21.2
Papine-Mona
Aqueduct (1758),
Jamaica (photo by
A. Dolland, 2008)

(2007) in Guyana and the Angostura Museum (1999) in Trinidad are but a few examples of sites where tours are offered and where visitors can witness the distilling process and taste the results. Many museums in the territories under review feature artefacts relating to the sugar industry, but some museums are dedicated solely to this aspect of the region's history, for example, the Sir Frank Hutson Sugar Museum (1982) in Barbados. With the closure of Trinidad and Tobago's national sugar production company Caroni (1975) Limited, plans are afoot to use one of its former factory sites to set up a sugar museum as a testament to the country's long history with the industry.

Figure 21.3
Sir Frank Hutson
Sugar Museum
(1982), Barbados
(photo by A. Dolland, 2008)

## Lime

Throughout the Caribbean, lime was produced for use in the sugar fields, both for purifying cane juice and as a key element in mortar. Designed to produce lime on a huge scale, kilns ranged from small and simple to elaborate structures in territories such as Jamaica. They often had a substantial super-structure of dressed stone and an internal egg-shaped chamber lined with heat-resistant bricks, within which limestone was burned at high temperatures in order to produce lime (Buisseret 1983). In the territories under review, relics of this industrial activity can be found at Port Henderson and Prospect Pen in Jamaica, Britton Hills in Barbados and Courland Bay in Tobago.

## Cocoa, Coffee and Indigo

Smaller landowners who lacked sufficient capital to establish sugar plantations sometimes chose crops such as indigo, which required a smaller capital invest-ment. The extreme care with which the indigo plant needed to be cultivated was matched only by the difficulty of refining it into dye (Burns 2005). Dur-ing the seventeenth and eighteenth centuries, much indigo was produced in many of the territories of the Caribbean, and its production left behind a sys-tem of cisterns, vats and interconnecting pipes. Although in many of the ter-ritories it was a thriving industry from which great fortunes were made, it disappeared quickly in the face of competition from other dyes, and today it is hard to detect vestiges of the industry. One of the few surviving relics of large indigo works can be found in the Hellshire Hills of Jamaica (Buisseret 1983).

Other crops which proved lucrative include coffee and cocoa. The high quality of these products in both Trinidad and Jamaica has caused them to be in high demand globally. The remains of both drying platforms and grinding houses used in the coffee industry can still be found at Clydesdale and in the Cinchona Botanical Gardens in Jamaica (Gravette 2000). Visitors can also tour coffee plantations on the island that are still in operation. Cocoa, on the other hand, has left fewer material remains attesting to past industrial activity. Despite this, some Caribbean territories contain barbecues or drying racks characteristic of cocoa production, sometimes taking the shape of rolling plat-forms which can be moved according to the state of the weather (Buisseret 1983). Several of these can still be seen at the Lopinot Estate and in several cocoa villages in the Montserrat Valley of Trinidad.

## Logging

The logging industry and its associated downstream activities represent a profitable industrial enterprise. Recognized during colonization as a rich resource, commercially produced timber was used for constructing dwellings and ships, as well as for fuel. This resource was quickly depleted in the smaller Caribbean territories. In Guyana, however, the industry is still lucrative, given the fact that this South American country boasts some 168,000 square kilometres of forested land (Guyana 2000). One local monument which stands as testimony to this logging heritage is the Christianburg Waterwheel (1855).

**Figure 21.4**
The Christianburg Waterwheel (1855), Guyana (photo by A. Dolland, 2008)

## Infrastructure Development

Economic activity has always served as a catalyst for development of the infrastructure required to house, transport and protect the people involved. The architecture of the region, much of it built from the wealth of the plantations, provides many examples of great houses, churches, government buildings and schools. These structures reflect the style of the ruling European nations of the time, displaying Gothic, Romanesque, Baroque, Georgian or Victorian influences (Gordon and Hersh 2005; Tarr 1978). The vernacular structures provide examples of how European architecture was adapted to suit the demands of a tropical climate (Gravette 2000). The survival of hundreds of these structures serves as testament to the quality of the engineering techniques applied, which enabled them to withstand the destructive hurricanes and earthquakes that have affected the region over the centuries.

## Fortifications

Forts were built to protect the territories and the wealth they generated. Strategically placed by the various European rivals, these military outposts collectively tell the story of European rivalry across the whole region, providing a chain of defence stretching from Trinidad in the south to Cuba in the north (UNESCO World Heritage Centre 2005b, 2006b). These forts were joined by heavily fortified British and American military bases in the twentieth century, which were aimed at protecting the interests of Britain and its allies (Kelshall 1988; Metzgen and Graham 2007) as they waged war against their enemies in the Caribbean. Some of these sites still operate as local military bases and airports, while others have been adapted or redeployed for civilian purposes.

Many of the old forts have been converted into museums and successful heritage tourism sites which depict past and present strategies for land, sea and air defence in the Caribbean. The Jamaica National Heritage Trust has some nineteen forts on its list of heritage assets, while the Barbados National Trust has had Bridgetown and its garrison listed by UNESCO as a world heritage site. The National Trust of Guyana currently has three forts listed as national monuments. These are Fort Kyk-Over-Al, Fort Nassau and Fort Zeelandia, which all date back to the early seventeenth century. In Trinidad,

**Figure 21.5** Ruins of Fort Kyk-Over-Al (circa 1623), Guyana (photo by A. Dolland, 2008)

vestiges of several old forts form part of the tourism landscape. Prime examples are Fort King George, Fort Milford, Fort James, Fort Bennett, Fort Granby and Fort Cambleton in Tobago as well as Fort Chacon, Fort Picton and Fort San Andres in Trinidad. Apart from the forts, museums such as the Chaguaramas Military Museum in Trinidad, the Fort Charles and Defence Force (Military) Museums in Jamaica and the National Military and John Campbell Police Museums in Guyana provide useful insights into the region's military heritage (JNHT 2009; NTG 2009; BNT 2009; Barbados World Heritage Task Force 2005).

## Utilities: Water and Electricity

**Figure 21.6** Sluice gate (*koker*) at the seawall (n.d.), Uitvlugt, Guyana (photo by A. Dolland, 2008)

Access to both water and power has always influenced settlement patterns and socio-economic development. Apart from the aqueducts and dams in the territories under review, more specialized drainage and irrigation systems were also developed. One such system was developed in Guyana by the original Dutch sugar-estate owners – the Dutch were noted for their drainage and land reclamation expertise in the sixteenth and seventeenth centuries. This network was used for both drainage and irrigation of estates located along the

coast, which lies 0.5 to 1.1 metres below sea level. This was made possible by sea and river sluices (*kokers*) which were opened during low tide. Today the irrigation system consists of primary and secondary canals with a seawall (Guyana 2000). The design of this network and its many components is a prime example of technical and construction knowhow; they have survived the elements and remain critical to economic activity in Guyana to this day.

Modern water distribution and treatment systems continue to be of central importance to commercial and industrial activities throughout the region, intimately affecting the quality of life of each Caribbean citizen. As in other islands, state-of-the-art technologies have evolved in Trinidad. Since 2002 it has boasted a desalination plant with one of the largest seawater reverse osmosis (SWRO) systems in the western hemisphere (Rodriguez 2003).

Electricity came to Jamaica in 1892. In Trinidad, Port of Spain was officially lit up in 1895 (Anthony 1985), but electricity was first used in Tobago only in 1946 (T&TEC 2006). Generation activities in Guyana began before the turn of the twentieth century, with several individual private and government enterprises providing their own power. The forerunner of the Barbados Light and Power Company Limited, the Barbados Electric Supply Corporation (BESC), was formed in 1909 (BLPC 2009). Electrification of the territories under review transformed business and everyday life in the region, and today another transformation has begun. High oil prices and a global movement towards renewable energy resources have created a sense of urgency in non-oil-producing countries in the region, leading them to explore options such as solar, wind, geothermal and biomass energy. The cultural, social and technical aspects of this area of industrial heritage are yet to be adequately explored.

## Transportation: Shipping, Railways and Bridges

The transportation infrastructure constructed to move goods and people constitutes a tangible manifestation of industrial heritage. Features of this network include roads, railways, tramways, ports, harbours, jetties and "stellings", as well as shipyards for construction and repair of the mighty sea vessels.

Colonial railways were an essential part of economic development (Coulls, Divall and Lee 1999; Satchell 2003). The railways that were constructed in the territories under review were used to transport people and freight (sugar, bauxite, etc.) to large, centrally located factories, and to harbours in some cases. Many old railway stations, railway lines and machines in Trinidad, Guyana, Barbados and Jamaica have been converted to offices or have become stand-alone exhibits or showcased in museums. One such example is the main transportation hub in Port of Spain, Trinidad – the City Gate,

**Figure 21.7** Arima Railway Station, Trinidad, 1895 (photo courtesy Alma Jordan Library, University of the West Indies, St Augustine)

formerly the Trinidad Government Railway headquarters. Yet others remain abandoned to the ravages of time in the absence of resources to devote to their preservation. This heritage is worthy of exploration and preservation.

Maritime activity, piracy and colonial control were all contributory factors in the development of harbours and the capacity for repairing and building ships in the Caribbean (Evans 2005, 2007). These facilities and skills were available in all the territories under review. Research has shown that vernac-

**Figure 21.8** Loading rum at the sugar wharf, Jamaica, circa 1900 (photo courtesy National Library of Jamaica)

ular Jamaica sloops were custom designed, built with indigenous wood and utilized by Caribbean colonists in the late seventeenth century (Evans 2005, 2007). Guyana celebrates its shipbuilding industry at the National Museum. One exhibit showcased the MV *Independence*, one of the first aluminium cargo vessels in the world, constructed in 1966 and believed to be among the first vessels designed and outfitted in Guyana. Trinidad also boasted a successful shipbuilding industry (Jackson 1904). These industries continue to be viable today, and drydocks, marinas and shipyards abound throughout the region.

Bridges are also central to the development of transportation infrastructure. Since ancient times, bridges have been one of the tangible manifestations of the craft of engineering (DeLony 1996). Their value and significance cannot be overlooked in the study of industrial heritage artefacts worthy of preservation. The Mahaica, Mahaicony, Abary and Boeraserie railway bridges of Guyana stand as tangible reminders of one of the first railways constructed in South America; all were erected in the nineteenth century. The Demerara Harbour Bridge was built in the late twentieth century, and the Takutu River Bridge, linking Guyana and Brazil, and the Berbice River Bridge were both built in the new millennium. The Berbice bridge is the sixth longest floating bridge in the world (Ullah 2008), and the Demerara bridge is the fourth longest (Stabroek News 2007). Jamaica also boasts of historic bridges, such as the historic cast-iron bridge which spans the Rio Cobre River (1801) and the Flat Bridge in St Catherine, which dates back to the eighteenth century.

**Figure 21.9** Mahaicony railway bridge (1897), Guyana (photo by A. Dolland, 2008)

They are both listed by the Jamaica National Heritage Trust as national heritage sites, but many other bridges lie abandoned and deteriorating. These large artefacts also require the attention of those charged with preserving heritage.

## Mining and Manufacturing

### The Bauxite Industry

The early twentieth century brought to the Caribbean a new era of industrial development. It was during this period that bauxite was discovered in Guyana and Jamaica. Mining began in Guyana in 1917 at the Three Friends Mine south of Mackenzie, now called Linden (Campbell 1985). With its large reserves, Guyana became an important source of bauxite in the global market, and by the end of the 1940s it had become one of the world's largest producers (Guyana 2000). Bauxite production began in Jamaica much later. Although there had been an awareness of the mineral's existence in Jamaica since 1867 (JGCL 2008), the first shipment from Jamaica came in 1952 (Young 1965). From then on production rapidly increased, with Jamaica also becoming a leading world producer of both bauxite and alumina.

**Figure 21.10** Commissioning of a wheel excavator, Mackenzie, Guyana, 1962 (photo courtesy Linden Industrial Heritage Museum, Guyana)

**Figure 21.11** A new type of hopper car loading bauxite at Port Esquivel, Jamaica, circa 1960 (photo courtesy National Library of Jamaica)

Bauxite mining has left a distinct footprint on the landscapes of Guyana and Jamaica: huge tracts of land surface have been transformed forever. The challenge of rehabilitating mining sites is now part of the agenda of policy developers, as industry operations have created an awareness of the need to protect the natural environment from the ravages of mining. This is evidenced by vehement protests against plans to explore the bauxite potential of Cockpit Country in Jamaica. Rich in biodiversity, this unique karst landscape is also a profound symbol of Jamaica's proud history; in the Maroon Wars of 1670–1796, the British fought bands of escaped slaves in this treacherous landscape (Day 2004).

There is also an awareness of the need to showcase and preserve bauxite heritage. In Guyana, the Linden Industrial Heritage Museum provides a chronology of the development of the industry in Mackenzie, Wismar and Christianburg. The museum boasts a unique collection of company documents that provide unique insight into the industry's history and operations at the time.

While the bauxite industry in both Guyana and Jamaica has diminished on the global market over the past few decades, it still remains of central importance to the economies of both countries.

## Gold and Diamonds in Guyana

In addition to bauxite, Guyana has gold and diamonds. Mining came to the fore with the discovery of gold in the Cuyuni and Mazaruni districts in the 1860s (Mangar 2008). Gold was initially produced in Guyana by "porknockers", who used hand mining methods based on ground sluicing, the long tom and the gold pan. This method was later supplemented, and to an extent mechanized, by the introduction of jet dredges, which could mine the river bottoms under the guidance of aqualung-equipped divers (Guyana 2000). Couple-jet units have now been largely superseded by remote-controlled diverless gravel pumps or missile dredges, which possess the capacity to mine deeper channels and riverbanks and to explore river bottoms more efficiently. However, because the riverbeds are becoming exhausted, a larger percentage of local production is increasingly being derived from land dredges, which work the large pits where spent ores are stockpiled for additional treatment at a later date (Guyana 2000). Development of the sector continues today, with foreign companies still being granted large-scale licences to mine gold.

**Figure 21.12** Mining for gold on the Demerara River, Guyana, 2008 (photo by A. Dolland, 2008)

Diamonds were first reported in 1887 from the Puruni River area and in 1890 from the Putareng River. By the 1920s diamond production averaged 200,000 carats annually (Guyana 2000). Production has fluctuated over the years but the industry has continued to be a viable source of government revenue. Greener approaches are now being sought for both the gold and diamond industries, which have been plagued by poor environmental prac-

tices such as the continued use of mercury in exploitation of the country's gold resources.

The need for land rehabilitation of mining sites has been an ongoing concern. Converting dormant sites into industrial heritage sites would be challenging, given the scarcity of available resources and the remoteness of many of the locations. Guyana's museums contain many artefacts associated with both gold and diamond mining. Agencies such as the National Heritage Trust and the Guyana Geology and Mines Commission (GGMC) periodically showcase the country's mining heritage through travelling exhibits and public oral presentations. Much more can be done, however, to document this unique regional industrial heritage.

## Petroleum and Asphalt

For decades Barbados, Jamaica and Guyana have prospected for oil with little or no real success. While exploration continues in those economies, the Republic of Trinidad and Tobago has had a relatively long and successful history as a petroleum economy. The birth of the petroleum industry is closely linked with another resource: a natural asphalt lake which according to current estimates holds an estimated ten million tons (LATT 2007). Some of the first descriptions of asphalt in Trinidad were contained in the diaries of Sir Robert Dudley and Sir Walter Raleigh in 1595 (Attwooll and Broome 1935; Higgins 1996). At that time the material was used to caulk ships, and it was not until 1825 that export of asphalt on a commercial scale began in Trinidad (Higgins 1996).

A type of asphaltite (manjak) was mined in Barbados in the late 1800s. Mining occurred in areas such as the College Estate; Spring Vale, in the parish of St Thomas; and Bruce Vale, in the parish of St Joseph (Cave Shepherd 1911). Exports were used for paving as well as the manufacture of varnishes and paints. In the Scotland district of Barbados, one of the nominated sites for the tentative World Heritage list, manjak, the blackest of the asphalts, still rises to the surface (UNESCO 2009a). The industry thrives today in both Barbados and Trinidad; the latter has an estimated four-hundred-year reserve (LATT 2007).

The Pitch Lake in Trinidad has long been a tourist attraction and has an onsite exhibit showcasing the industry's history. Lake Asphalt of Trinidad and Tobago, the company managing the resource, on its website provides the public with information on the development of the industry, adding colour by including Amerindian legends pertaining to creation of the lake.

The story of oil in Trinidad actually begins with the use of asphalt to create fuel (Higgins 1996). It is therefore not surprising that the first attempts to

**Figure 21.13** Governor Sir George Le Hunte visits the Guayaguayare oil production site, Trinidad, 1909 (photo courtesy Alma Jordan Library, University of the West Indies, St Augustine)

find oil were focused on areas in the vicinity of the Pitch Lake. It is well accepted by many in Trinidad and Tobago that the country's first well was drilled by Walter Darwent's Merrimac Company in the vicinity of the La Brea Pitch Lake in 1857 (GSTT 2008). The drilling of this particular well symbolized the beginning of one of the oldest petroleum industries in the world, even though there was no commercial exploitation until 1902. By 1930 Trinidad had produced more than 30 per cent of the British Empire's oil (Jones 1981), and up to 1934 it was the world's eleventh largest oil producer (Renwick 2008). After the Second World War, more exploratory drilling was conducted, using improved technologies in the areas of engineering, geophysics, geochemistry and chemistry. This led to discovery of new and deeper wells and the first exploitation of marine resources. More recently, the focus of the energy sector has been on increased production and utilization of natural gas in both energy and non-energy applications (Manning 2007).

Efforts at preserving the tangible manifestations of this industrial heritage in Trinidad have, to date, been modest. They have included research and publication of several seminal works on the industry's development. Vestiges of old wells and other, similar types of infrastructure remain scattered throughout the south of the island, abandoned and in need of attention. The National Museum and Art Gallery does showcase the development of the oil industry, and so too does the Petroleum Company of Trinidad and Tobago (Petrotrin), which maintains an onsite exhibit with artefacts from past eras. Given that the oil and natural gas industries have formed the basis of the country's economic development for more than a century and have transformed the

industrial landscape, much more can be done to create an appreciation of this industrial heritage.

## Manufacturing

Apart from the industrial activities already identified, the late nineteenth century saw different types of manufacturing enterprises spring up in the territories under review. These ranged from match factories (Richardson 2004) to factories manufacturing soap, beer, ice, biscuits, cigars and cigarettes (Jackson 1904), edible oils, lard, aerated beverages and aromatic bitters. Since then, the territories of the Caribbean have developed mature, thriving industries, having harnessed their human and natural resources to maximize their revenue-earning potential. These industries range from cement and textiles to iron and steel, chemicals, plastics and so on. Showcasing this type of industrial heritage could enhance brand image and create positive associations of quality and environmental consciousness, and even enhance national pride in indigenous products.

## The Human Factor

Often-overlooked aspects of industrial heritage are the human skills and inventiveness utilized in various industrial activities throughout the centuries. Every well-run plantation needed a cadre of highly skilled workers, such as carpenters, smiths, pitters, boilers, clarifiers, clayers, distillers, coopers, potters, millwrights, wheelwrights, masons, plumbers, coppersmiths and engineers (Shepherd 2002; Satchell 2004; Dunn 2000; Sheridan 1974). By taking over skilled plantation tasks which were initially performed by white artisans, the enslaved blacks demonstrated a high degree of adaptability to changing sugar technology (Sheridan 1989; Hayes 2008). The region was not merely a consumer of technology: evidence of technical innovation in sugar and rum production methods can be seen in patents filed throughout the history of the industry (Satchell 2002a, 2002b, 2004; France 1984).

Allied to the activities of skilled workers and professionals is the evolution of industrial relations legislation, practice and case law in the region. Over time, the major industries have given birth to the most powerful trade unions, which from very early on joined in political struggles for voting rights, public education, social equality and, later on, political independence for the former British colonies (Goolsarran 2003, 2006; Weekes 1988). These unions, and the people they represent, continue to profoundly affect the region's socio-economic development.

## Conclusion and Recommendations

The richness and variety of Caribbean industrial heritage is evidenced by the many surviving sites and artefacts. Many obstacles continue to face those who seek to preserve this type of industrial heritage. Some citizens and even governments fail to recognize the intrinsic value of these assets because of their limited aesthetic appeal, while others avoid investing in their preservation because of what is perceived as limited income-generation potential. Many are rejected because of their associations with colonial oppression and slavery (Gupta 2004). But perhaps the greatest obstacle to progress in this area is the scarcity of adequate human and financial resources for research, conservation, preservation and adaptive reuse of heritage sites and artefacts. However, stakeholders continue to persevere in preservation efforts. Successes have been achieved by academic institutions, international agencies, community groups, professional associations, tourism development agencies and government property management/development entities, as well as authorities entrusted with the overall management of national heritage trusts, foundations, museums and historical and archaeological societies.

The Jamaica National Heritage Trust, in existence since 1959, has more than two hundred sites listed, while the Barbados National Trust and the National Trust of Guyana, both established in 1961, have eight and nine respectively. In Trinidad and Tobago, the Act to Establish the National Trust (TTNT) was passed in 1991, amended in 1999 and assented to in 2000, but the trust itself became fully functional only in 2003 (Long 2006a). Despite severe local criticism of its performance with regard to heritage issues (Bagoo 2008a–c; Balgobin 2007; Balroop 2008; Kenny 2004a–c, 2006a–c; Long 2006b, 2006c), the TTHT has managed to make some strides in the evaluation and restoration of heritage sites. In 1992 the Tobago House of Assembly (THA) created the Tobago Trust to manage preservation of the archaeological, historical and natural sites in that island (Williams 2008). To date the Trinidad and Tobago government does not have any sites listed as properties of interest.

Throughout the Caribbean, the academic community has played an integral role in preserving the region's industrial heritage. The ongoing work of archaeologists, palaeontologists, historians and cultural anthropologists has served to increase public awareness of heritage issues, as evidenced by the increasing number of published works in the area. The body of work generated thus far has contributed significantly to the creation of a knowledge base to support related legal frameworks and policy development. It has also done much to enhance the level of cultural consciousness in the Caribbean community. To further increase appreciation of our industrial heritage assets, specialist professional training in the methodological, theoretical and historical aspects of industrial heritage should be provided at tertiary learning institutions. Educational material about the region's industrial heritage should also be produced for students at the primary and secondary levels.

The work of international agencies such as UNESCO has complemented heritage conservation programmes carried out by governments in the Caribbean (UNESCO World Heritage Centre 2001, 2004, 2005a, 2005c, 2006a, 2006b). This work has helped to raise public awareness of heritage issues, provide technical expertise and training, and support collaborative efforts aimed at resolving problems commonly faced by heritage managers in the region. UNESCO's work has substantially increased networks that link decision-makers, heritage managers, researchers, heritage foundations and various other stakeholders. Both the International Council on Monuments and Sites and the International Council of Museums have expanded their operations considerably throughout the Caribbean. As signatories to the 1972 Convention Concerning the Protection of the World Cultural and Natural Heritage – better known as the World Heritage Convention (see table 21.1) – many English-speaking territories have sought to have their heritage assets inscribed on the World Heritage List. Many have been successful, including Barbados, Belize, Dominica, St Kitts and Nevis, and St Lucia (table 21.2), while others have submitted to UNESCO tentative lists for consideration (table 21.3). Despite the successes of UNESCO in the area of heritage preservation, research has shown that one of the most consistently underrepresented types of property on the World Heritage List has been technological and industrial heritage sites and landscapes (ICOMOS 2005; TICCIH 2008).

**Table 21.1** World Heritage Convention Ratification Status in the Caribbean

| State Party | Date* | Type of Instrument |
|---|---|---|
| Antigua and Barbuda | 01/11/1983 | Ac |
| Barbados | 09/04/2002 | Ac |
| Belize | 06/11/1990 | R |
| Cuba | 24/03/1981 | R |
| Dominica | 04/04/1995 | R |
| Dominican Republic | 12/02/1985 | R |
| Grenada | 13/08/1998 | Ac |
| Guyana | 20/06/1977 | Ac |
| Haiti | 18/01/1980 | R |
| Jamaica | 14/06/1983 | Ac |
| St Kitts and Nevis | 10/07/1986 | Ac |
| St Lucia | 14/10/1991 | R |
| St Vincent and the Grenadines | 03/02/2003 | R |
| Suriname | 23/10/1997 | Ac |
| Trinidad and Tobago | 16/02/2005 | R |

*Date of deposit of ratification (R), acceptance (Ac), accession (A) or of the notification of succession (S).

*Note:* This convention entered into force on 17 December 1975. It subsequently entered into force for each state three months after the date of deposit of that state's instrument, except in cases of declarations of succession, indicated by the letter (S), where the entry into force occurred on the date on which the state assumed responsibility for conducting its international relations.

*Source:* United Nations 2008a (UNESCO World Heritage Centre: http://whc.unesco.org/en/statesparties; accessed 17 February 2008).

**Table 21.2** World Heritage List Sites in the Caribbean

| Country | World Heritage Site | Year | Type |
|---|---|---|---|
| Belize | Belize Barrier Reef Reserve System | 1996 | ● |
| Cuba | Old Havana and its fortifications | 1982 | ■ |
|  | Trinidad and the Valley de los Ingenios | 1988 | ■ |
|  | San Pedro de la Roca Castle, Santiago de Cuba | 1997 | ■ |
|  | Desembarco del Granma National Park | 1999 | ● |
|  | Viñales Valley | 1999 | ■ |
|  | Archaeological landscape of the first coffee plantations in the south-east of Cuba | 2000 | ■ |
|  | Alejandro de Humboldt National Park | 2001 | ● |
|  | Urban historic centre of Cienfuegos | 2005 | ■ |
| Dominica | Morne Trois Pitons National Park | 1997 | ● |
| Dominican Republic | Colonial City of Santo Domingo | 1990 | ■ |
| Haiti | National History Park – Citadel Laferrière, Sans Souci Palace Ruins, Ramiers | 1982 | ■ |
| St Kitts and Nevis | Brimstone Hill Fortress National Park | 1999 | ■ |
| St Lucia | Pitons Management Area | 2004 | ● |
| Suriname | Central Suriname Nature Reserve | 2000 | ● |
|  | Historic Inner City of Paramaribo | 2002 | ■ |

*Legend:* Type of site:  ■ Cultural site   ● Natural site

*Source:* United Nations 2008d (UNESCO World Heritage Centre: http://whc.unesco.org/en/list; accessed 18 March 2008).

**Table 21.3** Sites in the Caribbean for Tentative World Heritage List Consideration

| Country | Nominated Site | Date |
|---|---|---|
| Barbados | Bridgetown and its Garrison | 18/01/2005 |
| | The Industrial Heritage of Barbados: The Story of Sugar | 18/01/2005 |
| | The Scotland District of Barbados | 18/01/2005 |
| Cuba | Ciénaga de Zapata National Park | 28/02/2003 |
| | Historic Center of Camagüey | 28/02/2003 |
| | National Schools of Art, Cubanacán | 28/02/2003 |
| | Reef System in the Cuban Caribbean | 28/02/2003 |
| Dominican Republic | Archaeological and Historical National Park of Pueblo Viejo, La Vega | 21/11/2001 |
| | Archaeological and Historical National Park of the Villa of La Isabela, Puerto Plata | 21/11/2001 |
| | Boca De Nigua Sugar Mill (#) [Ruta de Los Ingenios] | 21/11/2001 |
| | City of Azúa de Compostela | 21/11/2001 |
| | Historical Centre of Puerto Plata | 21/11/2001 |
| | Jacagua, Villa of Santiago | 21/11/2001 |
| | Jaragua National Park | 21/11/2001 |
| | Monetarist | 21/11/2001 |
| | Nuestra Señora de Monte Alegre or la Duquesa Sugar Mill [Ruta de Los Ingenios] | 05/04/2002 |
| | Parque Nacional del Este | 21/11/2001 |
| | Sanate Sugar Mill [Ruta de Los Ingenios] | 05/04/2002 |
| | The Ancient Big House of Palavé [Ruta de Los Ingenios] | 21/11/2001 |
| | The Ancient Diego Caballero Sugar Mill [Ruta de Los Ingenios] | 05/04/2002 |
| | The Sugar Mill of Engombe [Ruta de Los Ingenios] | 21/11/2001 |
| Grenada | Grenadines Island Group | 05/08/2004 |
| | St George Fortified System | 05/08/2004 |
| | St George Historic District | 05/08/2004 |

**Table 21.3** Sites in the Caribbean for Tentative World Heritage List Consideration (*cont'd*)

| Country | Nominated Site | Date |
|---|---|---|
| Guyana | City Hall, Georgetown | 15/11/1995 |
| | Fort Zeelandia (including Court of Policy Building) | 15/11/1995 |
| | Georgetown's Plantation Structure and Historic Buildings | 28/01/2005 |
| | Shell Beach (Almond Beach) Essequibo Coast | 15/11/1995 |
| | St Georges Anglican Cathedral | 15/11/1995 |
| Haiti | Centre historique de Jacmel | 21/09/2004 |
| Jamaica | Blue and John Crow Mountains National Park | 28/08/2006 |
| St Kitts and Nevis | City of Charlestown | 17/09/1998 |
| | Historic Zone of Basseterre | 17/09/1998 |
| Suriname | The Settlement of Joden Savanne and Cassipora Cemetery | 30/06/1998 |

*Source:* United Nations 2008c (UNESCO World Heritage Centre: http://whc.unesco.org/en/tentativelist/; accessed 17 March 2008).

To facilitate greater focus on industrial heritage, Caribbean territories need to conduct detailed studies in order to prepare an inventory of technological objects and landscapes in the principal productive sectors. Harnessing state-of-the-art technologies such as geographical information systems (GIS), global positioning systems (GPS) and so forth could be useful in this regard (Reid 2008). These efforts should be accompanied by sustained efforts to educate the public about the meaning and value of industrial heritage. The documentary heritage associated with the various types of industrial activities should also be given serious consideration by all stakeholders. Photographs, technical drawings and technical documents pertaining to the acquisition, installation and design of machinery and the construction of industrial facilities provide detailed insights into many aspects of industrial heritage. Company records detailing industrial processes, coupled with oral histories regarding the experiences of all categories of personnel, are also a critical data source (Rojas-Sola 2008). Sample specimens of the products may be useful as well, to both collect and display. Particular focus needs to be given to developing a better understanding of how both technologies and work practices responded to local conditions and traditional practices.

Also essential is a review of the effectiveness and appropriateness of existing national legal and institutional frameworks and policies for industrial heritage preservation and management. A framework to facilitate the full participation of all stakeholders is critical. With the overlap in responsibilities among government ministries, statutory authorities and other relevant bodies, these entities may sometimes find themselves duplicating preservation efforts or working at cross-purposes.

Greater collaboration among Caribbean territories is also of key importance, since for many of the small territories in the region, the scale of the problem exceeds the capabilities of some of the local heritage organizations. Cooperative strategies for industrial heritage preservation should help maximize available intellectual, financial and human resources. The issue could be included on CARICOM's agenda. One collaborative project that might be undertaken is the creation of a Caribbean Route of Industrial Heritage, similar to one being currently developed in Europe. The European Route of Industrial Heritage (ERIH) is a network or theme route of the most important industrial heritage sites in Europe. The aim of the project is to create interest in the common European heritage of industrialization and its remains. ERIH also seeks to promote regions, towns and sites that exemplify industrial history and market them as visitor attractions in the leisure and tourism industry (Miller, Vandome and McBrewster 2010). Participation in the work of more specialized agencies such as the TICCIH would also help further industrial heritage preservation goals by opening up possibilities for networking and accessing global expertise and experience.

Many sites face constant threats of vandalism, hurricanes, earthquakes, floods and neglect. For those that cannot be saved or have already gone, virtual reality technologies may one day represent the only way of bringing them back to life. In this way historic sites and events can be recreated for such purposes as education and entertainment.

There is no doubt that regional industrial landscapes can function as public cultural spaces, and that their interpretation, preservation, celebration and commemoration are critical elements of the national identities of Caribbean countries. To ensure the preservation of this category of heritage assets, policymakers must give industrial heritage equal status with other types of heritage in the region. While collaboration among national and regional stakeholders remains key, each Caribbean territory is ultimately responsible for charting its way forward in the research, preservation, promotion and utilization of its own industrial heritage.

# References

Anthony, M. 1985. *First in Trinidad*. Port of Spain: Circle Press.

Attwooll, A.W., and D.C. Broome. 1935. *Trinidad Lake Asphalt*. London: Banyard Press.

Bagoo, A. 2008a. "$63M Gingerbread House". *Trinidad and Tobago's Newsday*, 16 February. http://www.newsday.co.tt/.

———. 2008b. "Red House Unprotected". *Trinidad and Tobago's Newsday*, 24 February. http://www.newsday.co.tt/.

———. 2008c. "TT Behind in Landmark Preservation". *Trinidad and Tobago's Newsday*, 2 March. http://www.newsday.co.tt/.

Balgobin, D. 2007. "$12M to Restore Nelson Island". *Trinidad and Tobago's Newsday*, 20 August. http://www.newsday.co.tt/.

Balroop, P. 2008. "Boissiere House Heritage Site". *Trinidad Guardian*, 24 February. http://www.guardian.co.tt/.

Barbados Light and Power Company Limited (BLPC). 2009. "Our History". http://www.blpc.com.bb/.

Barbados National Trust (BNT). 2009. "The Barbados National Trust". http://trust.funbarbados.com/.

Barbados World Heritage Task Force. 2005. "The Industrial Heritage of Barbados: The Story of Sugar", 18 January. UNESCO World Heritage Centre. http://whc.unesco.org/.

Buisseret, D. 1983. "Tourism and Historical Architecture in the Caribbean". In *Final Report: OAS/CTRC Regional Seminar Cultural Patrimony and the Tourism Product: Towards a Mutually Beneficial Product*, International Trade and Tourism Division, Department of Economic Affairs, Organization of American States, 17–28. Washington, DC: OAS.

Burns, W.E. 2005. *Science and Technology in Colonial America*. Westport, CT: Greenwood.

Campbell, D.C. 1985. *Global Mission: The Story of ALCAN*. Vol. 1, *To 1950*. Toronto: Ontario Publishing.

Cave Shepherd Company. 1911. "Barbados (Illustrated): Historical, Descriptive and Commercial". Barbados: Cave Shepherd Company. http://ia340916.us.archive.org/.

Coulls, A., C. Divall and R. Lee. 1999. "Railways as World Heritage Sites". Paris, France: International Council on Monuments and Sites. http://www.icomos.org/.

Day, Michael J. 2004. "Military Campaigns in Tropical Karst". In *Studies in Military Geography and Geology*, edited by Douglas R. Caldwell, Judy Ehlen and Russell S. Harmon, 79–88. New York: Springer.

DeLony, E. 1996. "Context for World Heritage Bridges". Paris, France: International Council on Monuments and Sites and TICCIH. http://www.icomos.org/.

Dunn, R.S. 2000. *Sugar and Slaves: The Rise of the Planter Class in the English West Indies, 1624–1713*. Chapel Hill: University of North Carolina Press.

Evans, A.M. 2005. "Institutionalized Piracy and the Development of the Jamaica Sloop, 1630–1743". MA thesis, Florida State University. http://www.etd.lib.fsu/.

———. 2007. "Defining Jamaica Sloops: A Preliminary Model for Identifying an Abstract Concept". *Journal of Maritime Archaeology* 2, no. 2: 83–92.

France, L.G. 1984. "Sugar Manufacturing in the West Indies: A Study of Innovation and Variation". MA thesis, College of William and Mary.

Geological Society of Trinidad and Tobago (GSTT). 2008. *Historical Facts on the Petroleum Industry of Trinidad and Tobago.* http://www.gstt.org/history/chronology .htm.

Goolsarran, S.J. 2003. "International Labour Standards and Labour Relations in the Caribbean Public Service". Port of Spain: International Labour Organization Caribbean Office, May. http://unpan1.un.org/.

————, ed. 2006. "Industrial Relations in the Caribbean: Issues and Perspectives". Port of Spain: International Labour Office, Caribbean. http://www.ilocarib.org.tt/.

Gordon, S., and A. Hersh. 2005. *Searching for Sugar Mills: An Architectural Guide to the Caribbean.* Oxford: Macmillan Caribbean.

Gravette, A. 2000. *Architectural Heritage of the Caribbean: An A–Z of Historic Buildings.* Kingston: Ian Randle.

Gupta, Divay. 2004. "The State of Industrial Heritage in India", *TICCIH Bulletin* 25, no. 1. http://www.mnactec.cat/ticcih/.

Guyana. 2000. "Guyana National Development Strategy, 2001–2010". http://www .sdnp.org.gy/.

Hayes, David. 2008. "Industrial Heritage and Archaeology in the Caribbean". *TICCIH Bulletin* 41: 4–5. http://www.mnactec.cat/ticcih/.

Higgins, G.E. 1996. *A History of Trinidad Oil.* Port of Spain: Trinidad Express Newspapers.

International Council on Monuments and Sites (ICOMOS). 2005. "The World Heritage List: Filling the Gaps. An Action Plan for the Future", compiled by Jukka Jokilehto with Henry Cleere, Susan Denyer and Michael Petzet. Paris, France: ICOMOS.

Jackson, T.B., ed. 1904. *The Book of Trinidad.* Trinidad: Muir Marshall.

Jamaica Gleaner Company Limited (JGCL). 2008. "Jamaican History: Mining and Mining Resources". http://www.discoverjamaica.com/mining.htm.

Jamaica National Heritage Trust (JNHT). 2009. "Jamaica National Heritage Trust: A Mission Begun in 1958". http://www.jnht.com/.

Jones, G. 1981. *The State and the Emergence of the British Oil Industry.* London: Macmillan.

Kelshall, Gaylord. 1988. *The U-Boat War in the Caribbean.* Port of Spain: Paria Publishing.

Kenny, J. 2004a. "Heritage Vision, Heritage Hope". *Trinidad and Tobago Express,* 27 April. http://www.trinidadexpress.com.

————. 2004b. "The Ortinola Way". *Trinidad and Tobago Express,* 3 February. http://www.trinidadexpress.com/.

————. 2004c. "Our Vanishing Heritage". *Trinidad and Tobago Express,* 13 April. http://www.trinidadexpress.com/.

————. 2006a. "Built Heritage Tragedies". *Trinidad and Tobago Express,* 2 May. http://www.trinidadexpress.com/.

————. 2006b. "Contrasts in Heritage Care". *Trinidad and Tobago Express,* 22 August. http://www.trinidadexpress.com/.

————. 2006c. "Lighthouse Lessons". *Trinidad and Tobago Express,* 17 January. http://www.trinidadexpress.com/.

Lake Asphalt of Trinidad and Tobago (LATT). 2007. "The Pitch Lake (Trinidad Natural Asphalt)". http://www.trinidadlakeasphalt.com/.

Long, S. 2006a. "Building Heritage: National Trust Aims to Preserve and Promote Historical Sites". *Trinidad Guardian,* 10 August. http://www.guardian.co.tt/.

————. 2006b. "Mille Fleurs's Decline Symbolic of Country's Attitude to History". *Trinidad Guardian,* 20 July. http://www.guardian.co.tt/.

————. 2006c. "Stollmeyer's Castle: Long Road Back to Glory". *Trinidad Guardian,* 31 August. http://www.guardian.co.tt/.

Mangar, Tota C. 2008. "Post Emancipation Economic Development in Colonial British Guiana". *Stabroek News,* 28 August. http://www.stabroeknews.com/.

Manning, P. 2007. "Feature Address by the Honourable Patrick Manning, Prime Minister of the Republic of Trinidad and Tobago, at the Opening Ceremony for the Conference on the Future Development of the Oil and Gas Industry in Trinidad and Tobago at the Trinidad Hilton, 13 August 2007". http://www.opm.gov.tt/.

Metzgen, Humphrey, and John Graham. 2007. *Caribbean Wars Untold: A Salute to the British West Indies.* Kingston: University of the West Indies Press.

Miller, Frederic P., Agnes F. Vandome and John McBrewster. 2010. *European Route of Industrial Heritage.* Mauritius: VDM Publishing.

National Trust of Guyana (NTG). 2009. "National Trust of Guyana: Safeguarding the Nation's Patrimony". http://www.nationaltrust.gov.gy/ (accessed 20 May 2008).

Reid, Basil A. 1988. *Archaeology and Geoinformatics: Case Studies from the Caribbean.* Tuscaloosa: University of Alabama Press.

Renwick, D. 2008. *Trinidad and Tobago Energy Industry.* Trinidad: UTC Energy Fund. http://www.ttutc.com/.

Richardson, B.C. 2004. *Igniting the Caribbean's Past: Fire in British West Indian History.* Chapel Hill: University of North Carolina Press.

Rodriguez, Stacy. 2003. "SWRO Desalination Plant Supplies High-Quality Water in Trinidad: Innovative Seawater Reverse Osmosis Design Coupled with Proven Pre-treatment Technology Produces Affordable Water Supply for Trinidad". *Water and Waste Water International,* 1 Nov 2003. http://www.pennnet.com/.

Rojas-Sola, José Ignacio. 2008. "Infografical Techniques for Industrial Engineering as an Integral Tool for Industrial Archaeology". *TICCIH Bulletin* 42: 3–4.

Satchell, Veront M. 2002a. "Innovations in Sugar Cane Mill Technology in Jamaica, 1760–1830". In *Working Slavery, Pricing Freedom: Perspectives from the Caribbean, Africa and the African Diaspora,* edited by Verene A. Shepherd, 93–111. Kingston: Ian Randle.

————. 2002b. "Steam for Sugar-Cane Milling: The Diffusion of the Boulton and Watt Stationary Steam Engine to the Jamaican Sugar Industry, 1809–1830". In *Jamaica in Slavery and Freedom: History, Heritage and Culture,* edited by Kathleen E.A. Monteith and Glen L. Richards, 242–58. Kingston: University of the West Indies Press.

————. 2003. "The Rise and Fall of Railways in Jamaica, 1845–1975". *Journal of Transport History* 24, no. 1: 1–21.

————. 2004. "Estate Ruins as Loci for Industrial Archaeology in Jamaica". *Industrial Archaeology Review* 26, no. 1: 37–45.

Satchell, Veront, and Shani Roper. 2007. "The William James Foundry, 1817–1843: An Exposé of Local Metallurgical Enterprise". *Industrial Archaeology Review* 29, no. 2: 105–13.

Sheridan, R.B. 1974. *Sugar and Slavery: An Economic History of the British West Indies, 1623–1775.* Barbados: Caribbean Universities Press.

————. 1989. "Changing Sugar Technology and the Labour Nexus in the British Caribbean, 1750–1900, with Special Reference to Barbados and Jamaica". *New West Indian Guide* 63, nos. 1–2: 59–93.

Shepherd, Verene A. 2002. *Working Slavery, Pricing Freedom: Perspectives from the Caribbean, Africa and the African Diaspora*. Kingston: Ian Randle.

*Stabroek News*. 2007. "Berbice Bridge Taking Shape". 19 October. http://www.stabroeknews.com/.

Tarr, J.A. 1978. "The Architecture of the Caribbean: Great Houses, Sugar Mills and Fortresses". *America*, June–July, 37–43.

TICCIH (International Committee for the Conservation of the Industrial Heritage). 2008. "TICCIH and the World Heritage List: A Strategy for Advising on Industrial and Technical Cultural Properties". http://www.mnactec.cat/.

Trinidad and Tobago Electricity Commission (T&TEC). 2006. "A Historical Perspective". http://www.ttec.co.tt/.

Ullah, Shabna. 2008. "Berbice Bridge Opened". *Stabroek News,* 12 December. http://www.stabroeknews.com/.

UNESCO World Heritage Centre. 2001. "Regional Experts Meeting on Plantation Systems in the Caribbean, Paramaribo, Suriname (17 to 19 July 2001)". Convention Concerning the Protection of the World Cultural and Natural Heritage, World Heritage Committee Twenty-Fifth Session, 11–15 December, Helsinki, Finland. http://unesdoc.unesco.org/.

———. 2004. "Summary Report of the Conference on the Development of a Caribbean Action Plan in World Heritage, Castries, Saint Lucia (23 to 27 February 2004)". Convention Concerning the Protection of the World Cultural and Natural Heritage, World Heritage Committee Twenty-Eighth Session, 28 June–7 July, Suzhou, China. http://whc.unesco.org/.

———. 2005a. "Caribbean Archaeology and World Heritage Convention". World Heritage Papers 14. http://whc.unesco.org/.

———. 2005b. "Caribbean Wooden Treasures: Proceedings of the Thematic Expert Meeting on Wooden Urban Heritage in the Caribbean Region, 4–7 February 2003, Georgetown, Guyana". World Heritage Papers 15. http://whc.unesco.org/.

———. 2005c. "Meeting of Experts on Cultural Landscapes in the Caribbean: Identification and Safeguarding Strategies, 7–10 November, Santiago de Cuba". Concept paper. http://whc.unesco.org/.

———. 2006a. "The State of the World Heritage in Latin America and the Caribbean". World Heritage Papers 18. http://whc.unesco.org/.

———. 2006b. "American Fortifications and the World Heritage Convention". World Heritage Papers 19. http://whc.unesco.org/.

———. 2009a. "Tentative Lists". http://whc.unesco.org/.

———. 2009b. "World Heritage List". http://whc.unesco.org/.

Weekes, G. 1988. *Oilfields Workers' Trade Union: 50 Years of Progress, 1937–1987*. San Fernando, Trinidad: Vanguard.

Williams, E.S. 2008. "Macro-economic Management in a Hydrocarbon Economy". Address to the Trinidad and Tobago Petroleum Conference by the governor of the Central Bank of Trinidad and Tobago, 25 February 2008. http://www.centralbank.org.tt/.

Young, B.S. 1965. "Jamaica's Bauxite and Alumina Industries". *Annals of the Association of American Geographers* 55, no. 3: 449–64.

**Part 5.**

ARCHAEOLOGY AND MUSEOLOGY

# 22.

# Creativity in Maritime Heritage Management in the Cayman Islands

MARGARET E. LESHIKAR-DENTON AND DELLA A. SCOTT-IRETON

*In the past three decades, foundations for maritime heritage management have been laid in the Cayman Islands through a series of steps: a 1979–80 Institute of Nautical Archaeology shipwreck survey, laws establishing the Cayman Islands National Museum and the National Trust for the Cayman Islands, research on the "Wreck of the Ten Sail", hiring an archaeologist, enlarging the national shipwreck inventory, recording maritime sites and advocating for new legislation. The National Museum, the National Trust, the National Archive and the Department of Environment formalized the Maritime Heritage Partnership in 2002 to combine heritage, education, and recreational tourism through a three-tiered approach to protecting, managing and interpreting the islands' maritime heritage sites. The partnership has created a land-based interpretive trail, has worked towards developing an offshore shipwreck preserve system, and aspires to focus special attention on sensitive and significant sites. A dedicated government-sponsored maritime archaeology programme is proposed. The public, both citizens and visitors, are envisioned as stakeholders – guardians of the past, empowered by new awareness of their maritime heritage and culture.*

## Introduction

Rich and diverse underwater and maritime archaeological sites abound throughout Latin America and the Caribbean. Today many countries in this collective region are endeavouring to protect, manage, research and interpret their heritage resources. Despite significant difficulties, considerable progress is being made (Leshikar-Denton 2011; Leshikar-Denton and Luna Erreguerena 2008). This chapter describes past progress, current directions and future challenges for heritage resource management and protection in the Cayman Islands, a British overseas territory located in the western Caribbean Sea.

In the past three decades, the foundations for maritime heritage management have been laid in the Cayman Islands through a series of steps:

- a shipwreck survey to identify and inventory submerged cultural resources (1979–80);
- laws to establish the Cayman Islands National Museum (1979) and the National Trust for the Cayman Islands (1987);
- completion of research on the "Wreck of the Ten Sail" (1993); and, since the early 1990s,
- employing an archaeologist,
- enlarging the national shipwreck inventory,
- recording maritime sites, and
- advocating for new legislation. (Leshikar-Denton 2002, 2004, 2006, 2011; Leshikar-Denton and Luna Erreguerena 2008, 25–53, 221–44)

The museum, trust and National Archive, with the Department of Environment, formalized a maritime heritage partnership in 2002 to combine heritage, educational and recreational tourism through a three-tiered approach to protecting, managing and interpreting the islands' maritime heritage sites (Leshikar-Denton and Scott-Ireton 2007, 2008). The partnership has created a land-based interpretive trail, has worked towards developing an offshore shipwreck preserve system, and aspires to focus special attention on sensitive and significant sites. A dedicated government-sponsored maritime archaeology programme is proposed to administer the islands' maritime cultural resources for the public benefit. The public, both citizens and visitors, are envisioned as stakeholders – guardians of the past, empowered by a new awareness of the Cayman Islands' maritime heritage and culture.

In developing this chapter, the authors chose to focus on heritage issues for which the Cayman experience might provide lessons or models. While every Caribbean country has unique issues and challenges related to heritage management, we feel that some of the ideas explored in the Cayman Islands can provide examples that may prove useful for other areas. These topics include both traditional and creative approaches to managing archaeological and other heritage sites, through both legislation and education; the role of tourism in heritage management and promotion; the contributions of local organizations and how they can and should be included in management policy and practice; the importance of promoting the value of heritage resources to both citizens and visitors; and the future of historical and archaeological preservation in the Cayman Islands.

## Archaeological Heritage Management

Heritage management in the Cayman Islands is inextricably linked to its maritime archaeology. No evidence of pre-European contact has been discovered on the islands, although the remains of historical activities abound both on land and underwater (Craton 2003; Leshikar-Denton 2002, 2004, 2006, 2011; Leshikar-Denton and Luna Erreguerena 2008, 25–53, 221–44; Leshikar-Denton and Scott-Ireton 2007, 2008; Smith 2000). Many sites are connected to the uniquely maritime culture of Cayman, including turtle fishing, provisioning areas, anchorages, careenages, forts, lighthouses, boatyards, slipways and turtle pens, or *kraals*. Because the Cayman Islands are a natural ship trap, located in the midst of the western Caribbean Sea and fringed with coral reefs, an abundance of Cayman's known archaeological sites are shipwrecks.

In order to effectively manage heritage sites, they must be located and recorded. The first systematic effort to record shipwrecks was conducted by Texas A&M University's Institute of Nautical Archaeology in 1979–80, at the request of the Cayman Islands government. This survey identified the remains of seventy-seven ships and maritime sites and initiated what became the National Shipwreck Inventory, a list that has been further developed in the past two decades by the National Museum. Today the inventory includes more than 140 shipwreck sites representing fifteen nations and perhaps five centuries. Some of these shipwrecks have been more thoroughly investigated, such as the "Turtle Wreck", probably associated with a privateer attack on the eighteenth-century turtling village at Little Cayman (Smith 2000, 91–103). Additionally, the National Museum and the Department of Environment have partnered with institutions such as Florida State University to record some shipwrecks, including the Norwegian barque *Glamis,* built in Dundee, Scotland, in 1876 and lost on Grand Cayman in 1913 (Ho 2004; Leshikar-Denton and Ho 2004).

One of the best-documented events in Caymanian history is the Wreck of the Ten Sail: the loss of HMS *Convert* plus nine ships and brigs of its merchant-ship convoy, wrecked on the East End reef in 1794 and the topic of a doctoral study by Leshikar-Denton (1993, 2005, forthcoming; Leshikar-Denton and Pedley 2004). On the bicentenary of the disaster, in 1994, the Islands commemorated the event with a museum exhibition, a National Archive publication, a postage stamp issue and a commemorative coin. Queen Elizabeth II visited the exhibition and dedicated a park to the Wreck of the Ten Sail. Further research is needed to better understand most of Cayman's shipwrecks, particularly significant vessels such as a possible sixteenth-century site off Grand Cayman's East End and HMS *Jamaica*, lost in North Sound in 1715 while on patrol for pirates.

**Figure 22.1** This historic well was created by cutting steps into the limestone bedrock to enable access to fresh water (photo courtesy Margaret Leshikar-Denton).

Currently the Cayman Islands' approach to management of its heritage sites is through creative use of existing legislation, education and research carried out by various governmental and non-governmental cultural and environmental departments and organizations. Current legislation, while not perfect, provides the legal framework for management and protection, while public education initiatives encourage interest and concern at a grassroots level. One of the most interesting recent projects involved the discovery of an historic step well in downtown George Town (*Caymanian Compass Weekender* 2003). The well, created by cutting steps into the limestone bedrock to enable people to reach fresh water, was uncovered in 2003 during construction of a new shopping mall on the historic waterfront (figure 22.1). The builder halted excavation while the National Museum conducted test excavations to record the well and to mitigate loss of other historic resources located in the path of construction. Local media that covered the project indicated that the well could be destroyed because it was on privately owned land. Resulting public interest in the work of the heritage professionals and volunteers from the museum and related heritage and environmental organizations, and growing interest in the fate of the well, provided an incentive for the landowner to preserve this unusual feature, which was incorporated into the mall as a public exhibit.

## Heritage and Tourism

The Cayman Islands are a very popular tourist destination in the Caribbean, and the nation's economic success is based in large part on recreational tourism. Cruise ships and water sports – especially diving and snorkelling – bring tens of thousands of people annually to the islands (Cayman Islands 2001, 59). The resulting development and construction to support these visitors and to maintain the islands' infrastructure place immense pressure on Cayman's historic resources. One of the best ways to focus attention on these fragile non-renewable resources is to encourage citizens and visitors alike to visit places of historic interest and to learn about how the sites relate to Caymanian culture and heritage (Leshikar-Denton and Scott-Ireton 2007, 2008). Working on the hypothesis that understanding leads to appreciation and appreciation leads to preservation, heritage organizations and managers have developed a proactive approach to heritage tourism.

In 2002 the National Museum, the National Trust, the Department of Environment and the National Archive joined forces as the Cayman Islands Maritime Heritage Trail Partners. The partners worked together with the authors to research and develop the Cayman Islands Maritime Heritage Trail, which opened in 2003 (Cayman Islands Maritime Heritage Trail Partners 2003;

Figure 22.2 The Cayman Islands Maritime Heritage Trail's "Sister Islands" brochure, showing the poster side (courtesy Cayman Islands Maritime Heritage Trail Partners).

Leshikar-Denton 2006; Leshikar-Denton and Scott-Ireton 2007, 2008; Scott-Ireton 2005). The Trail features thirty-six sites of maritime significance on all three islands that are accessible to students, local residents and tourists; they are interpreted through signs and two colourful brochures that include a poster on one side and a trail map with site interpretations on the other (figure 22.2). The Trail has proven to be a successful endeavour in educating the public and in raising awareness of the need to protect the Cayman Islands' remaining cultural resources.

The next step is the proposed development of shipwreck preserves – underwater archaeological sites interpreted for divers and snorkellers by means of submerged signs and markers, informational brochures and site guides. The interpreted shipwrecks will tie heritage tourism into the already popular underwater ecotourism enjoyed by scuba divers, snorkellers and submarine passengers. The first site proposed to become a preserve, *Glamis*, has been mapped and researched in preparation for development of interpretive materials (Leshikar-Denton and Ho 2004; Leshikar-Denton 2006, 24–25; Leshikar-Denton and Scott-Ireton 2007, 75–83, 2008, 236–42) (figure 22.3).

A land-based trail accessible by all, a shipwreck preserve system for the adventurous public, and interpretation of rare heritage sites through exhibitions and publications create a layered approach to protection and management of heritage sites. Local people who understand and are inspired by their

**Figure 22.3** The wreck of *Glamis* is ideally suited for a shipwreck preserve, as it features extensive remains and a vibrant ecosystem (photo courtesy Alexander Mustard).

history make great stewards for protection of heritage sites. Tourists who learn about the history of the places they visit gain a greater appreciation for all heritage sites. This approach, focusing on long-term preservation through education, also results in sustainable tourism through use and interpretation of heritage sites, which has consequences for enduring economic growth.

## Heritage and the Law

In addition to the challenges of managing heritage sites that are in the path of construction, as described above, the Cayman Islands government, like many Caribbean nations, has had to deal with individuals who are not opposed to destroying the islands' cultural sites for personal gain. Tales of pirate gold and Spanish treasure have lured treasure hunters and commercial salvagers to Cayman's shores. In response to requests received in the early second half of the twentieth century for official permission to hunt for treasure, the government developed legislation to regulate recovery of material from historic shipwrecks. In 1966 the resulting Abandoned Wreck Law (Cayman Islands 1997) allowed some commercial salvage; ultimately it was judged too lenient to provide the protection needed to prevent exploitation of the islands' submerged cultural resources. The law provides that all historical shipwrecks that have been on the seabed for more than fifty years are vested in the British Crown; this is used to protect sites but falls short of recognizing shipwrecks as cultural property. If the government enters into an agreement with a prospector, it must return at least half of the value of the wreck to the prospector, and to retain salvaged artefacts, it must pay the prospector a percentage of their appraised value, thus giving up rights to more than 50 per cent of a shipwreck and then paying the prospector to buy it back. Fortunately the government has not granted licences to treasure hunters, and in 2002 there were prosecutions for violations.

The Ministry of Culture eventually appointed a Marine Archaeology Committee, which reviewed the Abandoned Wreck Law in the 1990s and decided that it was inadequate. New legislation is proposed and fortunately can now take into consideration the standards of two international instruments, the International Council on Monuments and Sites International Charter on the Protection and Management of Underwater Cultural Heritage (1996) and the UNESCO Convention on the Protection of the Underwater Cultural Heritage (2001). One of the most progressive ideas for protection and management of Cayman's maritime resources is the proposed Cayman Islands Maritime Archaeology Programme. With legislative support and governmental funding, this program has the potential to establish an official office that will administer research of maritime sites, respond to discoveries of new sites, prepare and interpret shipwreck preserves, distribute and maintain preserve-related information materials, and manage Cayman's underwater heritage resources for the public benefit. Additionally, the programme could provide a model for similar programs in other Caribbean nations.

## Cultural Landscapes and Caribbean Heritage

The entire nation of the Cayman Islands can be considered a maritime cultural landscape. Both its culture and history are tied to the sea, and evidence of maritime heritage is located all over the islands (Craton 2003; Leshikar-Denton 2002, 2004, 2006, 2011; Leshikar-Denton and Luna Erreguerena 2008, 25–53, 221–44; Leshikar-Denton and Scott-Ireton 2007, 2008; Smith 2000). From turtle *kraals* and *barcaderes* (boat slips) cut into the ironshore to naturally occurring caves in Cayman Brac's cliff, used for protection from hurricanes (both historically and as recently as 2004's Hurricane Ivan and 2008's Paloma), the landscape of the Cayman Islands has been used and modified to accommodate the maritime industries and needs of the islanders. Many of these sites are featured on the Cayman Islands Maritime Heritage Trail, but many more have been obliterated by construction and development. Ongoing management of the remaining sites is needed to prevent their loss as well. Governmental agencies and non-governmental organizations are moving in the right direction, but more proactive means are desirable.

The Government of the Cayman Islands aggressively protects the extensive coral reef ecosystem for which the islands are famous and which draws many millions of dollars in diving tourism. Embedded within the coral are historic shipwrecks, which links their protection to the responsibilities of the Department of Environment. The department is one of the Maritime Heritage Trail Partners and was instrumental in development of the Trail. Operational support of the Department of Environment in the proposed new Cayman Islands Maritime Archaeology Programme is envisioned to create a dynamic force for protection of Cayman's historic shipwrecks, from the installation of mooring buoys to prevent anchor damage to cooperative projects and research on reefs and wrecks. Once again, legislation is needed to provide equal protection for cultural as well as natural resources.

## Archaeological and History Organizations

In addition to the Maritime Heritage Trail Partners, Cayman is home to several organizations dedicated to specific elements of island history and culture. The Cayman Catboat Club and Cayman Maritime Heritage Foundation are non-profit cultural preservation organizations. The Seafarer's Association is composed of Caymanians who have been in occupations involving seamanship and a livelihood dependent on the sea. These organizations, although small, boast enthusiastic members who are committed to ensuring that locally designed and built schooners and catboats, for example, will never be forgotten and are appreciated as part of Caymanian culture. These sorts of societies are a vibrant part of Cayman Islands life and offer links to a past that many young people will never experience otherwise. Further, the members of these organizations are often extremely knowledgeable about local history and are inherently interested in preserving their community's past; they offer perfect opportunities for cooperative heritage stewardship under governmental programmes such as the proposed Cayman Islands Maritime Archaeology Programme.

Caymanians have long demonstrated a deep interest and pride in their unique heritage. The National Trust, established in 1987, has proven a leader in historic preservation initiatives. The trust developed historic walking trails in George Town and established a Heritage Register of historical buildings. Its Historic Sites Committee, which included heritage professionals from multiple organizations, was instrumental in guiding the restoration of Pedro St James. The oldest house still standing in the Cayman Islands, Pedro St James was the site of such important events as the announcement of the abolition of slavery in Cayman. Today Pedro St James is an innovative, technologically advanced heritage experience that features a multimedia theatre devoted to Caymanian history, a beautifully restored plantation house, and interpretive exhibits. The site hosts thousands of visitors annually and is a model of historic preservation and heritage tourism.

## Values and Attitudes to Heritage

Cayman Islanders value their heritage, as can be seen in their historical societies, their support for projects such as the Maritime Heritage Trail and their pride in successful historic preservation endeavours such as Pedro St James and Fort George, the ruins of which, dating from 1780, are preserved on extremely valuable commercial waterfront property. As descendants of the seafarers who first colonized these three small islands and founded their maritime culture, present-day Caymanians are stakeholders and guardians of their heritage; their preservation efforts serve as excellent examples of successful community-level activism.

One of the Cayman Islands' advantages relative to many Caribbean nations is its economic ability to foster and fund historic preservation and cultural initiatives. Because Cayman is not obliged to dedicate all its available resources to issues such as poverty and unemployment, the nation can afford to invest in preserving its past. This good fortune perhaps brings with it a responsibility to research and develop effective model programmes, legislation and funding strategies that can be utilized by other nations. The Maritime Heritage Trail, shipwreck preserves and the proposed Cayman Islands Maritime Archaeology Programme are all steps towards this goal. In this way Cayman can not only respond to the needs of its own heritage preservation but can also offer assistance, ideas and examples to others, particularly in the Caribbean region.

## Conclusion

The nations of the Caribbean hold a vast array of unique heritage sites, from evidence of prehistoric cultures to colonial shipwrecks, from plantation ruins to local architecture and the emergence of local identities and communities. The region's long and often tumultuous history is also evident in archaeological remains found underground and underwater. Today these cultural sites offer opportunities not only to better understand the region's past but also to promote economic prosperity through heritage tourism. The economic value of heritage sites can only be realized, however, through long-term, government-sponsored management to ensure that the sites are protected for future generations. We hope the avenues for heritage management and promotion explored in the Cayman Islands will provide some ideas for other nations in the Caribbean and elsewhere.

# References

*Caymanian Compass Weekender.* 2003. "Uncovering Fragments of Cayman's Rich Past", 21 March, A1, A12–13.

Cayman Islands. 1997. *Abandoned Wreck Law* (5 of 1966, 1997 revision).

———. 2001. *Cayman Islands 2000: Annual Report and Official Handbook.* George Town: Government Information Services.

Cayman Islands Maritime Heritage Trail Partners. 2003. "The Cayman Islands Maritime Heritage Trail, Grand Cayman" and "The Cayman Islands Maritime Heritage Trail, Sister Islands [Cayman Brac and Little Cayman]". Brochures. Cayman Islands Maritime Heritage Trail Partners.

Craton, Michael. 2003. *Founded upon the Seas: A History of the Cayman Islands and Their People.* Kingston: Ian Randle.

Ho, Bert. 2004. "An Archaeological Study of *Glamis*: The Role of a 19th Century Iron Barque". MA thesis, Florida State University.

International Council on Monuments and Sites (ICOMOS). 1996. International Charter on the Protection and Management of Underwater Cultural Heritage. Paris: ICOMOS. www.international.icomos.org/charters/underwater_e.htm (accessed 1 December 2010).

Leshikar, Margaret E. 1993. "The 1794 'Wreck of the Ten Sail': A Historical Study and Archaeological Survey". PhD diss., Texas A&M University.

Leshikar-Denton, Margaret E. 2002. "Problems and Progress in the Caribbean". In *International Handbook of Underwater Archaeology*, edited by C. Ruppe and J. Barstad, 279–98. New York: Kluwer Academic/Plenum Press.

———. 2004. "The Situation in the Caribbean". In *Patrimonio cultural subacuático / Underwater Cultural Heritage*, edited by V. Marín, 80–85. Havana: UNESCO.

———. 2005. "Tracing the Wreck of the Ten Sail". In *Beneath the Seven Seas*, edited by G.F. Bass, 206–9. London: Thames and Hudson.

———. 2006. "Foundations in Management of Maritime Cultural Heritage in the Cayman Islands". In *Underwater Cultural Heritage at Risk*, edited by R. Grenier, D. Nutley and I. Cochran, 23–25. Paris: International Council on Monuments and Sites. http://www.international.icomos.org/risk/2006/index.html (accessed 1 December 2010).

———. 2011. "Caribbean Maritime Archaeology". In *The Oxford Handbook of Maritime Archaeology*, edited by A. Catsambis, B. Ford and D.L. Hamilton, 629–59. New York: Oxford University Press.

———. (Forthcoming). *The Wreck of the Ten Sail.* Gainesville: University Press of Florida.

Leshikar-Denton, Margaret E., and Pilar Luna Erreguerena. 2008. *Underwater and Maritime Archaeology in Latin America and the Caribbean.* Walnut Creek, CA: Left Coast Press.

Leshikar-Denton, Margaret E., and Bert Ho. 2004. *The Probable* Glamis *Site: Archaeological Mapping and Potential for a Shipwreck Preserve, Grand Cayman, Cayman Islands* (with contributions by D. Scott-Ireton, A. Evans and W. Anderson), Shipwreck Preserve Series 1. George Town: Cayman Islands National Museum.

Leshikar-Denton, Margaret E., and Philip E. Pedley, eds. 1994. *Our Islands' Past.* Vol. 2, *The Wreck of the Ten Sail.* George Town: Cayman Islands National Archive and Cayman Free Press.

Leshikar-Denton, Margaret E., and Della A. Scott-Ireton. 2007. "A Maritime Heritage Trail and Shipwreck Preserves for the Cayman Islands". In *Out of the Blue: Public Interpretation of Maritime Cultural Resources,* edited by J.H. Jameson and D.A. Scott-Ireton, 64–84. New York: Springer.

———. 2008. "The Cayman Islands' Experience: Yesterday, Today and Tomorrow". In *Underwater and Maritime Archaeology in Latin America and the Caribbean,* edited by M.E. Leshikar-Denton and P. Luna Erreguerena, 221–44. Walnut Creek, CA: Left Coast Press.

Scott-Ireton, Della A. 2005. "Preserves, Parks, and Trails: Strategy and Response in Maritime Cultural Resource Management". PhD diss., Florida State University.

Smith, Roger C. 2000. *The Maritime Heritage of the Cayman Islands.* Gainesville: University Press of Florida.

UNESCO (United Nations Educational, Scientific and Cultural Organization). 2001. Convention on the Protection of the Underwater Cultural Heritage. Paris: UNESCO. http://portal.unesco.org/culture/en/ev.php-URL_ID=34114&URL_DO=DO_TOPIC&URL_SECTION=201.html (accessed 1 December 2010).

# 23.

# Regulating the Movement of Cultural Property Within and Out of Jamaica

ANDREA RICHARDS

*Considering the worldwide issues in the trading of cultural objects, and with some countries signing bilateral agreements for the return of particular objects, there remains a great deal to contend with in regard to monitoring the movement of particular objects. Some countries have already adopted the 1970 UNESCO Convention on Illicit Trafficking, but Jamaica has yet to deal fully with this problem. There is no control system related to this area of trading. The focus of this chapter is therefore to examine particular constraints with regard to the protection of Jamaica's movable cultural heritage in light of recent trends in the worldwide illegal trading of such objects. It also seeks ways to combat this problem using both current legislation and development of necessary programmes.*

## Introduction

Cultural property, as defined by UNESCO's 1970 Convention on Illicit Trafficking (Article 1), refers to "property which, on religious or secular grounds is specifically designated by each state as being of importance for archaeology, prehistory, literature, art or science". It has long been recognized that unregulated movement of such property results in serious losses to the cultural heritage of many countries and has contributed to an ongoing worldwide illicit trade in cultural objects (Brodie and Walker Tubb 2002). In response, the international community has established several major initiatives to control illicit trafficking of cultural property, including the 1970 UNESCO and 1995 UNIDROIT (International Institute for the Unification of Private Law) conventions and Interpol's cultural property programme. The International Council of Museums has also established guidelines for action and has implemented various programmes in this regard (for example, International Museums Day in 1996 and 1997 focused on illicit trafficking of cultural objects). The council has also published a code of ethics (UNESCO 2004) that governs museum practice and has signed agreements with the World Customs Organization and Interpol.

In Jamaica, no similar actions have been taken regarding regulating the movement and transfer of cultural objects or even the theft of these objects. This unregulated movement of cultural objects from Jamaica is seen to have begun as early as the period of European colonization, when there were no legal restrictions on conducting archaeological excavations. Objects of cultural significance were arbitrarily acquired and moved to outside Jamaica; an example is the three Taíno zemis discovered in 1792, which are presently housed in the British Museum (Saunders and Gray 1996; Lester 1958).

This chapter highlights the major areas of concern related to regulating the movement of Jamaica's material cultural heritage, largely through the implementation of a movable cultural property programme. These areas include

1.  defining what is significant and requires regulation;
2.  addressing inadequate or non-existent legislative controls over the movement of these objects;
3.  streamlining the ownership of objects in private collections and encouraging more productive dialogue with individuals and groups; and
4.  addressing the exportation of objects and illegal removal of objects from archaeological sites, museums and other such places.

## Ownership of Cultural Objects

As is the case in many countries worldwide, the situation in Jamaica highlights various categories of ownership. *Public ownership* refers to objects owned by the state and held in trust for the public. They are either housed as collections available to the public in national institutions – such as the Institute of Jamaica (IOJ), through its Museums Division or the National Gallery, or government-regulated historic sites such as Seville Heritage Park – or housed in more closed collections in government buildings such as Kings House and Gordon House. *Private ownership* includes heritage objects owned by individuals or groups that constitute part of the heritage of institutions – such as schools, churches and non-governmental historic structures – or a family's heritage.

## Rights to Ownership

Established by the Jamaica National Heritage Trust Act of 1985, the Jamaica National Heritage Trust (JNHT) is the only institution mandated to authorize archaeological investigations in Jamaica. This authorization is, however, limited to areas that have been declared national monuments or protected national heritage. In the nineteenth and earlier decades of the twentieth centuries, both amateur and professional archaeologists conducted excavations on public and private lands without any regulation (see, for example, Archaeological Society of Jamaica 1966–91; Cotter 1970; Duerden 1897). This has unfortunately resulted in objects of special significance, such as rare pre-Colombian and Spanish occupation period artefacts, becoming part of private collections while knowledge of their existence remains unknown to both the Jamaican public and heritage managers. During this earlier period, no legislation made random excavations illegal or even prohibited removal of these cultural objects to other countries. The issuing of permits governing excavations at national monuments or protected national heritage sites began only in 1992, with the system of archaeological research permits introduced by the JNHT (Dorrick Gray, Archaeology Division, JNHT, personal communication, 2005).

Towards the end of the twentieth century, archaeological research in Jamaica became more organized, with registration of permitted excavations. Despite this, the reports continue of illegal excavations and objects being sold to known collectors or private museums; a smaller number of persons have sought to sell objects to the IOJ or the JNHT. Collectors are often from the "educated and elite" classes and, having developed an interest in Jamaican archaeology and its relics, are searching for rare pieces for their growing collections. While it is known that important finds from archaeological excavations and other sources have left or are leaving the country, the extent of their movement across Jamaica's borders is unknown, as no monitoring system is currently in place. A particular challenge exists with monitoring the movement of certain categories of objects such as Taíno pottery, wooden sculptures and ethnographic pieces. These are often from private collections and, although they are significant to Jamaica's heritage, customs officers at our ports are not able to identify what is significant and what is not. Furthermore, identification of these objects by customs personnel is merely one part of the solution, as they need to know the legal framework they are operating within.

At present there are few restrictions on individuals travelling into or out of the island with archaeological or historical objects. Items emanating from permitted excavations must be given written permission by the JNHT, while restrictions imposed under Jamaica's Trade Board cover certain categories of objects[1] such as antique furniture and paintings. Objects from excavations not overseen by the JNHT are not regulated. For public institutions, the export and import of cultural objects are governed by policies formulated according to international museum practices. For example, from time to time public museums and institutions (National Gallery, Museums Division, Devon House) enter into loan agreements with local or overseas institutions with similar mandates whereby objects are sent to or received from them for exhibitions or research.

## Legislation Governing Jamaica's Cultural Heritage

Currently Jamaica has not ratified the UNESCO 1970 Convention, which would give guidance in the development of national legislation and procedures relating to implementation of this convention. At present the five pieces of legislation either concerned with or referring to cultural property are the JNHT, IOJ, Customs, Trade and Natural Resources Conservation Authority (NRCA) Acts. However, no single piece of legislation at present specifically refers to or governs terms and conditions for the movement of cultural property within or out of Jamaica. The JNHT Act (Section 17) provides guidelines for objects declared national monuments or protected national heritage, and these guidelines may in turn influence the Trade, Customs and NRCA Acts.

### Jamaica National Heritage Trust Act (1985)

Aspects of the JNHT Act refer to the protection of material cultural property:

4. (1) The functions of the Trust shall be –
   (a) to promote the preservation of national monuments and anything designated as protected national heritage for the benefit of the Island;
   . . .
   (d) to record precious objects or works of art to be preserved . . .
   (3) . . . do anything and enter into any transaction, which . . . is necessary to ensure the proper performance of its functions . . .

17. Every person who . . .
   (d) removes any national monument or protected national heritage to a place outside of Jamaica . . . shall be guilty of an offence . . .

19. (1) Where the Minister is satisfied in relation to any structure . . .
   (b) that it is in danger of destruction or removal or damage from neglect or injudicious treatment . . . (Jamaica 1985)

Provisions are made for the JNHT to initiate necessary actions for the protection and preservation of the country's material cultural heritage. However, very often the focus is solely on the built heritage environment. The JNHT is hampered in part because the Act that governs the organization contains no broad categories of what is considered protected heritage, such as Taíno or Spanish artefacts. If an object of national significance becomes known to an officer of the trust, legislative provisions do exist for the object (very often a historical structure) to be protected, whether it is on public or private property.

The JNHT Act at present does not address excavations on private lands, although some individuals conducting research have sought first to obtain permission from the landowner and then an archaeological permit from the JNHT. It is evident, then, that if an individual locates a significant object on his or her land or chooses to conduct excavations, and the land in question is not public land or designated protected national heritage, he or she is not required by law to notify the JNHT. However, if the JNHT wishes to conduct excavations on private lands which may be of interest, permission must be sought from the landowner.

## Institute of Jamaica Act (1978)

Section 4, paragraph 2, states that the purpose of the IOJ is, among other things, "to establish . . . collections and preservations of cultural, scientific and historical works, illustrations and artefacts" and "to provide . . . for the dissemination, encouragement and development of culture . . ." (Jamaica 1978). Critical to the IOJ fulfilling its mandate of establishing collections and preserving such objects is an awareness of the movement of these objects, particularly of significant pieces for which official records are non-existent.

## Jamaica Customs Act and Trade Act

The Customs Act (1941) and the Trade Act (1955) prohibit exportation of anything deemed illegal by any other piece of Jamaican legislation. The Trade Board, as the certifying authority for goods to be exported, maintains an Export Control List. An object designated protected national heritage or a national monument (JNHT Act, Section 17[d]) would therefore be legislatively protected from export under the Jamaica Customs[2] and Trade[3] Acts.

## Natural Resources Conservation Authority Act (1991)

Section 5, paragraph 1(b) of the NRCA Act states: "The Minister may, on the recommendation of the Authority after consultation with the JNHT, by order published in the Gazette, designate any area of land or water as a protected area in which may be preserved any object (whether animate or inanimate) . . . that is of aesthetic, educational, historical or scientific interest" (Jamaica 1991).

## Establishing Procedures and Guidelines for Implementing Change

The importance a nation places on its cultural heritage will be evident in a relevant and effective protective framework and its enforcement. International guidelines such as those of UNESCO and UNIDROIT are able to stimulate the environment necessary for amendment of existing legislation or implementation of new laws aligned with international standards and requirements. Ratification of these international conventions also encourages cooperation and dialogue among nations, leading to agreements which will assist in the return of cultural objects.

Revision of or amendments to the JNHT and IOJ Acts are necessary and critical to regulating this area. Any amendment should be complementary on the part of both pieces of legislation and should contain similar definitions of "significant movable national heritage" and statements as to how such objects will be treated. The JNHT Act should be revised to ensure that archaeological impact assessments are required for land-based development projects, particularly for large-scale engineering works. And where cultural objects are found, the Act should require that they be remitted to the relevant institution, in this case the Institute of Jamaica. At present, impact assessments are not mandatory, and very often artefacts are lost because of this.

With its mandate to establish collections, the IOJ Act should speak to regulation of all museums open to the public and the objects used to establish them. Guidelines should also be incorporated into the Act to address how private collections are to be treated. While object and collection loans made by the Institute of Jamaica are conducted according to approved international museum practices, these guidelines should be fully incorporated into the Act to ensure that they are acknowledged as the accepted procedure.

In tandem with the amendment of existing legislation, it may be necessary to implement new legislation which addresses all the stated areas of concern with regard to the import and export of cultural property. Appropriate movable cultural property protection legislation will set standards and guidelines for regulating the trading of cultural property and its import and export, and will establish incentives (funding for community projects, tax relief, etc.) to encourage individuals to donate (or sell) important objects they currently own to the relevant institutions. Such legislation would establish ownership of objects, the rights and obligations of those with custodial responsibilities (such as museums, antique dealers and art galleries), categories of significant movable national heritage, objects prohibited from export, and criteria for obtaining permits to export. It is also crucial that legislation addresses how stolen objects will be treated, as well as the treatment of objects in private collections and the assessment and loan of objects by and to the Institute of Jamaica.

In 2009 the JNHT commenced public consultations in all parishes in order to facilitate review of and amendments to the JNHT Act. New sections have been proposed relating to

- ensuring that all artefacts are registered with the JNHT;
- incorporating provisions to regulate the conservation, exportation and importation of cultural property;
- licensing all archaeological explorations, whether on a declared/designated site or otherwise;
- designating all artefacts as property of the Government of Jamaica; and
- giving the JNHT authority to require an impact assessment on any land (including those not designated) once there is reasonable likelihood that the land could contain heritage assets.

This review process is continuing, and incorporating these suggested amendments into the JNHT Act would signal a positive step in regulating the movement of cultural objects.

Although the United States ratified the 1970 UNESCO Convention in the 1980s, there continue to be problems with the illicit antiquities market. There has, however, been one positive result, which is the signing of treaties with individual countries to combat the problem of illicit trading. Unfortunately there exists a large group of private collectors and art and antiquities dealers in the United States who continue to use metal detectors on heritage sites, particularly government-owned sites. The Archaeological Resources Protection Act (1979) – and before that the Antiquities Act (1906) – and the 1990 Native American Graves Protection and Repatriation Act were therefore established for the protection of artefacts on both public and Native American lands (United States 1906, 1979, 1990).

Objects found on private lands belong to the property owner even when excavated with public funds, and are handled at the discretion of the owner. This is currently the situation in Jamaica. The object(s) may, however, be donated by the owner to a recognized conservation facility. A permit system and prohibitions are in effect for public lands on which materials are located and excavated with a permit. Under the law, such objects go to a state agency with collections management responsibility.

Although minimal progress has been made with regard to the monitoring of objects within the cultural heritage field in Jamaica, effective examples can be drawn from the National Environment and Planning Agency (NEPA) and from implementation of the Convention on the International Trade in Endangered Species of Wild Fauna and Flora (CITES)[4] in Jamaica. NEPA has addressed the problem through

- ratifying the requisite international convention – CITES – and ensuring that the relevant pieces of national legislation are in place (Endangered Species Act, Plants Regulation Act, etc.).
- enforcing legislation through wardens, the police and ports of entry/exit officials. Each region is overseen by an enforcement officer and further monitored by the Enforcement Branch at NEPA's central office. Significant fines have been established for trading in or harming endangered species.
- establishing guidelines to ensure change (for example, permits for field research and exportation of specimens).
- training personnel to ensure that the necessary information is disseminated, awareness is stimulated and monitoring and enforcement are facilitated (by customs officials and game wardens, for example).
- establishing an ongoing public awareness campaign informing members of the public regarding endangered species, why it is prohibited to trade in or export them and also the relevant fines for breaking the law. A CITES website and a Jamaican biodiversity database were also established.

This ongoing programme has contributed significantly to a reduction in the problems previously experienced. However, it was found that some individuals collecting plants would work outside their stated agreement, and it is not always possible to monitor collectors in the field. Also, at the ports of exit, customs officers may not always thoroughly check inventories.

## Conclusion

A programme similar to the implementation of CITES in Jamaica would significantly address the problems associated with the movement of cultural objects and should address the following issues:

- the establishment of criteria for what is to be regarded as significant cultural property;
- the role of agencies and institutions such as the Ministry of Culture, the IOJ, the JNHT, the Jamaica Trade Board, UNESCO, Jamaica Customs, the Jamaica Constabulary Force, the University of the West Indies and other national and international bodies in ascertaining the extent of the issue in Jamaica and beginning to seek solutions;

- recording and regulating the removal of movable cultural heritage within Jamaica through a national registry and sensitization programme and implementing the steps necessary to protect significant cultural objects from trade by utilizing export licences and legislation;
- expanding the export licensing list of Jamaica's Trade Board to include other categories of objects – as the organization that regulates export, a permit would be required from the Trade Board for any object which falls under the Board's Export Control List;
- conducting and promoting public initiatives to raise awareness (such as education of enforcement personnel) and establishing and making public the various categories of significant objects and educating the public regarding their significance;
- establishing a central registry for cultural objects in both public and private collections and keeping track of stolen objects; a positive relationship between private collectors and the national collections institution is critical to the success of this programme; and
- initiating contact on matters concerning the return or restitution of cultural objects from other countries and institutions. The ratification of international conventions in this area will offer assistance if both countries are party to the relevant convention.

Difficulties will be experienced in encouraging private collectors to come on board, especially in the current climate of mistrust and increases in the theft of cultural objects. A campaign based on "You have it; we want to record it" would prove useful while making it clear what exactly it is we want to record and why. This process will hopefully encourage private collectors and other individuals and institutions to positively contribute to safeguarding Jamaica's material cultural heritage.

## Notes

1. The current export licensing list includes scrap metal (including scrap batteries), scrap gold and silver, coffee and pimentos, live animals, endangered species, brown sugar, petroleum oils, ammunition (explosives and firearms), eggs ("N.O.P." [not otherwise provided for]), antique furniture, ores (minerals and metals, including bauxite, alumina and gypsum), paintings (antique), plasma (in any form), wood (lignum vitae and logwood only), motor vehicles, jewellery (excluding that made from earth metals) and shells (subject to the Convention of International Trade in Endangered Species and administered by NEPA). See http://www.tradeboard.gov.jm/tb/exp_lic/Lic_items.html (accessed 25 August 2011).

2. "If any person shall put on board any coasting aircraft or ship, or put off, or put into any vessel to be put on board any coasting aircraft or ship, or bring to any aerodrome, customs area, quay, wharf or any place whatever in the island for carriage . . . any goods prohibited to be carried coastwise, or any goods the carriage coastwise of which is restricted, contrary to such restriction, or attempt to perform or be knowingly concerned in the performance of any of the aforesaid acts, he shall incur a penalty . . ." (Jamaica Customs Act 1941, Section 180).

3. "Nothing in this Act shall make it lawful to import or export goods when such importation or exportation is unlawful under any other enactment . . ." (Jamaica Trade Act 1955, Section 19).

4. CITES was adopted by Jamaica on 23 April 1997 and entered into force on 22 July 1997. http://www.nepa.gov.jm/conventions/index.asp.

## References

Archaeological Society of Jamaica. 1966–91. *Archaeology Jamaica*.

Brodie, N., and K. Walker Tubb. 2002. *Illicit Antiquities: The Theft of Culture and the Extinction of Archaeology*. London: Routledge.

CITES (Convention on International Trade in Endangered Species of Wild Fauna and Flora). 1973. http://www.cites.org/eng/disc/what.shtml (accessed 2 July 2008).

Cotter, Charles S. 1970. "Sevilla la Nueva: The Story of an Excavation". *Jamaica Journal* 4, no. 2: 15–22.

Duerden, J.E. 1897. "Aboriginal Indian Remains in Jamaica". *Journal of the Institute of Jamaica* 2, no. 4: 1–51.

International Council of Museums (ICOM). 2004. "ICOM Measures Concerning the Fight against the Illicit Traffic of Cultural Property". Seoul: ICOM and UNESCO. http://icom.museum/measure.html (accessed 2 July 2008).

Jamaica. 1978. Institute of Jamaica Act. http://www.moj.gov.jm/laws/statutes/The%20 Institute%20of%20Jamaica%20Act.pdf (accessed 2 July 2008).

———. 1941. Jamaica Customs Act (amended 2003). http://www.moj.gov.jm/laws/ statutes/The%20Customs%20Act.pdf (accessed 2 July 2008).

———. 1955. Trade Act. http://www.moj.gov.jm/laws/statutes/Trade%20Act.pdf (accessed 2 July 2008).

———. 1985. Jamaica National Heritage Trust Act. http://www.jnht.com/act_ 1985.php (accessed 2 July 2008).

———. 1991. Natural Resources Conservation Authority Act. http://www.nepa .gov.jm/legal/nrca_act_Ipart1.htm (accessed 2 July 2008).

———. 2001. *Towards a National Strategy and Action Plan on Biodiversity in Jamaica*. Green Paper 3/01, Ministry of Land and Environment.

Jamaica National Heritage Trust. 2009. Jamaica National Heritage Trust Act: A Review. A Document to Guide the Discussions on the Proposed Amendments to the Act (November 2009)". http://www.jnht.com (accessed 30 August 2010).

———. N.d. "Guidelines for Application for Archaeological Permit". http://www. jnht.com/guidelines_ap.php (accessed 2 July 2008).

Lester, S. 1958. "Jamaican Treasures in London". *West India Review* 4: 30.

Saunders, Nicholas, and Dorrick Gray. 1996. "Zemis, Trees and Symbolic Land-scapes: Three Taíno Carvings from Jamaica". *Antiquity* 70: 270.

UNESCO. 1970. Convention on the Means of Prohibiting and Preventing the Illicit Import, Export and Transfer of Ownership of Cultural Property.

———. 2004. "Code Which Outlines the Principles Governing Museums and the Museum Profession, Acquisitions and Transfers of Ownership of Collections". UNESCO General Assembly, Seoul. http://icom.museum/measure.html (accessed 2 July 2008).

UNIDROIT (International Institute for the Unification of Private Law). 1995. Convention on Stolen and Illegally Exported Cultural Objects.

United States. 1906. Antiquities Act. http://www.cr.nps.gov/archeology/tools/laws/AntAct.htm (accessed 2 July 2008).

———. 1979. Archaeological Resources Protection Act. http://www.cr.nps.gov/local-law/fhpl_archrsrcsprot.pdf (accessed 2 July 2008).

———. 1990. Native American Graves Protection and Repatriation Act. http://www.cr.nps.gov/local-law/fhpl_nagpra.pdf (accessed 2 July 2008).

# 24.

# Imagined History

## Colonialism and Caribbean Museums

ALISSANDRA CUMMINS

*Colonialism, as a project of imperial control, infused the established canon for West-ern approaches to museum collection and display in order to rationalize the emerg-ing natural diversity of the New World and to prescribe a more "scientific" way of seeing objects or specimens from foreign territories. Public institutions established in the latter half of the nineteenth century were at the same time influenced by the philanthropic notion of emancipation through education, though only a vocational, Christian-oriented education was regarded as acceptable. Graeme Davison has posited that "The museum, together with the public library and the university, was one of the means by which colonial statesmen hoped to create an enlightened, vir-tuous and orderly society" (Davison 2002, 2). Such were the earliest origins of the museum in the West Indies, created as part of the "universal" story fostered by empire, a process which profoundly shaped regional institutions well into the first half of the twentieth century.*

## Introduction

As Bermuda's newly appointed governor (later governor of the West Indies) in 1839, Lieutenant Colonel (later Sir) William Reid arrived in the arena of recently emancipated Caribbean Atlantic territories. Given a mandate to improve the deplorable condition of the colony's agriculture, Reid found that the project required meticulous identification, categorization, promotion and transportation of colonial products to supply the needs of both the British Empire's population and its trading partners (Drayton 2000, 62). For this he needed institutional bases to collect, collate and compile the data required.

These he created with legislation to establish a public library and museum in the colony, predicated on the imperial government's intention to ensure control over a properly subjugated territory (Cummins 1994, 194; 1995, 2). Remembered as Bermuda's "good governor", Reid epitomized the "improving" British imperialism which emerged at the end of the eighteenth century, a new species of governance based on "the idea that colonization was an enterprise of amelioration" and a firm "faith in its capacity and right to increase the happiness of barbarians" (Drayton 2000, 92–93). With his primary motive being the "securing of the loyal support of the people . . . through their own self interest, by enabling them to prosper under British rule", Reid had by 1846 (when he was appointed governor of the Windward Islands) initiated promulgation of similar bills for the development of these institutions in Barbados, Grenada and St Lucia (Cummins 1994, 194).

## Museums in the Nineteenth Century

In a critical sense, West Indian collections and museums were created by commercial and political leaders as early promotional campaigns designed to attract new audiences within the colonies, as well as new clients and new investors from the metropole. Thus, like many similar institutions throughout the British colonial empire, early museums in the region primarily collected and displayed natural history and "curiosities". Donald Fleming has posited that the study of natural history "was a fundamental part of the quest for a national identity in societies where the cultural differentiation from Britain was insecure and the sense of the land correspondingly important for self-awareness" (quoted in Sheets-Pyenson 1988, 15). Many of the early institutions within the region were founded on the basis of natural history and geological collections amassed through systematic surveys. Duplicate specimen collections assembled variously for Kew Gardens and, to a lesser extent, the British Museum also provided impetus for the development or expansion of local collections.

Between the 1840s and 1870s, private arts and scientific societies rapidly proliferated throughout the region. By 1868 British Guiana's Royal Agricultural and Commercial Society had opened the doors of its newly constructed "permanent home of science, art and industry" (Munro 2004), which later became the Guyana National Museum (Cummins 1994, 196–97). The General Agricultural Society in Jamaica was one of the founding agencies of the Royal Society of Arts and Agriculture in 1864 (DuQuesnay 1965). In 1873 its museum collections were handed over to the government together with the Sawkins and Brown geological collection; together these became in 1879 the nucleus of the Institute of Jamaica (Cummins 1994, 197). These entities were

**Figure 24.1** The Jamaica Exhibition of 1891 (photo courtesy Institute of Jamaica)

all part of a collecting economy with extensive links to mother institutions in Britain (and sister institutions in the United States and elsewhere) that existed within a system of international trade in objects and specimens.

Colonial and international exhibitions initiated in Europe during the nineteenth century, which displayed the resources and opportunities available in the different nations or colonies, also gave impetus to the development of various museums and art galleries. Their popularity with huge audiences on the Continent drove public demand for exhibitions in North America and the Caribbean as well, the 1891 Jamaica Exhibition, opened by the Prince of Wales, being a prime example of the power and significance of these events (see figure 24.1). Martin Prösler has observed that "the world-wide diffusion of museums was tied in with European colonialism and imperialism. Their expansion, then, occurred in close connection with those political factors in globalization which have provided the contemporary *world order* with its basic structure" (1996, 22).

Territorial governments were inspired to either duplicate or buy many of the exhibits, thus establishing the technological and industrial collections which eventually founded (or found their way into) colonial museums by the end of the century. This resulted in the ongoing export and display (both in the colonies and in the metropole) of objects illustrating the natural history and indigenous peoples of these territories, and that led to a change in the role of museums. The Trinidad Society of Arts and Sciences, established in 1870, joined with the Trinidad Field Naturalists Club in spearheading the creation in 1892 of the Royal Victoria Institute (later the National Museum and Gallery of Trinidad and Tobago; see figure 24.2), which was a vocational training institute and museum modelled along the lines of the Victoria and Albert Museum (Cummins 1994, 198).

**Figure 24.2** The Royal Victoria Institute, later the National Museum and Gallery of Trinidad and Tobago (photo courtesy Alma Jordan Library, University of the West Indies, St Augustine)

P.T. Barnum's importation of "live" aboriginal people from Dominica and St Vincent fuelled a frenzy of popular interest in West Indian archaeology and ethnology, and proved a successful investment for the shrewd showman. Both Amerindian culture and people were appropriated by non-indigenous populations for "scientific" as well as entertainment purposes. The movement of objects (and bodies) from these exotic cultures reinforced the specific relationship between master and subaltern histories and cultures. These global expositions (and the museums which emanated from them) were more often seen as places of "curiosity"– sites of peculiarity and promotion. Amerindian artefacts were being collected mainly for their novelty value, and they served to demonstrate the complete "inferiority" of indigenous cultures in comparison to European civilization. Amerindians were treated as "living fossils" and displayed in the nineteenth-century manner of taxonomic classification identically to other flora and fauna. Their artefacts were relegated to the ranks of stuffed birds, animals and other curiosities, divorced from the indigenous people who had created them. These attitudes were in evidence and influenced museum development throughout the nineteenth and well into the twentieth centuries, perpetuating the social mores and inequities of the period.

Consequently, Caribbean museums were predominantly museums of natural history and science. They were not history museums, and few had significant collections designed to relate to the human history of their respective countries. Of course, in some of the museums there did exist items which would now be considered historical material, such as tools and farming implements, yet these were in no sense collected with the aim of representing the human development of the country. As Tony Bennett indicates, when compared to European national pasts, the colony "could not lay claim to a past which might be represented on the same footing as the pasts of other nations within the militarised modes of national commemoration which were dominant at the time" (1988, 6). In this sense the colony did not have a "nation" on which to base its historical collections.

By the end of the nineteenth century, however, museums were seen as institutions of power and instruments of education, enlightenment and social salvation. They took their place alongside libraries, churches and schools as a means of providing sound intellectual and moral culture to the working classes. At the same time, these museums were seen as a vital part of the colonial culture, as they could order and make "comprehensible the newness of the 'natural world'" (Healy 1997, 85).[1] The early museums were thus transformed primarily for enlightening the general public about the wonders of the nineteenth-century industrial world. They also served to reaffirm the colonies' place within British and imperial progress and history.

None of these institutions held a significant historical collection representing the human development of its respective community or country. The indigenous population was generally regarded as outside civilized time and history, while pirate, plebeian or planter ancestors were regarded as not worthy of preservation or commemoration, and certainly not the appropriate foundation upon which to build a national identity.[2] The white population still generally saw themselves as being British or European and were largely content to have their history rooted there. The black majority was not merely marginalized within the scope of museum interpretation; it quite simply did not exist in any formal consideration of colonial history. West Indian museums thus developed in the colonial manner, whereby they celebrated the dominance of European culture and society – organized primarily around the exploits of monarchs, great statesmen and military heroes – over "primitive" indigenous populations. This served to confirm the West Indies' place as part of the Empire, reinforcing the sense of imperial identity, and also reaffirmed the colonies as part of the continuum of Europe's white history.

## The Twentieth Century

While museums of natural history, science and art continued to grow and flourish up to the outbreak of the First World War, it was the experience of that war which provided the first substantive basis upon which West Indians (both white and, to a lesser extent, black) could envisage a national ideal – one which relied on a "real" lived history. From these catalytic events, their own heroes might be fashioned and their history shaped, similar to those histories upon which the nations of Europe had been built. Nevertheless, the West Indian museum remained little changed in the decades which followed.

In the early 1930s the Carnegie Corporation of New York funded a number of surveys of museums and art galleries in Commonwealth countries, including the Caribbean. Conducted by the Museums Association of the United Kingdom, the Empire Survey report and directories highlighted the fact that the absence of historical collections was "one of the most notable gaps in the whole of the existing museum collections". More important, the commissioners indicated that "the islands of the British Empire present one of the most difficult problems in the realm of cultural services, and in the following reports the recommendations that are made are put forward with the hope that in at least one area efforts will be made to evolve the ideal museum and art gallery policy for an island colony" (Miers and Markham 1933, 8). The survey's recommendations had a major impact on the professional development of the region's museums. The Carnegie Corporation provided further funding to implement recommendations for recruitment and training of curators, provision of showcases and, in some instances, model buildings meant to fulfil the educational mission of modern-day museums.

After the Second World War, public interest in heritage and the past began to escalate globally. Impetus was provided by many of the developments indicative of a postcolonial society. These included a steady increase in emigration following the war and the gradual assertion of feminist and labour histories, all illustrative of a widening historical consciousness and a search for alternative histories. The beginnings of the national trust movement, towards the end of the 1950s, also provided new impetus for the development of historic sites and open-air "living history" museums.[3] These kinds of museums marked a new direction in the interpretation of history. Like the traditional museum, however, the living history museums were also generally monocultural, usually concentrating on European material culture and history from the colonial period, with little acknowledgement of indigenous, maroon or enslaved populations.

## Conclusions

Museums in the Caribbean region developed originally as colonial institutions that illustrated the progress of Western civilization and emphasized the dominant colonial power. This invariably meant either neglecting the presence and contributions of the indigenous, enslaved, indentured and migrant communities or relegating them to a place in the "natural history" of the country. At the same time, the histories of the white populations since European settlement were not regarded as being suitable material to be collected or presented. Consequently, the focus of the region's museums was largely on natural history, science and technology. By disregarding the value and meaning of indigenous and migrant cultures, they helped support the image that to be a West Indian was to be white and British.

After the Second World War, various factors combined both to challenge these common interpretations of *nation* and to position history in an increasingly important role in society, both culturally and politically. There was also a growing awareness of the need to acknowledge the presence of different groups within society and within different interpretations of society. Such factors were also indicative of the increasingly problematic nature of national identity and a growing preoccupation with defining the nation.

## Notes

1. Here the author is speaking of the experience of Australia, but these observations are equally applicable to the trajectory of West Indian museum development.
2. The colonies did, however, strive to show the progress they had made, particularly through the exhibitions, which in some ways can be seen as being typical of nationalism.
3. A. Acworth's report on the historic buildings of the region, published in 1951, provided impetus for the heritage preservation movement.

## References

Bennett, T. 1988. "Out of Which Past? Critical Reflections on Australian Museum and Heritage Policy". Cultural Policy Studies Occasional Paper no. 3. Brisbane: Institute for Cultural Policy Studies, Griffith University.

Cummins, Alissandra. 1994. "The 'Caribbeanization' of the West Indies: The Museum's Role in the Development of National Identity". In *Museums and the Making of "Ourselves": The Role of Objects in National Identity*, edited by Flora Kaplan. London: Leicester University Press.

———. 1995. "Confronting Colonialism: The First 60 Years at the BMHS". In *Journal of the Barbados Museum and Historical Society* 42.

Davison, Graeme. 2002. "Museums and National Identity". Paper presented at Museums Australia National Conference, Adelaide.

Drayton, Richard. 2000. *Nature's Government: Science, Imperial Britain, and the "Improvement" of the World*. New Haven: Yale University Press.

DuQuesnay, Frederick J. 1965. "Museums of Jamaica". Jamaican Family Search Genealogy Research Library. http://jamaicanfamilysearch.com/Samples/fred01 .htm.

Healy, C. 1997. *From the Ruins of Colonialism: History as Social Memory*. Melbourne, Australia: Brown Prior Anderson.

Miers, Henry A., and Sydney F. Markham, comps. 1933. Introduction to *Reports on the Museums of Ceylon, British Malaya, the West Indies, etc. to the Carnegie Corporation of New York*. London: Museums Association.

Munro, Arlene. 2004. "A Short History of the National Museum". *Stabroek News*, 26 February.

Prösler, Martin. 1996. "Museums and Globalisation". In *Theorizing Museums: Representing Identity and Diversity in a Changing World*, edited by Sharon Macdonald and Gordon Fyfe, 21–44. Oxford: Blackwell and Sociological Review.

Sheets-Pyenson, Susan. 1988. *Cathedrals of Science: The Development of Colonial Natural History Museums during the Late Nineteenth Century*. Kingston and Montreal: McGill-Queen's University Press.

# 25.

# Identity Forged

## The Museum's Role in the Creation of Identity in the English-Speaking Caribbean

KEVIN FARMER AND ALISSANDRA CUMMINS

*The years after independence have seen the development of national "identity" as part of the fabric of developing nation-states in the Caribbean. Nation building has brought with it development at the economic and social level and prompted calls for review as well as an assertion of an identity separate from that established during the colonial era. The creation of an independent national identity is fraught with contestation over who it purports to represent. This chapter examines that contested identity through the creation of new museums in the region and their role in identity creation. A comparative critique of established institutions in the region, specifically Barbados, will take into account institutions created during the colonial and independence eras and allow for a critical examination of institutional input into the development of national identity in the region. This comparative study will also signal the path ahead.*

## Introduction

The independence experiment in the English-speaking Caribbean emerged fully during the 1960s, continued evolving into the 1980s and has apparently reached a plateau as we enter the second decade of the twenty-first century. This experiment has resulted in the creation of independent multi-party democratic states that depend mostly on tourism, and to a lesser extent agriculture and its by-products, for their livelihood. The exception to this is the twin republic of Trinidad and Tobago, whose GNP is secured mostly by the oil industry and its derivatives. The demography of the region primarily comprises persons of African, European and Asian descent, with some countries

– notably Dominica, St Vincent, Belize and Guyana – nurturing pockets of descendants of the indigenous people of the region. Culturally diverse, the region shares a common pre- and post-colonization history, though nuanced by the peculiar local histories and geographies of the individual countries.

Once they had settled down to governing their countries, the emerging anglophone Caribbean nation-states turned their attention (reluctantly in some cases) to the creation of a national identity that went beyond designing a flag, singing a national anthem and reciting a national pledge. The role of identity creation became the core mandate of cultural institutions, which in many instances were museums. Whilst the pre-independence museum had been the offspring of elitist societies, the post-independence institution was expected to respond to popular calls to provide a reflection of the nation in a cultural form. Governments of the day, by default, assumed that museums would reflect all the actors and agencies involved in the narration of national histories – a mission which, though embraced by reformists, was and still is (to a certain extent) resisted by conservatives. These differing approaches emerge in the case studies which follow.

## Popularizing History and Culture

The earliest form of popular mass museum in the region is seen in the creation of the People's Museum of Craft and Technology (originally called the Folk Museum of Jamaica) in 1961, located in the old capital of Spanish Town, San Jago de la Vega. Its mandate and purpose were to celebrate the creativity and industry of the now "emancipated" people as they fashioned a new life for themselves in towns and rural villages across Jamaica. The exhibition offered visitors a truly nostalgic trip down memory lane, back to "ole time Jamaica" to reminisce and enjoy. In reading its mandate, one is perhaps confronted by its strident call "to truly appreciate our foreparents' triumph over enormous odds to secure our future in modern Jamaica". Such naked nationalism was the mantra of museums created during the post-independence phase. Another, later incarnation of this approach was the St Lucian Folk Research Centre. Though not a museum per se (plans for a museum are ongoing), the Centre is the de facto folk museum of the island; it was created in 1973 to combat the "anglicization" of St Lucia. The stated objectives of the Centre are as follows: "The Folk Research Centre (FRC) is a non-governmental organization established in 1973 to preserve and promote the cultural heritage of St. Lucia and registered as a non-profit company in 1985. FRC has sought to promote the role of folk arts as a vehicle for change and to illustrate the development potential of cultural heritage, particularly in the field of education and in economic development."

The Folk Research Centre, like the Museum of Craft and Technology in Jamaica, used forceful language in describing its mission and mandate to champion aspects of the island's traditional culture. Some forty years after the beginning of the independence movement, such fervent nationalism seems almost a call to arms for the people to defend themselves against unchecked colonialism.

At a national level, these museums sought to distil a national identity that was accessible to all, and increasingly so to the visitor as economic development shifted to tourism. This was juxtaposed against a strong academic stance that the past must be engaged in order for a new type of nationalism to strive. Social partnerships developed whereby the professional curator, the antiquarian, both amateur and professional historians and others interested in heritage came together to forge or formulate policy for the operation of museums in the region. The museum was therefore evolving from an elitist institution to one which, in addressing populist concerns about representing the "common man", was now the preserve of an emergent elite middle class.

## The Post-independence Landscape

However, have these museums fulfilled their mandate? To answer this question, one must have an understanding of the forces that shaped this postcolonial ideology. The post-independence Caribbean, both ideologically and physically, was determined to discard and distance itself from the colonial past, in some cases going to extremes in dismantling the vestiges of empire, for example, through neglect (and ultimate destruction) of colonial-style buildings. A major catalyst for this ideological shift lay with the developing historiography of the region, disseminated by a new cadre of professionally trained historians returning from the metropole to teach at the newly developed and growing University College of the West Indies (now the University of the West Indies). These Caribbean historians thus had a stage from which they could confront the historiography of the region.

This new cohort of historians – Elsa Goveia, Phillip Sherlock, Roy Augier and, later, Bridget Brereton, Woodville Marshall, Keith O. Laurence, Hilary Beckles and Verene Shepherd – sought to interpret the history of the region from a postcolonial, gendered perspective and not that of empire. It was a reversal of the "great man" paradigm of history that had so engrained the writings and shaded the historiography to date. Their history "from the bottom" took on board the then prevailing ideology of the Annales School led by Durkheim, Bloch, Braudel and Febvre, intertwined with the ideology of Marx and Lenin, in seeking to deconstruct the history of the region. In so doing, Caribbean historians laid the foundation for a new historiography to emerge which focused on retrieval of the stories/voices of the majority of the population. Their research framed the paradigm under which historical research was carried out in the region. The fruits of such research began to inform, infiltrate and prescribe what and how museums presented and interpreted the history of the society they represented.

This emergent nationalism has also seen the co-option of colonial institutions in development of the newly independent nation-state, at the same time as the creation of new institutions to meet the challenges of development. That which was British became West Indian and eventually Caribbean, with some modification. One may well ask, how far removed from the colonial mentality are such institutions today? In asking this question, we need to recall the writings of Frantz Fanon (1967) in *Black Skins, White Masks* in analysing the colonial mindset, a mindset which perhaps has endured into the postcolonial era.

Alissandra Cummins (1994) notes that colonization was a process of "deculturalization", and such a process was reflected in the development of museums in the region. Born out of the Victorian desire to explain the world through science and to exhibit its progress, museums in the Caribbean became showcases of technological progress juxtaposed against all that was primitive. This dichotomy meant that invariably what was presented indicated that all that was European was good and all that was not (i.e., Amerindian, African and Asian) was bad. Created by the colonial elite, these often privately funded institutions were governed by a discriminatory mindset which continued to exist into the postcolonial era.

Post-independence West Indian governments, in their developmental thrust, invariably placed culture on the backburner. It was a feature that many governments, until at least the late 1990s, did not see as part of their countries' development, except for Carnival festivals, which were reintroduced as a means by which tourists could be enticed to the islands. Nationalism symbolically manifested itself politically with the election of majority non-white governments. Nationally this meant that the formerly disenfranchised black populace eventually became masters of their fate. In the experiment of nationalism in the Caribbean, the creation of this image of the region as comprising primarily descendants of Africa has seen the marginalization of certain other ethnic groups. Sometimes this marginalization has evolved into factionalized political parties, as witnessed in Trinidad and Tobago and Guyana following independence. Independence therefore witnessed the creation of a pro-black nation-state whose institutions and organs were organized to facilitate that shift in the politics of government business. The response has been an increasing intensity of ethnically oriented cultural activity, not least in the creation in 2006 of the Indian Caribbean Museum in Trinidad and Tobago.

## De-colonizing the Institution

Existing museums in the region were co-opted by postcolonial governments to become agents of identity creation. This saw existing institutions, such as the Barbados Museum and Historical Society (BMHS), change focus through government intervention to facilitate creation of a new national identity. The BMHS was started in 1933 out of the concerns of a select few who wished for a museum to showcase Barbadian history and to educate Barbadians about the rest of the world. Despite its twentieth-century origins, the Museum over the first five decades of its existence exhibited natural history, pre-Columbian archaeology, colonial art and ethnography of the island, as was typical for colonial institutions. The transition of that proto-colonial institution which marginalized the majority to a modern museum reflective of the entire society warrants our attention. Principally, the museum is a private institution that was created to "collect, preserve and publish matter relating to the history and the antiquities of Barbados, and to gather and preserve appropriate articles for collection" (BMHS 1934, 150).

The first fifty years of the Barbados Museum and Historical Society were concerned with great men, prehistory and industry, with little or no mention of the social history of the majority of persons who made up the community. This was to change with the advent of a museum development committee in the 1980s. This government-appointed committee, under the chairmanship of Professor Woodville Marshall, set out to critique the museum's development in terms of its representation of Barbadians and Barbados history. The committee's recommendations, contained in a museum development plan, advocated, among many things, the hiring and training of local professional staff, a focus on collections, and programmes that reflected the society to be included in the museum's interpretation and programming (Cummins 1994).

The 1980s saw the deliberate transformation of the BMHS into a de facto national museum, a hybrid of both colonial and postcolonial paradigms as Barbados refocused its national identity some sixteen years after independence. The government's vision was that the museum needed to reflect a developing nation-state which had realized the potential inherent in embracing and defining its culture. During this period, the Government of Barbados also formed the National Cultural Foundation to explore, develop and sustain the tangible and intangible aspects of Barbadian culture. This cultural awakening in the island was the catalyst for development of the Barbados Museum and Historical Society. Since then the museum has installed an African gallery, after seventeen years of having a temporary exhibit on Africa kept open by public demand. Such a departure from pre-colonial interpretation was even then met with concern and questioned in 2004 by some members of the

Society. The BMHS exemplifies the coming of age of a colonial museum within the postcolonial setting, and it has since evolved to meet the needs of its society. The Museum continues to meet the challenges of those who would contest its development by holding on to a "glorious past".

## Caribbean Nationalism

Caribbean nationalism, as constructed in the post-independence era, sought to combat the issue of the colonial self as inferior, replacing it with a notion of self as superior and therefore capable of running one's own country. However, there was also a need to face the reality of how to combat five hundred years of colonization practised and legitimized by the judicial, political and social machinery of the day. The Caribbean, then and now, can be framed within Lamming's concept of "Caliban bettering Prospero" (1960). This thesis posits that an emergent Caribbean consciousness, when awakened and rooted in a strong sense of self, is able to overthrow the weight of the colonial stereotype of ineptitude. The emergent Caribbean nation is still grappling with this concept of self-actualization and development of identity, and has turned to its museums to be agents of change. The question is, can they fulfil this role of redefining the national psyche?

The development of Caribbean museums has gone through several phases nuanced by temporal and spatial factors, and as such the region's museums cannot be simply labelled as pre- and postcolonial institutions. One such phase of museum development witnessed the colonial museum, formed in the nineteenth and early twentieth centuries, evolving into a postcolonial institution. This museum has been able to redress its imbalances internally without resorting to name change or being shuttered, and has readjusted to reflect the new society in which it now functions – the emerging independent nation-state. Concomitant with this is the development of site- or theme-specific museums, situated at restored plantation houses or historic, industrial or military sites, which focus on attracting the tourist, such as Sunbury Plantation in Barbados; Nelson's Dockyard, Antigua; the Jewish Nidhe Israel Museum, Bridgetown; and the Chaguaramas Military History and Aviation Museum in Trinidad and Tobago.

Similarly, the growth of private museums founded on the collecting focus of a single person – for example, the prehistoric archaeology museum founded by the late Dr Earl Kirby in St Vincent, sadly now in a state of disrepair, and the Dr Cecil Cyrus Museum of Caribbean medical specimens and equipment, set up next door – also merits our attention as a catalyst for developing small, specialized museums. At the same time, museum development in the region has witnessed the creation of "subaltern" museum spaces, constructed by persons or groups that see themselves as marginalized in society and seek to redress this imbalance through museum creation. Personal or community collections have found fertile ground, inspiring the emergence of "culture houses" in Belize, "negga houses" in Antigua and Barbuda and Amerindian museums in Dominica, Guyana, Belize and Trinidad.

## The Mirror Image

Within such an environment, the growth of national art galleries in the region must also be mentioned, as they signal a marked departure from the prints and paintings galleries to be found in the colonial museum. The latter adopted the European perspective of highlighting portraits of "great men" and the vast open landscapes they had conquered, while viewing the colonial person as the "other". Caribbean national art galleries, all formed in the postcolonial era, sought to confront that image of otherness in the work of regional and extra-regional artists. These artists interrogated contemporary issues of identity and forced both viewers and the general society to confront these issues through the "imaging of self by self". Such acquisitions and their exhibition in gallery spaces represented a conscious institutional approach to self-contemplation aimed at examining the aspirations of postcolonial society.

The adoption of this "mirror image" mentality by such institutions represents perhaps some of the more democratic examples of the postcolonial society's being critical of its own development. As such, the national art gallery joins that sphere of national, subaltern and personal institutions developed in the postcolonial era that have broken the tradition of colonial museums' image of the colonial person as "other", exotic and a creation of empire to be exploited for development of the metropole. The National Galleries of Jamaica and Guyana, and the later National Art Gallery of the Bahamas, are key exemplars of this project.

## Museums in the Postcolonial Era

How then does a museum established in the colonial period change to reflect the new postcolonial outlook? How does the Caribbean museum created in the postcolonial era confront the colonial past in order to chart a new direction and create a sense of identity in the community in which it is established? Such complex negotiations of space, time and context must be handled carefully, and in so doing ensure that there is no romanticizing of the past or of the contemporary, but instead a truthful discourse on the context that has formed these states.

These institutions were confronted with similar issues of interpretation, relevance to the communities they served and the "democracy" inherent in the creation of exhibits. Cannizzo (1987) states that museums are "negotiated realities" that reflect the fears and aspirations of those who create them. As elsewhere, museums in the Caribbean rely on their collections to frame the interpretation of history that the viewer will experience. Much of their new direction, however, is designed to lessen reliance on the tangible (where the preserved heritage tends to be largely colonial in origin and focus) and balance this with intangible memories and historical experiences based on family or community knowledge.

As such, the formulation of Caribbean museums as repositories and showcases of the region's economic and cultural diversity reflects the Enlightenment world view, advanced by the founders of colonial museums and expanded upon by the founders of the postcolonial museum. It must be noted that Amerindian peoples are still to a certain extent contemporarily viewed as the "other", and as such are still captives of a colonial mindset within which they are perceived as "primitive", a perception reinforced in exhibitions which continue to represent indigenous peoples as such. Such an attitude is even more apparent where indigenous peoples still live in the constructed nation-state, as in Guyana. Attempts at community museums seem to reflect a metaphorical "slumming" by the national museum, an imposition from above as opposed to a movement from below.

But all is not lost. The legacy of Garvey's pan-African movement is reflected in national governments' joint creation of the Order of National Heroes. This in turn has resulted in the establishment of "national heroes" monuments or galleries, for example, Barbados's Museum of Parliament and National Heroes Gallery. Essentially they are designed to commemorate the lives of persons chosen to be "heroes" for the national audience. Similarly, the Institute of Jamaica recently created a museum at Liberty Hall in honour of Marcus Garvey during his centenary anniversary. The privately owned Bob Marley Museum in Jamaica, while responding to a more opportunistic imperative, also broadens the base through memory and popular culture in the region.

## Discussion and Conclusion

Caribbean museums are not yet fully democratic, and it is their willingness to combat this lack of democracy and dependency on limited funding that will determine how these museums formulate and develop content, programmes and policies. Museums in the region need to become more reflexive if they are to be dynamic and relevant in the twenty-first century. This is particularly important in the face of developing globalization and a nascent neo-colonial mentality. The museum must be more than the sum of its collections. Regional museums must construct a hybrid between the traditional "tangible" orientation of the European model and the intangible modalities of African and Asian museums. They must embrace the oral tradition of storytelling and "ole talk" and maximize the masquerade festivals and their potential to engage peripheral communities. Most important, they must engage the community.

The development paradigm for museums in the contemporary Caribbean must be more inclusive or else they will be found wanting, as the colonial museum was on the eve of independence. They must become centres of discourse, willing and able to voice the concerns, fears and aspirations of the multiple voices of the people they represent, without bias or favour. They must reflect the development of the societies they represent and prepare themselves to question – and in some cases help resolve – societal problems through their programmes and heritage interpretation. Both the tangible and intangible components of the society must find equal space within the museum as it strives to give voice to varying constituents in the new century. The museum must not see itself as the singular authority in construction of national identity but must instead allow itself to be a conduit through which the often multiple voices of the society are heard. The curator is not gate-keeper but custodian by popular decree, not master but servant. The society should be encouraged to shape its national identity within the "negotiated reality" of the national museum.

## References

Barbados Museum and Historical Society (BMHS). 1934. *Journal of the Barbados Museum and Historical Society* 3: 150.

Cannizzo, Jeanne. 1987. "How Sweet It Is: Cultural Politics in Barbados". *Muse* 4 (Winter): 22–27.

Cummins, Alissandra. 1994. "The 'Caribbeanization' of the West Indies: The Museum's Role in the Development of National Identity". In *Museums and the Making of "Ourselves": The Role of Objects in National Identiy,* edited by Flora E.S. Kaplan. Leicester: Leicester University Press.

Fanon, Frantz. 1967. *Black Skin, White Masks.* New York: Grove.

Gathercole, P., ed. 1994. *The Politics of the Past.* London: Routledge.

Karp, I., ed. 1994. *Exhibiting Cultures.* Washington, DC: Smithsonian Institution Press.

Lamming, George. 1960. *The Pleasures of Exile.* London: Michael Joseph.

Walsh, Kevin. 1992. *The Representation of the Past.* London: Routledge.

# Glossary of Terms

## Abbreviations

| | |
|---|---|
| ACHEA | Association of Caribbean Higher Education Administrators |
| ACURIL | Association of Caribbean University and Research Institution Libraries |
| CARINDEX | Caribbean Index |
| CCFA | Centre for Creative and Festival Arts, University of the West Indies |
| NALIS | National Library and Information Systems Authority of Trinidad and Tobago |
| OPReP | Oral and Pictorial Records Project, Alma Jordan Library, University of the West Indies, St Augustine |
| UWI | University of the West Indies |

**Advocacy**. The act of pleading for, supporting or recommending.

**Aroid**. A perennial herb in the arum family, which includes anthurium, dieffenbachia and philodendron, that has tiny flowers fused to form a spike-like spadix that is subtended by a spathe.

**Arrivants**. Individuals or groups who arrived in the Caribbean as a result of either forced or voluntary migration or who made landfall by accident.

**Assistive technologies**. Technologies used by people with disabilities which enable them to perform key functions they would otherwise be unable to perform.

**Bract**. A leaf from the axil of which (where it joins the stem) a flower or floral axis arises.

**Bromeliad**. A member of the Bromeliaceae family, which has almost 2,600 species, among them pineapple (*Ananas comosus*) and Spanish moss (*Tillandsia usneoides*). All but one species is native to the tropics of the New World and to the West Indies. Many bromeliads are short-stemmed epiphytes and bear flowers in a long spike, with coloured bracts below or along the spike. See also *Epiphyte*.

**Calcium carbide**. A chemical compound ($CaC_2$) used primarily in the production of acetylene when added to water, and also as an explosive.

**Calycophyll**. A sepal which expands to resemble a petal, as in some species of the Rubiaceae family.

**Communal tenure**. A land ownership system in which the land rights are held indivisibly by a group as opposed to being held by an individual.

**Creole**. Originally used to refer to some post-Columbian peoples of the Americas, a word often used to refer to certain languages of the Caribbean and elsewhere. The word *creole* (lowercase) has come to be used to describe a number of vastly different languages across the globe whose types and features may or may not be similar and whose only point in common may be their relatively recent social history. The creole language varieties of the Caribbean, regardless of their vocabulary origins, share certain grammatical features, especially in the tense-mood-aspect verbal system. Caribbean creole languages are the combined and complex result of history, language change, language development (including preservation and innovation), and second-language acquisition. They are commonly thought to be highly and exceptionally divergent from the western European languages with which they share much vocabulary, and from the West African languages involved in the Caribbean contact situation. Creole (uppercase) is a proper name for specific languages such as Kriol (Belize), Creolese (Guyana), Créole/Kwéyòl (French Caribbean), Kreyòl (Haiti), and others. Elsewhere in the Caribbean, creole languages have names such as Dialect and Patois/Patwa. More and more Caribbean creole languages – traditionally oral media used alongside official standardized languages – have been used in writing and are undergoing various levels of codification and standardization. Their speakers are developing a wide range of literacy and literary materials. See also *Dialect; Standard language form.*

**Cultural identity**. Defined operationally in Culturometrics as a context-specific display of values.

**Cultural Index (CI)**. A Culturometric measure of cultural identity components such as the trans-generational components of cultural identity that define one's personal cultural heritage.

**Culturally relevant pedagogy.** An approach to teaching in which students' cultural knowledge and prior experiences are used to facilitate learning.

**Cultural resource/heritage management.** The management and preservation of cultural resources such as landscapes, archaeological sites, historical records, historic buildings, industrial heritage and artefacts.

**Culturometrics.** The measurement of cultural identity. Culturometrics gives a postmodernist and radical-constructivist definition of an individual's cultural heritage as a continued personal re-construction of trans-generational ethnic identity components. In multicultural societies this is achieved via a sociocultural bricolage. Culturometrics views the cultural heritage of a group as a socially negotiated aggregation of individuals' cultural heritages. These re-constructions and negotiations produce a dynamic cultural heritage that exhibits both developmental and historical change.

**Deciduous tree.** A tree which sheds its leaves during a prolonged period of very cold or dry weather, during which it becomes dormant.

**Defaunation.** The process of removal of species caused by the effect of human activities, including pollution, habitat alteration and reduction in food or potential mates.

**Dialect.** A variety or subset of a language that usually differs from other varieties at the levels of accent (phonology) and vocabulary (lexicon), with relatively minor differences at the level of grammar (morphosyntax). All languages, including creole languages, comprise dialects which may be sociolinguistically defined on regional, ethnic, gender and socioeconomic bases. Socially based dialects are also referred to as sociolects or social dialects. Speakers of different dialects of the same language usually understand each other, though sometimes they need time and effort to do so (depending on how different the dialects and accents are from each other, and depending on language attitudes, among other factors). In the Caribbean, Dialect (uppercase) is the proper name given to many English-lexicon creoles by their speakers (except for Jamaica, where English Creole is called Patwa). The term *dialect* (lowercase) is usually reserved for non-standard varieties of a language that encompass societal and regional differences in pronunciation, grammar and vocabulary. The term, whether capitalized or not, is often used disparagingly, not only in the officially English ("anglophone") Caribbean but throughout the English-speaking world. See also *Creole*.

**Diaspora.** Members of a population that share a common ethnic identity who have left their settled territory (voluntarily or forcibly) and become residents of other areas.

**Differently abled.** The preferred or "politically correct" term coined in the 1980s to replace the words *handicapped* and *disabled*.

**Diurnal**. Active during the daytime rather than at night.

**Echolocation**. The emission of pulses of sound and analysis of the returning echoes in order to find out what lies ahead, used by many bats and dolphins for hunting and navigating.

**Ecotourism**. Responsible travel on a small scale to fragile, pristine, often protected areas that causes as little disturbance as possible. Its goals include educating the traveller, supporting conservation, and economic development and political empowerment of local communities, as well as fostering respect for different cultures and human rights.

**Elfin Woodland**. A forest of epiphyte-laden, stunted trees at high elevations in tropical wet areas, where ferns, mosses and other relictual plants cover the forest floor. See also *Epiphyte*.

**Endemic species**. A species found in one particular region and nowhere else on Earth, often on an island or other isolated habitat.

**Epiphyte**. A plant that grows on another plant for physical support rather than as a parasite.

**Escathological**. Related to the meaning of life and death, the afterlife, concepts of heaven and hell, and the reward and punishment for good and evil respectively, used in reference to funerary practices.

**Family land**. A Caribbean form of communal tenure in which the members of the group belong by virtue of being related through some common descent line.

**Float**. A buoyant object used to keep equipment suspended near the surface of water. Several small floats are placed along the tops of fishing nets to keep the nets from sinking to the bottom.

**Fringing reef**. A tropical coral reef generally located directly offshore or connected to the shoreline without an intervening lagoon.

**Guanine**. An organic compound used to strengthen gold crystals and enhance their reflective/refractive or glittering quality.

**Heritage**. Something inherited, passed on or transferred from the past. The notion is distinct from that of history because it places more emphasis on a sense of ownership of the past than simply on knowledge of it, and distinct from the notion of tradition because, in the case of heritage, the past has contemporary significance, whereas this is not necessarily so with tradition. Different categories of heritage are commonly distinguished, for example, built heritage, which includes buildings and monuments; natural heritage, which includes landscapes and parks; and cultural heritage, which includes art and literature, cultural artefacts and distinctive ways of life. In certain circumstances popular music has also been included in the latter category.

**Heritage/cultural tourism.** Travelling to experience the places, artefacts and activities that authentically represent the stories and people of the past and present, including cultural, historic and natural resources.

**Holocene.** The second geological epoch of the Quaternary period, which began about 11,700 years ago and continues to the present.

**Ideology.** The assumptions, beliefs and rules which govern the way in which reality is interpreted by a society, influencing prevailing perceptions of who the society sees as powerful as well as who is discriminated against.

**Indigenous culture.** A term used to describe a group of people who inhabit a geographic region with which they have the earliest known historical connection.

**Industrial heritage.** The remains of industrial culture which are of historical, technological, social, architectural or scientific value, including buildings and machinery; workshops, mills and factories; mines and sites for processing and refining; warehouses and stores; places where energy is generated, transmitted and used; transport and all its infrastructure; and places used for social activities related to industry, such as housing, religious worship or education.

**Intertropical Convergence Zone.** A band of rainclouds with occasional thunderstorms that circle the globe near the equator. The ITCZ follows the sun, moving north in the northern summer and south in the northern winter, and is responsible for the wet and dry seasons in the tropics.

**Karst system.** A network of drainage fissures, caves and reservoirs that permeate soluble carbonate bedrock, including limestone, dolomite, and gypsum; its development is accelerated by acid rain.

**Keystone predator.** An animal that maintains species diversity in a community by feeding on species that would otherwise compete with each other.

**Laws of survivorship.** The legal process by which land is bequeathed to the remaining (surviving) members of a group of owners and not to the heirs of the deceased member of the group.

**Liana.** A woody vine rooted in the forest floor that uses trees for vertical support. While often described as climbers, many lianas begin life on the ground as creepers and are simply carried up into the canopy by the supporting tree. Lianas are found in many different plant families and are characteristic of tropical rainforests.

**Likert Scale.** The most widely used scale in survey research. Likert questionnaires require respondents to specify their level of agreement to a statement.

**Maritime cultural landscape.** An archaeological concept that combines sea and land in the study of maritime cultures.

**Mnemonic device**. A memory aid usually occurring in verbal form.

**Modernism**. Most broadly, modern thought, character or practice; more specifically, both a set of cultural tendencies and an array of associated cultural movements, originally arising from wide-scale and far-reaching changes to Western society in the late nineteenth and early twentieth centuries. The concept of heritage, like any other concept in modernist discourse, is an objectified and reified one, denoting a concept of the past as a place – as a "thing" with other things in it. Thus the concept of heritage in modernist world affairs centres on the creation of a "world museum" containing items deemed by UNESCO to be of "outstanding universal value" on behalf of the whole of humankind. See also *postmodernism*.

**Narrative perspective**. The viewpoint from which the events in a text are reported. Perspective thus answers the question "Who sees?" while the reader's job is to evaluate the reliability of the voice that tells the tale.

**Parody**. A concept comprising two dimensions: imitation of the defining features of the original work and insertion of new subject matter into the original form. The tension between the established form and the new subject matter creates the force of parody.

**Petroglyphs**. Images engraved on rocks and stones during prehistoric times, particularly the Neolithic, or Stone Age; often seen as a prehistoric form of art and referred to as "rock art".

**Pleistocene**. The first geologic epoch of the Quaternary period, from two million to 11,700 years ago, during which a series of continental glaciers advanced and retreated in the northern hemisphere, modern humans evolved and tool-making cultures developed.

**Popular romance**. A form of writing that focuses on a predictable pattern of attraction between a man and a woman who each embody to some degree societal ideals of beauty and power. This relationship is typically traced through a process of attraction, misunderstanding, estrangement and reconciliation. In the text *Ti Marie*, the formulaic structure of the popular romance is parodied and becomes on a larger scale a background against which the relationship between the Caribbean and the metropole is examined.

**Postmodernism**. A movement away from the viewpoint of modernism and, more specifically, a tendency in contemporary culture characterized by problematization of objective truth and inherent suspicion towards global cultural narrative or meta-narrative. It involves the belief that many, if not all, apparent realities are only social constructs, as they are subject to change inherent to time and place. It emphasizes the role of language, power relations, and motivations and in particular attacks the use of definitive classifications such as male versus female, white versus black, and imperial versus colonial. Rather, it holds realities to be plural, relative and multivocal. See also *modernism*.

**Radiocarbon date**. An estimated date of origin based on the remains of organic material found in archaeological sites.

**Security of tenure**. The ability to hold land rights and to fend off counter-claimants to those land rights. Objective security of tenure is documentary evidence held by land occupants that supports their claim to hold or use land. Subjective security of tenure describes the confidence of land occupants that their claim to hold or use the land will not be contested or rejected.

**Shipwreck preserves**. Underwater archaeological sites that include vessel wrecks and other cultural remains, interpreted for divers and snorkellers by submerged signs and markers, informational brochures and site guides.

**Standard language form**. The dialect of a language that has been chosen (gradually over time or consciously, or both) to be the representative form of a given language, often combining features of several dialects and usually considered to be neutral and unmarked, compared to other dialects of the same language. Part of the standardization process includes codification – establishing and/or normalizing the spelling system (orthography) – agreeing on acceptable grammatical norms, and selecting vocabulary appropriate to various domains. It is often the prestige variety, spoken by those with socio-political and financial power. In the English-official Caribbean, the terms *standard* (i.e., standard English) and *creole* (English Creole) are often erroneously pitted against each other, implying that Creole English is somehow a non-standard or substandard variety and that standard(ized) English is the only acceptable variety of English. See also *Creole; Dialect*.

**Tenure**. The way in which rights to land are held. See also *Security of tenure*.

**Vernacular language**. The variety of a language natively spoken by a community or group of people, now usually referring to the language of the home and sometimes contrasted with the literary language of a people (if the two are different and co-exist).

**Zoogeographic**. An adjective describing areas of similar distinct animals or the study of the distribution patterns of animals.

# Contributors

**Basil A. Reid** is Senior Lecturer in Archaeology, Department of History, University of the West Indies, St Augustine, Trinidad and Tobago. He is also the senior representative for the Caribbean and Latin America at the World Archaeology Congress. He is the author of *Myths and Realities of Caribbean History and Archaeology, GIS and Cultural Resource Management in Trinidad* and editor of *Archaeology and Geoinformatics: Case Studies from the Caribbean* and *A Crime-Solving Toolkit: Forensics in the Caribbean*.

**Estelle M. Appiah**, now retired, was Director of Legislative Drafting in the Ministry of Justice and Attorney General's Department, Accra, Ghana, where she is responsible for legislative drafting for the Republic of Ghana.

**Gregor Barclay** is Lecturer in Botany and Biomechanics, Department of Life Sciences, University of the West Indies, St Augustine, Trinidad and Tobago.

**Béatrice Boufoy-Bastick** is Senior Lecturer in French and TESOL, Department of Liberal Arts, University of the West Indies, St Augustine, Trinidad and Tobago. She is the author of several books on culture and numerous peer reviewed journal articles and research publications.

**Bridget Brereton** is Emerita Professor of History, University of the West Indies, St Augustine, Trinidad and Tobago. Her publications include *Race Relations in Colonial Trinidad, 1870–1900* and *A History of Modern Trinidad, 1783–1962*.

**Patrick Bryan** is retired Douglas Hall Professor of History, Department of History and Archaeology, University of the West Indies, Mona, Jamaica. His publications include *Philanthropy and Social Welfare in Jamaica, The Jamaican People: Race, Class and Social Control*, and, most recently, *Edward Seaga and the Challenges of Modern Jamaica*.

**Innette Cambridge** is Lecturer in the Social Work Unit, Department of Behavioural Science and Coordinator of the Social Policy Programme, University of the West Indies, St Augustine, Trinidad and Tobago. Her publications include *Youth, the Witnesses of Today: Nurturing a Caring Society, Creating Inclusive Societies* and, as co-editor, *Report on the Proceedings of the Think Tank*

*Conference on Disability, Integration and Development: The Way Forward in Education.*

**Beverly-Anne Carter** is Director of the Centre for Language Learning, University of the West Indies, St Augustine, Trinidad and Tobago. She is the author of *Teacher–Student Responsibility in Foreign Language Learning.*

**Alissandra C.B. Cummins** is Director of the Barbados Museum and Historical Society. She is the co-author, with Allison Thompson and Nick Whittle, of *Art in Barbados: What Kind of Mirror Image?*

**Allison Dolland** is Librarian, Engineering and Physical Sciences, University of the West Indies, St Augustine, Trinidad and Tobago. She co-editor, with Stella Sandy, Yacoob Hosein and Floris Fraser, of *Index to the Conference Papers of the Association of Caribbean Historians, 1989–2005.*

**Kevin Farmer** is Curator of History and Archaeology, Barbados Museum and Historical Society.

**Jo-Anne S. Ferreira** is Lecturer in Linguistics, Department of Liberal Arts, University of the West Indies, St Augustine, Trinidad and Tobago.

**Claudius Fergus** is Senior Lecturer in African History, Department of History, University of the West Indies, St Augustine, Trinidad and Tobago.

**Judith F. Gobin** is Lecturer in Marine Ecology, Department of Life Sciences, University of the West Indies, St Augustine, Trinidad and Tobago.

**Charisse Griffith-Charles** is Lecturer in Cadastral Systems, Land Administration and Surveying, Department of Geomatics Engineering and Land Management, University of the West Indies, St Augustine, Trinidad and Tobago.

**Susan Herbert** is Lecturer in Science Education and Head of Department, School of Education, University of the West Indies, St Augustine, Trinidad and Tobago.

**Sunil Lalloo** is a graduate research assistant, Department of Geomatics Engineering and Land Management, University of the West Indies, St Augustine, Trinidad and Tobago.

**Margaret E. Leshikar-Denton** is Director of the Cayman Islands National Museum. She is co-editor, with Pilar Luna Erreguerena, of *Underwater and Maritime Archaeology in Latin America and the Caribbean.*

**Sylvia Moodie-Kublalsingh**, now retired, was Senior Lecturer in Spanish, Department of Liberal Arts, and Director of the Centre for Language Learning, University of the West Indies, St Augustine, Trinidad and Tobago. She is the author of *The Cocoa Panyols of Trinidad: An Oral Record.*

**Lorraine M. Nero** is Special Collections Librarian, Alma Jordan Library, University of the West Indies, St Augustine, Trinidad and Tobago.

**Elizabeth Pigou-Dennis** is Senior Lecturer in the Caribbean School of Architecture, University of Technology, Jamaica.

**Andrea Richards** is Assistant Programme Specialist, Latin America and the Caribbean Unit, UNESCO World Heritage Centre.

**Laura B. Roberts-Nkrumah** is Lecturer in Crop Production, Department of Food Production, University of the West Indies, St Augustine, Trinidad and Tobago.

**Ian E. Robertson** is Professor of Linguistics University of the West Indies, St Augustine, Trinidad and Tobago. He is co-editor, with Hazel Simmons-McDonald, of *Exploring the Boundaries of Caribbean Creole Languages*.

**Gerard H. Rogers** is Head of Cataloguing and Metadata Service, Alma Jordan Library, University of the West Indies, St Augustine, Trinidad and Tobago.

**Courtenay Rooks** is a leading naturalist of Trinidad and Tobago and founder of the Paria Springs Trust and Eco-community.

**Margaret D. Rouse-Jones**, now retired, was Professor and University/Campus Librarian, University of the West Indies, St Augustine, Trinidad and Tobago. Her publications include *Inward Hunger Revisited: Guide to the Library and Archives of Eric E. Williams*, vol. 2, *Archives and Guide to Manuscripts, Special Collections and Other Research Resources for Caribbean Studies at UWI St Augustine.*

**Clement K. Sankat** is Pro Vice-Chancellor, Campus Principal, and Professor of Engineering, Department of Mechanical and Manufacturing Engineering, University of the West Indies, St Augustine, Trinidad and Tobago.

**Karen Sanderson-Cole** is Coordinator, English Language Foundation Programme, University of the West Indies, St Augustine, Trinidad and Tobago.

**Della E. Scott-Ireton** is Northwest Region Director, Florida Public Archeology Network.

**Godfrey St Bernard** is Senior Research Fellow, Sir Arthur Lewis Institute of Social and Economic Studies, University of the West Indies, St Augustine, Trinidad and Tobago. He is the co-author, with Selwyn Ryan and Roy McCree, of *Behind the Bridge: Politics, Power and Patronage in Laventille, Trinidad.*

**Brent Wilson** is Senior Lecturer in Palaeontology and Sedimentology, Department of Chemical Engineering, University of the West Indies, St Augustine, Trinidad and Tobago.

CPSIA information can be obtained at www.ICGtesting.com
Printed in the USA
BVOW030303040612

291556BV00002B/5/P

9 789766 402648